# CRITICAL INFRASTRUCTURE

# CRITICAL INFRASTRUCTURE

## Understanding Its Component Parts, Vulnerabilities, Operating Risks, and Interdependencies

## TYSON MACAULAY

CRC Press
Taylor & Francis Group
Boca Raton  London  New York

CRC Press is an imprint of the
Taylor & Francis Group, an **informa** business

CRC Press
Taylor & Francis Group
6000 Broken Sound Parkway NW, Suite 300
Boca Raton, FL 33487-2742

International Standard Book Number-13: 978-1-4200-6835-1 (Hardcover)

**Library of Congress Cataloging-in-Publication Data**

Macaulay, Tyson.
    Critical infrastructure : understanding its component parts, vulnerabilities, operating risks, and interdependencies / Tyson Macaulay.
        p. cm.
    Includes bibliographical references and index.
    ISBN 978-1-4200-6835-1 (hbk. : alk. paper)
        1. Emergency management. 2. Risk management. 3. Infrastructure (Economics)
I. Title.

HV551.2.M323 2008
363.6--dc22                                                          2008019715

**Visit the Taylor & Francis Web site at**
**http://www.taylorandfrancis.com**

**and the CRC Press Web site at**
**http://www.crcpress.com**

# Contents

# Preface

If intuition were a person, it would be instinct's egghead cousin. Intuition is the path of least resistance when comprehending complex issues. Often intuition is an excellent guide and necessary shortcut for rapidly dealing with intricate situations. Instinct and intuition are certainly valuable when dealing with fire, snakes, and heights, but using instinct and intuition to plan and manage macroeconomic interactions is different. Intuition has its limits: as Christina Stead (1902–1983) has noted "Intuition is not infallible; it only seems to be the truth." Currently, managing critical infrastructure (CI) interdependency threats and risks is largely done based on intuition.

This book is dedicated to moving past intuition when dealing with the threats and risks associated with interdependency between CI sectors. Despite all the technology currently arrayed against threats and risks in the world of 2008, old-fashioned intuition is the state-of-the-art when dealing with CI interdependency as a whole. Some excellent work has been done with regard to bilateral dependencies among CI sectors, especially the relationship between pipelines and electricity generation, for instance. But these efforts have all had a constrained perspective and did not present a 360 degree view of interdependencies among CIs. As a result, progress has been delayed as businesses, and especially governments, lacked sufficient logical foundation upon which to found plans and policy.

This work is first generational. In presenting this material to audiences, I frequently compare it to a steam engine. Steam engines were revolutionary during their time, but grossly underpowered and inefficient by the standards of today's power sources. Steam power has long since become obsolete, but it provided the initial impetus and industrial momentum to solve problems that allowed tougher problems to be approached and then solved. This work is merely a stepping stone and possesses flaws and inefficiencies that will be remedied in subsequent work by subsequent researchers. The point is to overcome the inertia associated with trying to form CI protection strategy and tactics using intuition.

Reticence in addressing CI interdependency is important because modern economies are ecosystems, with CI sectors being core, critical suppliers of goods and services not just to the public at large, but to each other as this book reveals. If one fails they are all affected and sooner or later will eventually collapse as cascading impacts in the supply chain compile and combine to the demise of even the most resilient CI players. In Canada, CI sectors generated over $750 billion for the economy, with approximately one third of the value consisting of intrasector trade and supply. In the United States, CI sectors represent over $10 trillion, with $4 trillion flowing among the sectors through supply chain relationships. It is extraordinary that policy and plans related to the threats and risks of CI interdependency, and therefore threats and risks to CI economic activity, are largely based upon intuition!

Why is intuition currently the rule and not the exception for managing CI interdependency threats and risk? One reason is CI interdependency risks are managed by the public sector but most CI is owned and operated by the private sector. These companies are concerned with managing threats and risks up to a demarcation point where their goods or services are handed off to a counterparty (client or delivery partner). At this point, the counterparty is responsible for the management of their own threats and risks; businesses are not their brother's keepers. To the extent that private sector CI firms are concerned with each other's assurance, they tend to manage these risks through contracted service levels and penalties. But in the end, a business does not want to collect a penalty—they want the goods or services they agreed to pay for! Some CI sectors do engage in cooperative, interdependency risk management on a bilateral basis, but this is an exception not a rule. In the end, the private sector views interdependency risk management as the mandate of government and a component of macroeconomic management. To government, intuition seems close enough to the truth—this book will show that intuition is fallible.

A second reason intuition prevails in assessing and managing CI interdependency risks is a function of the historical approach to the problem. To date, CI interdependency has often centered around risk assessment based upon well-understood and trusted methodologies such as threats risk assessments (TRAs), which utilize granular risk assessment techniques to understand CI interdependency. These TRAs typically focus on a discreet asset level of inquiry. What are the possible vulnerabilities and threats to this building? The generator in this building? The control system managing the generator in this building? Such assessment techniques end up with complex results that do not scale. They do not scale because by the time you perform a similar assessment on all assets for the purpose of comparison, the first assessments are grossly out of date. Similarly, the resulting data set is massive and usually incompatible unless all the assessors used identical assessment techniques and identical vulnerability, threat, and risk taxonomies. Efforts to assess CI interdependency through close-up TRAs stall and collapse under their own weight. Another approach to CI interdependency has been tabletop exercising where a group of CI stakeholders are gathered to walk-through a hypothetical disaster or crisis scenario. The objective is for participants to discuss what and how they would do things and to uncover sector-specific requirements, assumptions, and expectations, which are generally not understood by the other sectors. Tabletops are great ways to test recovery plans and train staff; however, they are not necessarily effective for the purposes of CI interdependency analysis. Tabletops produce few repeatable metrics upon which to compare tests and make hard decisions. But most importantly, any metrics that might be derived from tabletops are related to the specific crisis scenario being played out. These metrics will largely not apply to a different crisis, which greatly limits their ability to support planning—except for the crisis exercised.

Using intuition to establish policy and plans around CI interdependency risk management is especially dangerous because intuition is entirely biased by your frame of reference. A very simple proof of this is revealed in this book, where metrics and intuition diverge around the role of financial services and their criticality. Financial services are generally considered a lesser-priority infrastructure than energy and health by many people making CI risk management decisions based on intuition. Intuition tells them that energy is core to remaining operational and health is critical to personal safety. Yet, ask an executive in a private sector CI what is critical and they will probably tell you, in the end, its about remaining profitable, not just operational. There is no point being operational if you cannot sell and meter your goods and services—because you cannot give them away! This conflict between remaining operational and remaining profitable is a keystone to CI interdependency risk management and demonstrates the need to plan using metrics and not intuition.

Finally, the methodology presented in this book possesses far more staying power than the metrics themselves. The metrics are comprised of (a) quantitative measures that will be updated in the future by statistical agencies and (b) qualitative metrics-based executive perceptions, which will change as soon as they read the findings in this book. Therefore the metrics within this book will serve as a record against which to gauge progress over the years if and when subsequent editions are published with revised quantitative and qualitative metrics. The metrics will also improve over time as more granular quantitative data becomes available and CI sector definitions are refined (a major discussion point in Chapter 2).

# Acknowledgments

The author wishes to acknowledge all the hundreds of people who were consulted and interviewed in the course of this work. It has been the willingness of executives and managers from CI organizations to participate that made this book possible. Not everyone was willing, not everyone "got it," but many did. I cannot acknowledge many of these people because of confidentiality conditions, but several deserve special thanks. Some supported this work to the point of going public: Greg Solecki from the city of Calgary, Dave Baumken from Hydro One, and Rob Murray from the Bank of Canada are leaders in their sectors and were instrumental in this work.

Dave McMahon was essential in synthesizing many complex ideas into digestible and even philosophical observations, and he contributed to Chapter 5. Dave and I spent many hours jogging for miles through extremes in the Ottawa heat and cold and at lunches discussing these matters.

Derek Holmes was one of the first people who "got it" when I started writing this book in May 2006, and was a great supporter and enthusiastic sounding board throughout. Derek offered some of the most insightful business interpretations of the metrics dealt with in this book. Like Derek, Rob McClure was an indispensable source of the business and communications acumen necessary to getting interviews and asking the right questions to get the right answers. Rob was a key enabler at many meetings, which greatly improved this work.

Conversations with Brian Jackson, Sheri Fleeger, and Bruce Don from the RAND Corporation were remarkably productive and indicated directions which turned out to be critical to the outcomes of this book. It was a pleasure to meet and work with people of their caliber, even for a short period.

Defense Research and Development Canada became a key contributor to this work through the efforts of two premier scientists, Reg Sawill and Craig Burrell. Reg and Craig saw an opportunity to apply analytical algorithms to the CI metrics in this book (see Chapters 4 and 6) and showed astonishing speed and keenness in their collaboration. Their contribution cannot be overestimated.

Several people deserve my thanks for their ideas, assistance, and support at various times through this effort: Claire de Grasse, Hugh Ellis, Eugene Bacic, Paulette Hatch, Robert Sandor, Leroy Peirce, Barry Denofsky, and Phil Murray. Thank you! There are others but I regret that I cannot name them all. Last but not least, thanks to Public Safety Canada (PSC) for commissioning a project based upon this work. As a result, PSC was a catalyst for the refinement of the methodologies within this book, and has shown encouraging leadership in a little explored but important discipline of risk management: critical infrastructure interdependency.

# Author

**Tyson Macaulay** leads Bell Canada's critical infrastructure protection practice, and functions as a customer chief information security officer/security liaison officer. In these roles, he is responsible for technical and operational risk management solutions for Bell's largest enterprise clients. Tyson leads security initiatives addressing large, complex, technology solutions including physical and logical (IT) assets, and regulatory/legal compliance requirements. In this role, he leads worldwide engagements involving multinational companies and international governments.

Tyson's leadership encompasses a broad range of industry sectors from the defense industry to high-tech start-ups. His expertise includes operational risk management programs, technical services, and incident management processes. Tyson has successfully served as prime architect for large-scale security implementations in both public and private sector institutions, working on projects from conception through development to implementation. Tyson is a respected thought leader with publications dating since 1993. His published work has covered authorship of peer-reviewed whitepapers, on topics as diverse as policy papers on e-commerce and micropayments to legal papers on wireless regulatory reform to technical papers on hardening networks. In June 2006, he saw the publication of his first book, *Securing Converged IP Networks*, published in collaboration with British Telecom, Lucent Technologies, Gallagher Insurance, and InCode Wireless.

Tyson previously served as director of risk management for Electronic Warfare Associates, Canada, founded General Network Services (GNS), an IT security consultancy specializing in PKI services, and Peel Wireless, a WiFi (IEEE 802.11) security firm. GNS grew steadily and in 2000, the company was acquired by JAWZ Inc. Peel Wireless was acquired by EION Inc., in 2004. Tyson began his career as a research consultant for the federal Department of Communications (DoC) on information network where he helped develop the first generation of Internet services for the DoC in the early 1990s.

Tyson lives in Ottawa, Canada, with his wife Genevieve and their son and daughter. The support of his family is core to his work. Whitepapers and past publications from Tyson can be found at http://www.tysonmacaulay.com.

# 1 Critical Infrastructure: What, Who Cares, and Why

## INTRODUCTION TO CRITICAL INFRASTRUCTURE

Critical infrastructure (CI) is so important, so fundamental, that most people take it for granted. This is the irony of CI. It has always been there during our lifetime and it has rarely failed us. And when it did fail, it was not for long. It has been designed to be so dependable that we tend to assume it in our equations around the resiliency of our lives, lifestyles, and businesses. CI is a given; it is an assumption.

That is the experience of most people in the Western world, until recently. Good water, safe food, strong bridges, working phones, ambulances, police, the ability to buy and sell goods and services, power for gas pumps, refrigerators, the kid's night-lights, and the grandparent's lift-matic beds. This experience has been challenged just before the anticlimactic end of the twentieth century with events like the 1998 ice storm in Eastern Canada which required a continent-wide response effort, and the challenge has continued since. Perhaps it is the advent of modern, mass communications like BBC World, CNN, and the Internet, but for the last ten years the Western world has seen what seems a dramatic increase in events impacting CI and highlighted a simple fact: there can be consequences associated with our assumptions about CI.

Events such as, ice storms, hurricanes, pandemics, fuel shortages, border closures, food scares, banks ceasing to function due to systems failures, have all effected millions and millions of people in North America since 2000 because in each case, it was the CI that took the hit. Moreover, not just a single infrastructure, but often more than one because part of the simple fact is that CIs have mutual interdependencies; impact one and others will feel it. These second-order impacts that flow from one CI to another are poorly understood, even though they are the determining factor between a manageable failure and an out and out disaster. The management, governance, and regulation of CIs is parochial, which facilitates the conduction of impacts and risks across CI sector boundaries—like old movies where the police would stop pursuing a felon once he crossed the state line.

Interdependency among CIs is very much about the security and assurance of a given CI. As a result, information about interdependency is not commonly available and is considered highly sensitive by the people who possess it. A fair amount has been written about CIs, their respective interdependencies, and the potential threats and vulnerabilities they face; however, little to none of this material has been written by the infrastructure owners themselves. Most work in this area has been done by academia or not-for-profit associations or government entities; this is not to say it is illegitimate, but typically lacking in specifics and arguably valid metrics. Metrics, to the extent they exist in the contemporary body of literature, are highly qualitative in nature and based on assessments by indirect stakeholders using techniques like mass surveying or educated guesswork. Although the entities publishing these assessments may be knowledgeable of the CI under consideration, they are offering a best guess at the CI security profiles they are attempting to assess.

## ANTITHESIS

CI interdependency is a massively complex subject, which this book approaches through tools described as indicators: independently derived, correlated metrics, which serve as indicators for CI interdependency and thereby vulnerability assessment. An indicator is a variable used to infer the value of another variable which is of interest; in this case, the variable of interest is CI interdependency and related vulnerabilities. Rather than attempting to define and measure CI interdependency directly, we are collecting and analyzing metrics, which allow us to infer the interdependency status among CI sectors. These indicators might also be considered as "composite" metrics, where a single metric is derived by combining other indicator metrics through processes to be described herein.

The proxy indicators we propose in this chapter are econometrics and data-dependency metrics. These are good starting points for discussions of CI sector interdependency for two specific reasons: all sectors possess, product, spend, and manage money; and all sectors possess, produce, send, and receive information and data. Money and data are the lowest common denominators of modern economies and CI sectors. These are things that all business and sectors have and must use on a constant basis to remain operational. This notion of a lowest common denominator is important, because it allows for the measurement of bidirectional not just unidirectional relationships. For instance, you can ask how a bank buys services from an energy company and how an energy company buys services from a bank; but it would be absurd if you asked how much energy a bank produces and sells or how many financial services an energy company performs and sells. See interdependence versus dependence discussed later. This book therefore uses macroeconomic statistical information and its correlation with information and data dependency as a framework to understand interdependencies between CIs, and arriving at a single composite metric for CI interdependency. These concepts are explored later in this chapter and in great detail in Chapters 2 and 3. In Chapter 4, we move on to correlating the proxy indicators of input–output (I–O) analysis with data dependency metrics.

Why are we bothering with proxy indicators and composite metrics? Why not measure interdependency itself? Directly? For instance, why not go to the CI sector businesses and organizations and ask questions like how important is Energy to your business? Communications and IT? Food, Water, Health care, and Transport? Then collect these metrics and come out with a single, accurate picture rather than relying on inferences from proxy indicators?

A direct approach seems like the intuitive thing to do, except it does not work for at least two reasons: The first reason that indicators and composite metrics are appropriate is that we simply do not possess a single metric for CI interdependency.

CI interdependency is a concept not necessarily a quantifiable tangible, especially if the intent is to apply the same metric across all CIs. In the end, CI interdependency will always be derived from proxy indicators and composite metrics, but the indicators themselves and their management will become more and more effective with time. Second, indicators and composite metrics for CI interdependency analysis are necessary because the current state of research and understanding of CI interdependency does not yet allow for a direct approach on the issue. There are no publicly available 360 degree assessments of CI interdependency upon which to compare findings; there is no reference point. The direct approach solution is regularly proposed and attempted by risk professionals and academics alike looking for simple and precise answers to the complex problem of CI interdependency; unfortunately, simple and precise answers to CI interdependency do not exist for reasons of business, security, and comprehensiveness.

For those unconvinced that a frontal assault on CI interdependency will not work, consider the following challenges about trying to collect interdependency metrics directly as quantitative data:

1. Business: The value of understanding CI interdependencies is relative to the role of the person in an organization. The people with the raw, interdependency data are not the people who care. To understand in granular detail how each CI sector business rates the importance of all the different goods and services from all the different CI sectors requires a vast amount of internal company data. This data includes accounting information, inventory data, contract information, and management plans and assumptions. At least! Aside from dedicated risk managers, most CI businesses and organizations do not (at this time) see the reciprocal value of the final data set relative to the cost of compiling the information. They will not go to that extent.

2. Security: If business and organizations possess granular and accurate dependency information, they consider it commercially sensitive, a security issue, a matter of intellectual property, and an input into their competitiveness. If they have it, the instinct and typical response is to not release it for aggregation and assessment.*

3. Comprehensiveness: Dependency does not equal interdependency. You need two sides to every dependency story to understand interdependency and vulnerabilities. Individual CI sector players possess information about their own critical relationships (though typically not centralized and organized) but will have incomplete insight into how their partners, suppliers, regulators, or customers are actually dependent upon them. Accurate metrics about interdependency must be bidirectional. Just collecting data from one or two sectors will give a highly distorted picture of overall interdependency—even for these participating sectors! You have to work all sectors at the same time. Given points 1 and 2, the obstacles around direct measurement become highly problematic.

---

* See "Fearing Access leaks, energy companies wont share data with Ottawa", *Globe and Mail*, August 20, 2007 in which a federal government department explicitly admits that they cannot get the specific interdependency information then need to forward the current CI protection strategies.

**FIGURE 1.1**   Girl with a pearl earring, Mauritshuis, The Hague.

For these reasons, CI interdependency is too sensitive, complex, and expensive to try and assess with finality the first time out. Stakeholders need to be convinced of the following:

- There is something to learn from CI interdependency metrics, which will contribute to their business.
- Information can be managed securely.

CI interdependency is not something that can appear like a photograph transmitted through space from a distant planet. It must be built up with an inclusive and broad-based methodology and emerge like a classical painting, stage by stage. Classical paintings—like the intricate beauties seen in museums—by Dutch masters like Johannes Vermeer (1632–1675) (see Figure 1.1) were created in stages because of the complexity of working with the primitive pigments of the time. These artists were known to apply a technique which involved inventing (sketching), dead-coloring (under painting and toning the medium, for instance canvas, to support the picture), working-up (figures and colors), retouching (details of shadows and reflections, depth, and dimension), and glazing (applying highlights, tuning reflected light).*

Although not nearly as fetching, CI interdependency analysis must evolve as stages: from sketch and toning to the first brush strokes, which outline the subject and communicate information—but the details of the picture and the depth of information it conveys grow as more stages are completed and layers applied. The reason that CI interdependency must be undertaken in stages is directly related to the challenges

---

* http://essentialvermeer.20m.com/technique/technique_overview.htm.

associated with trying to obtain real interdependency metrics at the first attempt. At this time, we possess only primitive, first generation tools for assessing CI interdependency.

This book approaches CI interdependency analysis with this theory of staging deliberately in mind, and as a result of early lessons learned with stakeholders. If compared to the development of a classical painting, this work covers perhaps the two first stages and at least some of the third stage: we review the definitions of CI, which have been previously invented; we establish a context for assessing interdependency and tone the medium, and we also present initial outlines of the figures and terrain and work-up the CI interdependency picture. We will not go so far as to make affirmative declarations about sector dependencies and vulnerabilities (retouching?) or drawing conclusion about the specific impacts on specific industries of specific threats (glazing?). Enough information has not been collected to produce reliable results around retouching and glazing of CI interdependency analysis. But until this initial work is undertaken, the richer information required to draw detailed conclusions will not become available from the stakeholder for the reasons cited earlier.

Staging CI interdependency analysis increases the chances of success at each successive stage and therefore enables deeper broader work in the future. This book and the staged approach it applies to CI interdependency analysis have the following benefits:

- Approach shows upfront value to stakeholders for minimal investment.
- Approach requires little sensitive or proprietary information be disclosed.
- Approach allows for trust to be established with stakeholders for low stakes initially.
- Approach fosters management-understanding of the issues around CI inter-dependency with executive-level metrics and displays.
- Approach drives conclusions among stakeholders about the benefits of more in-depth work.

Based on the above discussion, we will not complete the CI interdependency painting in this book. We will start it—much work and many more brush strokes will be required to complete this highly complex picture—to the extent that it can be completed at all.

The CI interdependency picture will emerge over years of effort and constantly change as technologies, business-ownership, and regulatory structures change. The utility of this book is that even a partial picture can convey much information about the nature of the subject.

## CHAOS THEORY AND CRITICAL INFRASTRUCTURE

None too reassuringly, CI interdependencies show hallmarks of being a form of non-linear of chaotic systems, making the task ahead of us all that much more difficult. Nonlinear or chaotic systems have a long and deep academic and mathematical pedigree going back to the early 1900s when mathematicians studying the movement of planets discovered that, very simply put, minute influences (what might be considered rounding errors) on the inputs into equations can result in dramatically different, and even totally opposite outcomes. This is where the famous "butterfly" effect comes from; under nonlinearity theory, a butterfly flapping its wings in Brazil can generate a tornado in Texas in two years: minute changes in inputs can have dramatic results. The relationships become so complex that they are in effect impossible to calculate and the application of quantitative attempts to measure and predict is futile. But we still try, even though some of the greatest thinkers like Henri Poincaré in the area of nonlinearity ultimately came to the conclusion that discussions related to nonlinear systems can only be undertaken with qualitative measures.* Weather is a nonlinear system yet we still try to forecast it; if CI interdependency analysis reaches the level of forecasting accuracy obtained by weather forecasting, we might be doing well! Just as weather forecasting is now accurate enough to model emerging severe weather events, the most optimistic outcome of our CI methodology of determining interdependency risk would be to mitigate large-scale (detectable) catastrophic events.

## WHO SHOULD READ THIS BOOK?

Executives and senior management, policy makers, emergency responders, risk managers and assessors, finance and contract managers will all benefit from the material presented here. This material will provide increased understanding of how one business or industry interrelates to another business or industry. Why should the water company care if there is a pandemic and the hospitals are overwhelmed? Why should the slaughter house care if the phone company has a major fire in a core location? Through these sorts of insights, managers will be in a position to better respond to events and understand the potential flow down impacts between sectors: "What will the pandemic mean to me?"; "What will the central office fire mean to me?"

Through the possession of information related to interdependencies, managers can better understand the risks facing their organization in the form of supply-chain risk. Although most managers might have an idea of who and what is in the supply chain, they are not frequently prepared to understand how impacts to this supply chain might be delivered. This is where the process of understanding and managing operational risks to the business becomes monumental: how do you try and understand all the potential threats to all your suppliers?

Business managers will learn about how their supply chains are interwoven and how impacts within the economy as a whole may translate down to them. How does the derailment 1000 miles away potentially impact their suppliers and eventually them? Policy makers and emergency responders will gain a better insight into where the vulnerabilities in the economy, on the whole, may lie. An exhaustive range of vulnerabilities will not be documented in this book; there are too many and they are too idiosyncratic. Rather, an all-hazards approach to risk management will be explored and the cascading effects related interdependency are explored here.

---

* See Taleb, N.N., 2007. *The Black Swan: The Impact of the Highly Improbable*, Random House, New York, pp. 178–179; http://en.wikipedia.org/w/index.php?title = Henri_Poincar%C3%A9& oldid = 153446742.

This book is an advantage to business managers in the context of operational risk management and understanding the threat environment, leading to better overall management as defined by the financial institutions, which are assessing and rating business for credit and investment purposes. Not only are financial institutions assessing businesses on operational risk but they are also establishing the cost of capital (credit, loans, bonds, equity) and the cost of insurance (Directors and Officers [D&O], Errors and Omissions [E&O]) according to good or bad operational risk management.* For business managers, the sort of knowledge presented in this book one day may be the difference between a good risk rating from standard to poor, or a better risk rating.

Policy makers and emergency responders will already be familiar with the concept of CI interdependency. Although the concept has been well discussed, work in this area has been largely limited to case studies and anecdotes of bilateral relationships between CIs. Even less has been done in the way of defining metrics related to CI interdependencies. This book presents a metric-based approach to understanding CI interdependency to supplement (or supplant) the intuitive approach to interdependency assessment, which currently prevails.

Readers may find the following sorts of actionable items in this book:

Business continuity: How will apparently unrelated impacts on other businesses require that continuity plans be activated? The ability to understand the indications of an impending impact and activate plans just ahead of the event will result in dramatically improved results.

Inflection point of private versus public responsibility: Private sector organizations are only incentivized to spend resources on threats they can manage. These are the threats within their controls and therefore within their organizations, or threats manageable through legal, contracted agreements. Private sector organizations, while they are seriously concerned about CI interdependency, are not in a position individually to implement controls and safeguards for sectors as a whole. CI interdependency and the mitigating controls, which reduce risks to public and economic health, security, and safety are the preview of government. This book provides a much greater detail than was previously available for policy makers seeking to understand where the private sector finishes and the public sector might start when it come to CI interdependency risk management.

Service levels and contracting: Key suppliers may be in the position of being knocked out of commission due to impacts suffered by the supply chain. Service level stipulations should ensure that these suppliers take the necessary precautions— even if it means they have to educate themselves and read this book too!

Risk reporting: A clear understanding of operational risks as reported to the board, auditors, or investors will make the life of executives easier and professionally safer. Managers can put into place or augment threat and risk assessment programs to look more closely at the issues of interdependency, which were previously ignored or guesstimated.

---

* Macaulay, T., 2007, Additivity of Risk.

Achieve lower cost of capital: Operational risks impacting the entire organization can be better understood and managed. Sophisticated operational risk management can be reported to capital markets and financial institutions to lower the overall credit risk attributed to an organization.

Achieve lower cost of insurance: As with the cost of capital, better operational risk management can be reported to insurance providers to support better terms, conditions, and costs associated with insurance policies for large entities, which are essentially de rigueur—D&O insurance and E&O insurance.

## HOW TO READ THIS BOOK?

This book was written with the understanding that many readers will be interested in only a subset of the information initially, specifically, the interdependency information for their sector. For this reason there may appear to be a fair amount of repetition of concepts if you read this book cover to cover—this is intentional to allow readers to page directly to information about a specific sector and start reading at that point without losing context.

## WHAT ARE CRITICAL INFRASTRUCTURES?

CIs are the organizations delivering goods and services in an economy that is funda-mental to the functioning of society and the economy. The loss of a CI or an impact within a CI will generally be perceptible to many if not all people within the economy. Whether a school student, a business person, or retired widow, all CIs will be visible to one extend or another to all people either by virtue of consumption of the good or service, or by virtue of awareness (via a media report of a failure). All people consume most CI goods and services on a constant or frequent basis, whether this is electric or water or roads. When these goods and services become unavailable, you are acutely aware of the change. Some CIs are not consumed on a constant basis, they are in place for reasons related to personal and public health and safety; in these instances, people are concerned when a CI such as hospitals (Health sector) or police (Safety sector) is unavailable because of the vulnerability or exposure generated by its absence. The result is an intuitively understood and a perceived increase in the potential impact of hazards like fire, assault, food poisoning, car accidents, or any of the high-impact/low-prob-ability risks, and other daily calamities we are susceptible to when certain contingency CI sectors such as Health and Safety are impacts.

A CI may be geographically defined, but not necessarily. In fact, it is an especially serious mistake to think that cartographic (map) borders are an obstacle to CI disruptions. Some CIs are dependent upon specific infrastructure for the delivery of their goods or services, and the extent of a second-order* impact may

---

* A first-order impact is the outcome of an incident on the CI itself. What happened to the CI? A first-order impact is a relatively simple thing to observe, measure, estimate relative to second-order impacts, which are follow-on effects of the initial impact on all the people and businesses. How does the impact move through the supply chain and economy as a whole? Each subsequent chapter deals with this concept of second-order impacts in a variety of ways.

be confined to their service area. Other CIs will be so interlinked with other adjacent CIs within the same sector that impacts can conduct from one to the other almost seamlessly, without any regard for national borders of any sort.

CI is broadly identified by species according to the good or service produced and delivered by a particular CI. Any taxonomy of CI species is not absolute and at best reflects an aggregate of professional or policy-maker opinion. All national governments seem to group and name the critical goods and services within their economies similarly, but differently. Furthermore, these groupings seem to evolve and morph regularly depending on the administration in power. Below are several examples of definitions of CI sectors and the subsectors definitions cited by the relevant authorities.

The greatest shortcoming of all these CI taxonomies is that they appear arbitrary: they were not developed based upon any apparent methodology. The lack of a methodology to define CIs creates a fundamental weakness—we don't know if they actually include the right industries! Therefore, the first required step in trying to understand CI interdependency is to establish a defensible methodology to express CIs. Using the existing CI definitions as a starting point, we need to do a little reverse engineering and associate CI sector definitions with more established systems for classifying industries.

## NAICS-BASED CI DEFINITIONS

The first industrial classification schemes were developed post–World War II to meet government's need to establish a more comprehensive and fully integrated system of economic reporting, in support of postwar reconstruction programmes. Until 1994, the governments of Canada, the United States, and Mexico maintained similar but distinct classification schemes for describing the industries within their economies. In 1994, the advent of the North American Free Trade Agreement (NAFTA) generated a strong requirement for a harmonized classification scheme to support cross-border trade. The North American Industry Classification System (NAICS) was developed by Statistics Canada, Mexico's Instituto Nacional de Estadística, Geografía e Informática (INEGI), and the Economic Classification Policy Committee of the Office of Management and Budget. NAICS 2002 is an industry naming scheme now shared among NAFTA countries. NAICS contains classifications for 20 sectors, 103 subsectors, 328 industry groups, 728 industries, and 928 national industries. The NAICS classifications do not align with the CI sector definitions of any of the jurisdictions described above; each CI sector seems to contain industries from a variety of NAICS groups.

There are clear benefits to applying definitions of CI sectors that are mapped to NAICS groups and codes. In Chapter 2, translating CI sectors definitions to a deep, rich, and accepted scheme like NAICS will allow for at least two advantages. First, by starting with the existing definitions and using statistics to observe how the industries within a given sector consume good and services, we start to get an idea of which industries might be conspicuously absent from CI sector lists. A couple of quick examples—coal mining is not considered a CI, but 25–50 percent of North American electricity comes from burning coal and it is a major source of spending within the power sector. Another example is industrial gas: this is a multibillion dollar industry and a critical supply component to medical equipment (MRI scanners, cryogenic preservation systems) used in every modern hospital. Yet, this too is excluded under the existing CI definitions for critical industries of the Manufacturing sector. Missing industries are discussed in detail in Chapter 2. The second advantage of using a tool like NAICS to validate our CI definitions is that the breadth and depth of the NAICS data set of statistical information might be leveraged in the understanding of CI interdependency. The process of how macroeconomic statistical information might be employed for assessing CI interdependencies is explained later in this chapter. However, the first challenge is to demonstrate a mapping between the current definitions of CI sectors used by nations and NAICS.

One further point before we continue: why not abandon the current CI definitions altogether and adopt NAICS classifications and definitions? This is not an entirely appropriate solution because the current definitions of CI make a certain amount of sense intuitively and are therefore digestible by a wide audience of policy makers, private sectors bosses and risk managers, media, technical folks, and general lay people. Second, in order for this book to be relevant in the context of almost all the previous work done around CI, it is helpful to use the terms and taxonomies that are recognized. We are trying to build a bridge from intuitive but ad hoc definitions to a standards-based definition of CI.

To begin reconciling NAICS classifications with current CI definitions in use, let us propose a potential top level list of CI sectors. According to Table 1.1, ten sectors are mentioned, where at least two of three times in the comparison between the United States, Canada, and the European Union. These sectors are listed in Table 1.2.

## TABLE 1.1
## CI Sectors by Nation

| Sector Name | U.S.[a] Subsectors | Canadian[b] Subsectors | EU[c] Subsectors |
|---|---|---|---|
| Banking and Finance | Storage, investment exchange, and disbursement | Banking, securities, and investment | None specified |
| Information and Communications | Telecommunications and information technology | Telecommunications, broadcasting systems, software, hardware, and networks including the Internet | None specified |
| Transportation | Aviation, highways, mass transit, pipelines, rail, waterborne commerce | Air, rail, marine, and surface | None specified |

## TABLE 1.1 (continued)
## CI Sectors by Nation

| Energy | Electric power, oil and gas production, and storage | For example, electrical power, natural gas, oil production, and transmission systems | None specified |
|---|---|---|---|
| Safety and Security | None specified | For example, chemical, biological, radiological and nuclear safety, hazardous materials, search and rescue, emergency services, and dams | |
| Health services | Prevention, surveillance, laboratory services, and personal health services | Hospitals, health care and blood supply facilities, laboratories, and pharmaceuticals | None specified |
| Water supply | None specified | Drinking water and wastewater management | None specified |
| Government | None specified | Services, facilities, information networks, assets, and key national sites and monuments | |
| Manufacturing | | Defense industrial base and chemical industry | None specified |
| Food supply | | Safety, distribution, agriculture, and food industry | None specified |
| Research | | | None specified |

| United States | The taxonomy is drawn directly from the seminal U.S. Presidential Directive 63 in May 1998. In 2003 the Homeland Security Presidential Directive seven (HSPD7) was released which re-organized and sub-divided the original ten sectors into seventeen sectors. The original ten sectors will be used for the purposes of this work because they are inclusive of the HSPD-7 sectors and better support international comparisons. |
|---|---|
| Canada | Canada's definition for CIs dates back to approximately 2001, and is currently supported by Public Safety Canada. |
| European Union | The European Council requested in 2004 the development of a European Programme for CI protection. Since then, a comprehensive preparatory work has been undertaken, which has included the organization of relevant seminars, the publication of a Green Paper and discussions with both public and private stakeholders. |

[a] This taxonomy is taken from U.S. Presidential Decision Directive 63 (PDD 63) 1998 http://www.fas.org/irp/offdocs/pdd/pdd-63.htm. This taxonomy has been superseded by HSPD-7 2003 in which seventeen sectors were established from the original ten. See http://www.whitehouse.gov/news/releases/2003/12/20031217-5.html.

[b] Public Safety Canada, http://www.publicsafety.gc.ca/prg/em/nciap/about-en.asp.

[c] European Program for Critical Infrastructure Protection http://europa.eu/rapid/pressReleasesAction.do?reference=MEMO/06/477&format=HTML&aged=0&language=EN.

---

**TABLE 1.2**
**Harmonized CI Sectors**

Banking and finance
Energy
Information and Communications
Transportation
Safety and Security
Health services
Water supply
Government
Manufacturing
Food supply

---

Working from this list of CIs, the next requirement is for a proposal concerning how to map the 20 sectors, 103 subsectors, 328 industry groups, 728 industries, and 928 national industries under NAICS to these sectors. The subsectors currently used by the national definitions can be used as a starting point; Chapter 2 contains a more thorough mapping of the existing CI definitions to NAICS.

## WHAT IS INTERDEPENDENCY?

Now that we have described the contemporary working definition of CI and its limits, we can move onto the notion of interdependency among CI sectors.

Interdependency may best be understood in the context of dependency: to be partially or entirely reliant upon another for some good or service. Young children are dependent on parents, cars are (mostly) dependent on gasoline, and businesses are dependent on customers. Interdependency is a bidirection, two-way version of dependency with degrees of intensity: both are partially or entirely reliant upon each other. Interdependency is not necessarily a matter of equality; it is possible that between two interdependent parties, one is more dependent than another. (In fact, a core purpose of this book is to try and expose not only interdependencies but also the different degrees of dependency among CI sectors.)

## CASCADING IMPACTS: FIRST ORDER, SECOND ORDER, TERTIARY

First-order impacts are direct effects of an incident upon the entity, whether this be physical (fire, flood, earthquake, labor action) or logical (data loss, software bugs, network failures). An impact could be a fire in a building occupied by the entity, or it might be a server failure relied upon by the entity. The first-order impact is the catalyst that sets events in motion. This brings us to the second-order impacts.

Second-order impacts are the meat of interdependency analysis; they reflect what happens as a cascading result of the first-order impact. How are the risks of the impact in the first entity conducted outward into the client base or the supply chain? Just because an entity did not suffer a fire or a server failure does not preclude it from being indirectly impacted. Furthermore, second-order impacts are likely to arrive in the form of a completely distinct threat and risk from the original first-order impact.

A first-order impact may be a fire in entity A, resulting in a stoppage of services flowing to entity B (an availability impact), which in turn requires that production of goods slow or stop. To understanding cascading second-order impacts is a challenge addressed by this book because they are so difficult to predictably map.

A tertiary impact is basically a second-order impact of a second-order impact. It is the impact that will be conducted out of the second entity and into a third entity on account of the impact in the first entity. The fire results in the failure of services to arrive at a second entity which slows production and forces the cancellation of some just-in-time deliveries, which results in shortages of perishable hospital supplies. For instance, where second-order impacts are difficult to identify and assess, tertiary impacts are insidious to define and assess because there is an attenuation effect that must be accounted for. Attenuation under the presumption that the further from the source of the impact, the less the conducted threat, risk, and impact. This assumption is based upon a further assumption that controls and safeguards are effectively employed at each level of impact against risk conductance. Examples of tertiary impacts at work are provided in Chapter 4, but this is not to imply that impacts are limited in their cascading abilities to merely three levels of cascade: there is no limit to the number of cascading "hops" that an incident might achieve through CI. In fact, Chapter 4 presents new algorithms which have been specifically designed to model cascading impacts through CI sectors up into hundreds of hops, seeking to understand where the actual weight of an impact might settle after it has ricocheted around multiple CIs.

## INTERDEPENDENCY AND METRICS

The challenge with most of the CI analysis which has been done to date is that it is built upon anecdote and case studies rather than empirical evidence. In other words, the analysis tends to be an aggregation of personal experiences, expressed to analysts or journalists in unstructured fashions. To assess interdependency thoroughly, you need more than anecdote. You need metrics. It is human nature to both underestimate consequence and likelihood.

This book uses metrics in a variety of way to try and express interdependency relationships between CI sectors. To better understand the nature of these relationships and the amount of weight that they might possess, it is worthwhile to have a quick discussion about types of metrics. The value of this discussion is that it will allow readers and users of this information to better comprehend the limits of the techniques and the sample findings.

Qualitative and ordinal metrics are the first important pairing of concepts that will be deployed substantially in the methods of this book. A qualitative measure or metric is one that is based upon imprecise measures, namely poor, fair, good, very good, and best. By virtue of being imprecise in nature, these measures are also ordinal meaning that they describe a relative position in an established order but not necessarily specific information about the size of the interval between the values. How far is it from fair to good? Is it the same distance from very good to best? Qualitative metrics will almost always be coupled with ordinal values and as a result they should not be used like quantitative and cardinal metrics which are described in the following paragraph. Qualitative metrics should be considered less precise. But, when you are trying to extract, quantify, and measure knowledge from humans which is not measurable directly and requires the use of indicators—such as CI interdependency—qualitative metrics are remarkably useful. They allow simple questions to be answered simply, but validly. (A well-asked question will be understood the same way by just about all the people responding.) Qualitative metrics allow opinions to translate into numbers, which can be managed and manipulated as meaningful, aggregated data.

Quantitative and cardinal metrics are the second important pairing covered in this book and are extremely important because they are precise. Quantitative metrics are things like statistics related to the number events or clearly measurable units like dollars or widgets. How many times did it happen exactly? How many dollars were lost? How many minutes did the outage last? As opposed to qualitative metrics which are ordinal in nature, quantitative metrics should be cardinal in nature; the units of measure are precise and agreed upon, as are the distances between these units of measure: dollars, seconds, meters would all be quantitative and cardinal measures. Quantitative metrics tend to be precise but also large and more difficult to manage in the sense that the range of values may extend from zero into millions or billions and beyond. Quantitative metrics might also be organized into further descriptive units using other quantitative metrics such as hours or kilometers—or by devices, servers, networks—or by age group, income, etc. Quantitative measures and metrics can be harder to extract because they typically involve specific measurements which are not always transparent or easy to obtain. These measures may have been aggregated, weighted, and rolled-up into something for management digestion. When you do this (aggregate distinct quantitative metrics) you end up with a qualitative metric. If you add apples and oranges you get fruit, but it is no longer a naturally occurring fruit. Different qualitative metrics may be combined by an organization because there is a clear qualitative relationship between them, and a single metric is better than two stand-alone metrics.

Qualitative metrics should not be interpreted in the same manner as quantitative metrics. They are not as precise and tend to be best valued as indicative rather than conclusive. A qualitative metric can justifiably be calculated down to as many decimal points as the analyst feels is necessary. For instance, 22,567.25 barrels of oil on average are consumed hourly by logistics companies. To make the same sort of statement using qualitative metrics would exceed the accuracy limits of the underlying ordinal values. For instance, logistics companies rated the importance of oil supplies 9.86 out of 10 in importance to their business. Such a statement can be made based upon qualitative information gathered on a scale from one to ten and averaged—but the actual distinction between 9.86 and 8.86 must be interpreted with caution by analysts. Because of the underlying original values, possibly 9.86 is closer to 8.86 than to 10.

## APPLYING METRICS TO CRITICAL INFRASTRUCTURE INTERDEPENDENCY

This chapter proposes two types of metrics associated with CI interdependency and a means to apply them for the purposes of assessing the strength of dependency relationships among CI sectors. The metrics proposed in this chapter for assessing CI interdependency and generating a single composite metric are

1. National I–O statistics: quantitative and cardinal
2. Data dependency metrics: qualitative and ordinal

## NATIONAL INPUT–OUTPUT STATISTICS

National I–O statistics are generated or refreshed annually by all NAFTA countries and provide documentation of economic activity among NAICS industries including a breakdown of their inputs (what they buy) and outputs (what they sell) by both commodity and industry. How much value of a given commodity or from a given industry does an industry consume? Alternately, how much output (measured in currency units) does an industry consume from another industry? Commodities are defined according to preestablished lists which are harmonized between Organisation for Economic Co-Operation and Development (OECD) countries. NAICS codes are completely harmonized within NAFTA countries and partially harmonized throughout the OECD countries. Therefore, the NAICS codes again lend themselves well to both defining CI and assessing econometric dependency.

I–O statistics is the place proposed as the starting point for CI interdependency assessment because economic relationships can be demonstrated quantitatively. These relationships are also totalled across the economy and are broken down to significant detail, allowing for the industries to be aggregated and grouped into infrastructure sectors and their I–O values assessed for relationships with other sectors.

The assumption associated with I–O analysis is that increased value exchange equates to increased dependency. By itself, this is a flawed assumption because it does not take into account that dependency in the context of CI is defined as criticality in the course of hour-to-hour and day-to-day operations. An electricity producer might spend more money on the coal industry than any other industry in the supply chain. But it might also stockpile weeks of coal on site: they are dependent upon coal but not critically dependent on a day-to-day basis. Therefore, assessing CI interdependency based solely upon I–O statistics is informative but not sufficient alone. I–O statistical metrics, their collection, and assessment with regard to CI interdependency are discussed in detail in Chapter 2.

## DATA DEPENDENCY METRICS

In the communications-intensive world of modern economies, interdependent relationships are reflected by the exchange of data. By exchange of data we intent the deliberate exchange of data, where it is directed at a specific destination (customer, supplier, partner, regulator) as opposed to being released into the ether for general, public consumption. Consider a food retailer sending an order to a frozen food supplier for re-supply one week down the road. Even though there is not instantaneous action required by the supplier, in the electronic data world the communication or order cannot even be placed without proper responses and acknowledgments from the supplier's IT systems to the retailer's systems. In other words, an exchange of data—no matter how one-sided—requires a level of responsiveness from the receiving party. Without this responsiveness, the messages are not delivered and supply chains start to fray. Information and communications are a two-way, inter-dependent street. In the context of CI, data dependency is a measure of the sensitivity of infrastructure sectors to changes in the security profile of the data they exchange with other sectors: how have the properties of confidentiality, integrity, and avail-ability changed?

The counterpoint to interdependency associated with the exchange of data is the receipt of broadcast data such as media or public domain information that can be obtained in a wide variety of ways. This sort of data does not clearly result in interdependency, but at the same time it is not directed to a business partner. This is why data interdependency is a useful gauge of overall interdependency. Data is logical and unambiguous in its requirements for interchange: if the data is directed and targeted to a specific entity for a business purpose (or any purpose for that matter), then there will be a base level of interdependency required for the simple delivery of the data. The logical extension of this assessment is that if data is being deliberately sent and received, there is a business reason.

Monitoring and surveillance of a nations' communications traffic as a means for understanding relationships, intent, and dependencies have long been the primary means for establishing mapping vulnerabilities in military campaigns; this is the tried and true discipline of *Information Operations*.

A data dependency metric is a qualitative measure of the properties associated with the confidentiality, integrity, and availability of information flowing between CI sectors. Dependency metrics are gathered through structured management interviews across all sectors, applying qualitative metrics. Data dependency metrics are about the assurance requirements on the inter- and intrasector information exchanges. If you think about this as a $10 \times 10$ metrics (recall there are ten CIs for the purposes of this book) then that equates to 100 distinct dependency metrics among the CIs.

## TABLE 1.3
## Sample Dependency Matrix

|  | Banking | Energy | Info and Comms | Transp | Safety | Health | Water | Gov | Manufac | Food |
|---|---|---|---|---|---|---|---|---|---|---|
| Banking |  |  |  |  |  |  |  |  |  |  |
| Energy |  |  |  |  |  |  |  |  |  |  |
| Info and Comms |  |  |  |  |  |  |  |  |  |  |
| Transp |  |  |  |  |  |  |  |  |  |  |
| Safety |  |  |  |  |  |  |  |  |  |  |
| Health |  |  |  |  |  |  |  |  |  |  |
| Water |  |  |  |  |  |  |  |  |  |  |
| Gov |  |  |  |  |  |  |  |  |  |  |
| Manufac |  |  |  |  |  |  |  |  |  |  |
| Food |  |  |  |  |  |  |  |  |  |  |

Dependency metrics provide us a unique and profound piece of information that annualized I–O statistics cannot provide: how critical is one infrastructure on a day-to-day basis to the delivery of goods and services of another given infrastructure? The only people who can accurately address such questions are the sector stakeholders themselves. The people who earn their living in the sector and know what it takes to operate profitably, according to government regulations. The example of electricity and coal is used: an electricity manager knows that information and communications from coal suppliers are important, but if the delivery of the coal is delayed for three days they can possibly make it up in the following three days with larger deliveries; therefore, the information and data flow are considered mission critical until it has been disrupted for an extended period. Interdependency indications from I–O statistics and data dependency metrics would possibly not align in the above example, leading us closer to the real picture because we investigate and assess these misalignments among the metrics.

Dependency metrics possess a weakness because they are qualitative and therefore imprecise. The most significant challenge to data dependency metrics— and the reason they benefit so much from the company of quantitative I–O measures—is that they are limited by the knowledge, awareness, and mood of the people providing the metrics. Although the sector managers who are interviewed during the collection of dependency metrics may be sincere and serious professionals, they might not be security practitioners familiar with assessments around confidentiality, integrity, and availability. In the course of interviewing they may have to be schooled in these concepts to enable them to answer, which might reasonably be expected to impact the accuracy of their answers. Even the most (or especially) senior managers may not possess complete insight into all the facets of the business to answer accurately. Similarly, because the dependency metrics described in this book are a new means of assessing CI relationships, the fact there is little to no precedent information means that respondents do not have a benchmark or historical records upon which to find responses. If they had known what the typical response was from their peers, who they have answered the same way . . . ? Dependency metrics, their collection, and assessment with regard to CI interdependency are explained in great detail in Chapter 3.

## REQUIREMENT FOR COVARIANCE AND CORRELATION IN CRITICAL INFRASTRUCTURE INTERDEPENDENCY ASSESSMENT

Covariance is the degree to which two random variables will move in the same direction at the same time. Correlation is the amount of sameness in the movement. Do they move the same amount in the same direction? Or does one move a more or less than the other?

Either one of the proxy indicators/metrics discussed will provide some apparently interesting insights into CI interdependency and vulnerabilities, but will not alone be convincing. However, both the metrics, once analyzed methodically and correlated, will provide significantly more information with a greater overall

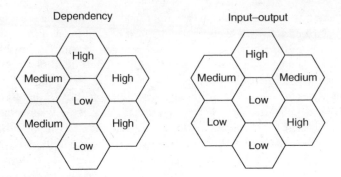

**FIGURE 1.2**   Independent metrics.

potential of being valid when presented as a single composite metric. Discussing correlated metric sets and composites may provide indications of interdependency, highlight possible flaws in measurement (due to very high or low correlations) or flaws in source data (statistics and interview materials), or even the compositions of CI sectors.

Figures 1.2 and 1.3 demonstrate how correlation of two independent metrics sets can provide a substantial amount of information about the variables involved and whether or not they are valid. When the assessment of CI interdependency—like any decision supported by metrics—is stronger, the more correlated metrics can be found to support observations. The combination of two metric set through the process of correlation will provide not only information about which measurements tend to support and reinforce each other but also which measurements conflict. Conflicting measures are especially interesting because they tend to narrow down problematic areas in methodology, whether that be measuring, sampling, analysis, or synthesis of data. Similarly, many conflicting metrics or weak correlations can be an indication that you are on the wrong track to begin with! Chapter 4 is concerned entirely with the correlation of the metrics discussion in Chapters 2 (econometric interdependency assessment) and 3 (data dependency assessment).

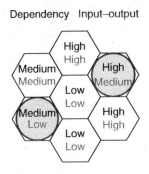

**FIGURE 1.3**   Correlating metrics.

## INTERDEPENDENCY AND CRITICAL INFRASTRUCTURE RISKS

Risk, as it is typically defined in the security world, is an outcome of applying the likelihood of the threat acting upon a vulnerability to create an impact. A baseline, entry-level qualitative risk scale that is easy to understand and frequently applied is shown in Table 1.4.

Depending on which security practitioner you speak with, threats are assessed against vulnerabilities, or vulnerabilities are assessed against threats. This means that you can start risk assessment either by looking at threats first, or vulnerabilities first. But you always have to consider both sides. This is not necessarily a "chicken or egg" situation, it is always optimal to understand your vulnerabilities to zoom in on the most applicable threats, especially if the population of threats is almost infinite.

CI interdependency is fundamentally about CI vulnerability. It is a conduit through which risk is conducted. This translates to an exposure. The fact that CI operations are impacted to a greater or lesser extend by the loss of another CI sectors' inputs means that they are vulnerable to events in other CI sectors. The degree of this vulnerability is the tough part to gauge, and represents at least half the challenge of understanding and managing CI interdependency. This book is primarily about understanding the vulnerabilities of CI sectors. Vulnerabilities are part of the CI risk picture that we are trying to ultimately manage.

Understanding CI vulnerabilities is also the starting point for managing CI risks. If you are concerned with CI risks then your job is facilitated substantially by a picture of the interdependencies—the vulnerabilities—before you start to consider threats. Most people concerned with CI risks (or just risks in general) want to go right to the threats. They want to know what the threats are, where they come from, who has done it, why, what do they want, etc., and then start to layer in controls and safeguards against these threats. This a mistake, and this is why it is a mistake especially in the context of managing CI risks.

CI interdependency is fiendishly complex, to the point we have compared it with mathematical theories about the complexity of the universe: nonlinearity and chaos theories. In the end, the best we can hope to achieve in the area of CI interdependency metrics are qualitative values (nonprecise, ordinal measurements) and not precise calculations.

The complexity of CI is a booby trap for those that wish to jump into CI threat analysis. Without methodological vulnerability data it is very easy to get diverted

---

**TABLE 1.4**

**Baseline Qualitative Risk Scale**

|  | Low Severity Vulnerability | Medium Severity Vulnerability | High Severity Vulnerability |
|---|---|---|---|
| High likelihood of threat event | Medium risk | High risk | High risk |
| Medium likelihood of threat event | Low risk | Medium risk | High risk |
| Low likelihood of threat event | Low risk | Low risk | Medium risk |

down to issues concerning threat agents and threat vectors (the tools and angles of attack for the threat agents) that are wasteful and misdirected. Why? Without perspective on the severity and known range of vulnerabilities, the extent of threats is essentially unbounded. It is unbounded in such a way that you cannot logically exclude or discount any threat agents or vectors; so you will need to consider them all. In CI and taking into account the complexity of these systems, this basically leaves an enormous scope of threats to try and assess and remediate. Without the context of CI vulnerability information, there is a very high probability that not only will some of the wrong (not applicable, very low likelihood) threats be considered but also some of the right (high likelihood) threats will be overlooked. When the vulnerabilities are treated largely based upon threat information, resources will invariably be invested in inappropriate safeguards while leaving some vulnerabilities entirely unaddressed. At the end of the day, it is most important to understand your CI vulnerabilities to assess CI threats.

## STRENGTHS AND LIMITS OF THIS BOOK

There are numerous elements of this book, which might fall under the strengths category. First, this book represents one of the first complete departures from anecdote in the discipline of CI protection and interdependency assessment. Most earlier works base conclusions and findings upon the observations from case studies, war stories, and subject matter expert opinion or limit the focus to specific CI sectors. Although we have reviewed and often consulted with such sources in the course of this work, we have derived none of the metrics in this book from such sources. Second, all metrics and CI interdependency findings are from quantitative and qualitative empirical data which has been gathered and assessed through methodologies exposed within this book. We have tried to be both systematic and transparent in our methods and conclusions, and present our data for others to refine and reinterpret accordingly. Third, unlike much of the existing body of work in CI protection, which tends to focus on a limited number of CI relationships among a limited number of industries (as opposed to sectors), this work deliberately and systematically attempts to cover all CI sectors and even refine the definition of CI sectors to make them more rational. The observations about vulnerabilities and risks related to CI sector interdependency offer a full 360 degree view of the environment as it is currently understood. Regardless of which sector a reader is most concerned with, they will find full treatment within these pages. Similarly, if the indications for a given sector lead stakeholders to want to know more about the vulnerabilities and risks of other interdependent sectors for the purposes of their own risk management, again, the information is here in equal measure. Fourth, this book focuses on a rather under-serviced but vital part of CI risk management—vulnerabilities. Attempts to assess threats have consumed much of the effort around CI protection, but threats are only half the equation of calculating risks—the other half is assessing and quantifying vulnerabilities. This book is an attempt to try and shed some light into the dark side of CI protection. A concluding strength of this book lies in what it leaves as a solid foundation for in the future. Much more work can be built on top of what is contained in this book. More detailed quantitative analysis and especially the gathering and assessment of industry-specific metrics would be beneficial. This chapter creates an underpinning upon which to build valid and repeatable CI risk management systems, and shows value to CI stakeholders which will encourage collaboration and participation—essential to the eventual success of any CI protection strategy.

What is yin without yang? This book has its limits which we openly acknowledge, and we take this opportunity to address a few of the more potent criticisms here and now. First, CI stakeholders are still looking for detailed threat information regardless of what we say about the need to understand vulnerabilities first. We do not provide anything near the level of detail about threats to CI as we do about vulnerabilities and consequently what we say about risks is generalized. Threat information is highly parochial, dynamic, and time sensitive. Experience has shown us that CI stakeholders don't want generalized threat information, but want details such as who, what assets, when, how, and why? If we undertook to publish such information, it would be out of date before we even finished proofreading the chapter. Detailed threat information is the domain of short-term assessment or real-time reporting systems. In Chapter 5 we address how threats to CI might be measured at significant levels of detail, but we don't provide specific threat data. Sorry. Second, this book contains a lot of numbers (but also a lot of pictures) that will result in a perception by some people that the kernels of valuable information are buried and inaccessible. As Andrew Jaquith in his recent book *Security Metrics* observes that executives in large businesses seem to have no trouble absorbing and making decisions about complex financial market indicators and metrics. So they should be able to apply those same skills to the comprehension of the graphics and visualization aids within this book that have been deliberately modeled upon financial visualization techniques. Having made that rather defensive remark, we admit that there is a lot of detail about CI in general but not as much about specific industries. For instance, we speak about the Transportation sector in detail—but not airlines in particular. This is as much an artifact of the way CI id defined as it is about the state of research. We are at the beginning.

Another potential criticism of this book is that it documents normal operating conditions and interdependencies under those circumstances, but what we need to know are the interdependencies under crisis conditions. Normal operating conditions are the ways in which CI sectors will probably spend 99.5 percent or more of their time functioning. Normal operating conditions are the point of departure when a crisis strikes; these are the conditions of preparedness and the interrelationships which characterize preparedness. Interdependency metrics based on normal operating conditions are the baseline from which distinct crisis metrics emerge, and can provide a basic order and latency of impact under an all-hazards approach to CI risk management.

Ideally, we would possess two distinct metrics for each CI interrelationship: normal operating conditions and crisis conditions. Unfortunately, each crisis is as different as the unlimited number of threat agents and events. Crisis metrics under one threat/scenario will be completely different from another threat/scenario. For this reason, collecting and presenting crisis interdependency metrics are an infinite undertaking and of limited value. Interdependency metrics under normal operating conditions provide the basis for appropriate, all-hazards risk management related to CI interdependency. Case studies provided in Chapter 6 utilize normal operating conditions to extrapolate to the likely, though amplified, levels of dependency during crisis conditions. The case studies show how the dependency metrics which have been analyzed and presented in detail in this book are applicable to crisis conditions versus normal operating conditions.

Finally, this book will rely upon a system of correlation where the resulting composite metrics are manually adjusted up or down according to indications from correlation analysis. Adjustments are applied according to subject matter expert opinion rather than through a pure, repeatable mathematical formula. This approach is used because it is typical in risk management for subject matter opinion to have the final say in assessments; mathematical formulas, though beautifully repeatable, are rarely if ever trusted for a final verdict on complex topics with many moving parts. For instance, in the world of financial risk management, mathematical quantitative formulas are routinely used as decision support tools, but human experts have the final call and make adjustments accordingly for all substantial transactions. (Even if they make the wrong call or provide faulty instructions for automatic execution.) Similarly, Standard & Poors—a rater of equity and debt—has definitely stated that risk management and assessment must include and be ultimately managed by human experts rather than machines applying formulas.* The resulting metrics and ratings used to assess trading trillions of dollars of risk daily are composites of quantitative and qualitative metrics—not unlike those proposed in this book.

## CHAPTERS TO COME

The chapters that follow delve deeply into the issues discussed in this introductory chapter on CI interdependency.

Chapter 2 attempts to refine and define CI sectors according to a methodology derived from economic statistical analysis. This chapter considers the existing definitions and discusses these definitions in light of the reality of economic interchange and business relationships. Chapter 2 reviews the pedigree of data dependency and the associated analytical methodology, and its linkages to previous, similar work. Once the definitions of CI sectors have been considered, an analysis of relative, indicated economic interdependency between the sectors will be undertaken. The basis of all this interdependency assessment is quantitative metrics derived from national I–O metrics. The I–O metrics will be sourced from Canada and the United States, with interdependency assessment metrics generated for each country independently. Following each set of economic dependency metrics will follow some brief analysis of the findings.

Chapter 3 explores qualitative metrics in the form of the data dependency assessment conducted against the ten defined CI sectors. Data dependency refers to the reliance of one sector upon the data flowing from other sectors for the continuance of normal operations. Data dependency is considered a second form of metric indicative of overall interdependency among CI sectors. Chapter 3 reviews the pedigree of data dependency and the associated analytical methodology, and its linkages to previous, similar work. The data dependency methodology itself will

---

* Standard and Poors, S&P completes initial "PIM" risk management review for selected U.S. energy firms, May 29, 2007, p. 4.

then be explained including some of the data-collections processes and tools. Chapter 3 discusses in detail the data dependency results from seminal North American work, including some analysis of the indications. Chapter 3, like Chapter 2, is intended to define and discuss a particular metric (information and data dependency) which can be used as a proxy indicator for CI interdependency.

Chapter 4 brings together the quantitative metrics presented in Chapter 2 with the qualitative metrics of Chapter 3 and correlates these metrics. The results are then discussed and assessed in detail. Results consist of primary two varieties of analysis: strong correlations and possible interpretations of the correlations; weak correlations and likely causes for the failure of correlation and possible corrective approaches. Chapter 4 introduces the concept of dependency latency—different sectors are impacted at different points in time by outages—and also proposes forms of cascading vulnerability flows among the sectors based dependency latency and the correlated interdependency metrics.

Chapter 5 is our threat chapter. It proposes a variety of methods and approaches to assessing CI threats from both physical and logical/technical perspectives. This chapter provides risk managers a boarder and deeper context from which to consider future risk management strategies and perhaps reconsider current strategies.

In Chapter 6, the correlated dependency metrics are applied to several case studies involving different type of incidents and include a discussion of possible risk to current CI sectors. The case studies are intended to provide examples of how to apply the material from the earlier chapters into risk assessment activities around CI sectors.

## CONCLUSION

It is certain that you need more than one metric about CIs to assess interdependency. You need multiple, distinct metrics that can arguably be shown to reflect properties of interdependency. Furthermore, the metrics that are selected need to show positive correlation to underpin validity or flag weaknesses of the interdependency assessment.

This book presents two methodologies for collecting empirical evidence about CI interdependency in the form of the two types of qualitative and quantitative metrics. Of these two sources of metrics, sample results are supplied for econometric data and data dependency, and the process of correlation and assessment of the findings are undertaken in Chapter 4.

For people working within the CI sectors, it may appear a legitimate question to ask: why do I need to understand all this information about other sectors? This is not an uncommon perspective among people working within sectors because the sectors by themselves are so often large that inputs from any other CI sector seem small relative to the overall operational scope. What they do not see, and is an objective of this work, is the interdependency among CI sectors that links them together such that there is a potential for cascading impacts which affect multiple sectors at the same time. This is the distinction that managers within CI sectors need to be aware of while no single sector might represent a direct and imminent threat to the delivery of goods and services, what combination of sectors impacts is a problem? If they lose safety infrastructure and food infrastructure at the same time, what does that mean? If both the Transportation and the Financial services sectors wobbled for reasons of their own interdependency, what does that mean to business? Analogous to this issue of multiple impacts is the phenomena we discussed of second-order and tertiary impacts, where a failure in one sector cascades and results in multiple impacts to other sectors.

# 2 Econometrics and Critical Infrastructure Interdependency

## INTRODUCTION

Abstract statistical information does not sway us as much as the anecdote—no matter how sophisticated the person.*

Since this chapter deals with lots of statistics, the translation of statistical observations into anecdotal analysis has been done wherever possible. It is of great interest to a few people, but possibly contains too many complex details for some readers. For these readers, the conclusion is recommended. The following pages take an in-depth look into the economic relationships between different industries designated as critical infrastructure (CI) within Canada and the United States and how these relationships impact the nature of CI and the interdependencies among CI sectors.

This chapter is a core part of understanding the proposed methodology for assessing CI independencies within this book, but it is not necessary to fully and completely review this chapter to understand the outcomes of this book.

If you are a policy maker, and insurer/risk manager or a contract lawyer this chapter will definitely interest you, because it reveals interdependencies from the perspective of dollar flows and service-level requirements. It also contains an assessment of interdependency as represented by the analysis of statistical data in Canada and the United States.

For the policy maker and possibly the regulator, this chapter outlines the flow of goods and services, measured by dollar value, among CI at the national-level and provides some indications of how Government itself consumes CI goods and services. This results in an insight into how Safety and Government especially require CI goods and services to continue operations. It also explores how the definitions of CI which are applied may require refinement based upon the observable flow of goods and services among sectors. For instance, the exclusion of certain industries from the current, formal CI definitions may be an obstacle to the development of effective policy around controls, safeguards, response, and remediation.

For the insurer or their counterparty, the risk manager, this chapter provides a sector-level view of supply-chain dependencies and the possibility of second-order impacts, which drive insurable losses. This results in understanding the types

---

* Taleb, N.N., 2007. *The Black Swan: The Impact of The Highly Improbable*, Random House, New York, p. 79.

of exclusions and insurance riders, which might be applied to protect either the insurance company from undue loss or the risk manager's firm from uninsured losses.

For the contract lawyer, this chapter provides a sector-level view of supply-chain dependencies and the application of appropriate contract terms to these relationships. For instance, the types of contracted service levels that might be applied to protect either the buyer or seller (depending on which side the lawyer is) from undue loss associated with service-level breaches caused by failures further down the supply chain.

CI interdependency is a highly complex topic to approach. Chapter 2 represents one of the two proposed, metric-based approaches to a difficult field of study. The input–output (I–O) analysis and observations presented here are not presented as conclusive, but as proposed proxy indicators for interdependency. Chapter 3 continues to present the second proposed proxy indicator to CI interdependency analysis. And Chapter 4 correlates the proxy indicators into a single, composite metric for CI interdependency applicable at the national level of analysis.

Finally, this approach to analysis of business patterns (e.g., patterns of CI interdependency) has its roots in the original I–O work of Wassily Leontief (1905–1999) at Harvard University during the 1950s.* Leontief was the first to show how "...the Input–Output Model of economics uses a matrix representation of a nation's (or a region's) economy to predict the effect of changes in one industry on others and by consumers, government, and foreign suppliers on the economy."[†] Later efforts to specifically address the assessment of CI interdependency using I–O econometrics can be observed in the work of Yacov Y. Haimes from the University of Virginia.[‡] However, Haimes focused on specific industries rather than infrastructure sectors and to the best of the author's knowledge, did not attempt correlation with other independent variables related to interdependency.

## CI SECTORS AND ECONOMETRIC INTERDEPENDENCY ANALYSIS

The chapter builds on the work done in Chapter 1, where existing CI sector definitions in Canada and the United States were expressed in terms of a well-understood classification scheme—North American Industry Classification System (NAICS)—which is briefly reviewed below. From this point, we will engage in high-level CI sector interdependency analysis based upon the I–O statistical interdependency analysis using the contemporary CI sector definitions. This analysis will be based upon both a comprehensive view of all sectors and their relationships to each other using tools, we refer to as "maps" and "tornados," for each individual CI sector. Initially, Canada and the United States will be reviewed and described individually, then compared side by side. Our statistical interdependency analysis

---

* Leontief, W.W., 1951. Input–output economics, *Scientific American*, October: 15–21.
[†] Leontief, W.W., http://en.wikipedia.org/w/index.php?title = Wassily_Leontief & oldid = 169820201.
[‡] Haimes, Y.Y., B.M. Horowitz, J.H. Lambert, J.R. Santos, K.G. Crowther, and C. Lian, 2005. Inoperability input–output model (IIM) for interdependent infrastructure sectors: Case study, *Journal of Infrastructure Systems*.

will also look at what is possibly overlooked by the current definitions of CI sectors—which industries appear to be critical within CI sector but not designated critical under the policy definitions currently in place and therefore the subject of government funded projects.

## LIMITS OF THIS APPROACH

Using NAICS and statistical information for CI interdependency assessment has some obvious limits. To begin with, the CI definitions which are currently used in Canada and the United States have not been developed with NAICS terminology in mind. As a result, some of the descriptions used for industries are not identical, so the mapping exercise performed in this chapter has had to engage in a certain amount of translation between the terms used by public safety entities dealing with CI issues and statistical entities dealing with NAICS schemes.

A further limit to this exercise is the depth to which the I–O statistics are available from Statistics Canada and the U.S. Bureau of Economic Analysis (BEA). Although current definitions of CI can be very specific in the description of the industries they include, e.g., wastewater treatments, I–O statistics are not provided for all of the 900+ defined industries. In fact, the 900+ industries defined by NAICS are grouped into an approximate of 120 I–O groups in the case of Canada and 70 aggregate groups in the case of U.S. data sets. This aggregation was done to make CI assessment easier. These aggregations sometimes group non-CI industries with CI industries and necessitated that the authors attempt to reverse engineer I–O data to separate certain needed data from data which might not be required and would bias results. This is the greatest limit of using generally available statistical I–O data for interdependency assessment. In future editions, significant improvements in analysis may be obtained with access to more detailed, customized I–O econometric information.

The final limit of this approach to CI interdependency assessment is that the definition of CI sectors is ad hoc. That is, they have apparently been developed without any defined methodology and are therefore subject to gaps: e.g., certain industries essentially not listed as critical are in fact critical to a sector by virtue of the strength of its relationship with other parts of the sector. For instance, coal mining is not listed as a CI, though 50 percent of U.S. electricity is generated with coal.

The limits inherent in this approach to CI interdependency assessment make the findings associated with this chapter not only interesting and informative, but also merely indicative. However, the correlation of these findings with those from Chapter 3, which discusses dependency assessment, provides two independent and random metric associated with CI interdependency, which together provide indicators with much stronger foundation.

## MAPPING NAICS TO CI SECTORS

A caveat: Safety and Government sector have been combined into a single CI sector for much of this book because available I–O data does not allow police and fire (Safety sector) to be separated from other government spending. (This is not to say that someone in the BEA or Statistics Canada does not have this information at their fingertips. Someone probably does! But the author failed to ever find these people and their data after months of effort. If you do exist—please contact us so we can apply them as revised analysis in this book!)

The following mappings are at the "L-level" (link level) of statistical description as defined by Statistics Canada for the NAICS I–O metrics, or the "summary" level as defined by the Bureau of Economic Information for the United States. A very wide variety of statistics is available from both Statistics Canada and the BEA related to economic interrelationships. The type of statistics that was sought for the purposes of this analysis was the industry-by-industry spending or gross output. The reason why industry by industry was employed (as opposed to industry by commodity or commodity by commodity) was that CI is mostly privately owned. Companies generally describe themselves and their supply chains along industrial lines as opposed to using commodity definitions.

The Canadian and United States statistics were not available at the same level of detail for the same years due to different census and survey calendars between the two countries. However, the following mapping that has been applied represents the most detailed, the most recent statistics available as of Q1 2008.

Table 2.1 gives a better understanding of what the contemporary definitions of CI sectors can reasonably be assumed to contain in the context of a well-defined classification system, such as NAICS. For instance, when one considers the Food sector and its formalized definition of production, processing, distribution, and safety, you might not immediately make a leap to soft drink bottling. Yet this is a very reasonable inclusion given established NAICS classifications in Canada and the United States. Has anyone bothered to tell the bottlers that they are considered CI? Similarly, tobacco and alcohol products are grouped very tightly with food products under NAICS and in statistical products from Statistics Canada and the BEA (perhaps because they are also physically consumed by people). Yet it would appear absurd to consider tobacco and alcohol as CI, unless you are a gangster, smuggler, or pirate.

The Manufacturing sector definition contains defense industrial base, which is a fairly broad term that is translated for industrial classification purposes as aerospace and other transportation by Canada and the United States, respectively. However, this is not to imply that defense industrial base is comparable to defense spending. The numbers reflected in our analysis reflect spending within the classification aerospace and other transportation—not defense spending. Defense spending numbers are published by both Canada and the United States, but they are not broken down by industrial input for security reasons. In the case of the United States, defense spending is a classification in the I–O tables with a single (massive) input, federal government spending, and no listed outputs. In Canada, defense spending is simply aggregated with other federal government services. NAICS does support a code for defense services (code 9111) under the category public administration (code 91), but it is not used in I–O tables.

Industry-by-industry I–O tables, as previously mentioned, are not available at low levels of granularity. In fact, in several cases, segregations and inferences about sector inputs and outputs had to be manually generated using detailed

## TABLE 2.1
## Contemporary CI Sector Definitions under NAICS

| CI Sector and Harmonized Definitions | Canadian Statistics NAICS Mapping to CI Sectors | U.S. Statistics NAICS Mapping to CI Sectors |
|---|---|---|
| Finance (banking, storage, investment exchange, disbursement, and securities) | 5A01 Monetary authorities and depository credit intermediation | 521CI Federal reserve banks, credit intermediation, and related activities |
| | 5A02 Insurance carriers | 523 Securities, commodity contracts, and investments |
| | 5A06 Other finance, insurance and real estate and management of companies and enterprises | 55 Management of companies and enterprises |
| | | 524 Insurance carriers and related activities |
| | | 525 Funds, trusts, and other financial vehicles |
| Energy (electric power generation and transmission, oil and gas production and storage) | 2211 Electric power generation, transmission, and distribution | 22 Utilities (excluding water) |
| | 2111 Oil and gas extraction | 211 Oil and gas extraction |
| | 3241 Petroleum and coal products manufacturing | 324 Petroleum and coal products |
| | 4860 Pipeline transportation[a] | |
| Information and communications (telecommunications and information technology, broadcasting systems, software, hardware, and networks including the Internet) | 513A Pay TV, speciality TV and program distribution and telecommunications | 513 Broadcasting and telecommunications |
| | 541B Computer systems design and other professional, scientific, and technical services | 5415 Computer systems design and related services |
| Health care (hospitals, ambulances, blood banks, laboratories, surveillance, and personal health services) | 62A0 Health care services (except hospitals) and social assistance | 621 Ambulatory health care services |
| | GS11 Hospitals | 622HO Hospitals and nursing and residential care facilities |
| | 3254 Pharmaceuticals and medicine manufacturing | NA—pharmaceuticals are bundled with chemical manufacturing |
| Food (production, processing, distribution, and safety) | 11A0 Crop and animal production | 111CA Farms |
| | 1140 Fishing, hunting, and trapping | 311FT Food and beverage (except tobacco and alcohol products)[b] |

*(continued)*

**TABLE 2.1 (continued)**
**Contemporary CI Sector Definitions under NAICS**

| CI Sector and Harmonized Definitions | Canadian Statistics NAICS Mapping to CI Sectors | U.S. Statistics NAICS Mapping to CI Sectors |
|---|---|---|
| | 3111 Animal food manufacturing | |
| | 3113 Sugar and confectionary manufacturing | |
| | 3114 Fruit and vegetable preserving and speciality food manufacturing | |
| | 311A Miscellaneous food manufacturing | |
| | 312A Soft drink and ice manufacturing | |
| | 3115 Dairy product manufacturing | |
| | 3116 Meat product manufacturing | |
| | 3117 Seafood product manufacturing | |
| Water (drinking water and wastewater management treatment) | 221A Natural gas distribution, water, sewage, and other systems | 2213 Water, sewage, and other systems[c] |
| Transport (aviation, mass transit, rail, marine, and road) | 4810 Air transportation | 481 Air transportation |
| | 4820 Rail transportation | 482 Rail transportation |
| | 4830 Water transportation | 483 Water transportation |
| | 4840 Truck transportation | 484 Truck transportation |
| | 4850 Transit and ground passenger transportation | 485 Transit and ground passenger transportation |
| | | 486 Pipeline transportation[d] |
| | NA—Couriers, messengers, and postal services are excluded from Canadian CI definitions | 487OS—Other transportation services[e] |
| Safety (law enforcement, fire, search and rescue, and emergency services) | GS40—Other municipal government services | GFG Federal general government |
| | GS50—Other provincial government services | GSLG State and local government |
| | GS60—Other federal government services | |
| Government (social services, regulation) | GS40—Other municipal government services | GFG Federal general government |
| | GS50—Other provincial government services | GSLG State and local government |
| | GS60—Other federal government services | |

## TABLE 2.1 (continued)
## Contemporary CI Sector Definitions under NAICS

| CI Sector and Harmonized Definitions | Canadian Statistics NAICS Mapping to CI Sectors | U.S. Statistics NAICS Mapping to CI Sectors |
|---|---|---|
| Manufacturing (defense industrial base, chemical industry) | 325A—Miscellaneous chemical product manufacturing 3251—Basic chemicals 3364 Aerospace product and parts manufacturing[f] | 325 Chemical products  3364OT Other transportation equipment[g] |

[a] Canadian and U.S. grouping of pipelines under CIs differ very clearly. Canadian CI definitions state that transmission systems are part of the energy infrastructure. In Canada, transmission systems are regulated by the National Energy Board (NEB), which governs both electricity and pipeline transmission systems. The NEB is under the Natural Resources Minister of the Canadian federal government, which manages energy resources.

[b] The BEA industry by industry I–O information has grouped tobacco and alcohol products under Food 311FT. Data for this analysis has been inferred using the proportional I–O share of tobacco and alcohol products relative to all other products starting with prefix "311" from 1997, and applied this proportion to 2005 data for 311FT to create 311FT (excluding tobacco and alcohol) and 311FT (tobacco and alcohol).

[c] The BEA industry by industry I–O information does not include 2213 as a discreet item in records earlier than 1997—the last detailed census year. Data for this analysis has been inferred using the proportional I–O share of 2213 under 211 utilities from 1997, and applied this proportion to 2005 data for 221 to extract 2213.

[d] Canadian and U.S. groupings of pipelines under CIs differ very clearly. U.S. definitions of CI place pipelines under the Transportation sector are regulated by the Department of Transportation as transport systems for hazardous goods.

[e] Other transportation services were included to account for the U.S. postal services and courier and messenger services, that are considered to be part of CI in the United States, but not in Canada.

[f] Under Canadian CI definition, defense industrial base is considered a sector—but there is no obvious, equivalent NAICS industry group; similarly, there is no generally accepted definition for defense industrial base, which might provide clues to industries that are within such a base. However, industrial spending patterns available from the UK MOD (http://www.york.ac.uk/depts/econ/documents/research/DTIPUBFR.pdf) indicated that aerospace is the largest component of the defense industrial base at 23 percent, followed by electronics (13 percent), construction (12 percent), shipbuilding (11 percent), ordnance (4 percent), vehicles (4 percent), and miscellaneous (33 percent). For this reason, Aerospace is included under Manufacturing, because most Aerospace spending will be to either government (for defense) or Transportation sector. Electronics is at least partially if not fully covered under Communications and IT. Ordnance is a subgroup under NAICS 333—machinery, which is itself a massive sector too large to include without skewing results substantially. Similarly, shipbuilding and vehicle manufacturing are subgroups under NAICS 336—transportation equipment manufacturing, also a massive sector too large to include without skewing results.

[g] Similar to the Canadian situation, under U.S. CI definitions, defense industrial base is considered as a sector—but there is no obvious, equivalent NAICS industry group, or generally accepted definition for defense industrial base, which might provide clues for industries that are within such a base. In this instance, 3364OT Other Transporation equipment was the closest subgroup to the aerospace subgroup used for Canada under the reasoning applied in the previous note [f].

gross domestic product (GDP) statistics, For instance, to unbundle water and waste treatment from electricity generation (utilities) or tobacco and alcohol from food and beverage manufacturing. Additionally, the Safety sector and the Government are not apparently divisible on the basis of industry-by-industry I–O: they are lumped together by the statistical agencies. For this reason they have also been necessarily lumped together for interdependency analysis, bringing the total number of actual sectors from ten down to nine.

## CANADIAN I–O ECONOMIC INTERDEPENDENCY MAPPING

The exchange of goods and services among CI sectors is a quantitative indicator of interdependency. Using the definitions for CI sectors established in Table 2.1: contemporary CI sector definitions under NAICS, it has now become possible to reference directly to the I–O statistics generated and maintained by Canada and the United States and gain indications of interdependency.

As stated in Chapter 1, no single metric can form a credible picture of CI interdependency. More than one dimension can be used to create representations of reality and at least two dimensions for model reality. This section will assess the CI interdependencies, which might be interpreted using a purely econometric approach to analysis in the form of summary, but will not attempt to critique these indications. Chapter 4 will accomplish this task by correlating statistical dimension with data dependency dimension (Chapter 3) allowing for analysis of strength and weaknesses.

The econometric analysis of CI interdependency undertaken involved review and detailed analysis of over 10,000 distinct metrics for Canada. Statistics from the year 2004 were assessed for Canada (the latest available data at the time of writing). The resulting data sets are complex and the relationships between the sectors are equally complex and multilayered.

To try and steer clear vast matrixes of sterile numbers, we have adopted tools know as "treemaps"*—henceforth just maps—and tornados to try and display the relationships and interdependencies between the CI sectors. As we quoted at the beginning of the chapter "Abstract statistical information does not sway us as much as the anecdote…" therefore we are using maps and tornados as visual anecdotes for thousands and thousands of statistical metrics.

Figure 2.1 shows the total sector-to-sector consumption or use of goods and services by all CI sectors in Canada. Both the size and the shade of the box are an indication of the value. Although the size of the boxes is possibly useful in assessing interdependency, it is also an indication of the overall size of the sector in the Canadian economy. The size of the box indicates the overall relative value of spending by a sector with other sectors. The lighter the shade (with white being the lightest possible) the closer is the maximum value for consumption relative to all consumption from all sectors. The boxes within a sector box mostly tell how sectors

---

* Treemaps are tools developed by Ben Shneiderman at the University of Maryland in the 1990s to display complex and multilayer data sets. http://www.cs.umd.edu/hcil/treemap-history/.

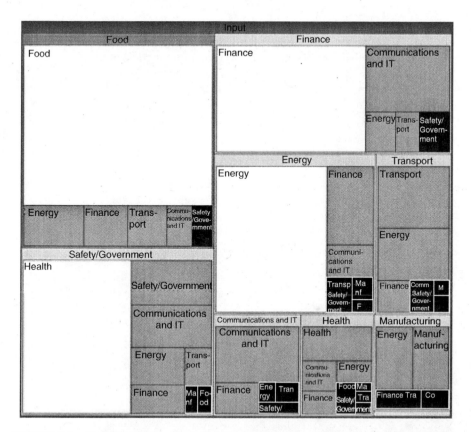

**FIGURE 2.1** Canadian CI economic "use" interdependency. White □ = high value inputs ($10 billion to a maximum value of $40 billion). Gray ▓ = medium value inputs ($1–$10 billion). Black ■ = lower value of inputs ($1 million to $1 billion). Each sector block is proportional to the size of its total value of economic inputs consumed by the sector. Each square within each sector block indicates the proportional size of economic inputs in dollars.

consume and are possibly interdependent on the goods and services produced by each other. Detailed sector analysis will occur shortly.

Figure 2.1 shows that the Food sector in Canada is the largest overall consumer of goods and services from other CI sectors because Food has the largest box within the map. Within the Food sector, we can also see that intrasector spending (Food-to-Food) in goods and services—a white box—is not only the largest component of Food spending, but also proportionally the largest sector-to-sector spending relative to all other sectors. Spending on inputs from Food to Food is greater than any other form of sector-to-sector spending in Canada under the contemporary definitions of CI.

Figure 2.1 also shows how all other sectors relate proportionally as far as the consumption of goods and services required from other CI sectors are to support the production of their own goods and services. Note that Figure 2.1 is not a representation of all goods and services consumed by all CI sectors, it only indicated consumption of goods and services from other CI sectors. Goods and services consumed from other non-CI industries may represent greater overall spending for certain sectors. The distinction between consumption of goods and services from CI sectors and non-CI sectors will be displayed and analyzed in depth later in this chapter.

Figure 2.2 shows the total sector-to-sector output or make of goods and services by all CI sectors in Canada. Both the size and the shade of the box are an indication of the value. Although the size of the boxes is possibly useful in assessing interdependency, it is also an indication of the overall size of the sector in the Canadian economy. The size of the box indicates the overall relative value of goods and services delivered by a CI sector to other CI sectors. The lighter the shade (with white being the lightest possible) the higher value of output relative to

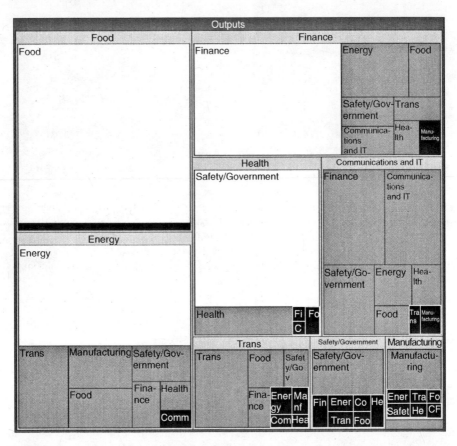

**FIGURE 2.2** Canadian CI economic "make" interdependency. White □ = high-value inputs ($10 billion to a maximum value of $40 billion). Gray ▤ = medium value inputs ($1–$10 billion). Black ■ = lower value of inputs ($1 million to $1 billion). Each sector block is proportional to the size of its total value of economic inputs consumed by the sector. Each square within each sector block indicates the proportional size of economic inputs in dollars.

all outputs to all sectors. The boxes within a sector box mostly indicate how sectors consume and how interdependent they are on the goods and services produced by each other.

Figure 2.2 shows that the Food sector in Canada is the largest overall producer of CI goods and services, and Food has the largest box within the map. Within the Food sector, we can also see that intrasector spending in goods and services—a white box— is not only the largest component of Food spending, but that direct consumption of Food, goods and services by the other CI sectors is almost negligible by contrast. Spending on inputs from Food to Food is greater than any other form of sector-to-sector spending in Canada under the contemporary definitions of CI.

The Safety and Government box is also very small in Figure 2.2 because the size of services sold by Canadian government to CI sector is relatively small. However, this calculation does not include the taxes paid by CI sectors. Services sold to CI sectors would include licenses, processing charges, and other miscellaneous service charges.

Figure 2.2 also shows how all other sectors relate proportionally as far as the production of goods and services destined for other CI sectors is concerned. Note that Figure 2.2 is not a representation of all goods and services produced by all CI sectors—it only indicates production of goods and services destined for other CI sectors. Goods and services consumed by other non-CI industries and consumers may represent greater overall spending. The distinction between consumption of goods and services from CI sectors and non-CI sectors will be displayed and analyzed in depth later in this chapter.

## SECTOR-BY-SECTOR I–O (USE VERSUS MAKE)

Sector-by-sector discussion represents analysis of the levels and types of interdependency indicated by economic analysis of CI sectors. Each sector is described using economic input and output tornado figures, and ratio metrics. These figures and numbers do not indicate total consumption or production, which would necessarily include non-CI sector goods and services, and consumer consumption.

Tornado figures show the economic inputs from all the CI sectors to the given sector, from the largest input to the smallest input among the conventionally defined CI sectors. A tornado illustrates the manner in which a sector consumes and supplies goods and services from other CI sectors. Note, this is not a measure of all goods and services consumed by a sector, but a measure of only the goods and services from other CI sectors. Values are in Canadian dollars from the recently available detailed I–O data from Statistics Canada prepared in 2003. The Canadian dollar was worth between approximately \$65 and \$78 during that year.

An I–O ratio is also generated to support analysis of sector-to-sector interdependency analysis. An I–O ratio is simply the input value of a given sector divided by the output value of a given sector. For instance, the dollar value of goods and services consumed by Energy from Finance (inputs) divided by the dollar value of goods and services consumed by Finance from Energy (outputs). This ratio shows relative weight of consumption versus supply among sectors and is useful in spotting the strength and direction of dependency as indicated by value flows.

The assumption underlying tornados and I–O ratios is that the more lopsided the flow of money between two given sectors, the more lopsided the dependency relationship may be. For instance, if Energy spends significantly more on Communications and IT than vice versa, it is an indication that Energy may be more dependent upon Communications and IT than vice versa.

I–O ratios are useful for high-level, at-a-glance analysis but are certainly not definitive because, as we will examine shortly, a flawed sector definition can exclude certain high-value inputs or outputs from overlooked industrial sectors and skew the I–O ratio. Furthermore, I–O ratios ignore the relative value of the inputs and outputs. If there is an I–O ratio of 2.0 resulting from a $1 billion of inputs versus $500 million in outputs between two sectors, this is a much more significant observation that $1 million in inputs versus $500,000 in outputs. Although the I–O ratio in both instances is 2.0, the difference of half a million dollars in trade between two entire sectors is more an indication of no significant relation has opposed to any form of dependency from one sector to another. I–O ratios should be considered in the context of the values shown input and output Tornados—not in isolation.

## ENERGY SECTOR IN CANADA

Figure 2.3 depicts the I–O analysis for Energy sector in Canada.

Total value of sector inputs consumed from other CI sectors is $31.4 billion—fourth largest gross consumer of CI goods and services.

Total value of sector outputs required by other CI sectors is $36.7 billion—second largest gross supplier to other CI sectors.

### Dependency Observations

- Energy is mostly dependent on goods and services flowing within its own sector—intrasector dependency.
- Energy spends significantly more on goods and services from the Communications and IT sector than what the Communications and IT sector spends on Energy. The indication is that Energy may be more dependent upon Finance than visa versa.
- Energy spends significantly more on goods and services from the Finance sector than what the Finance sector spends on Energy. The indication is that Energy may be more dependent upon Communications and IT than vice versa.
- Health, Food, and Safety/Government appear to have substantial spending and therefore reliance upon Energy with a very low, reciprocal relationship from Energy. The indication is that Health, Food, and Safety/Government are substantially more dependent upon Energy than vice versa.

### Non-CI Sector Inputs to Energy

Although our analysis must necessarily revolve around the contemporary definitions of CI sectors discussed in Chapter 1, an examination of other significant industrial inputs is required. In general, understanding what might be missing from

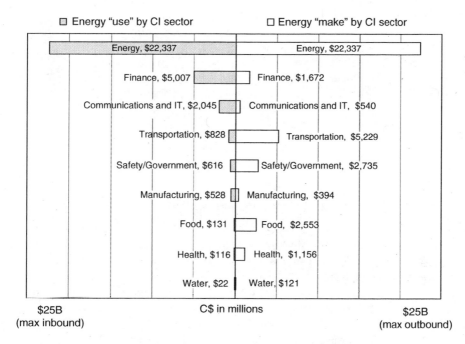

**FIGURE 2.3**   Energy sector tornado.

| | **Energy** | **Communications and IT** | **Finance** | **Health** | **Food** | **Water** | **Transportation** | **Safety/ Government** | **Manufacturing** |
|---|---|---|---|---|---|---|---|---|---|
| I–O ratio | 1.00 | 3.79 | 2.99 | 0.10 | 0.04 | 0.18 | 0.16 | 0.23 | 0.15 |

the current definitions of CI sectors will help assess the accuracy and validity of the dependency findings.

Assessment of the non-CI sector inputs is assessed here specifically for Energy, but will be aggregated across all sectors and discussed in detail toward the end of this Chapter. Figure 2.4 is a waterfall of the top 15 industrial inputs to the Energy sector in Canada, including both CI and non-CI sectors.

## Key Observations Related to Non-CI Sector Inputs

Regarding the short-term delivery of the Energy sector's core goods and services and the industries, which are direct operational inputs, the following observations are made:

- Wholesale and retail trades together are the fourth largest input to Energy— only slightly less than Communications and IT. This reflects the importance of the distribution of nonelectric Energy goods such as liquid fuels and

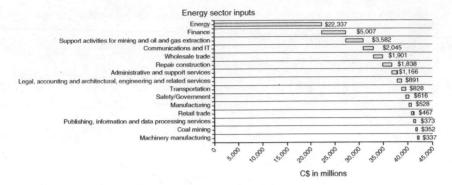

**FIGURE 2.4**   Energy sector inputs—top 15 industries.

compressed gases, which are accounted under these trade industries. Wholesale and retail trades are not considered part of a CI under current definitions.

- Coal mining is not considered a CI, although it is the 14th largest input in Canada to Energy and 25 percent of Canadian energy is generated with coal. Coal mining is not considered part of a CI under current definitions.
- Publishing, information and data processing services are a large input into the Energy. Such services are listed under NAICS 5182 (data processing, hosting and related services) and includes "establishments primarily engaged in providing infrastructure for hosting or data processing services. These establishments may provide specialized hosting activities, such as web hosting, streaming services or application hosting, provide application service provisioning, or may provide general time-share mainframe facilities to clients. Data processing establishments provide complete processing and specialized reports from data supplied by clients or provide automated data processing and data entry services."* Information and data processing is not considered a CI under current definitions.

**Note:**   See Conclusions and Indicated Risks of this chapter for a roll-up of all non-CI inputs.

## Communications and IT Sector in Canada

Figure 2.5 depicts the I–O analysis for Communications and IT sector in Canada.

Total value of sector inputs consumed by Communications and IT internally and from other CI sectors is $10.7 billion—sixth largest gross consumer of CI goods and services among the CI sectors.

Total value of sector outputs required by other CI sectors is $25.6 billion—fifth largest gross supplier to other CI sectors among the sectors.

---

* http://www.census.gov/epcd/naics02/def/NDEF518.HTM#N5182.

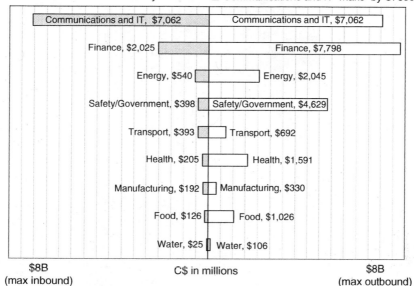

☐Communications and IT "use" by CI sector   ☐ Communications and IT "make" by CI sector

| | |
|---|---|
| Communications and IT, $7,062 | Communications and IT, $7,062 |
| Finance, $2,025 | Finance, $7,798 |
| Energy, $540 | Energy, $2,045 |
| Safety/Government, $398 | Safety/Government, $4,629 |
| Transport, $393 | Transport, $692 |
| Health, $205 | Health, $1,591 |
| Manufacturing, $192 | Manufacturing, $330 |
| Food, $126 | Food, $1,026 |
| Water, $25 | Water, $106 |

$8B
(max inbound)                    C$ in millions                    $8B
                                                                (max outbound)

**FIGURE 2.5**   Communications and IT sector tornado.

| | Energy | Communications and IT | Finance | Health | Food | Water | Transportation | Safety/ Government | Manu- facturing |
|---|---|---|---|---|---|---|---|---|---|
| I–O ratio | 0.26 | 1.00 | 0.26 | 0.13 | 0.09 | 0.24 | 0.57 | 0.09 | 0.49 |

## Dependency Observations

- Energy and Finance both appear to have heavily dependent relationships with Communications and IT based upon the fact that they spend four times more with Communications and IT than Communications and IT spends on their goods and services.
- Transportation is the closest sector to equilibrium between inputs and outputs and is the fourth largest supplier to Communications and IT—indicating equal levels of awareness and responsibilities to each others' priorities.

## Non-CI Sector Inputs to Communications and IT

Although our analysis must necessarily revolve around the contemporary definitions of CI sectors discussed in Chapter 1, an examination of other significant industrial inputs is required. Understanding what might be missing from the current definitions of CI sectors will help assess the accuracy and validity of the dependency findings.

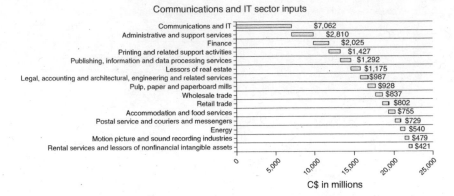

**FIGURE 2.6**  Communications and IT sector inputs—top 15 industries.

At present, the non-CI sector inputs are assessed specifically for Communications and IT, but later will be aggregated across all sectors toward the end of this chapter. Figure 2.6 is a waterfall of the top 15 industrial inputs to the Communications and IT sector in Canada, including both CI and non-CI sectors.

## Key Observations

Regarding the short-term delivery of the sector's core goods and services and the industries, which are direct operational inputs, the following observations are made:

- Wholesale and retail trades are major inputs to Communications and IT reflecting the requirement to distribute specific tangible goods (phones, modems, computers, and software) to deliver and support the core services (bandwidth, connectivity, and customer support). Wholesale and retail trades are not considered part of a CI under current definitions.
- Publishing, information and data processing services are a larger input into the Communications and IT CI sector than Energy. Such services are listed under NAICS 5182 (data processing, hosting, and related services) and includes "establishments primarily engaged in providing infrastructure for hosting or data processing services. These establishments may provide specialized hosting activities, such as web hosting, streaming services or application hosting, provide application service provisioning, or may provide general time-share mainframe facilities to clients. Data processing establishments provide complete processing and specialized reports from data supplied by clients or provide automated data processing and data entry services."* Information and data processing is not considered a CI under current definitions.

---

* http://www.census.gov/epcd/naics02/def/NDEF518.HTM#N5182.

- Postal service, couriers, and messengers are larger inputs than Energy. These services are almost indistinguishable from other transportation industries in the movement of goods (but not people, which they do not transport). Postal services, couriers, and messengers are considered non-CI in Canada.
- Printing, paper, and recording industries are all within the top 15 for Communications and IT reflecting the intensity of documentation, advertising, and promotion to the Communications and IT business—including many consumer services such as mobile phones and software, which are very important to both service delivery and commercial services. Though from a CI perspective this is not material. Printing, paper, and recording industries are not considered part of a CI under current definitions.

**Note:** See the end of this chapter for a roll-up of all non-CI inputs.

## FINANCE SECTOR IN CANADA

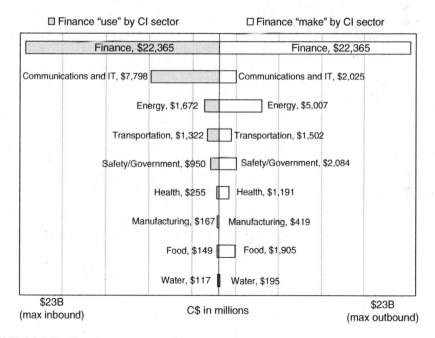

**FIGURE 2.7** Finance sectors tornado.

| | Energy | Communications and IT | Finance | Health | Food | Water | Transportation | Safety/ Government | Manufacturing |
|---|---|---|---|---|---|---|---|---|---|
| I–O ratio | 0.33 | 3.85 | 1.00 | 0.21 | 0.06 | 0.60 | 0.88 | 0.46 | 0.22 |

Total value of sector inputs consumed by Finance from other CI sectors is $34.7 billion—third largest gross consumer of CI goods and services.

Total value of sector outputs required by other CI sectors is $36.7 billion—third largest gross supplier to other CI sectors.

## Dependency Observations

- Finance spends almost four times as much with Communications and IT as Communications and IT spends on Finance services. This is an indication that for Finance, Communications and IT is by far the most important supply sector—almost five times more important than the nearest other supplier—Energy.
- All other sectors are net consumers of Financial services.

## Non-CI Sector Inputs to Finance

Although our analysis must necessarily revolve around the contemporary definitions of CI sectors discussed in Chapter 1, an examination of other significant industrial inputs is required. Understanding what might be missing from the current definitions of CI sectors will help assess the accuracy and validity of the dependency findings.

The non-CI sector inputs assessed here are specifically for Finance, but will be aggregated across all sectors in the Conclusions and Indicated Risks of this chapter. Figure 2.8 is a waterfall of the top 15 industrial inputs to the Finance sector in Canada, including both CI and non-CI sectors.

## Key Observations

Regarding the short-term delivery of the sector's core goods and services and the industries, which are direct operational inputs, the following observations are made:

- Finance, as a service industry appears to consume more services from suppliers than tangible goods. The top five suppliers to Finance are producers of services and non-tangible goods.

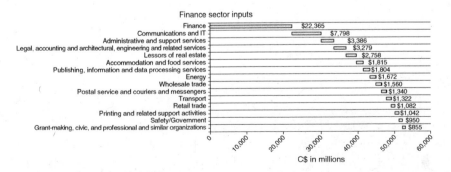

**FIGURE 2.8**   Finance sector inputs—top 15 industries.

- Publishing, information and data processing services are a larger input into the Finance CI sector than Energy. Such services are listed under NAICS 5182 (data processing, hosting, and related services) and includes "establishments primarily engaged in providing infrastructure for hosting or data processing services. These establishments may provide specialized hosting activities, such as web hosting, streaming services or application hosting, provide application service provisioning, or may provide general time-share mainframe facilities to clients. Data processing establishments provide complete processing and specialized reports from data supplied by clients or provide automated data processing and data entry services."* Information and data processing is not considered a CI under current definitions.
- Postal service, couriers, and messengers are a larger input than Transportation. These services are almost indistinguishable from other transportation industries in the movement of goods (but not people, which they do not transport). Postal services, couriers, and messengers are considered non-CI in Canada.

**Note:** See the end of this chapter for a roll-up of all non-CI inputs.

## HEALTH SECTOR IN CANADA

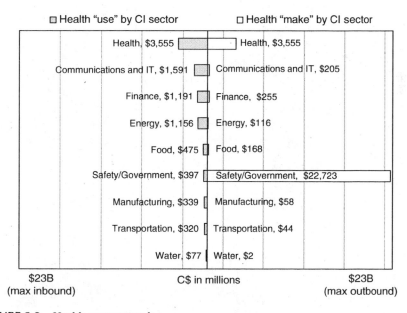

**FIGURE 2.9**   Health sector tornado.

---

* http://www.census.gov/epcd/naics02/def/NDEF518.HTM#N5182.

| | Energy | Communications and IT | Finance | Health | Food | Water | Transportation | Safety/ Government | Manufacturing |
|---|---|---|---|---|---|---|---|---|---|
| I–O ratio | 9.97 | 7.76 | 4.67 | 1.00 | 2.03 | 38.50 | 7.27 | 0.02 | 0.27 |

Total value of sector inputs consumed by Health from other CI sectors is $9.1 billion—sixth largest gross consumer of CI goods and services among the CI sectors.

Total value of sector outputs required by other CI sectors is $27 billion—fourth largest gross supplier to other CI sectors among the sectors.

## Dependency Observations

- Vast majority of Health resources are spent outside CI sectors, with Government transferring revenues to the Health sectors as part of socialized medical services in Canada.
- Communications and IT, Finance, and Energy are the most CI to Health. In the case of Communications and IT, this would be a reflection of the wide variety of players and communications mediums, which are employed to deliver Health services such as wireless, fixed line, and satellite.

## Non-CI Sector Inputs to Communications and IT

Although our analysis should necessarily revolve around the contemporary definitions of CI sectors, discussed in Chapter 1, an examination of other significant industrial inputs is required. Understanding what might be missing from the current definitions of CI sectors help assess the accuracy and validity of the dependency findings.

The non-CI sector inputs assessed here are specifically for Health, but will be aggregated across all sectors toward the end of this chapter. Figure 2.10 is a waterfall of the top 15 industrial inputs to the Health sector in Canada, including both CI and non-CI sectors.

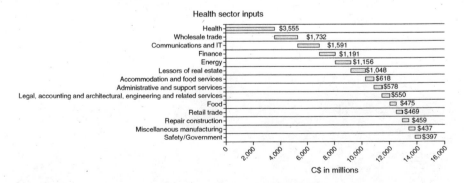

**FIGURE 2.10**  Health sector inputs—top 15 industries.

## Key Observations

Regarding the short-term delivery of the sector's core goods and services and the industries, which are direct operational inputs, the following observations are made:

- Accommodation and Food services is the sixth largest overall input— 50 percent larger than the Food industry itself. This reflects the large degree of outsourcing associated with the preparation and delivery of food within the Health sector. Accommodation and Food services are not considered part of a CI sector under current definitions.
- Wholesale and retail trades are the major inputs to Health reflecting distribution system for many medical goods that do not go directly from manufacturer to end-consumer (for instance, hospitals). Wholesale and retail trades are not part of a CI under current definitions.

**Note:** See the end of this chapter for a roll-up of all non-CI inputs.

### FOOD SECTOR IN CANADA

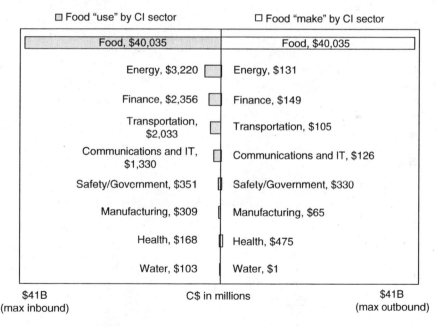

☐ Food "use" by CI sector                    ☐ Food "make" by CI sector

| Food, $40,035 | Food, $40,035 |
|---|---|
| Energy, $3,220 | Energy, $131 |
| Finance, $2,356 | Finance, $149 |
| Transportation, $2,033 | Transportation, $105 |
| Communications and IT, $1,330 | Communications and IT, $126 |
| Safety/Government, $351 | Safety/Government, $330 |
| Manufacturing, $309 | Manufacturing, $65 |
| Health, $168 | Health, $475 |
| Water, $103 | Water, $1 |

$41B
(max inbound)                    C$ in millions                    $41B
(max outbound)

**FIGURE 2.11**  Food sector tornado.

| | Energy | Communications and IT | Finance | Health | Food | Water | Transportation | Safety/Government | Manufacturing |
|---|---|---|---|---|---|---|---|---|---|
| I–O ratio | 24.58 | 10.56 | 15.81 | 0.49 | 1.00 | 103.00 | 19.36 | 1.06 | 3.22 |

Total value of sector inputs consumed by Food from other CI sectors is $44.3 billion—the largest gross consumer of CI goods and services among the CI sectors.

Total value of sector outputs required by other CI sectors is $38.1 billion—the largest gross supplier to other CI sectors among the sectors.

## Dependency Observations

- Overwhelming amount of the Food sector inputs and outputs are consumed within the Food sector itself—83 percent. This level of intrasector trade indicates that the movement and goods, and the logistical communications associated with the movement of goods may make Transportation and Communications at least as important as other sectors with higher inputs—such as Energy and Finance.
- Health is the largest purchaser of goods from the Food sector as a result of the patient food programs, although Government would be a large purchaser for purposes such as the police and military. Other sectors do not routinely supply meals to staff and clients.

## Non-CI Sector Inputs to Food

Although our analysis must necessarily revolve around the contemporary definitions of CI sectors discussed in Chapter 1, an examination of other significant industrial inputs is required. Understanding what might be missing from the current definitions of CI sectors will help assess the accuracy and validity of the dependency findings.

The non-CI sector inputs assessed here are specifically for Food, but will be aggregated across all sectors toward the end of this chapter. Figure 2.12 is a waterfall of the top 15 industrial inputs to the Food sector in Canada, including both CI and non-CI sectors.

## Key Observations

Regarding the short-term delivery of the sector's core goods and services and the industries, which are direct operational inputs, the following observations are made:

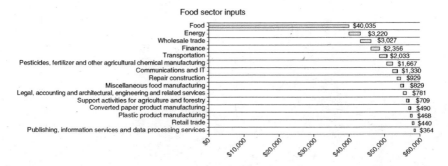

**FIGURE 2.12**   Food sector inputs—top 15 industries.

- Converted paper products and plastic products are the major inputs to food—together larger than Communications and IT inputs. These industries provide packaging to the Food industry, which cannot prepare food for distribution without packaging inputs. Packaging inputs such as converted paper and plastics are not part of a CI under current definitions.
- Wholesale and retail trades are major inputs to Food reflecting distribution system for many perishable goods, which do not go directly from manufacturer/farmer to consumer. Wholesale and retail trades are not part of a CI under current definitions.

**Note:** See the end of this chapter for a roll-up of all non-CI inputs.

## WATER SECTOR IN CANADA

Water is a challenging sector for the purposes of econometric I–O analysis because much of the spending that industry sector might otherwise engage in with Water is supplanted by municipal taxes, which are in part levied to pay for Water infrastructure. For this reason especially, indications from this sector must be understood to be represent an important but incomplete picture of CI sector dependencies on Water.

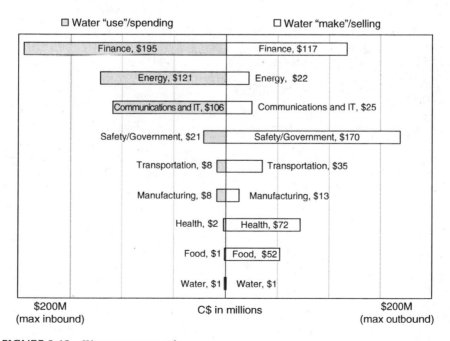

**FIGURE 2.13**  Water sector tornado.

| | Energy | Communications and IT | Finance | Health | Food | Water | Transportation | Safety/ Government | Manufacturing |
|---|---|---|---|---|---|---|---|---|---|
| I–O ratio | 5.50 | 4.24 | 1.67 | 0.03 | 0.01 | 1.00 | 0.23 | 0.12 | 0.10 |

Total value of sector inputs consumed by Water from other CI sectors is $460 million—the smallest gross consumer of CI goods and services among the CI sectors.

Total value of sector outputs required by other CI sectors is $628 million—the smallest gross supplier to other CI sectors among the sectors.

## Dependency Observations

- Water is unique among CI sectors in that it is its own smallest input as opposed to the largest—which is typical for other CI sectors. This reveals the extent to which Water infrastructures are almost entirely autonomous in operations. Operations are also typically monopolies within well-defined geographic boundaries defined by political economic or engineering necessity.
- Large input from the Finance sector is likely a reflection of the fact that some water and waste facilities may be owned by private holding companies that are considered Financial industries under NAICS. This, as opposed to services is purchased directly from Water sector.
- Health and Food both have large I–O ratio because they do not own water or waste facilities, but are apparently the largest consumers of these services after government (municipal primarily), which purchases for general populations which it in turn might tax.

## Non-CI Sector Inputs to Water

Although our analysis must necessarily revolve around the contemporary definitions of CI sectors discussed in Chapter 1, an examination of other significant industrial inputs is required. Understanding what might be missing from the current definitions of CI sectors will help assess the accuracy and validity of the dependency findings.

The non-CI sector inputs assessed here are specifically for water, but will be aggregated across all sectors toward the end of this chapter. Figure 2.14 is a waterfall of the top 15 industrial inputs to the Water sector in Canada, including both CI and non-CI sectors.

## Key Observations

Regarding the short-term delivery of the sector's core goods and services and the industries, which are direct operational inputs, the following observations are made:

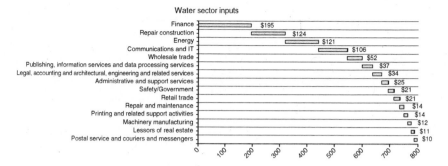

**FIGURE 2.14**   Water sector inputs—top 15 industries.

- Manufacturing (as officially defined) does not make the top 15 industrial inputs despite the fact that chemicals such as chlorine are core inputs to municipal water systems. This may indicate that the bulk costs of water infrastructure are related to dams, waterway management, and the disposal of wastewater. Alternately, it may indicate that the bills for chemicals are paid by municipal governments directly rather than the Water infrastructures.

**Note:** See the end of this chapter for a roll-up of all non-CI inputs.

## Transport Sector in Canada

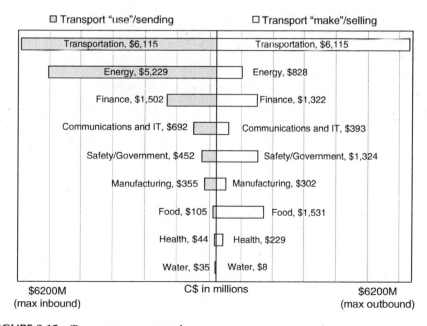

**FIGURE 2.15**   Transport sector tornado.

| | Energy | Communications and IT | Finance | Health | Food | Water | Transportation | Safety/ Government | Manufacturing |
|---|---|---|---|---|---|---|---|---|---|
| I–O ratio | 6.32 | 1.76 | 1.14 | 0.14 | 0.05 | 4.38 | 1.00 | 0.34 | 0.68 |

Total value of sector inputs consumed by Transport from other CI sectors is $14.5 billion—fifth largest gross consumer of CI goods and services among the CI sectors.

Total value of sector outputs required by other CI sectors is $12.8 billion—sixth largest gross supplier to other CI sectors among the sectors.

## Dependency Observations

- Energy is almost as large an input to Transport as the sector is to itself, which is unusual because intrasector trade is typically substantially larger than all other inputs. This finding in combination with the low I–O ratio for Energy indicates one of the strongest dependency relationships among all sectors between Transport and Energy, with Transport being the dependent sector.
- Food is the largest consumer of Transport services outside the Transport sector, using almost 15 times the value of service that Transport purchases from Food. This relationship reflects the nature of the Food production system, which starts with many small producers, is centralized with large processors with finished goods returning to small wholesale and retail distributors.

## Non-CI Sector Inputs to Transport

Although our analysis must necessarily revolve around the contemporary definitions of CI sectors discussed in Chapter 1, an examination of other significant industrial inputs is required. Understanding what might be missing from the current definitions of CI sectors will help assess the accuracy and validity of the dependency findings.

The non-CI sector inputs assessed here are specifically for Transport, but will be aggregated across all sectors toward the end of this chapter. Figure 2.16 is a waterfall

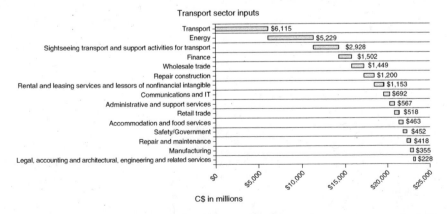

**FIGURE 2.16**  Transport sector inputs—top 15 industries.

of the top 15 industrial inputs to the Transport sector in Canada, including both CI and non-CI sectors.

## Key Observations

Regarding the short-term delivery of the sector's core goods and services and the industries, which are direct operational inputs, the following observations are made:

- Wholesale and retail trades are major inputs to Transport reflecting the importance of the sale and distribution of items such as spare parts and even fare tickets to both private and business consumers. Wholesale and retail trades are not part of a CI under current definitions.

**Note:** See the end of this chapter for a roll-up of all non-CI inputs.

### SAFETY AND GOVERNMENT SECTOR IN CANADA

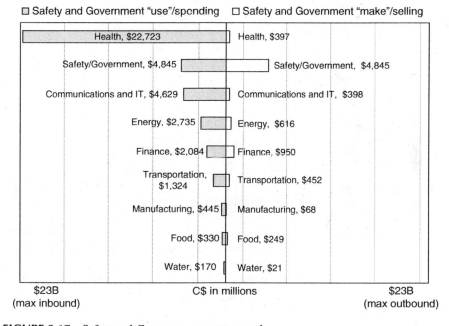

FIGURE 2.17 Safety and Government sector tornado.

| | Energy | Communications and IT | Finance | Health | Food | Water | Transport | Safety/ Government | Manufacturing |
|---|---|---|---|---|---|---|---|---|---|
| I–O ratio | 4.44 | 11.63 | 2.19 | 57.24 | 0.94 | 8.10 | 2.93 | 1.00 | 2.47 |

Total value of sector inputs consumed by Safety and Government from other CI sectors is $39.1 billion—the second largest gross consumer of CI goods and services among the CI sectors.

Total value of sector outputs required by other CI sectors is $12.1 billion—the seventh largest gross supplier to other CI sectors among the sectors.

## Dependency Observations

- Health is largely a socialized service in Canada and paid for by the government, explaining Health as the largest sector expenditure.
- Safety and Government does not have an I–O ratio of greater than 1.0 with any CI sector indicating that no sector is more dependent upon Safety and Government than Safety and Government is upon any other given sector.
- Safety and Government spends significantly on Transportation, this indicates the size of publicly funded urban transportation as opposed to direct consumption by the Safety and Government sector.

## Non-CI Sector Inputs to Safety and Government

Although our analysis must necessarily revolve around the contemporary definitions of CI sectors discussed in Chapter 1, an examination of other significant industrial inputs is required. Understanding what might be missing from the current definitions of CI sectors will help assess the accuracy and validity of the dependency findings.

The non-CI sector inputs assessed here are specifically for Safety and Government, but will be aggregated across all sectors toward the end of this chapter. Figure 2.18 is an input tornado of the top 15 industrial inputs to the Safety and Government sector in Canada, including both CI and non-CI sectors.

## Key Observations

Regarding the short-term delivery of the sector's core goods and services and the industries, which are direct operational inputs, the following observations are made:

- Wholesale and retail trades are major inputs to Safety and Government reflecting the importance of the consumption large amounts of goods from

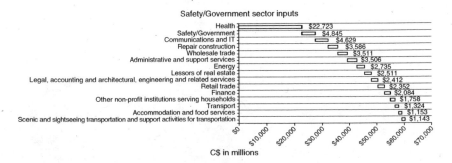

**FIGURE 2.18**   Safety and Government sector inputs—top 15 industries.

all sectors for both Health and military purposes (military expenditures are included in the I–O metrics from Statistics Canada). Wholesale and retail trades are not part of a CI under current definitions.

**Note:** See the end of this chapter for a roll-up of all non-CI inputs.

## MANUFACTURING SECTOR IN CANADA

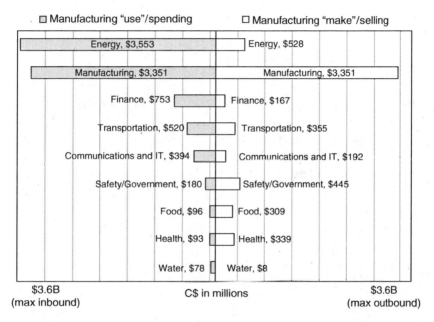

**FIGURE 2.19**  Manufacturing sector tornado.

|  | Energy | Communications and IT | Finance | Health | Food | Water | Transportation | Safety/ Government | Manufacturing |
|---|---|---|---|---|---|---|---|---|---|
| I–O ratio | 6.73 | 2.05 | 4.51 | 0.27 | 0.31 | 9.75 | 1.46 | 0.40 | 1.00 |

Total value of sector inputs consumed by Manufacturing from other CI sectors is $2.5 billion—the second smallest gross consumer of CI goods and services among the CI sectors.

Total value of sector outputs required by other CI sectors is $2.5 billion—the second smallest gross supplier to other CI sectors among the sectors.

### Dependency Observations

- Manufacturing is heavily dependent upon the Energy sector according to I–O ratios, possessing a very large deficit in absolute terms.

- Health and Food are the most dependent upon Manufacturing, due to the consumption of industrial gases (categorized under NIACS 325A Miscellaneous Chemicals). Gases critical to anesthesia, and for operating advanced but widespread devices such as magnetic resonance imaging (MRI) machines that liquify gases for cooling. To Food, industrial gases would be applied to packaging and preservation.

## Non-CI Sector Inputs to Manufacturing

Although our analysis must necessarily revolve around the contemporary definitions of CI sectors discussed in Chapter 1, an examination of other significant industrial inputs is required. Understanding what might be missing from the current definitions of CI sectors will help assess the accuracy and validity of the dependency findings.

The non-CI sector inputs assessed here are specifically for Manufacturing, but will be aggregated across all sectors toward the end of this chapter. Figure 2.20 is a waterfall of the top 15 industrial inputs to the Manufacturing sector in Canada, including both CI and non-CI sectors.

## Key Observations

Regarding the short-term delivery of the sector's core goods and services and the industries, which are direct operational inputs, the following observations are made:

- Manufacturing sector as defined under the CI definitions is limited to chemicals and aerospace (Other Transportation under NAICS). However, it is apparent that these industries are themselves dependent upon other forms of non-CI manufacturing such as metals, plastics, and resins. None of these other contributing manufacturing industries are considered CIs under the current definitions.

**Note:** See the end of this chapter for a roll-up of all non-CI inputs.

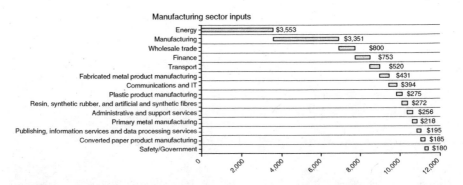

**FIGURE 2.20**   Manufacturing sector inputs—top 15 industries.

## CANADIAN I–O CI SECTOR ECONOMIC DEPENDENCY MATRIXES

The following data is a different means of visualizing the economic dependency information presented in Figure 2.1. Having reviewed the specifics of each sector, these alternate, more numerically focused, and specific views are presented to support greater scrutiny and in-depth analysis.

The 9 × 9 matrix in Table 2.2 is the detailed I–O metrics that resulted from mapping CI sectors to the NAICS and applying the industry-by-industry I–O econometrics available from Statistics Canada.

Table 2.2 is the rolled-up all-sector representation of the previous sections that presented each sector's finding and summary analysis individually. Although Table 2.2 is a specific representation of the Canadian spending among CI sectors, which is of interest to some readers, it does not readily display dependency relationships. The reason why the I–O ratio was developed in this book. Recall that with an I–O ratio, a number greater than 1 indicates that a sector is spending more within a given sector than the other sector is buying from the first sector. This spending relationship is assumed to be a potential indication of negative sector dependency on the part of the sector with the I–O ratio over 1. The greater the number is above 1, the more profound the spending imbalance between the two CI sectors. If a sector posses an I–O ratio of less than 1, then it is in a positive trade flow with the other sector, and this is assumed to be a potential indication of positive sector dependency on the part of the sector with the I–O ratio less than 1. The greater the number is below 1, the more profound the spending imbalance between the two CI sectors.

Table 2.3 summarizes all the I–O ratios captured in the pervious section. The table brings economic relationships and interdependencies into stark contrast, making some patterns appear where they may have been obscured within large numbers and decimal places.

## TABLE 2.2
## Canadian I–O CI Sector Dependencies in C$ Millions

| | Energy $ | Comms $ | Fin $ | Health $ | Food $ | Water $ | Trans $ | Safety/Gov $ | Manf $ |
|---|---|---|---|---|---|---|---|---|---|
| Energy | 22,337 | 540 | 1,672 | 1,156 | 3,220 | 121 | 5,229 | 2,735 | 3,553 |
| Comms | 2,045 | 7,062 | 7,798 | 1,591 | 1,330 | 106 | 692 | 4,629 | 394 |
| Fin | 5,007 | 2,025 | 22,365 | 1,191 | 2,356 | 195 | 1,502 | 2,084 | 753 |
| Health | 116 | 205 | 255 | 3,555 | 234 | 2 | 44 | 22,723 | 93 |
| Food | 131 | 126 | 149 | 475 | 40,035 | 1 | 105 | 330 | 96 |
| Water | 22 | 25 | 117 | 77 | 103 | 1 | 35 | 170 | 78 |
| Trans | 828 | 393 | 1,322 | 320 | 2,033 | 8 | 6,115 | 1,324 | 520 |
| Safety/ Gov | 616 | 398 | 950 | 397 | 351 | 21 | 452 | 4,845 | 180 |
| Manf | 528 | 192 | 167 | 339 | 309 | 8 | 355 | 445 | 3,351 |

**TABLE 2.3**

**Canadian I–O CI Sector Dependencies in C$ Millions**

|          | Energy | Comms | Fin  | Health | Food  | Water | Trans | Safety/Gov | Manf |
|----------|--------|-------|------|--------|-------|-------|-------|------------|------|
| Energy   | 1.00   | 0.26  | 0.33 | 27.28  | 19.49 | 5.50  | 6.32  | 4.44       | 1.10 |
| Comms    | 3.79   | 1.00  | 3.85 | 20.20  | 8.14  | 4.24  | 1.76  | 11.63      | 2.31 |
| Fin      | 2.99   | 0.26  | 1.00 | 5.62   | 12.79 | 1.67  | 1.14  | 2.19       | 3.25 |
| Health   | 0.04   | 0.05  | 0.18 | 1.00   | 0.04  | 0.01  | 0.12  | 62.40      | 0.08 |
| Food     | 0.05   | 0.12  | 0.08 | 27.19  | 1.00  | 0.02  | 2.02  | 1.33       | 0.50 |
| Water    | 0.18   | 0.24  | 0.60 | 72.00  | 52.00 | 1.00  | 4.38  | 8.10       | 2.17 |
| Trans    | 0.16   | 0.57  | 0.88 | 8.48   | 14.58 | 0.23  | 1.00  | 2.93       | 0.87 |
| Safety/Gov | 0.23 | 0.09  | 0.46 | 0.02   | 0.75  | 0.12  | 0.34  | 1.00       | 0.22 |
| Manf     | 0.91   | 0.43  | 0.31 | 0.08   | 2.00  | 0.46  | 1.15  | 4.59       | 1.00 |

*Notes:*

White ☐ (highly positive I–O ratio < 0.5) indicates that the sector in the adjacent row is strongly independent. That is, it sells much more than it spends with a given sector in the adjacent row.

Light gray ▨ (moderate positive I–O ratio > 0.5 < 1.0) indicates that the sector in the adjacent row is somewhat independent. That is, it sells more than it spends with a given sector in the adjacent row.

Dark gray ▨ (moderate negative I–O ratio < 1.0 > 1.5) indicates that the sector in the adjacent row is somewhat dependent. That is, it sells less than it spends with the sector in the adjacent row.

Black ■ (highly negative I–O ratio > 1.5) indicates that the sector in the adjacent row is strongly dependent. That is, it sells much less than it spends with the sector in the adjacent row.

Table 2.3 highlights the apparent polarity of relationships between the CI in Canada, where majority of the I–O ratios are either white or black. Safety and Government are clearly a major factor, weighing this table toward black due to the nature of I–O data that shows Safety and Government as completely dependent consumers of CI goods and services, although apparently returning relatively few services in return. We know this is not the case. Clearly, Safety and Government provide critical services to other CI sectors, but for the most part they do not charge directly for them.

Similar to Safety and Government, the Health CI sector is dominated by intense dependency relationships with all other sectors. This indication is best interpreted as an artifact of how Health services are funded in Canada, with massive inputs directly from government and a consumption relationship with all other CI sectors except Manufacturing.

Food, like Health and Government, appears to be a heavy overall consumer of CI goods and services, but the dependency relationships do not take into full account that 83 percent of all Food inputs come from within the Food sector itself. The result is that dependency relationships, such as that with Water, might appear more intense than they really are. Food, for instance has a very dependent I–O ratio with Water, but Water in fact represents 1/10 of 1 percent of Foods total sector inputs.

The only sector that does not possess any negative trade relationships with other sectors is the Communications and IT sector. Even the other high profile CI sectors such as Finance and Energy experience some intense dependency relationships with other sectors.

## U.S. I–O SECTOR ECONOMIC INTERDEPENDENCY MAPPING

The exchange of goods and services among CI sectors is a quantitative indicator of interdependency. Using the contemporary CI sector definitions under NAICS in Table 2.1, it has now become possible to reference directly the I–O statistics generated and maintain by the United States and gain indications of interdependency.

As stated in Chapter 1, no single metric can even start to form strongly credible picture of CI interdependency; more than one dimension can be used to create representations of reality. You need at least two dimensions and ideally three to model reality. This section will assess in a summary fashion the CI interdependencies, which might be interpreted using a purely statistical approach to analysis, but will not attempt to critique these indications: Chapter 4 will accomplish this task through the combination of this statistical dimension with a second data dependency dimension of Chapter 3, allowing for a correlation of results and analysis of strength and weaknesses.

The statistical analysis of CI interdependency undertaken involved review and detailed analysis of more than 10,000 distinct metrics for the United States. Statistics for the year 2005 was assessed for the U.S. BEA. The resulting data sets are complex and the relationships between the sectors that they indicate are themselves complex and multilayered.

To try and steer clear the vast matrixes of sterile numbers, tools known as treemaps* and tornados were adopted to try and display the relationships and interdependencies between the CI sectors. As quoted at the beginning of this chapter, "Abstract statistical information does not sway us as much as the anecdote..." therefore we are using maps and tornados as visual anecdotes for thousands and thousands of statistical metrics.

Figure 2.21 shows the total sector-to-sector consumption or use of goods and services by all CI sectors in the United States. Both the size and the shade of the box are an indication of the value. Although the size of the boxes is possibly useful in assessing interdependency, it is also an indication of the overall size of the sector in the American economy. The size of the box indicates the overall relative value of spending by a sector with other sectors. The lighter the shade (with white being the lightest possible) the closer to the maximum value for consumption relative to all

---

* Treemaps are tools developed by Ben Shneiderman at the University of Maryland in the 1990s to display complex and multilayer data sets. http://www.cs.umd.edu/hcil/treemap-history/.

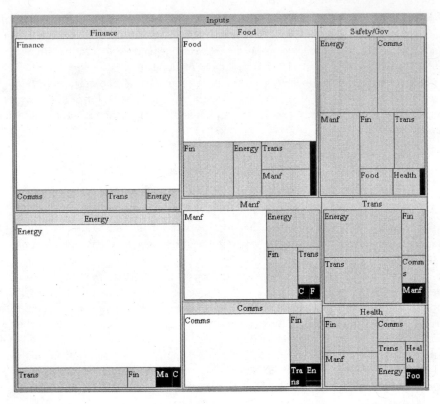

**FIGURE 2.21** U.S. CI economic "use" interdependency. White □ = high-value inputs ($100 billion to a maximum value of $500 billion). Gray ▦ = medium value inputs ($10–$100 billion). Black ■ = lower value of inputs ($1 million to $10 billion). Each sector block is proportional to the size of its total value of economic inputs consumed by the sector. Each square within each sector block indicates the proportional size of economic inputs in dollars.

consumption from all sectors. The boxes within a sector box mostly explain how sectors consume and are possibly interdependent on the goods and services produced by each other. Detailed sector analysis will be discussed shortly.

Figure 2.21 shows that the Finance sector in the United States is the largest overall consumer of goods and services from other CI sectors because finance has the largest box within the map. Within the Finance sector, we can also see that intrasector spending in goods and services—a white box—is not only the largest component of Finance spending, but also proportionally the largest intrasector spend relative to all other sectors. Spending on inputs from Finance to Finance is greater than any other form of sector-to-sector spending in the United States under the contemporary definitions of CI. Sector-by-sector analysis is to follow shortly in this chapter.

Figure 2.21 also shows how all other sectors relate proportionally as far as the consumption of goods and services required from other CI sectors to support the production of their own goods and services are concerned. Note that Figure 2.21 is not a representation of all goods and services consumed by all CI sectors—it only indicated consumption of goods and services from other CI sectors. Goods and services consumed from other non-CI industries may represent greater overall spending for certain sectors. The distinction between consumption of goods and services from CI sectors and non-CI sectors will be displayed and analyzed in depth later in this chapter.

Figure 2.22 shows the total sector-to-sector output or make of goods and services by all CI sectors in the United States. Both the size and the shade of the box are an indication of the value. Although the size of the boxes is possibly useful in assessing interdependency, it is also an indication of the overall size of the sector in the American economy. The size of the box indicates the overall relative value of goods and services delivered by a CI sector to other CI sectors. The lighter the shade (with white being the lightest possible) the higher the value of output relative to all outputs to all sectors. The boxes within a sector box mostly explain how sectors consume and are possibly interdependent on the goods and services produced by each other.

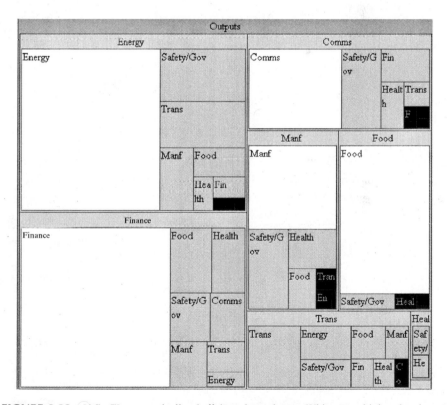

**FIGURE 2.22** U.S. CI economic "make" interdependency. White □ = high-value inputs ($100 billion to a maximum value of $500 billion). Gray ▨ = medium value inputs ($10–$100 billion). Black ■ = lower value of inputs ($1 million to $10 billion). Each sector block is proportional to the size of its total value of economic inputs consumed by the sector. Each square within each sector block indicates the proportional size of economic inputs in dollars.

Figure 2.22 shows that the Energy sector in the United States is the largest overall supplier of goods and services to CI sectors; Energy has the largest box within the map. Within the Energy sector, we can also see that intrasector spending on goods and services—a white box—is not only the largest component of Energy spending, but that direct consumption of Energy goods and services by all the other CI sectors is less than half by contrast. Spending on inputs from Energy to Energy is greater than any other form of sector-to-sector spending in the United States under the contemporary definitions of CI.

Figure 2.22 also shows how all other sectors relate proportionally as far as the production of goods and services destined for other CI sectors. Note that Figure 2.22 is not a representation of all goods and services produced by all CI sectors—it only indicates the production of goods and services destined for other CI sectors. Goods and services consumed by other non-CI industries and consumers may represent greater overall spending. The distinction between consumption of goods and services from CI sectors and non-CI sectors will be displayed and analyzed in depth later in this chapter.

## Sector-by-Sector I–O (Use versus Make)

The following sector-by-sector discussion represents analysis of the levels and types of interdependency indicated by economic analysis of CI sectors. Each sector is described using economic input and output tornado figures, and ratio metrics. These figures and numbers do not indicate total consumption or production, which would necessarily include non-CI sector goods and services, and consumer consumption.

Tornado figures show the economic inputs from all the CI sectors to the given sector, from the largest input to the smallest input among the conventionally defined CI sectors. A tornado illustrates the manner in which a sector consumes goods and services from other CI sectors. Note, this is not a measure of all goods and services consumed by a sector, but a measure of only the goods and services consumed from other CI sectors. A tornado also illustrates how the goods and services from the Energy sector are consumed by the other CI sectors; again, this is not a measure of total output, merely outputs consumed by other CI sectors. Values are in U.S. dollars from the most recently available detailed I–O data from the BEA prepared in 2005. The U.S. dollar was worth between approximately C$1.35 and C $1.22 at that time.

An I–O ratio is also generated to support the analysis of sector-to-sector interdependency. An I–O ratio is simply the input value of a given sector divided by the output value of a given sector—for instance, the dollar value of goods and services consumed by Energy from Finance (inputs) divided by the dollar value of goods and services consumed by Finance from Energy (outputs). This ratio shows relative weight of spending versus selling among sectors and is useful in spotting the strength and direction of dependency as indicated by value flows.

The assumption underlying I–O ratio analysis is that the more lopsided the flow of money between two given sectors, the more lopsided the dependency relationship may be—for instance, if Energy spends significantly more on Communications and

IT than vice versa, it is an indication that Energy may be more dependent upon Communications and IT than vice versa.

I–O ratios are useful for high-level, at-a-glance analysis but are certainly not definitive because, as will be examined shortly, a flawed sector definition can exclude certain high-value inputs or outputs from overlooked industrial sectors and skew the I–O ratio. Furthermore, I–O ratios ignore the relative value of the inputs and outputs. If there is an I–O ratio of 2.0 resulting from a $1 billion of inputs versus $500 million in outputs between two sectors, this is a much more significant observation that $1 million in inputs versus $500,000 in outputs. Although the I–O ratio in both instances is 2.0, the difference of half a million dollars in trade between two entire sectors is more an indication of no significant relation has opposed to any form of dependency from one sector to another. I–O ratios should be considered in the context of the values shown in the tornados—not in isolation.

## ENERGY SECTOR IN THE UNITED STATES

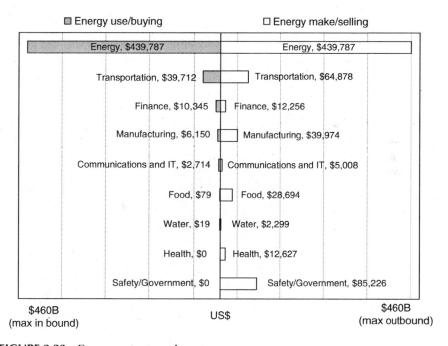

**FIGURE 2.23**  Energy sector tornado.

| | Energy | Communications and IT | Finance | Health | Food | Water | Transportation | Safety/ Government | Manufacturing |
|---|---|---|---|---|---|---|---|---|---|
| I–O ratio | 1.000 | 0.542 | 0.844 | 0.000 | 0.003 | 0.008 | 0.526 | 0.000 | 0.154 |

Total value of sector inputs consumed from other CI sectors is $485 billion—second largest gross consumer of CI goods and services.

Total value of sector outputs required by other CI sectors is $695 billion—the largest gross supplier to other CI sectors.

## Dependency Observations

- More than 93 percent of inputs to the Energy sector in the United States are from other Energy sector entities—intrasector dependency.
- Safety and Government consume more Energy that even the Transportation sector, indicating that Safety and Government are more susceptible to impacts if the Energy sector is damaged.
- Energy does not show an I–O ratio of over 1.0 except for intrasector trade, indicating that Energy sells more than it buys from every other CI sector. This drives toward an impression that Energy is in a dominant position relative to all other CI sectors.

## Non-CI Sector Inputs to Energy

Although our analysis must necessarily revolve around the contemporary definitions of CI sectors discussed in Chapter 1, an examination of other significant industrial inputs is required. Understanding what might be missing from the current definitions of CI sectors will help assess the accuracy and validity of the dependency findings.

The non-CI sector inputs assessed here are specifically for Energy, but will be aggregated across all sectors and discussed in detail toward the end of this chapter. Figure 2.24 is a waterfall of the top 15 industrial inputs to the Energy sector in the United States, including both CI and non-CI sectors.

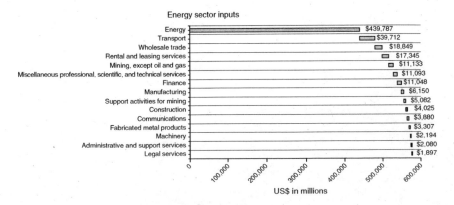

**FIGURE 2.24** Energy sector inputs—top 15 industries.

## Observations Related to Non-CI Sector Inputs

Regarding the short-term delivery of the Energy sector's core goods and services and the industries, which are direct operational inputs, the following observations are made:

- Miscellaneous professional, scientific, and technical services are equal to 13 percent of full-time employee compensation in U.S. Energy industries indicating that contractors are likely a critical input to Energy.
- Wholesale trade in the largest overall input to energy—almost as large as Finance and Transport combined—the closest CI sectors to the top inputs. This reflects the importance of the distribution of nonelectric Energy goods such as liquid fuels and compressed gases, which are accounted under these trade industries.
- Mining (not including oil and gas) is not considered a CI, although it is the fourth largest input in the United States to Energy and 50 percent of American energy is generated with coal.* Coal mining is not considered part of a CI under current definitions.

**Note:** See the end of this chapter for a roll-up of all non-CI inputs.

## COMMUNICATIONS AND IT SECTOR IN THE UNITED STATES

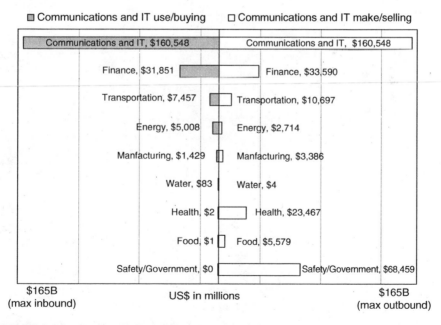

**FIGURE 2.25**   Communications and IT sector tornado.

---

* American Coal Foundation, http://www.teachcoal.org/aboutcoal/articles/faqs.html.

| | Energy | Communications and IT | Finance | Health | Food | Water | Transportation | Safety/ Government | Manufacturing |
|---|---|---|---|---|---|---|---|---|---|
| I–O ratio | 1.845 | 1.000 | 0.948 | 0.000 | 0.000 | 19.757 | 0.559 | 0.000 | 0.422 |

Total value of sector inputs consumed by Communications and IT from other CI sectors is $204 billion—sixth largest gross consumer of CI goods and services among the CI sectors.

Total value of sector outputs required by other CI sectors is $308 billion—third largest gross supplier to other CI sectors among the sectors.

## Dependency Observations

- Energy has a substantially stronger position relative to Communications and IT in the United States than in Canada, where it is clearly more dependent from an I–O perspective: a net buyer of services. In the United States the reverse is true.
- Finance is the closest sector to equilibrium between inputs and outputs and is the largest supplier to Communications and IT—indicating a strong, mutually dependent production relationship.

## Non-CI Sector Inputs to Communications and IT

Although our analysis must necessarily revolve around the contemporary definitions of CI sectors discussed in Chapter 1, an examination of other significant industrial inputs is required. Understanding what might be missing from the current definitions of CI sectors will help assess the accuracy and validity of the dependency findings.

The non-CI sector inputs assessed here are specifically for Communications and IT, but will be aggregated across all sectors toward the end of this chapter. Figure 2.26 is a waterfall of the top 15 industrial inputs to the Communications and IT sector in the United States, including both CI and non-CI sectors.

## Observations

Regarding the short-term delivery of the sector's core goods and services and the industries, which are direct operational inputs, the following observations are made:

- Miscellaneous professional, scientific, and technical services are equal to 26 percent of full-time employee compensation in U.S. Communications and IT industries, indicating the criticality of contractors.
- Motion picture, sound recording, and performing arts are all within the top 15 for Communications and IT reflecting broadcasting and entertainment elements associated with Communications and IT business. Though from a CI perspective this may not be material. Motion picture, sound recording

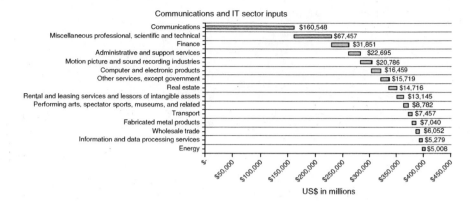

FIGURE 2.26 Communications and IT sector inputs—top 15 industries.

and performing arts industries are not considered part of a CI under current definitions.

- Wholesale trade is a major input to Communications and IT reflecting the requirement to distribute specific tangible goods (phones, modems, computers, software) to deliver and support the core services (bandwidth, connectivity and customer support). Wholesale and retail trades are not considered part of a CI under current definitions.
- Information and data processing services are a larger input into the Communications and IT CI sector than Energy. Such services are listed under NAICS 5182 (data processing, hosting, and related services) and includes "establishments primarily engaged in providing infrastructure for hosting or data processing services. These establishments may provide specialized hosting activities, such as web hosting, streaming services or application hosting, provide application service provisioning, or may provide general time-share mainframe facilities to clients. Data processing establishments provide complete processing and specialized reports from data supplied by clients or provide automated data processing and data entry services."* Information and data processing is not considered a CI under current definitions.

**Note:** See the end of this chapter for a roll-up of all non-CI inputs.

## FINANCE SECTOR IN THE UNITED STATES

Figure 2.27 depicts the I–O analysis for Finance sector in the United States.

Total value of sector inputs consumed by Finance from other CI sectors is $517 billion—the largest gross consumer of CI goods and services.

Total value of sector outputs required by other CI sectors is $657 billion—second largest gross supplier to other CI sectors.

---

* http://www.census.gov/epcd/naics02/def/NDEF518.HTM#N5182.

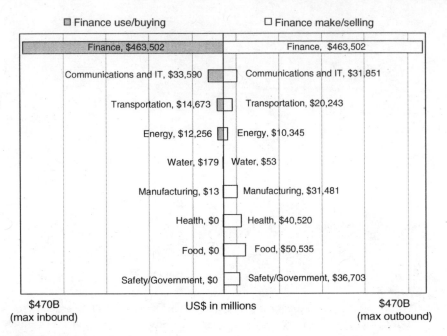

**FIGURE 2.27**   Finance sector tornado.

|     | Energy | Communications and IT | Finance | Health | Food | Water | Transportation | Safety/ Government | Manufacturing |
|-----|--------|----------------------|---------|--------|------|-------|----------------|--------------------|---------------|
| I–O ratio | 1.185 | 1.055 | 1.000 | 0.000 | 0.000 | 3.367 | 0.649 | 0.000 | 0.000 |

## Dependency Observations

- Finance spends nothing directly on Health care services; such expenditures are considered personal consumption and are accounted for as benefits to employees. However, the Health sector is the third largest consumer of Financial services among the CI sectors, indicating a substantial amount of dependency by Health.
- Finance spends so little directly on Food services that the I–O ratio value is essentially zero. However, the Food sector is the second largest consumer of Financial services among the CI sectors second only to intrasector trade, indicating a substantial amount of dependency by Food.
- Information and data processing services are a larger input into the Financial CI sector than Energy. Such services are listed under NAICS 5182 (data processing, hosting, and related services) and include "establishments primarily engaged in providing infrastructure for hosting or data processing services. These establishments may provide specialized hosting activities, such as web hosting, streaming services or application hosting, provide application service

provisioning, or may provide general time-share mainframe facilities to clients. Data processing establishments provide complete processing and specialized reports from data supplied by clients or provide automated data processing and data entry services."* Information and data processing is not considered a CI under current definitions.

- There is an inbound dependency relationship expressed between Finance and Energy and Finance and Communications and IT due to the fact that Finance consumes more from these sectors than vice versa.

## Non-CI Sector Inputs to Finance

Although our analysis must necessarily revolve around the contemporary definitions of CI sectors discussed in Chapter 1, an examination of other significant industrial inputs is required. Understanding what might be missing from the current definitions of CI sectors will help assess the accuracy and validity of the dependency findings.

The non-CI sector inputs assessed here are specifically for Finance, but will be aggregated across all sectors toward the end of this chapter. Figure 2.28 is a waterfall of the top 15 industrial inputs to the Finance sector in the United States, including both CI and non-CI sectors.

## Observations

Regarding the short-term delivery of the sector's core goods and services and the industries, which are direct operational inputs, the following observations are made:

- Miscellaneous professional, scientific, and technical services are equal to 24 percent of full-time employee compensation in U.S. Finance industries, indicating the criticality of contractors.

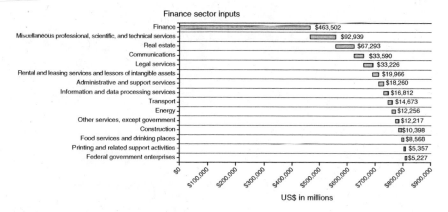

FIGURE 2.28  Finance sector inputs—top 15 industries.

* http://www.census.gov/epcd/naics02/def/NDEF518.HTM#N5182.

- Information and data processing services are a larger input into the Financial CI sector than Energy. Such services are listed under NAICS 5182 (data processing, hosting, and related services) and includes "establishments primarily engaged in providing infrastructure for hosting or data processing services. These establishments may provide specialized hosting activities, such as web hosting, streaming services or application hosting, provide application service provisioning, or may provide general time-share mainframe facilities to clients. Data processing establishments provide complete processing and specialized reports from data supplied by clients or provide automated data processing and data entry services." Information and data processing is not considered a CI under current definitions.

**Note:** See the end of this chapter for a roll-up of all non-CI inputs.

## HEALTH SECTOR IN THE UNITED STATES

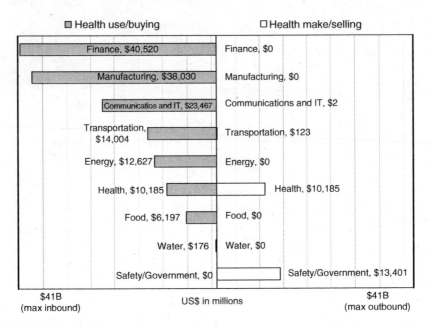

**FIGURE 2.29**   Health sector input tornado.

| | Energy | Communications and IT | Finance | Health | Food | Water | Transportation | Safety/ Government | Manufacturing |
|---|---|---|---|---|---|---|---|---|---|
| I–O ratio | Infinity | 11733 | 101300 | 1.0 | Infinity | Infinity | 109 | 0.0 | Infinity |

Total value of sector inputs consumed by Health from other CI sectors is $142 billion—seventh largest gross consumer of CI goods and services among the CI sectors.

Total value of sector outputs required by other CI sectors is $23.7 billion—sixth largest gross supplier to other CI sectors among the sectors.

## Dependency Observations

- Energy, Food, Water, Manufacturing, and Finance buy no Health sector services directly and therefore their I–O ratio is not possible to be calculated because anything divided by zero equals infinity.
- Vast majority of Health resources are spent outside CI sectors, with Government transferring revenues to the Health sectors as part of socialized medical services in the United States.
- Financial service inputs would necessarily include insurance services for institutions and practitioners.
- Manufacturing inputs would include not only basic chemicals associated with medical care but also pharmaceuticals suppliers. Pharmaceutical manufacturing is not considered CI under the current U.S. Health sector definitions but is not divisible from other chemical manufacturing inputs (NAICS 325) under the I–O data available from the BEA at the time of writing.

## Non-CI Sector Inputs to U.S. Health Sector

Although our analysis must necessarily revolve around the contemporary definitions of CI sectors discussed in Chapter 1, an examination of other significant industrial inputs is required. Understanding what might be missing from the current definitions of CI sectors helps us to assess the accuracy and validity of the dependency findings.

The non-CI sector inputs assessed here are specifically for Health, but will be aggregated across all sectors toward the end of this chapter. Figure 2.30 is a waterfall

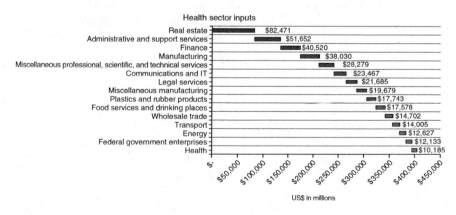

**FIGURE 2.30** Health sector inputs—top 15 industries.

of the top 15 industrial inputs to the Health sector in the United States, including both CI and non-CI sectors.

## Observations

Regarding the short-term delivery of the sector's core goods and services and the industries, which are direct operational inputs, the following observations are made:

- Miscellaneous professional, scientific, and technical services are equal to 5 percent of full-time employee compensation in U.S. health industries, indicating the importance of contractors.
- Food services is the tenth largest overall input—and at least 50 percent larger than the Food industry itself, which does not make the top 15 inputs to the Health sector in the United States. This reflects the large degree of outsourcing associated with the preparation and delivery of food within the Health sector. Food services are not considered part of a CI sector under current definitions.
- Wholesale trade is a major input to Health reflecting distribution system for many medical goods which do not go directly from manufacturer to consumer (IE, hospitals). Wholesale and retail trades are not part of a CI under current definitions.
- Miscellaneous Manufacturing includes goods such as industrial gas suppliers and are the eighth largest input to Health sector at $20 billion in sales directly to the sector: twice the value of health-to-health trade. Miscellaneous is not part of a CI under current definitions.

**Note:** See the end of this chapter for a roll-up of all non-CI inputs.

## FOOD SECTOR IN THE UNITED STATES

Figure 2.31 depicts the I–O analysis for Food sector in the United States.

Total value of sector inputs consumed by Health from other CI sectors is $395 billion—the third gross consumer of CI goods and services among the CI sectors.

Total value of sector outputs required by other CI sectors is $288 billion—the fourth largest gross supplier to other CI sectors among the sectors.

### Dependency Observations

- Overwhelming amount of the Food sector inputs and outputs are consumed within the Food sector itself—67 percent. This level of intrasector trade indicates that the movement of goods and the logistical communications associated with the movement of goods may make Transportation and Communications at least as important as sector with higher inputs—such as Finance.
- Government is the largest purchaser of goods from the Food sector as a result of the purchasing for the purposes of police and military food programs, although Health would be a large purchaser for purposes such

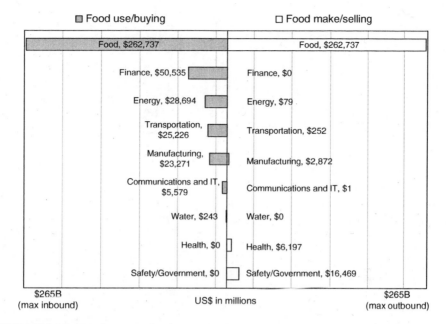

**FIGURE 2.31**  Food sector tornado.

| | Energy | Communications and IT | Finance | Health | Food | Water | Transportation | Safety/Government | Manufacturing |
|---|---|---|---|---|---|---|---|---|---|
| I–O ratio | 365.0 | 4648.7 | 168451.3 | 0.0 | 1.0 | 38024.0 | 38.1 | 0.0 | 8.1 |

as in-patient food programs. Other sectors do not routinely supply meals to staff and clients, who would feed themselves.

## Non-CI Sector Inputs to Food

Although our analysis must necessarily revolve around the contemporary definitions of CI sectors discussed in Chapter 1, an examination of other significant industrial inputs is required. Understanding what might be missing from the current definitions of CI sectors will help assess the accuracy and validity of the dependency findings.

The non-CI sector inputs assessed here are specifically for Food, but will be aggregated across all sectors toward the end of this chapter. Figure 2.32 is a waterfall of the top 15 industrial inputs to the Food sector in the United States, including both CI and non-CI sectors.

## Observations

Regarding the short-term delivery of the sector's core goods and services and the industries, which are direct operational inputs, the following observations are made:

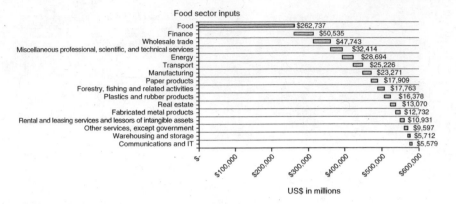

**FIGURE 2.32**  Food sector inputs—top 15 industries.

- Miscellaneous professional, scientific, and technical services are equal to 30 percent of full-time employee compensation in U.S. food industries, indicating the criticality of contractors.
- Paper and plastic products are major inputs to food—both larger than Communications and IT inputs. These industries provide packaging to the Food industry, which cannot prepare food for distribution without packaging inputs. Packaging inputs such as converted paper and plastics are not part of a CI under current definitions.
- Wholesale trade is a major input to Food reflecting distribution system for many perishable goods that do not go directly from manufacturer/farmer to consumer. Wholesale trade is not part of a CI under current definitions.

**Note:**  See the end of this chapter for a roll-up of all non-CI inputs.

## WATER SECTOR IN THE UNITED STATES

The Water sector information was bundled with 22 utilities I–O data from the BEA 2005 information used in this research. Water sector data was manually extracted by the author from utilities by applying GDP ratios between power generation, natural gas distribution, and water, sewage, and other systems to the I–O data for the roll-up of these three industries (utilities). As a result, the analysis in this sector is based upon independently derived data, based upon BEA data. Ambiguities are present and obvious ambiguities will be mentioned in the text.

Figure 2.33 depicts the I–O analysis for Water sector in the United States.

Total value of sector inputs consumed by Water from other CI sectors is $2.9 billion—the smallest gross consumer of CI goods and services among the CI sectors.

Total value of sector outputs required by other CI sectors is $3.2 billion—the smallest gross supplier to other CI sectors among the sectors.

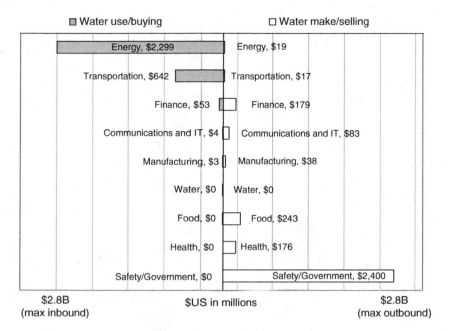

**FIGURE 2.33** Water sector input tornado.

| | Energy | Communications and IT | Finance | Health | Food | Water | Transportation | Safety/ Government | Manufacturing |
|---|---|---|---|---|---|---|---|---|---|
| I–O ratio | 123.101 | 0.051 | 0.297 | 0.000 | 0.000 | 1.000 | 38.290 | 0.000 | 0.092 |

## Dependency Observations

- Water is unique among CI sectors in that it is one of the smallest inputs to itself as opposed to one of the largest—which is typical for other CI sectors. This reveals the extent to which Water infrastructures are almost entirely autonomous in operations. Operations are also typically monopolies within well-defined geographic boundaries by either economic or engineering necessity.
- Energy is by far the largest input in Water, a logical observation given that the purification and pumping processes would all be energy-intensive industrial processes. This relationship may be overstated because Water statistics had to be derived from 22 utilities as discussed earlier.
- Transportation appears to be a large input in Water due to the logistics associated with equipment and chemicals used for water purification.
- The large input from the Finance sector is likely a reflection of the fact that some water and waste facilities may be owned by private holding companies that are considered Financial industries under NAICS. This, as opposed to services purchased directly from Water.

- Health and food both have large I–O ratio because they do not own water or waste facilities, but are apparently the largest consumers of these services after government, which purchases for general populations which in turn might tax.
- Manufacturing sector is a critical supplier of industrial gases to Water such as chlorine for purification purposes. Spending by the Water sector on Manufacturing goods is obscured by the relationship between Water and Safety/Government, where Water is a municipal government service with some bill such as those from Manufacturing being attributed to Government consumption rather than Water.

**Note:** See the Safety and Government discussion to follow.

## Non-CI Sector Inputs to Water

Although our analysis must necessarily revolve around the contemporary definitions of CI sectors discussed in Chapter 1, an examination of other significant industrial inputs is required. Understanding what might be missing from the current definitions of CI sectors will help assess the accuracy and validity of the dependency findings.

The non-CI sector inputs assessed here are specifically for Water, but will be aggregated across all sectors toward the end of this chapter. Figure 2.34 is a waterfall of the top 15 industrial inputs to the Water sector in the United States, including both CI and non-CI sectors.

## Key Observations

Regarding the short-term delivery of the sector's core goods and services and the industries, which are direct operational inputs, the following observations are made:

- Miscellaneous professional, scientific, and technical services are equal to 3.7 percent of full-time employee compensation in U.S. Water industries— significantly smaller than other CI sectors, possibly reflecting a lower dependency on contractors.

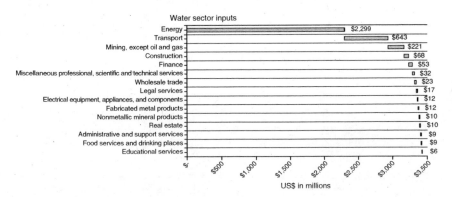

**FIGURE 2.34**   Water sector inputs—top 15 industries.

- Presence of mining, except oil and gas is almost certainly an artifact related to how the author had to derive the Water statistics (see above), and is likely not a major input to the Water sector.

**Note:** See the end of this chapter for a roll-up of all non-CI inputs.

## TRANSPORT SECTOR IN THE UNITED STATES

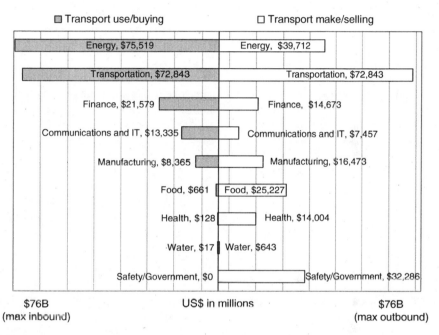

☐ Transport use/buying    ☐ Transport make/selling

Energy, $75,519    Energy, $39,712
Transportation, $72,843    Transportation, $72,843
Finance, $21,579    Finance, $14,673
Communications and IT, $13,335    Communications and IT, $7,457
Manufacturing, $8,365    Manufacturing, $16,473
Food, $661    Food, $25,227
Health, $128    Health, $14,004
Water, $17    Water, $643
Safety/Government, $0    Safety/Government, $32,286

$76B                US$ in millions            $76B
(max inbound)                            (max outbound)

**FIGURE 2.35** Transport sector input/output tornado.

| | Energy | Communications and IT | Finance | Health | Food | Water | Transportation | Safety/ Government | Manufacturing |
|---|---|---|---|---|---|---|---|---|---|
| I–O ratio | 1.9 | 1.8 | 1.4 | 0.1 | 0.03 | 0.03 | 1.0 | 0.0 | 0.51 |

Total value of sector inputs consumed by Transport from other CI sectors is $127 billion—the seventh largest gross consumer of CI goods and services among the CI sectors.

Total value of sector outputs required by other CI sectors is $139 billion—the sixth largest gross supplier to other CI sectors among the sectors.

## Dependency Observations

- Energy is a larger input to Transport as the sector is to itself, which is unusual because intrasector trade is typically substantially larger than all other inputs.

• Food is the largest consumer of Transport services outside the Safety/ Government and Transport sectors, using almost 20 times the value of service that Transport purchases from Food. This relationship reflects the nature of the Food production system, which starts with many small producers, is centralized with large processors with finished goods returning to small wholesale and retail distributors.

## Non-CI Sector Inputs to Transport

Although our analysis must necessarily revolve around the contemporary definitions of CI sectors discussed in Chapter 1, an examination of other significant industrial inputs is required. Understanding what might be missing from the current definitions of CI sectors will help assess the accuracy and validity of the dependency findings.

The non-CI sector inputs assessed here are specifically for Transport, but will be aggregated across all sectors toward the end of this chapter. Figure 2.36 is a waterfall of the top 15 industrial inputs to the Transport sector in the United States, including both CI and non-CI sectors.

## Key Observations

Regarding the short-term delivery of the sector's core goods and services and the industries which are direct operational inputs, the following observations are made:

• Miscellaneous professional, scientific, and technical services are equal to 10 percent of full-time employee compensation in U.S. Transport industries, indicating a significant dependency on contractors.
• Food as a sector is not part of the top 15 inputs into Transport—but Food services and drinking places does make the top 15. This indicates the importance of prepared foods and catering to Transportation, passenger services. (Note: Foods services and drinking places is a $532 billion dollar

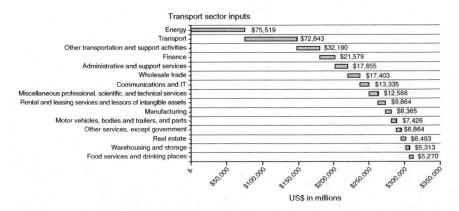

**FIGURE 2.36**   Transport sector inputs—top 15 industries.

industry in the United States, consuming $272 billion in inputs—30 percent of these inputs come directly from the Food Sector.)
- Wholesale and retail trades are major inputs to Transport reflecting the importance of the sale and distribution of tickets to both private and business consumers. Wholesale and retail trades are not part of a CI under current definitions.

**Note:** See the end of this chapter for a roll-up of all non-CI inputs.

## SAFETY AND GOVERNMENT SECTOR IN THE UNITED STATES

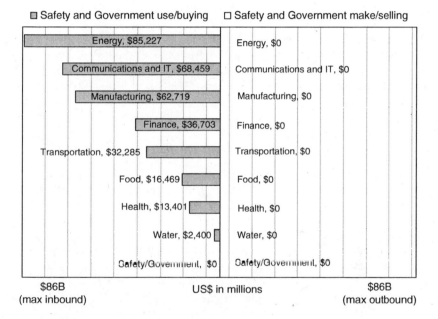

**FIGURE 2.37**   Safety and Government sectors input tornado.

| | Energy | Communications and IT | Finance | Health | Food | Water | Transportation | Safety/ Government | Manufacturing |
|---|---|---|---|---|---|---|---|---|---|
| I-O ratio | NA | NA | NA | NA | NA | NA | NA | NA | NA |

Total value of sector inputs consumed by Safety and Government from other CI sectors is $316 billion—fourth largest gross consumer of CI goods and services among the CI sectors.

Total value of sector outputs required by other CI sectors is zero dollars.*

---

\* Bureau for Economic Analysis (BEA) industry by industry I–O statistics only show government spending by sector—unlike Canadian I–O statistics, no data is provided on transfer to government other than "taxes on production and imports, less subsidies."

## Dependency Observations

- According to NAICS I–O and existing CI sector definitions, no goods or services are sold by the U.S. government, indicating that government services to CI sectors are largely provided free of charge. Safety and Government does not have an I–O ratio because all outputs are listed as zero in the BEA I–O tables and therefore a ratio cannot be obtained.
- Safety and Government spending on Manufacturing is distinct between different levels of government according to BEA statistics and together account for the third largest input: Federal government spends a bulk of its Manufacturing expenditures on other transportation, which is generally aerospace and defense-type goods. Recall that Defense spending is a distinct line item in the I–O statistics but no breakdown of sector spending is provided—only a single value is attributed to federal government inputs/resources. State and Local Government spending on manufacturing is largely on chemicals, likely for use in sectors like Water. In this case, certain inputs that should be attributed to Water may be attributed to Safety and Government due to lack of available detail about spending rationale. This will likely contribute to correlation weaknesses seen in Chapter 4.

## Non-CI Sector Inputs to Safety and Government

Although our analysis must necessarily revolve around the contemporary definitions of CI sectors discussed in Chapter 1, an examination of other significant industrial inputs is required. Understanding what might be missing from the current definitions of CI sectors will help assess the accuracy and validity of the dependency findings.

The non-CI sector inputs assessed here are specifically for Safety and Government, but will be aggregated across all sectors toward the end of this chapter. Figure 2.38 is a waterfall of the top 15 industrial inputs to the Safety and Government sector in Canada, including both CI and non-CI sectors.

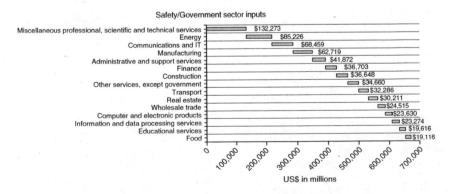

FIGURE 2.38   Safety and Government sector inputs—top 15 industries.

## Observations

Regarding the short-term delivery of the sector's core goods and services and the industries, which are direct operational inputs, the following observations are made:

- Number 1 input to Safety and Government appears to be professional and technical services at $132 billion. Given that federal government compensation to employees is $341 billion, and State and Local Government compensation to employees is $864 billion, indicating that 11 percent of the operational manpower of Safety and Government is attributed to non-employees. Professional and technical services are not considered part of CI under current definitions.
- Communications and IT is the third largest input to Safety and Government, and the second largest CI sector contribution. However, other industries directly related to Communications and IT such as computer and electronic products, and information processing services are also within the top 15 inputs. If these sectors were considered part of the Communications and IT sector, then this sector would surpass Energy as a top input to Safety and Government by over 20 percent.
- Wholesale and retail trades are major inputs to Safety and Government reflecting the importance of the consumption large amounts of goods from all sectors for both Health and nonmilitary purposes (military expenditures are included in the I–O metrics from Statistics Canada). Wholesale and retail trades are not part of a CI under current definitions.

**Note:** See the end of this chapter for a roll-up of all non-CI inputs.

### MANUFACTURING SECTOR IN THE UNITED STATES

Figure 2.39 depicts the I–O analysis for Manufacturing sector in the United States.

Total value of sector inputs consumed by Manufacturing from other CI sectors is $242 billion—fifth largest gross consumer of CI goods and services among the CI sectors.

Total value of sector outputs required by other CI sectors is $287 billion—fifth largest gross supplier to other CI sectors among the sectors.

## Dependency Observations

- Manufacturing appears to have polarized dependency relationships among the CI sectors; either it has a strong dependency upon a CI sector or the sector has a heavy dependence upon Manufacturing. In the cases of both Safety and Government, they supply no goods or services to Manufacturing (at least paid for goods or services) but are some of the largest consumers of goods from Manufacturing. The converse relationship applied to Finance especially, where large sums are spent on Financial Services but very little

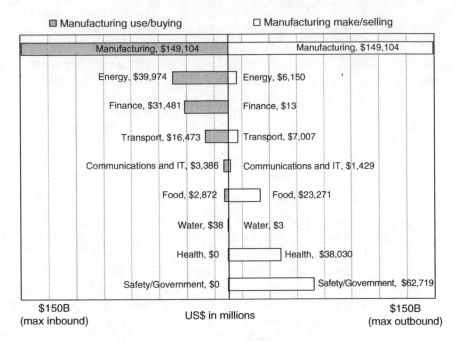

**FIGURE 2.39** Manufacturing sector input tornado.

| | Energy | Communications and IT | Finance | Health | Food | Water | Transportation | Safety/ Government | Manufacturing |
|---|---|---|---|---|---|---|---|---|---|
| I-O ratio | 6.50 | 2.37 | 2478.83 | 0.00 | 0.12 | 10.92 | 1.97 | Infinity | 1.00 |

is spent directly by Finance. In the case of Safety and Government, part of this large percentage spent must be attributed to the procurement of inputs from the Water sector such as chlorine for purification purposes.

## Non-CI Sector Inputs to Manufacturing

Although our analysis must necessarily revolve around the contemporary definitions of CI sectors discussed in Chapter 1, an examination of other significant industrial inputs is required. Understanding what might be missing from the current definitions of CI sectors will help assess the accuracy and validity of the dependency findings.

The non-CI sector inputs assessed here are specifically for Manufacturing, but will be aggregated across all sectors toward the end of this chapter. Figure 2.40 is a waterfall of the top 15 industrial inputs to the Manufacturing sector in the United States, including both CI and non-CI sectors.

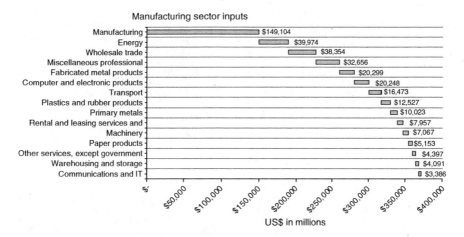

**FIGURE 2.40** Manufacturing sector inputs—top 15 industries.

## Observations

Regarding the short-term delivery of the sector's core goods and services and the industries, which are direct operational inputs, the following observations are made:

- Miscellaneous professional, scientific, and technical services are equal to 25 percent of full-time employee compensation in the U.S. Manufacturing sector, indicating the criticality of contractors.
- Manufacturing sector as defined under the CI definitions is limited to chemicals and aerospace (other Transportation). However, it becomes apparent that these industries are themselves dependent upon other forms of non-CI manufacturing such as fabricated metal products, machinery, plastics, and rubber products. None of these other contributing manufacturing industries are considered CIs under the current definitions.
- Computer and electronic components are six times larger than Communications and IT, which is barely within the top 15 overall inputs for Manufacturing. Though fundamental to the delivery of Communications and IT goods and services, computers and electronic components are not considered CIs under the current definitions.

**Note:** See the end of this chapter for a roll-up of all non-CI inputs.

## U.S. I–O CI Sector Economic Dependency Matrix

The $9 \times 9$ matrix in Table 2.4 below is the detailed I–O metrics that result from mapping CI sectors to the NAICS and applying the industry-by-industry I–O econometrics available from Statistics Canada.

Table 2.4 is the rolled-up all-sector representation of the previous sections, which presented each sector's finding and summary analysis individually. Although

**TABLE 2.4**

**U.S. I–O CI Sector Dependencies in Millions**

|            | Energy $ | Comms $ | Fin $ | Health $ | Food $ | Water $ | Trans $ | Safety/Gov $ | Manf $ |
|------------|---------|---------|---------|---------|---------|---------|---------|---------|---------|
| **Energy** | 439,787 | 5,008 | 12,256 | 12,627 | 28,694 | 2,299 | 75,519 | 85,226 | 39,974 |
| **Comms** | 2,714 | 160,548 | 33,590 | 23,467 | 5,579 | 4 | 13,335 | 68,459 | 3,386 |
| **Fin** | 10,345 | 31,851 | 463,502 | 40,520 | 50,535 | 53 | 21,579 | 36,703 | 31,481 |
| **Health** | 0 | 2 | 0 | 10,185 | 0 | 0 | 128 | 13,401 | 0 |
| **Food** | 79 | 1 | 0 | 6,197 | 262,737 | 0 | 661 | 16,469 | 2,872 |
| **Water** | 19 | 83 | 179 | 176 | 243 | 0 | 17 | 2,400 | 38 |
| **Trans** | 39,712 | 7,457 | 14,673 | 14,004 | 25,227 | 643 | 72,843 | 32,286 | 16,473 |
| **Safety/Gov** | 0 | 0 | 0 | 0 | 0 | 0 | 0 | 0 | 0 |
| **Manf** | 6,150 | 1,429 | 13 | 38,030 | 23,271 | 3 | 8,365 | 62,719 | 149,104 |

Table 2.4 is a specific representation of the United States spending among CI sectors, which is of interest to some readers, it does not readily display dependency relationships. The reason why the I–O ratio was developed in this book. Recall that with an I–O ratio, a number greater than 1 indicates that a sector is spending more within a given sector than the other sector is buying from the first sector. This spending relationship is assumed to be a potential indication of negative sector dependency on the part of the sector with the I–O ratio greater than 1. The greater the number is above 1, the more profound the spending imbalance between the two CI sectors. If a sector posses an I–O ratio less than 1, then it is in a positive trade flow with the other sector, and this is assumed to be a potential indication of positive sector dependency on the part of the sector with the I–O ratio less than 1. The greater the number is below 1, the more profound the spending imbalance between the two CI sectors.

Table 2.5 is a summation of all the I–O ratio captured in the pervious section, with the following coding applied. It brings economic relationships and interdependencies into stark contrast, making some patterns appear where they may have been obscured within large numbers and decimal places.

The view offered by Table 2.5 is interesting because it highlights the apparent polarity of relationship between the CIs in the United States, with a majority of the I–O ratios being either white or black. Safety and Government are clearly a major factor weighing this table toward black due to the nature of I–O data, which shows Safety and Government as almost complete consumers of CI goods and services without actually returning any service in return. We know this is not the case. Clearly, Safety and Government provided critical services to other CI sectors, but they do not charge for them. (Infinity is indicated where the output to the sector is

## TABLE 2.5
## U.S. I–O CI Sector Dependencies in Millions

| | Energy | Comms | Fin | Health | Food | Water | Trans | Safety/Gov | Manf |
|---|---|---|---|---|---|---|---|---|---|
| Energy | 1.000 | 1.845 | 1.186 | infinity | 365.092 | 123.101 | 1.902 | infinity | 6.500 |
| Comms | 0.542 | 1.000 | 1.055 | 11733.650 | 4648.750 | 0.051 | 1.788 | infinity | 2.370 |
| Fin | 0.844 | 0.948 | 1.000 | 101300.000 | 168451.333 | 0.297 | 1.471 | infinity | 2478.835 |
| Health | 0.000 | 0.000 | 0.000 | 1.000 | 0.000 | 0.000 | 0.009 | infinity | 0.000 |
| Food | 0.003 | 0.000 | 0.000 | infinity | 1.000 | 0.000 | 0.026 | infinity | 0.123 |
| Water | 0.008 | 19.757 | 3.367 | infinity | 38024.099 | 1.000 | 0.026 | infinity | 10.923 |
| Trans | 0.526 | 0.559 | 0.649 | 109.494 | 38.144 | 38.290 | 1.000 | infinity | 1.969 |
| Safety/Gov | 0.000 | 0.000 | 0.000 | 0.000 | 0.000 | 0.000 | 0.000 | infinity | infinity |
| Manf | 0.154 | 0.422 | 0.000 | infinity | 8.103 | 0.092 | 0.508 | infinity | 1.000 |

*Notes*:

White ☐ (highly positive I–O ratio $< 0.5$) indicates that the sector in the adjacent column is strongly independent, i.e., it sells much more than it spends with a given sector in the adjacent row.

Light gray ▦ (moderate positive I–O ratio $> 0.5 < 1.0$) indicates that the sector in the adjacent column is somewhat independent, i.e., it sells more than it spends with a given sector in the adjacent row.

Dark gray ▨ (moderate negative I–O ratio $< 1.0 > 1.5$) indicates that the sector in the adjacent column is somewhat dependent, i.e., it sells less than it spends with the sector in the adjacent row.

Black ■ (highly negative I–O ratio $> 1.5$) indicates that the sector in the adjacent column is strongly dependent, i.e., it sells much less than it spends with the sector in the adjacent row.

zero, and anything divided by zero, is infinity according to high school mathematics. Conversely, where a sector input from Safety and Government or any other sector is zero, then the resulting I–O is zero because zero divided by anything—input/output—is still zero.)

Like Safety and Government, the Health CI sector is dominated entirely by intense dependency relationships with all other sectors. This indication is best interpreted as an artifact of how health services are funded in the United States and not necessarily the fragility of health services.

The Water column in Table 2.5 is also remarkable because all the squares are either white (highly independent of other sectors) or black (highly dependent on other sectors). For Water this reinforces the observation that Water infrastructures operate as largest autonomous CI industries with just a couple of strong dependencies from Energy and Transport; Energy to run the massive machinery and transport to deliver the chemicals and additives needed to purify water and waste.

## COMPARISON OF CANADA–U.S. CI SECTORS BY I–O RATIO

The following section is a side-by-side comparison of Canadian and Unites States' I–O ratios for CI sectors. This comparison is useful because it may either reinforce observations seen in the data of both the countries or will possibly bring certain errors in measurement to the surface where they may have remained ambiguous without this comparison.

A comparison of Canadian and U.S. indications around CI interdependency provides insights into the potential from cross-border interdependency analysis, where the scope and scale of cross-border interdependency is largely unmeasured across sectors. The Canadian and U.S. border is highly porous and many industrial supply-chains span this border. If there is a high degree of similarity among Canadian and U.S. CI sectors and their interdependency, then it must be assumed that the similarity in industrial structures coupled with cross-border supply chains is highly relevant to the study of cross-border dependencies and vulnerabilities.

### ENERGY

Table 2.6 is a side-by-side comparison of Energy sector I–O ratios in Canada and the U.S. In Canada, the Energy sector appears to be significantly dependent upon the Communications and IT and Finance sectors, with I–O ratio indicating that Energy spends almost four times as much on Communications and IT as Communications and IT spends on Energy. In the case of Finance, it is almost three times of what is spent. In the United States, the dependency relationship for Energy appears reversed, with Energy selling more to both Communications and IT and the Finance sector.

Manufacturing in Canada, like Manufacturing in the United States has a dependency relationship with Energy. However, it is much more balanced in Canada, although the relationship in the United States shows Energy to be much more dominant toward the Manufacturing sector.

These differences within Communications and IT and Finance between Canada and the United States may indicate that these industries are substantially different in organizations and management between Canada and the United States. It may also

### TABLE 2.6
### Canada–U.S. Energy Sector I–O Ratio Comparison

|                        | Canada | United States |
|------------------------|--------|---------------|
| Energy                 | 1.00   | 1.000         |
| Communications and IT  | 3.79   | 0.542         |
| Finance                | 2.99   | 0.844         |
| Health                 | 0.10   | 0.000         |
| Food                   | 0.04   | 0.003         |
| Water                  | 0.18   | 0.008         |
| Transportation         | 0.16   | 0.526         |
| Safety/Government      | 0.23   | 0.000         |
| Manufacturing          | 0.15   | 0.154         |

indicate that the I–O information applied is significantly different at levels of aggregation not visible based upon publicly available data sets.

## COMMUNICATIONS AND IT

Table 2.7 is a side-by-side comparison of Communications and IT sector I–O ratios in Canada and the U.S. Communications and IT in Canada appears to support an entirely positive dependency relationship with all other CI sectors, meaning that it sells more to the sectors than it buys. In the United States, this is certainly not the case because Communications and IT appear to buy significantly more from the Energy than it sells. The difference between Canada and the United States in this sector-to-sector relationship is striking because both Communications and IT and Energy are very large; therefore the spending on Energy by U.S. Communications and IT industries is significantly larger than that in Canada—even when considered proportionally (as accomplished with the I–O ratio). This difference may possibly be explained by the fact that radio and television broadcasting is apparently included in the I–O data set for Communications and IT from the U.S. BEA, although it is separated in the Canadian data set. Radio and television broadcasting is substantially smaller in Canada than in the United States.

The Finance sector is proportionally a much larger supplier to the U.S. Communications and IT sector than in Canada, with the Communications and IT sector in the United States spending nearly four times as much proportionally. This may be an indicator of the much larger number of service providers in the United States, versus Canada with few but larger Communications and IT service providers. Again, this may be a function of the inclusion of radio and television broadcasting within the U.S. I–O data.

Water again appears as a major outlier in an I–O comparison between Canada and the United States, but must be considered carefully because the total value of this trade is minor in the larger picture. However, this indication might point to the fact that Water is simply a less expensive input in Canada, because technologies employed in Canada and the United States in the delivery of Communications and IT are substantially the same.

**TABLE 2.7**

**Canada–U.S. Communications and IT Sector I–O Ratio Comparison**

|  | Canada | United States |
|---|---|---|
| Energy | 0.26 | 1.845 |
| Communications and IT | 1.00 | 1.000 |
| Finance | 0.26 | 0.948 |
| Health | 0.13 | 0.000 |
| Food | 0.09 | 0.000 |
| Water | 0.24 | 19.757 |
| Transportation | 0.57 | 0.559 |
| Safety/Government | 0.09 | 0.000 |
| Manufacturing | 0.49 | 0.422 |

## TABLE 2.8
## Canada–U.S. Finance Sector I–O Ratio Comparison

|                      | Canada | United States |
|----------------------|--------|---------------|
| Energy               | 0.33   | 1.185         |
| Communications and IT| 3.85   | 1.055         |
| Finance              | 1.00   | 1.000         |
| Health               | 0.21   | 0.000         |
| Food                 | 0.06   | 0.000         |
| Water                | 0.60   | 3.367         |
| Transportation       | 0.88   | 0.649         |
| Safety/Government    | 0.46   | 0.000         |
| Manufacturing        | 0.22   | 0.000         |

## FINANCE

Table 2.8 is a side-by-side comparison of Finance sector I–O ratios in Canada and the U.S. One of the most interesting observations from the I–O data related to the Finance sector in Canada and the United States is the difference within Communications and IT. Communications and IT is certainly a critical component to the delivery of Financial services that are increasingly virtual in nature. In Canada, Communications and IT sells almost four times as much value to Finance as it purchases. In the United States this relationship is almost entirely in balance. Similarly, in Canada Finance sector sells three times as much as it buys from Energy sector, in the United States the relationship between Finance and Energy appears again nearly balanced.

The Finance sector is proportionally a much larger supplier to the U.S. Communications and IT sector than in Canada, with the Communications and IT sector in the United States spending nearly four times as much proportionally. This may be an indicator of the much larger number of service providers in the United States versus Canada with few but larger Communications and IT service providers. Again, this may be a function of the inclusion of radio and television broadcasting within the U.S. I–O data.

Within the United States, Finance does not possess any fundamentally weak dependency relationships with any sector except Water, but the value flowing from Finance to Water 0.3 percent (less than a third of 1 percent) of Finance's total inputs. This makes Finance one of the most independent infrastructures in the United States as a function of trade flows among CI sectors. In Canada Finance is strong but not the strongest CI sector. In Canada, the sector with the most apparent independence by the value of trade flows among CI sectors is Communications and IT (see previous section).

## HEALTH

Table 2.9 is a side-by-side comparison of Health sector I–O ratios in Canada and the U.S. Although the numbers derived from the Canadian and the U.S. I–O ratios for the Health sector appear to be widely different, they in fact tell us a closely aligned story that Health is a large net consumer of goods and services from other CI sectors

**TABLE 2.9**
**Canada–U.S. Health Sector I–O Ratio Comparison**

|  | Canada | United States |
|---|---|---|
| Energy | 9.97 | Infinity |
| Communications and IT | 7.76 | 11733.650 |
| Finance | 4.67 | 101300.000 |
| Health | 1.00 | 1.000 |
| Food | 2.03 | Infinity |
| Water | 38.50 | Infinity |
| Transportation | 7.27 | 109.494 |
| Safety/Government | 0.02 | 0.000 |
| Manufacturing | 0.27 | Infinity |

with the exception of government, which funds the sector in part or whole. The ratios are numerically larger in the United States than in Canada because much Health spending in the form of employee health-plan coverage in the United States is attributed to personal expenditures under U.S. I–O data, while Canadian I–O data attributed health-plan expenses to the industry paying the benefit.

### FOOD

Table 2.10 is a side-by-side comparison of Food sector I–O ratios in Canada and the U.S. Like the Health sector, the Food sectors in Canada and the United States are closely aligned in their patterns of dependency upon the other CI sectors, despite what appear to be large differences in the I–O ratios. These differences are uniformly positive and negatively dependent between these two countries, with the United States showing larger I–O ratios relative to Canada's I–O ratios for Food. This difference will be explained in part by the nature of the distribution and retail systems in the two countries, with U.S. Food sector industries selling directly to other CI sectors only very rarely.

Health, and Safety and Government are the two CI sectors, which have dependent relationships with food, however, specific comparisons between Canada and the

**TABLE 2.10**
**Canada–U.S. Food Sector I–O Ratio Comparison**

|  | Canada | United States |
|---|---|---|
| Energy | 24.58 | 365.092 |
| Communications and IT | 10.56 | 4648.750 |
| Finance | 15.81 | 168451.333 |
| Health | 0.49 | 0.000 |
| Food | 1.00 | 1.000 |
| Water | 103.00 | 38024.099 |
| Transportation | 19.36 | 38.144 |
| Safety/Government | 1.06 | 0.000 |
| Manufacturing | 3.22 | 8.103 |

United States are difficult for two reasons. First, industries not defined as official CI play an important, if not critical, role in the delivery of Food goods and services—particularly in distribution and preparation. This means their inputs into sectors such as health, and Safety and Government cannot be gauged and applied to the I–O ratio. Second, in the case of the United States, government spending on Food is largely for the defense forces. In Canada this information is bundled under the Canadian NAICS code GS60—other federal government services. If the U.S. defense spending is not bundled under federal government spending and is part of a simple, single output code of the federal government.

## WATER

Table 2.11 is a side-by-side comparison of Water sector I–O ratios in Canada and the U.S. The United States I–O ratios for Water were challenging for the purposes of doing the I–O dependency assessment, because Water statistics had to be derived from larger statistical aggregations of BEA I–O data sets, and the resulting estimates may lack a certain degree of precision. As a result, conflicts between the Canadian and U.S. I–O data for Water may be the result of errors in deriving Water I–O data, or may reflect actual differences as discussed below.

In Canada, Water is 0.25 of 1 percent of all CI inputs into other CI sectors. In the United States, Water is 0.12 of 1 percent of all CI sector inputs into other CI sectors. Based upon the relatively small weight of the Water sector from an I–O perspective, indications from this sector should be assessed cautiously. For instance, based upon the I–O ratios from both countries, it is probably safe to say that Water is negatively dependent upon Energy—but it would not be appropriate to say that Water need Energy 22.3 times more in the United States than in Canada (123/5.5).

In the case of Communications and IT, and Finance there is a divergence between the Canadian and U.S. I–O ratios, which might be explained by a greater expense associated with Water in the United States. In these cases, it is difficult to tell what is an artifact of market conditions, versus a real industrial requirement for the delivery of goods and services from Communications and IT and Finance. Correlation work discussed in Chapter 4 will seek to address where the truth may lie.

**TABLE 2.11**

**Canada–U.S. Water Sector I–O Ratio Comparison**

|  | Canada | United States |
|---|---|---|
| Energy | 5.50 | 123.101 |
| Communications and IT | 4.24 | 0.051 |
| Finance | 1.67 | 0.297 |
| Health | 0.03 | 0.000 |
| Food | 0.01 | 0.000 |
| Water | 1.00 | 1.000 |
| Transportation | 0.23 | 38.290 |
| Safety/Government | 0.12 | 0.000 |
| Manufacturing | 0.10 | 0.092 |

Transportation is a similar case to Communications and IT, and Finance in relation to Water, where the I–O ratios from Canada to the United States are opposite in their indications. In Canada, the I–O ratio indicates that Water is a net-supplier to the Transportation sector at almost a five to one supply to buy factor. The opposite is indicated by the U.S. I–O ratio, where Water appears to procure 2.4 times as much from Transportation as it sells. Again, correlation work discussed in Chapter 4 will seek to address where the truth may lie.

## TRANSPORTATION

Table 2.12 is a side-by-side comparison of Transportation sector I–O ratios in Canada and the U.S. There is strong alignment between Canada and the United States for Transportation of the input ratios of the CI sectors of Energy, Communications and IT, and Finance. These three sectors together make up a majority of Transport inputs and are the largest suppliers, making the relationships and resulting I–O ratios appear strong. However, in the sectors of Food, Water, and Manufacturing, the I–O ratios between Canada and the United States go in opposite directions.

In the case of Water, the divergence between Canada and the United States may possibly be attributed to an error in statistical assessment as discussed above in the section on Water.

Manufacturing under the current CI definitions includes aerospace—aircraft—and chemicals. Clearly the aerospace portion of Manufacturing would be a significant input into Transportation. The fact that Transportation in Canada appears to be more dependent than the Transportation in the United States from an I–O perspective can possibly be attributed to the greater use of intermediaries such as leasing companies among U.S. Transport sector firms. This would have the effect of reducing the I–O ratio of Transport to Manufacturing for the United States, but increasing the Finance to Transport dependency—which is in fact what is shown: Transport in Canada has a lower I–O dependency with Finance than Transport in the United States, possibly compensating for the higher I–O ratio with Manufacturing as a result of more direct purchasing.

## TABLE 2.12
## Canada–U.S. Transportation Sector I–O Ratio Comparison

|  | Canada | United States |
|---|---|---|
| Energy | 6.32 | 1.902 |
| Communications and IT | 1.76 | 1.788 |
| Finance | 1.14 | 1.471 |
| Health | 0.14 | 0.009 |
| Food | 0.05 | 0.026 |
| Water | 4.38 | 0.026 |
| Transportation | 1.00 | 1.000 |
| Safety/Government | 0.34 | 0.000 |
| Manufacturing | 0.68 | 0.508 |

**TABLE 2.13**

**Canada–U.S. Safety and Government Sector I–O Ratio Comparison**

|                        | Canada | United States |
|------------------------|--------|---------------|
| Energy                 | 4.44   | Infinity      |
| Communications and IT  | 11.63  | Infinity      |
| Finance                | 2.19   | Infinity      |
| Health                 | 57.24  | Infinity      |
| Food                   | 0.94   | Infinity      |
| Water                  | 8.10   | Infinity      |
| Transportation         | 2.93   | Infinity      |
| Safety/Government      | 1.00   | 1.0           |
| Manufacturing          | 2.47   | Infinity      |

## SAFETY AND GOVERNMENT

Table 2.13 is a side-by-side comparison of Safety and Government sector I–O ratios in Canada and the U.S. Infinity appears in the U.S. Safety and Government column because although the federal, state, and local governments consume goods and services from CI, the I–O data set from the BEA do not indicate any paid-for services from Safety and Government to these industries; therefore anything divided by zero equals infinity. As a result, no meaningful comparison between Canadian government I–O with CI sectors, and U.S. government I–O with CI sectors can be undertaken.

## MANUFACTURING

Table 2.14 is a side-by-side comparison of Manufacturing sector I–O ratios in Canada and the U.S. An interesting observation about the Manufacturing sector is that the sector in Canada consumes approximately the same value in Communications and IT services as Finance and Energy. Yet, in the United States, Manufacturing consumes

**TABLE 2.14**

**Canada–U.S. Manufacturing Sector I–O Ratio Comparison**

|                        | Canada | United States |
|------------------------|--------|---------------|
| Energy                 | 6.73   | 6.500         |
| Communications and IT  | 2.05   | 2.370         |
| Finance                | 4.51   | 2478.835      |
| Health                 | 0.27   | 0.000         |
| Food                   | 0.31   | 0.123         |
| Water                  | 9.75   | 10.923        |
| Transportation         | 1.46   | 1.969         |
| Safety/Government      | 0.40   | Infinity      |
| Manufacturing          | 1.00   | 1.000         |

communications and IT services at approximately 10 percent the rate of Finance and Energy consumptions. Where the Manufacturing sector in the United States consumes roughly $31 billion in Finance service, it consumes merely $3 billion in Communications and IT under current definitions.

As discussed in the section on Transportation, there appears to be a dependency flip around the Finance sector in the Transportation and Manufacturing sectors. This flip may be due to the greater use of certain intermediaries in the Finance sector acting as financers of purchases of aerospace equipment for the Transport sector from the Manufacturing sector. This has the effect in Canada (where the Transport companies by directly) having a stronger positive I–O ratio in Manufacturing to Transportation trade than the United States.

## UNDESIGNATED INDUSTRIES

In the initial discussion on the limits of statistical interdependency analysis we approached the issue of certain industries being inappropriately excluded from CI sector definitions—they are undesignated. This section discusses specifically which industries might be considered for inclusion as critical industries based upon analysis of I–O data sets from Canada and the United States. This is an important matter because the resiliency and assurance of the CI sectors relies not only on the controls and safeguards around the industries themselves, but also around their most important suppliers. A CI definition that overlooks critical contributors within a given sector is a weak concept that will likely prove ineffective for the purposes of managing security and especially crises.

The best indicator of an oversight related to undesignated, but in reality critical industries is the consideration of the overall sector input values that were covered after each sector's I–O analysis. Those sector-specific observations noted that certain industries were major suppliers to currently designated CI industries.

### CANADIAN INDICATIONS OF CRITICAL, UNDESIGNATED INDUSTRIES

Table 2.15 is a summation of the undesignated industries in Canada, which appeared as statistically large inputs to designated CI sectors and are themselves bona fide industrial entities. This table is not a recital of all undesignated, major inputs to each CI sector; certain major inputs come from industries, which by their nature do not appear to have time-sensitive and direct inputs into the supply chain and production process of CI sectors. For instance, leasers of real estate are major inputs to Health and Government, but are generally not real-time inputs to any production processes.

Following Table 2.15 is Figure 2.41, which is a waterfall diagram of the top 15 undesignated industries without qualification, and their total inputs to all CI sectors. The figure, therefore, looks at which undesignated CI sectors are the largest inputs and elements within the CI sectors' supply chains.

Considering the information from Table 2.15 and Figure 2.41, evidence starts to emerge based upon I–O analysis of CI sectors that the following industries at a minimum are significant inputs to multiple sectors and major overall inputs to CI

## TABLE 2.15

## Major Undesignated Industries Supplying CI Sectors in Canada

| Sector Name | Major Supply Industries not Considered CI in Canada |
|---|---|
| Energy | Wholesale and retail trades; coal mining |
| Finance | Postal services, courier, and messengers; information and data processing services |
| Communications and IT | Wholesale and retail trades; postal services, courier, and messengers |
| Health | Accommodation and food services; wholesale and retail trades |
| Food | Converted paper products and plastic products; wholesale and retail trades |
| Water | No observations |
| Transportation | Wholesale and retail trade; food services and drinking places |
| Safety/Government | Wholesale and retail trade; pharmaceutical and medicine manufacturing |
| Manufacturing | Metals, plastics, and resins |

supply chains in Canada. The undesignated industries are not presented in any specific order or intended priority.

1. Wholesale and retail trades: It is, in fact, a distribution system for the goods and services generated by many CI sectors. Distribution industries are not included within existing CI sector definitions, particularly for sectors such as Energy and Food, which utilize inputs from these sectors extensively.
2. Publishing, information and data processing services: Although this industrial group is an artifact of NAICS, components of it are clearly important inputs to CI sector. Services such as data-center management, application hosting, and other forms of IT outsourcing are very large business and a major component of many CI sector operations, especially Finance, Communications and IT, and Energy.

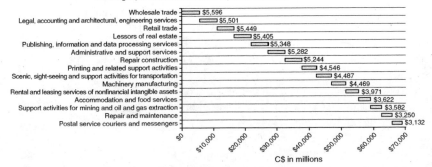

FIGURE 2.41 Undesignated Canadian industrial inputs to CI sectors.

3. Postal services, couriers, and messengers: These services form the backbone of logistics for most private sector firms and act as an interface for many of the other Transportation sector assets. These services are conspicuously absent from Canadian definitions.
4. Paper and plastic are forms of manufacturing which are undesignated but emerge as very important to a variety of sectors but especially critical to packaging for Food production and distribution.
5. Food services are important inputs to both Health and Transportation to the point that neither of the services would remain viable for public service-delivery if Food Services were unavailable for extended periods. Food services include not only restaurants but also Food contractors, caterers, and mobile food services.

**Note:** See Professional and Technical Services of this chapter for a discussion related to legal, accounting and architectural, and engineering services.

## U.S. Indications of Critical, Undesignated Industries

Table 2.16 is a summation of the undesignated industries in the United States, which appeared as statistically large inputs to designated CI sectors are themselves bona fide industrial entities. This table is not a recital of all undesignated, major inputs to each CI sector; certain major inputs come from industries which by their nature do not appear to have time-sensitive and direct inputs into the supply chain and production process of CI sectors. For instance, construction is a major input to Energy and Government, but are generally not real-time, short-term inputs to any production processes.

---

**TABLE 2.16**

**Major Undesignated Industries Supplying CI Sectors in the United States**

| Sector Name | Non-Critical Major Supply Industries in the United States |
|---|---|
| Energy | Wholesale trade; mining; miscellaneous professional, technical and scientific services |
| Finance | Information and data processing services; other transportation and support activities |
| Communications and IT | Wholesale trade; information and data processing services |
| Health | Food services; wholesale trade, miscellaneous manufacturing (industrial gas suppliers); pharmaceutical manufacturing (but bundled with NAICS aggregations for 325 chemicals under this assessment) |
| Food | Paper products; plastic products; wholesale trade |
| Water | No observations |
| Transportation | Food services and drinking places; wholesale trade; retail trade |
| Safety/Government | Computer and electronic products; information processing services; wholesale trade |
| Manufacturing | Wholesale trade, fabricated metal products, plastics and rubber products; computer and electronic components |

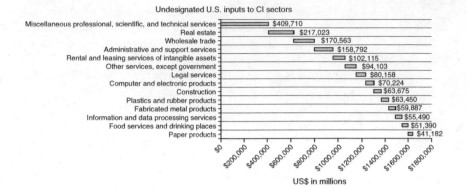

**FIGURE 2.42**   Undesignated CI inputs in the United States.

Following Table 2.16 is Figure 2.42, which is a waterfall diagram of the top 15 undesignated industries without qualification, and their total inputs to all CI sectors. Figure 2.42 therefore looks at which undesignated CI sectors are the largest inputs and elements within CI sectors' supply chains.

Considering the information from Table 2.16 is Figure 2.42, evidence starts to emerge based upon I–O analysis of CI sectors that the following industries at a minimum are significant inputs to multiple sectors and major overall inputs to CI supply chains in the United States. The undesignated industries are not presented in any specific order or intended priority.

1. Wholesale and retail trade: It is, in fact, a distribution system for the goods and services generated by many CI sectors. Distribution industries are not included within existing CI sector definitions, particularly for sectors such as Energy and Food, which utilize inputs from these sectors extensively.
2. Information and data processing services: Although this industry grouping is an artifact of NAICS, components of it are clearly important inputs to CI sector. Services such as data-center management and application hosting and other forms of IT outsourcing are very large business and a major component of many CI sector operations, especially Finance, Communications and IT, and Energy.
3. Paper and plastic are forms of manufacturing, which are undesignated but emerge with high importance to a variety of sectors but especially critical to packaging for Food production and distribution.
4. Computer and electronic products are undesignated but emerge as very important to Government, Manufacturing, and Communications and IT.
5. Food services are important inputs to both Health and Transportation to the point that neither service would remain viable for public service-delivery if Food services were unavailable for extended periods. Food services include not only restaurants but also Food contractors, caterers, and mobile food services.

**Note:** See Professional and Technical Services, the following section for a discussion related to miscellaneous professional, scientific, and technical services.

## PROFESSIONAL AND TECHNICAL SERVICES

A very notable finding associated with a review of the undesignated industries is that professional services, which are not applied against a particular CI sector, top the charts for both Canada and the United States. This is in addition to the fact that professional services specific to Communications and IT are already contained within the sector definition (for Canada this is "541B—Computer Systems Design and Other Professional, Scientific and Technical Services" and in the United States this is "5415—Computer systems design and related services").

In Canada, the aggregated industry classification of legal, 541A—Accounting and Architectural, Engineering Services is the second largest CI sector, second only to wholesale trade which is merely 1.7 percent larger.

In the United States, the comparable sector aggregation is 5412OP—miscellaneous professional, scientific, and technical services is almost 90 percent larger than the nearest undesignated CI sector input, real estate.

If the partially designated professional services (those counted within CI sector definitions) and undesignated professional services industries are combined as a whole, they become the dominant CI sector input across most sectors.

The dominance of professional services represents a challenge to CI assurance: professional services are more likely to be delivered by small businesses, making them more difficult to coordinate for assurance purposes and less able to absorb the overhead associated with planning and preparedness. Therefore, professional services are not particularly easy industrial inputs to manage from a business continuity and resiliency perspective.

## CONCLUSIONS AND INDICATED RISKS

This chapter started with the admission that statistics are difficult to grasp and not as convincing as anecdotes. A lot of data has been quoted throughout this chapter and it is only fit that we attempt to roll-up and conclude with simpler, visual anecdotes.

### CANADIAN INDICATIONS

The following discussion is a summary of the Canadian statistical indications on CI interdependency, which was covered in depth throughout this chapter.

Figure 2.43 is a high-level display of the results of CI interdependencies based upon statistical analysis of inputs and outputs (make versus use) for each defined CI sector. This analysis is based upon existing definitions of CI sectors.

Figure 2.43 shows the position of each Canadian CI sector relative to the value of their output to other Canadian CI sectors (make) and the value of the goods and services each consumes (use) from other CI sectors. The size of each sector bubble is relative to the total value of all goods and services either bought or sold to or from other Canadian CI sectors (make + use).

Interdependency risk is the risk that operations will be negatively impacted due to an impact in another CI sector, based upon statistical I–O data. The top right quadrant contains the sectors indicating the highest interdependency risk. The

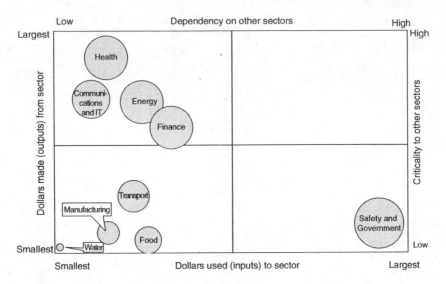

**FIGURE 2.43**   Canadian CI sector dependency risk.

bottom left indicates low risk. The top left quadrant contains sectors more likely to initiate cascading impacts, while the bottom right quadrant contains sectors more likely to be impacted through cascading impacts from interdependent sectors.

Figure 2.43 shows how Safety and Government in Canada is clearly the largest consumer of CI goods and services itself highly dependent upon other services under I–O analysis. However, the influence of government is so intense that the relationships and potential vulnerabilities among other CI sectors are obscured.

By extracting Safety and Government I–O data, a different picture of dependency risk emerges as seen in Figure 2.44. This analysis is based upon existing definitions of CI sectors.

Interdependency risk is the risk that operations will be negatively impacted due to an impact in another CI sector, based upon statistical I–O data. The top right quadrant contains the sectors indicating the highest interdependency risk. The bottom left indicates low risk. The top left quadrant contains sectors more likely to initiate cascading impacts, while the bottom right quadrant contains sectors more likely to be impacted through cascading impacts from interdependent sectors.

Interdependency risk as indicated in Figure 2.44 is about the risk of an initial impact to a single sector—as determined by its reliance on inputs from other CI sectors and the reliance among the other sector of the outputs of a given sector. Using inputs and outputs as the raw measures, Water appears to pose the smallest aggregated risk to CI sectors as a whole in Canada, occupying the bottom left quadrant. Similarly, Manufacturing is a slightly greater risk to the other CI sectors. However, Finance because of the large amount of its services consumed by the other CI sectors coupled with its own consumption is the largest source of risk to CI in Canada.

Consider now an alternate view of the same Canadian I–O data. If the reader wishes to simply consider the one-to-one intensity of dependency from the Canadian

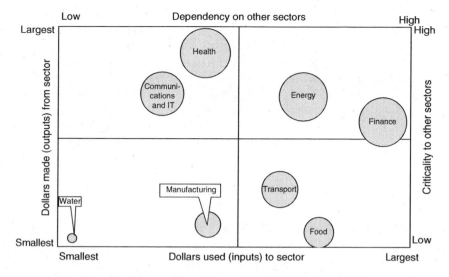

**FIGURE 2.44**  Canadian CI sector dependency risk without Safety and Government.

I–O relationships in Table 2.3, a picture of the potential for cascading impacts starts to emerge as displayed in Figure 2.45. One-to-one intensity is based upon the sectors with the fewest negative dependency relationships (I–O ratio > 1), tracing downward according to which sectors have the strongest overall I–O dependency with the top sector (I–O ratio < 1).

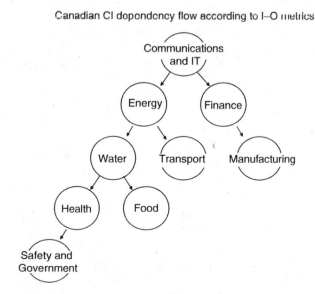

**FIGURE 2.45**  Canadian CI dependency flow according to I–O data.

In Canada, a specific picture emerges from the review of dependency relationships indicated by I–O data. If the relationships are organized starting with the sector
with the lowest sum of I–O ratios and the strongest dependency is shown with
arrows, the picture in Figure 2.45 emerges. Figure 2.45 indicates several pieces of
information about the CI interdependency and risk in Canada: (1) From an I–O
assessment perspective, Communications and IT is the top CI, a failure which is most
likely to impact other sectors both directly and through the possibility of cascading
failures. (2) Those failures further down the chain can still result in cascading
failures, especially in Energy and Water. (3) At the end of the chain are the CI
sectors less likely to initiate cascading impacts with CI sectors, Safety and Government, Food, Transport, and Manufacturing; this is not to minimize the overall impact
a failure in these sectors.

## U.S. INDICATIONS

The following discussion is a summary of the U.S. statistical indications around CI
interdependency, which have been covered in depth throughout this chapter.

Figure 2.46 is a high-level display of the results of CI interdependencies based
upon statistical analysis of inputs and outputs (make versus use) for each defined CI
sector. This analysis is based upon existing definitions of CI sectors.

Figure 2.46 shows the position of each U.S. CI sector relative to the value of
their output to other U.S. CI sectors (make) and the value of the goods and services
each consumes (use) from other CI sectors. The size of each sector bubble is relative
to the total value of all goods and services either bought or sold to or from other U.S.
CI sectors (make and use).

Interdependency risk is the risk that operations will be negatively impacted due
to an impact in another CI sector, based upon statistical I–O data. The top right

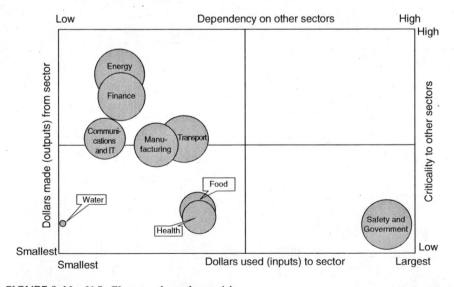

**FIGURE 2.46**   U.S. CI sector dependency risk.

quadrant contains the sectors indicating the highest interdependency risk. The bottom left indicates low risk. The top left quadrant contains sectors more likely to initiate cascading impacts, while the bottom right quadrant contains sectors more likely to be impacted through cascading impacts from interdependent sectors.

Figure 2.46, when compared with Figure 2.43: Canadian CI sector dependency risk starts to reveal the similarities between the Canadian and U.S. economic structures based upon I–O analysis.

Figure 2.46 shows how Safety and Government in the United States is clearly the largest consumer of CI goods and services itself highly dependent upon other services under I–O analysis. However, the influence of government is so intense that the relationships and potential vulnerabilities among other CI sectors are obscured.

By extracting U.S. Safety and Government I–O data, a different picture of dependency risk emerges as seen in Figure 2.47. This analysis is based upon existing definitions of U.S. CI sectors.

Interdependency risk is the risk that operations will be negatively impacted due to an impact in another CI sector, based upon statistical I–O data. The top right quadrant contains the sectors indicating the highest interdependency risk. The bottom left indicates low risk. The top left quadrant contains sectors more likely to initiate cascading impacts, while the bottom right quadrant contains sectors more likely to be impacted through cascading impacts from interdependent sectors.

Interdependency risk as indicated in Figure 2.47 is about the risk of an initial impact to a single sector—as determined by its reliance on inputs from other CI sectors and the reliance among the other sector of the outputs of a given sector. Using inputs and outputs as the raw measures, Water (as in Canada) appears to pose the smallest aggregated risk to CI sectors as a whole in the United States, occupying the bottom left quadrant. Transportation, because of the large amount of its services

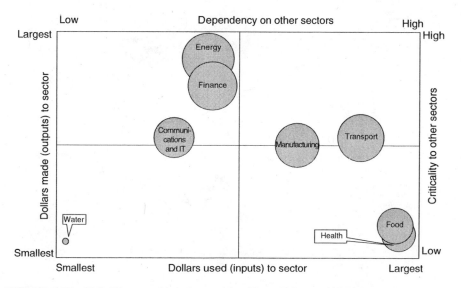

**FIGURE 2.47** U.S. CI sector dependency risk without Safety and Government.

consumed by the other U.S. CI sectors (primarily Health, Food, and Safety and Government) coupled with its own consumption, is the largest source of risk to CI in the United States.

Consider now an alternate view of the same U.S. I–O data. If the reader wishes to simply consider the one-to-one intensity of dependency from the U.S. I–O relationships contained in Table 2.3, a picture of the potential for cascading impacts starts to emerge as displayed in Figure 2.45. One-to-one intensity is based upon the sectors with the fewest negative dependency relationships (I–O ratio > 1), tracing according to which sectors have the strongest overall I–O dependency with the top sector (I–O ratio < 1).

In the United States, a different picture from Canada emerges during the review of dependency relationships indicated by I–O data. If the relationships are organized starting with the sector with the lowest sum of I–O ratios and the strongest dependency is shown with arrows, the picture in Figure 2.48 emerges. Figure 2.48 indicates at least one important piece of information about the CI interdependency and risk in the United States: From an I–O assessment perspective, Energy is the top CI, a failure most likely to impact at least five other sectors directly and the other remaining three sectors through the possibility of cascading failures.

U.S. CI dependency flow according to I–O metrics

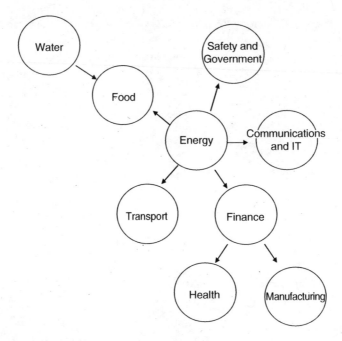

**FIGURE 2.48**   U.S. CI dependency flow according to I–O data.

# 3 Information and Data Dependency Analysis

## INTRODUCTION

Chapter 3 represents a different approach to assessing critical infrastructure (CI) interdependency from Chapter 2. Chapter 2 examined the spending and financial flows among CI sectors according to government statistics, whereas this chapter considers information and data flows among infrastructure sectors as an indicator of interdependency. It discusses findings in the area of data interdependency, where data is the exchange of information and communications to support the delivery of goods and services, and not the actual delivery of a sector's goods and services. For example, data interdependency is not about the delivery of electricity to a factory; it is about the data exchanged between a factory and the various parts of the electricity supply chain to manage, facilitate, and enable the delivery of electricity to the factory.

As discussed in Chapter 1, CI interdependency is a massively complex subject and initial approaches in this book rely upon indicators and correlations. In this chapter, we examine in detail the indicator of data dependency and the resulting interdependencies. In Chapter 4, we move on to correlating the indicators of input–output (I–O) analysis with information and data dependency analysis.

The production of goods and services is enabled by data exchanges among CI sectors and is the focus of this dependency assessment. Data interdependency does not focus on communications networks themselves because these pipes are in place to move data—not just for their own sake. If the network goes down, people do not miss the network—they miss the data! The benefit to CI owners of possessing data dependency information is new insight into the business risks associated with interdependence. From an operational risk perspective, production safety, efficiency, quality, and resilience are increased through better risk management. As a result, profitability is improved as losses are reduced.

In contrast to Chapter 2, the material in this chapter is possibly more accessible to a wider variety of people. Similar to Chapter 2, it will be of great interest to a few people, and possibly contain highly complex details for some readers, for whom the chapter summary is recommended. In the following pages we will dig deeply into the information and data dependency relationships between different industries designated as CI within Canada and the United States and how these relationships impart the nature of CI and the interdependencies among CI sectors. Unlike Chapter 2, the metrics in this chapter were collected from many North American multinations and are less specific to Canada or the United States.

For an executive or manager within a CI, this chapter is of great interest because it reveals common perceptions about interdependencies as expressed through executive interviews. This chapter contains an interdependency assessment based upon analysis of inbound and outbound information and data dependency metrics provided by Canadian and U.S. CI executives.

As in Chapter 2, there is much here for the policy maker and regulator: this chapter lays bare some common business perceptions upon which the management of CI industries is based. For the insurer or their counterparty, the risk manager, this chapter provides a sector-level view of perceived supply-chain management dependencies and the vulnerability to second-order impacts, which may result in insurable losses. The value-added by this chapter is insight into the types of exclusions, and insurance riders, which might be applied to protect either the insurance company from undue loss or the risk manager's firm from uninsured losses. Finally, for the contract lawyer, this chapter may provide very useful insight into how interdependencies are perceived at the management level and the impact and risks that might arise as these perceptions make their ways into legal agreements in the form of service-level commitments and related assumptions.

This chapter is a critical counterpoint to the material and indications discussed in Chapter 2. Neither this chapter nor the I–O econometrics information of Chapter 2 can stand alone as valid predictors of CI interdependency; they must be considered together. If one had taken the trouble to read Chapter 2 in its entirety, he or she should certainly read this chapter.

## INFORMATION OPERATIONS AND DATA DEPENDENCY

The ideas contained in this chapter about the applicability of data flows to CI analysis have its roots in the discipline of electronic warfare and information operations, which can be traced back through military history where resources were applied to gathering and assessing information focused on observed communications patterns of counterparties.* More broadly, information operations is about assessing the interdependence of assets based on communications linkages; a strategy as old as war itself. Information operations is now a well-defined discipline and directly influences the methodology applied to CI interdependency analysis through the concept of information assurance. Within information operations disciplines, information assurance is about the properties that define communications among different entities and assets, both friend and foe. By understanding the properties of information assurance, an organization is in a much better position to defend its assets or exploit weaknesses in an enemy's defenses through information superiority.

> When it exists, the information available to commanders allows them to accurately visualize the situation, anticipate events, and make appropriate, timely decisions more effectively than adversary decision makers. In essence, information superiority enhances commanders' freedom of action and allows them to execute decisions, and maintain the initiative, while remaining inside the adversary's decision cycle. However, commanders

---

* Major Joseph L. Cox, 2006. *Information Operations in Operations Enduring Freedom and Iraqi Freedom—What Went Wrong?* School of Advanced Military Studies, Fort Leavenworth, Kansas.

recognize that without continuous IO designed to achieve and maintain information superiority, adversaries may counter those advantages and possibly attain information superiority themselves.*

In the context of CI interdependency and the ability to prevent, detect, respond, and recover from cascading impacts among CI sectors, data dependency is a fundamental component of information superiority for CI owners and operators.

## INFORMATION AND DATA DEPENDENCY ASSESSMENT METHODOLOGY

Data dependency is a measure of how sensitive a CI sector is to the properties of availability, confidentiality, and integrity of data flowing among the CI sectors. Breaking this down to more granular component parts, dependency reflects the one-way data-assurance requirements of one CI sector upon another. Interdependency simply extends the relationship into a fully bidirection framework of information and data-assurance requirements among CI sectors.

The data dependency assessment methodology employed for the development of metrics in this chapter targeted CI sector entities with significant scope and scale of operations and which are defined as large enterprises (more than 500 employees) under the North American Industry Classification System (NAICS), or aggregators of sector opinion such as sector associations. The intent was to obtain broad coverage of the subsectors within a given CI sector. The companies were selected from industry groups drawn from the NAICS-based definitions developed in Chapter 1.

In total, over 150 face-to-face interviews were conducted with executives and senior managers from the ten defined CI sectors as defined in Chapter 1. Each respondent enterprise in the data dependency assessment was asked the same three questions to answer on a scale from 1 to 10. The three questions dealt with the data dependency of the firm upon other CI sector entities. The specific questions addressed were phrased as follows:

The numerical results of the three questions on dependency were then combined with equal weighting (33.33 percent) to generate a metric ranging from 1 to 10 representing the dependency of a CI sector on data from each other CI sector.†

These cyber-dependency metrics were gathered through an interview process, which established normal operating conditions as the context for response. Abnormal operating conditions, such as crisis conditions, would have resulted in substantially different results. Normal operating conditions were selected because it is this profile that establishes the baseline for day-to-day interdependency and is the departure point for incident/crisis events. Any changes or improvements in the assurance of interdependent relationships will necessarily focus upon the regular day-to-day operations. The performance of subsequent work related to abnormal operating

---

* Joint Publication 3–13, *Information Operations*, U.S. DOD Joint Chiefs of Staff, February 2006, Chapter 11 p. 22.
† The other six questions in the Public Safety Canada report are related to controls and safeguards and not dependency. As a result, they are not germane to this work and will not be discussed or used here.

conditions would nonetheless represent substantial value, because the change in associated metrics may better expose possible vulnerabilities in a nation's macroeconomic structure; however, for every crisis condition, there is a unique set of crisis metrics. Thus, attempting to gather crisis metrics is essentially an infinite and fraught task.

A concern during the design of executive interviews and the collection of cyber-interdependency metrics was that only questions that stood a good chance of being answered, and answered accurately, should be asked to maximize validity and response rates across all the CI sectors, including the most parochial and sensitive sectors. Based upon the feedback received to the sampled CI stakeholders, the question set in Table 3.1 was arrived at, which represents the level of questioning

## TABLE 3.1
## Data Dependency Questionnaire

| Question | CI Sector | Response Metric |
|---|---|---|
| On a scale from 1 to 10, where 1 is none or public domain data only, 3 is less important, 5 is important, 7 is very important, and 10 is critical. | | |
| How important is the provision of telemetry/real-time or other data from the following CIs? | Financial | 1..2..3..4..5..6..7..8..9..10 |
| | Communications and IT | 1..2..3..4..5..6..7..8..9..10 |
| | Energy | 1..2..3..4..5..6..7..8..9..10 |
| | Public health | 1..2..3..4..5..6..7..8..9..10 |
| | Water | 1..2..3..4..5..6..7..8..9..10 |
| | Food | 1..2..3..4..5..6..7..8..9..10 |
| | Transportation | 1..2..3..4..5..6..7..8..9..10 |
| | Safety | 1..2..3..4..5..6..7..8..9..10 |
| | Manufacturing | 1..2..3..4..5..6..7..8..9..10 |
| | Government | 1..2..3..4..5..6..7..8..9..10 |
| How sensitive to disclosure is the telemetry/real-time or other data received from other CIs? | Financial | 1..2..3..4..5..6..7..8..9..10 |
| | Communications and IT | 1..2..3..4..5..6..7..8..9..10 |
| | Energy | 1..2..3..4..5..6..7..8..9..10 |
| | Public health | 1..2..3..4..5..6..7..8..9..10 |
| | Water | 1..2..3..4..5..6..7..8..9..10 |
| | Food | 1..2..3..4..5..6..7..8..9..10 |
| | Transportation | 1..2..3..4..5..6..7..8..9..10 |
| | Safety | 1..2..3..4..5..6..7..8..9..10 |
| | Manufacturing | 1..2..3..4..5..6..7..8..9..10 |
| | Government | 1..2..3..4..5..6..7..8..9..10 |
| How sensitive to corruption or change is the telemetry/real-time or other data you received from those CIs? | Financial | 1..2..3..4..5..6..7..8..9..10 |
| | Communications and IT | 1..2..3..4..5..6..7..8..9..10 |
| | Energy | 1..2..3..4..5..6..7..8..9..10 |
| | Public health | 1..2..3..4..5..6..7..8..9..10 |
| | Water | 1..2..3..4..5..6..7..8..9..10 |
| | Food | 1..2..3..4..5..6..7..8..9..10 |
| | Transportation | 1..2..3..4..5..6..7..8..9..10 |
| | Safety | 1..2..3..4..5..6..7..8..9..10 |
| | Manufacturing | 1..2..3..4..5..6..7..8..9..10 |
| | Government | 1..2..3..4..5..6..7..8..9..10 |

and metrics which could be effectively collected. The queries refrained from delving into specifics concerning elements such as

- Identification of key assets within individual sectors and companies
- Identification of the key sensitivities (e.g., asset criticality, potential hazards) of the key assets for each sector

Additionally, the use of qualitative metrics was deemed most viable for the reasons cited in Chapter 1. A baseline set of common questions and associated metrics are developed and validated.* These questions and metrics are then converted into tools for interviewers to collect respondent data. These tools consisted first of the conversion of the undefined metric values associated with specific questions into qualitative scales and values for respondents to choose from on a scale from 1 to 10. In this manner, the responses are bounded to allow comparison but still flexible enough to allow significant variance between respondents and CI sectors. Interviewers gathered information in the course of interview discussions by reading the short questions directly to interviewees, and populated the response templates using direct instructions from the respondents.

## BOUNDARIES OF ANALYSIS

To collect information from respondents effectively and interpret indications, a definition of data and the associated infrastructure were applied for the purposes of CI data interdependency analysis. Data infrastructure typically refers to the composition of two distinct elements: information assets (data) and network infrastructure.

Information assets are the central component of data interdependency analysis because communications assets are in effect data. The role of network infrastructure in the context of CI interdependency assessment is to transport information and data assets within and among CI sector organizations. CI organizations are not dependent upon network infrastructure itself; they are dependent upon the information assets that network infrastructure makes available to their means of production. For instance, businesses do not buy Internet connections because it is an industrial input; they buy an Internet connection to send and receive information and data, which is an industrial input.

### SHARED NETWORK INFRASTRUCTURE

The data interdependency analysis considered specifically CI organizational communications assets that traverse the shared, core telecommunications infrastructure (such as those owned and managed by Tier 1 carriers) on their way either to internal network destinations or other CI sector players. For instance, a communication asset, such as process control information, might originate from a pipeline-terminal owned by a CI sector organization, travel through the core infrastructure to a central

---

* Ibid.

processing facility also owned by the CI organization. Alternately, an electronic data interchange (EDI) transaction from a customer CI to a supplier CI travels through the core infrastructure, which is the physical and logical linkage between the two organizations.

Physical, core infrastructure is transparent to communications assets. CIs are interdependent based upon the communications assets (information) which they exchange over the core data infrastructure, not on the infrastructure itself. Data assets originate and terminate (end their trip) on systems that may interface directly with the core network, or on internal systems that interface with the shared, core data infrastructure. It is the communications assets, not the data infrastructure itself, which engender cyber-interdependency between CIs.

In approaching executives within CI sector organizations, the context for questioning was established as communications assets which traverse the shared, core telecommunications networks. These are the networks controlled and managed by telecommunications firms. The dedicated, private, internal networks run by individual organizations were not a focus of the executive interviewing for at least two important reasons: (1) these networks are highly variable and information about them is especially sensitive and closely held and (2) the line of questions was not technical and focused on business communications assets as opposed to technical infrastructure. Including internal infrastructure in the discussions might have led to fruitless levels of technical detail not relevant to higher-level task of assessing data interdependency.

Core national network assets—data infrastructure—is different from an internal company network because they are not dedicated to a single entity; they are shared among many, potentially millions, different organizations and individual users. Core networks are provisioned by a telecommunications company.* Core networks are also entirely IP (Internet protocol) in modern service providers. As a result of being all-IP, core infrastructure does not just carry the public Internet traffic, but just about all communications assets traversing between autonomous organizations (CI sectors or otherwise): data, voice, process control information, and any other type of communications asset. For instance, organizations connect distant offices, equipment, and physical assets through networks essentially rented from, and provisioned by telecommunications firms. It is also characteristic of many CI sectors that offices, equipment, and physical assets are geographically dispersed. Consequently, core telecommunications infrastructure is invariably used by most CI entities for the movement of communications assets within the sector and among the sectors. Data infrastructure need not be part of the Internet; yet the data assets they transport will typically traverse network devices that are simultaneously routing the traffic from other entities. In this way, the core infrastructure is shared even though the data assets have no logical interface with each other (i.e., they do not mix).

---

* Legacy switched voice infrastructure is not considered part of cyberspace because it lacks many of the fundamental characteristics of IP that have allowed cyberspace to exist: easy and cheap extensibility, interoperability, robust routing, self-healing.

The demarcation point between a national carrier core network infrastructure and the internal infrastructure of a business is by convention called the customer edge (CE) and physically represented by a router. The logic for this demarcation point for analytical purposes is twofold: First, the internal organizational networks past the CE are not relevant to other organizations because localized, internal networks do not conduct risks,* that is, risks due to information and data dependency will conduct to other CI sectors over the shared networks, which join internal networks together. If CIs have data interdependencies with other CIs, the interdependencies will be related to the data assets—not internal network elements themselves because they do not physically or logically interface with each other. They interface only with the shared, core data infrastructure. In other words, the core infrastructure joins CI sectors together and enables the communications and the exchange of information assets which all CI organizations rely upon to one extent or another. Unless CI organizations are colocated, these internal networks never touch each other; they merely exchange data through the core.

Second, the CE demarcation point is a useful context for executive interviews in that it has become a generally accepted demarcation point for the purposes of regulatory compliance, specifically, with Sarbanes–Oxley (SOX). In the course of fulfilling reporting and assurance obligations under SOX, many firms have had to undergo audits associated with the assurance of their data infrastructure—both physical infrastructure and data assets. In the course of this compliance push, a convention has arisen that core/shared network infrastructure as described above is a distinct element from strictly internal informatics infrastructure, and not part of the company-specific compliance audit requirements. This convention represents the business and regulatory reality that all modern business relies on shared network infrastructure, which is for the most part beyond their direct control. Figure 3.1 is a graphical illustration of the data dependency limits of scope based upon the argument posited above.

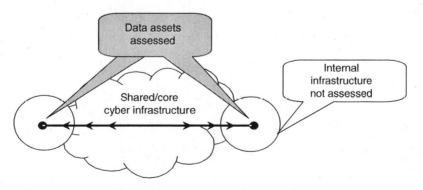

**FIGURE 3.1** Limits of data interdependency analysis.

---

* Macaulay, T., 2007. Risk conductors, *ISC2 Journal*, January.

## A WORD ABOUT VOICE

Voice services are often still provisioned and represented by the legacy public switched telephone network (PSTN) and analogue services which support the last mile connection infrastructure. This means that the final network segment connecting a telephone to the core network infrastructure is not IP-based nor part of a converged IP network, instead, plenty of voice services use the legacy analogue technology originally developed (but substantially refined) more than 125 years ago. However, the core of all modern telecommunications networks is IP-based; thus voice and data applications are transparent to this core network. Voice services are considered data and in-scope for the executive interviews because they are technically considered as communications assets.

## ANALYSIS OF SURVEY DATA

The data dependency analysis technique investigated the strength of inter-CI sector dependency and intra-CI sector dependency of all CI sectors relating to the information and data assets flowing among CI sectors. The analysis employed qualitative metrics for data dependency metrics selected in large part due to the influence of Kunreuther and Heal.*

In the work of Kunreuther and Heal, a formulaic expression for assessing interdependent security systems and incentives for investment in security was proposed. The interdependent systems discussed were airlines and baggage-handling processes, where one airline screening baggage faces risks associated with other non-screening airlines that transfer bags to screening airlines. Is it worth investing in security screening if interdependent parties do not similarly invest? The formulas proposed by Kunreuther and Heal presented the potential losses as variables that organizations could then apply to industry-specific metrics. The Kunreuther–Heal formula, which gained wide acceptance as a framework for interdependent security systems, is currently and frequently cited by the National Institute of Standards and Technology (NIST) for the purposes of risk management related to CIs and extreme events.[†]

The data dependency methodology employed used Kunreuther and Heal's variable $q$ (contagion) which is to be considered the indicator of inter/intradependence between CIs and was the focus of information collection in this work. The methodology did not propose to collect or manage empirical data associated with the other variables in the Kunreuther–Heal formula such as $p$, probability; $L$, potential loss; $Y$, potential earnings; and $c$, cost. These variables are heavily dependent on the threat, the timing, the circumstances, and the CI sector under consideration. The methodology proposed that $q$, the contagion metric, was the key variable of interdependency. Contagion is treated as the likelihood that an impact in one CI entity will be

---

* Kunreuther, H. and Heal, G. You can only die once: Public–private partnerships for managing the risks of extreme events, White paper for conference on Risk Management Strategies in an Uncertain World, Palisades, 2002, New York.
† NIST GCR 04 871—Risk analysis for extreme events: Economic incentives for reducing future losses.

passed to another CI entity—through the inter/intradependence on data assets and shared cyber infrastructure.

## DEFINING INBOUND AND OUTBOUND DEPENDENCY AMONG CI OWNERS

The following section discusses the inbound versus outbound dependency phenomena, and how outbound reflects a less understood but substantial business risk to CI owners.

### INBOUND DATA DEPENDENCY

Inbound data dependency is about information and data being delivered to and consumed by a CI sector organization. Information and data is traversing the core data infrastructure such as voice calls, Internet services, EDI services, fax, and even cellular calls, which are trunked through the core telecommunications infrastructure. Inbound information may be solicited (like a request for delivery schedules from suppliers which arrive through e-mail or fax); or inbound data may be unsolicited or unscheduled (such as a customer call for support or to place an order). Call centers and Web portals are established explicitly to support inbound information and data—especially unsolicited or unscheduled communications from customers and potential customers.

Inbound dependency is therefore about the assurance properties of data assets required by CI sector organizations to continue the production of goods or service according to contracted or regulated specifications. For instance, how long can a Water plant continue to operate safely without information from testing laboratories (Health sector)? How long will a bank elect to operate if confidentiality of the customer data arriving from retailers, transactions processors, or other banks is threatened? How serious is the impact to a telecommunications carrier if routing information from interconnected carriers is corrupted? Inbound dependency is about the interdependency vulnerabilities of a CI sector.

### OUTBOUND DATA DEPENDENCY

Outbound data dependency is about information and data leaving a CI sector, destined for another CI sector and traversing the core data infrastructure such as voice calls, Internet services, EDI services, fax, and even cellular calls, which are all trunked through the core telecommunications infrastructure. Outbound information may be solicited (such as response to a request for delivery schedules from customers which is sent out through e-mail or fax); or outbound data may be unsolicited or unscheduled (such as a call to a supplier for support or to place an order). Web sites are information assets established in part to address outbound data on a self-serve basis.

Outbound dependency is therefore about the assurance properties of data assets that other consuming CI sectors place upon the suppliers of information and data; however, these assurance properties may or may not be known to the source/supplying CI sector. In other words, outbound dependency is substantially different from inbound dependency because the source of information may not necessarily be aware of how it is consumed at the destination, and therefore be aware of the assurance placed upon it by the consuming CI sector. For instance, how long can the Health sector operate safety without information from Water? Does Health place a reciprocal importance on information and communications from Water as Water does on information and communications from Health? Outbound dependency is about the interdependency threat that a CI can pose to other CI sectors.

## DEPENDENCY MATRIXES

A dependency matrix is a means of tracking the intersector and intrasector dependencies related to the data assets (Table 3.2). A dependency matrix reveals the potential vulnerability of a given CI to the loss, corruption, or compromise of data assets from an interdependent CI, regardless of the status of the shared data infrastructure. In other words, what happens in the event when a single CI has its data assets being made unavailable, corrupted, or disclosed, due to an incident even though the data infrastructure continues to function?

The sample matrix in Table 3.2 provides the information that is collected for the purposes of CI data dependency analysis. Both inbound and outbound dependencies are presented through this single tool. Together, inbound and outbound dependencies equal interdependence.

The columns for each CI sector represent how a sector rates its dependency on information and data coming into the organization—inbound dependency. Most organizations intuitively understand the assurance requirements of the information they consume in the course of business.

The rows for each sector represent how dependent consuming CI sectors are on information and data from a sector, according to their own assessments—outbound

## TABLE 3.2
## Sample Data Dependency Matrix for the Ten CI Sectors

|  | CI Sector | Energy | Comms and IT | Finance | Health | Food | Water | Transport | Safety | Gov | Manf |
|---|---|---|---|---|---|---|---|---|---|---|---|
|  |  | Inbound Dependencies | | | | | | | | | |
| Outbound Dependencies | Energy | EdE | CdE | FindE | HdE | FdE | WdE | TdE | SdE | GdE | MdE |
|  | Comms and IT | EdC | CdC | FindC | HdC | FdC | WdC | TdC | SdC | GdC | MdC |
|  | Finance | EdFin | CdFin | FindFin | HdFin | FdFin | WdFin | TdFin | SdFin | GdFin | MdFin |
|  | Health | EdH | CdH | FindH | HdH | FdH | WdH | TdH | SdH | GdH | MdH |
|  | Food | EdF | CdF | FindF | HdF | FdF | WdF | TdF | SdF | GdF | MdF |
|  | Water | EdW | CdW | FindW | HdW | FdW | WdW | TdW | SdW | GdW | MdW |
|  | Transport | EdT | CdT | FindT | HdT | FdT | WdT | TdT | SdT | GdT | MdT |
|  | Safety | EdS | CdS | FindS | HdS | FdS | WdS | TdS | SdS | GdS | MdS |
|  | Gov | EdG | CdG | FindG | HdG | FdG | WdG | TdG | SdG | GdG | MdG |
|  | Manuf | EdM | CdM | FindM | HdM | FdM | WdM | TdM | SdM | GdM | MdM |

dependency. Unlike inbound dependency, most organizations do not have a great deal of insight into how all other CI sectors actually need the information and data they produce—other than provisions which may be expressed in service-level agreements.

Table 3.2 is intended to expose the interdependency relationships between CI sectors according to the data they exchange bilaterally and the security and assurance properties of this data. Each cell in the table is a metric, which represents a sector-to-sector (bilateral) inbound data dependency value (for the sector in the column) and at the same time, an outbound data dependency value (for the sector in the row).

Here, the dependency factor is indicated using the format *xqy*, where *x* and *y* are two CI sectors and *d* is the dependency. The shaded diagonal indicates the intrasector dependencies among sectors.

## Data Dependency Metrics

Over 4000 distinct data dependency metrics were gathered from CI stakeholders around interdependency within CI sectors. These metrics were weighted and placed into the dependency matrix in Table 3.3. Table 3.3 is intended to expose the interdependency relationships between CI sectors according to the data they exchange bilaterally and the security and assurance properties of this data.

In Table 3.3, higher scores (metrics) indicate stronger data dependence between CI sectors, while lower scores indicate less data dependence.

Dependency analysis illustrates how organizations are dependent upon data flowing to and from each other: the higher the number in the columns, the greater the dependency on data into a sector; the higher the number in a row the greater the dependency on data flowing out of the sector.

**TABLE 3.3**
**Dependency Matrix for the Ten CI Sectors**

| | | Inbound Dependencies | | | | | | | | | |
|---|---|---|---|---|---|---|---|---|---|---|---|
| | CI Sector | Energy | Comms & IT | Fin | Health Care | Food | Water | Trans | Safety | Gov | Manf |
| Outbound Dependencies | Energy | 9.37 | 3.63 | 2.48 | 3.88 | 2.06 | 3.08 | 4.25 | 3.23 | 3.36 | 3.24 |
| | Comms & IT | 6.96 | 8.82 | 4.48 | 5.11 | 2.32 | 3.42 | 4.41 | 4.62 | 3.96 | 7.08 |
| | Fin | 7.13 | 7.19 | 8.95 | 4.23 | 8.23 | 5.01 | 6.78 | 4.02 | 5.18 | 7.96 |
| | Health Care | 4.12 | 2.43 | 2.99 | 8.25 | 1.80 | 4.43 | 3.33 | 5.78 | 5.06 | 2.57 |
| | Food | 1.47 | 1.66 | 1.94 | 3.76 | 6.45 | 1.83 | 2.48 | 1.05 | 2.71 | 1.99 |
| | Water | 4.90 | 1.84 | 1.96 | 3.60 | 1.30 | 5.78 | 3.18 | 1.20 | 2.87 | 2.16 |
| | Trans | 6.82 | 3.95 | 4.23 | 4.95 | 5.06 | 2.96 | 7.49 | 3.78 | 4.66 | 5.84 |
| | Safety | 7.85 | 3.96 | 3.60 | 5.71 | 1.02 | 4.54 | 5.35 | 8.23 | 5.73 | 4.96 |
| | Gov | 5.85 | 5.05 | 7.00 | 6.12 | 4.76 | 5.05 | 7.61 | 6.43 | 8.78 | 5.96 |
| | Manf | 5.87 | 3.75 | 4.66 | 5.01 | 4.50 | 3.43 | 4.53 | 1.17 | 3.63 | 7.15 |

The metrics in Table 3.3 use the same scale against which the executive respondents in the survey answered on a scale from 1 to 10. Under this aggregation, a value of 1 indicates no data dependence or that all information from the other CI sectors was derived from public domain sources like the Internet or the media. It also indicates that the production of goods and services is largely independent from information and data communications with other CI sector stakeholders. A value of 10 means that information and communications arriving from a given sector is critical to the production of goods and services. If one sector's information or data were to stop flowing, be corrupted or disclosed, an impact would occur. Zero was not a response option, but is shown in the charts so that standard deviations can be fully displayed.

There is no precise interpretation or definition of differences between values of 1 and 10. These values are qualitative and ordinal in nature. Later, we consider more granular sector-by-sector assessments which expose more granular details about how the aggregated numbers are produced and what they reveal about dependencies are among sectors.

A reviewer notes that while metrics are presented to the second decimal place, these metrics are derived from executive interviewing and are fundamentally qualitative in nature: concrete distinctions should not be inferred from small numerical differences.

## Inbound Data Dependency Chart

Figure 3.2 shows the median results for inbound dependency for all CI sectors. Each sector is considered independently with a median data dependency metric shown (median is the metric with an equal number of scores occurring above and below). For each sector, the standard deviation is also displayed for each median score. The standard deviation is the average range within which all the individual dependency scores for that sector fall. Further, the smaller the standard deviation, the tighter the grouping of scores and the more overall consistency among the dependency score for a given sector. For instance, if a given sector has a series of dependency metrics like 3.5, 4, 3.5, 4, and 4.2 then the median score is 4 with a standard deviation of ±32. IE, the most representative score for the data set is 4 ± 32. Table 3.4 is the numeric inbound–outbound ratio for the data presented in Figure 3.2.

Data dependency results for the ten CI sectors are displayed from the highest score (most inbound data dependency) to the lowest score (least inbound data dependency). These scores represent the highest level of aggregation available without obscuring sector-to-sector differences.

Aggregated inbound findings are shown in Figure 3.2 and Table 3.4, where all inbound metrics are combined into a median score to present a single metric for each sector. This aggregation is useful in the context of a general assessment of sector dependency and for comparison across sectors.

The aggregation indicates that the Food sector has the lowest overall inbound dependency vulnerabilities on information and data from other CI sectors. Food executives perceive their business as being least dependent upon outside information and communications. Food executives consider that the delivery of their

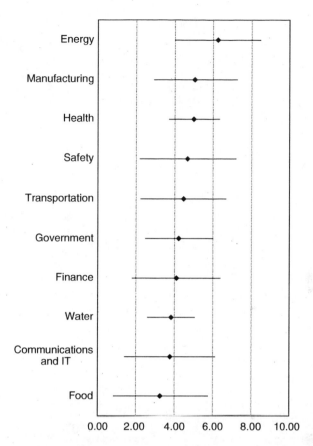

**FIGURE 3.2** Inbound data dependency. ◆ = median (same number of responses above as below this point) and — = standard deviation (average range in all scores from median). A score of 10 indicates all data and information from all sectors is critical to operations and the delivery of goods and services. A score of 1 indicates that no data is consumed, or all data and information is derived from public domain sources and is almost immaterial to continuity of operations. Zero is indicated to fully display standard deviations.

## TABLE 3.4
### Inbound Data Dependency Metrics—Aggregated

| | Food | Commu- nications and IT | Water | Finance | Govern- ment | Transpor- tation | Safety | Health | Manufac- turing | Energy |
|---|---|---|---|---|---|---|---|---|---|---|
| Median | 3.27 | 3.77 | 3.84 | 4.09 | 4.23 | 4.47 | 4.67 | 5.00 | 5.03 | 6.24 |
| High | 5.70 | 6.11 | 5.08 | 6.39 | 6.01 | 6.31 | 7.19 | 6.36 | 7.16 | 8.47 |
| Low | 0.83 | 1.43 | 2.60 | 1.79 | 2.45 | 2.63 | 2.14 | 3.64 | 2.90 | 4.00 |
| Standard deviation | 2.44 | 2.34 | 1.24 | 2.30 | 1.78 | 1.84 | 2.52 | 1.36 | 2.13 | 2.23 |

sector's goods (both processed and unprocessed foods) to be substantially autonomous in their means of production relative to the other CI sectors. This is not to claim that Food can continue operations if all information and data flows cease (including flows among the Food sector organizations themselves), because the sector still rates itself substantially above 1. Food executives considered that coordination of activities and the exchange of information with other CI sectors were not a critical part of preserving the assurance of their operations. See the following sector-by-sector analysis for a more detailed discussion of the Food sector metrics. The indication is that Food faces the lowest overall interdependency vulnerability when using data dependency as a proxy metric for CI interdependency.

On the opposite end of the aggregation is the Energy sector which places the highest importance of the inbound flow of information and data from the other CI sectors. In interviews, Energy executives considered that coordination of activities and the exchange of information with other CI sectors were a critical part of preserving the assurance of their operations; however, this is distinct from the ability to continue operations in the absence of outside information and data. See the following sector-by-sector analysis for a more detailed discussion of the Energy sector metrics. The indication is that Energy faces the highest overall interdependency vulnerability when using data dependency as a proxy metric for CI interdependency.

Emerging from this discussion of inbound data dependency aggregation is this notion of a linkage between the assurance of operations and preservation of operations: to what extent can or should a sector continue to operate, and for how long, once the assurance of their operations starts to degrade? The clearest indication from the inbound data dependency aggregations is that different sectors face different decay-rates for operational assurance when information and communications flows from other sectors degrade or cease. Using data dependency as a proxy for overall interdependency, the inferred finding is that Energy is most dependent upon the inputs (goods and services—not just information and data) from other CI sectors to maintain the assurance of its operations. The follow-on implication is that Energy is most susceptible to second-order impacts due to incidents within the other CI sectors: therefore, the assurance of Energy goods and services is most likely to suffer second-order impacts due to incidents in other CI sectors. The overall vulnerability of the Energy sector increases the most when other CI sectors suffer incidents.

## Outbound Data Dependency Chart

Figure 3.3 shows the median results for all CI sectors. Each sector is considered independently and a median data dependency metric shown—the metric with an equal number of scores occurring above and below. For each sector, the standard deviation is also displayed for each median score. The standard deviation is the average range within which all the individual dependency scores for that sector fall. Further, the smaller the standard deviation, the tighter the grouping of scores and the more overall consistency among the outbound dependency score for a sector.

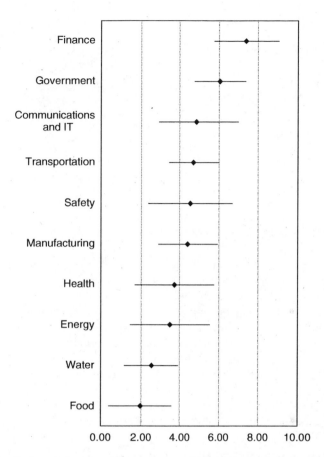

**FIGURE 3.3** Outbound data dependency. ◆ = median (same number of responses above as below this point) and — = standard deviation (average difference in all scores from median). A score of 10 indicates all data and information from all sectors is critical to operations and the delivery of goods and services. A score of one indicates that no data is consumed, or all data and information is derived from public domain sources and is almost immaterial to continuity of operations. Zero is indicated to fully display standard deviations.

For instance, if a given sector has a series of dependency metrics like 3.5, 4, 3.5, 4, and 4.2 then the median score is 4 with a standard deviation of ±32. IE, the most representative score for the data set is 4 ± 32. Table 3.5 is the numeric inbound–outbound ratio for the data presented in Figure 3.3 that uses the same scale against which the executive respondents in the survey answered.

Data dependency results for the ten CI sectors that are displayed from the highest score (most outbound data dependency) to the lowest score (least outbound data dependency). These scores represent the highest level of aggregation available without obscuring sector-to-sector differences.

Aggregated outbound findings are shown in Figure 3.3 and Table 3.5, where all outbound metrics are combined into a median score to present a single metric for

## TABLE 3.5
### Outbound Data Dependency Metrics—Aggregated

| | Food | Water | Energy | Health | Manufac- turing | Safety | Transpor- tation | Commu- nications and IT | Govern- ment | Finance |
|---|---|---|---|---|---|---|---|---|---|---|
| Median | 1.98 | 2.53 | 3.50 | 3.73 | 4.41 | 4.55 | 4.69 | 4.84 | 6.04 | 7.39 |
| High | 3.62 | 3.95 | 5.55 | 5.77 | 5.96 | 6.70 | 5.99 | 6.76 | 7.38 | 9.06 |
| Low | 0.33 | 1.12 | 1.45 | 1.69 | 2.85 | 2.41 | 3.40 | 2.91 | 4.71 | 5.73 |
| Standard deviation | 1.64 | 1.42 | 2.05 | 2.04 | 1.55 | 2.14 | 1.29 | 1.92 | 1.34 | 1.66 |

each sector. This aggregation is useful in the context of a general assessment of sector dependency and for comparison across sectors.

Recall that outbound dependency for any given CI sector is a measure of how the other CI sectors rate the importance of information and communications coming from the given sector. The outbound aggregation shows that the Food sector indicates the lowest overall outbound dependency on information and data from other CI sectors. As a whole, executives from all the other CI sectors perceived their business as facing the lowest dependency threat due to information and data from the Food sector. Executives consider that the delivery of their sector's goods and services to be most autonomous from the Food sector. This is not to claim that all sectors can continue unaffected operations if all information and data flows from the Food sector cease, because the outbound sector rating for Food is still above 1 (but not by much). Executives considered that coordination of activities and the exchange of information with the Food sector not a critical part of preserving the assurance of their sector's operations. The indication is that Food poses the lowest overall interdependency threat to other CI sectors when using data dependency as a proxy indicator for CI interdependency.

On the opposite end of the aggregation is the Finance sector, which possesses the highest outbound dependency assessment score for the information and data it sends to the other nine CI sectors. In interviews, executives from the CI sectors considered that coordination of transactions and the exchange of information with Finance were the most critical dependency relationship in terms of preserving the assurance of their business; however, this is distinct from the ability to continue operations in the absence of information and data. For executives interdependency is as much about remaining profitable as operational. The indication is that Finance poses the highest overall interdependency threat to all other CI sectors as an aggregate when using data dependency as a proxy metric for CI interdependency.

To what extent can or should a sector continue to operate, and for how long, once the assurance of their operations starts to degrade? The clearest indication from the outbound data dependency aggregations is that different sectors face different decay-rates for operational assurance when information and data flows from other sectors degrade or cease. Using data dependency as a proxy for overall interdependency, the inferred finding is that Finance is most critical provider of information and data inputs required by other CI sectors to maintain the assurance of their business. The follow-on implication is that CI as a whole is most susceptible to second-order impacts and service interruption due to incidents within the Finance sector: the overall vulnerability of all CI sectors increases the most when the Finance sector suffers incidents.

Government sector has the second highest outbound dependency but the smallest standard deviation, indicating that government information and data is universally agreed to be important to the delivery of goods and services from the other CI sectors. Conversely, government poses the second largest interdependency threat to CI sectors.

## INFORMATION AND DATA DEPENDENCY MAPS

This section will assess in summary fashion the CI interdependencies, which might be interpreted using information and data dependency findings. As stated in Chapter 1, no one single metric can start to form strongly credible picture of CI interdependency. More than one dimension can be used to create representations of reality. (We need at least two dimensions—height and width—to draw a picture on a piece of paper.) Therefore, we need at least two dimensions and ideally, three dimensions to model reality. This section provides interpretation but not attempt to critique indications: Chapter 4 accomplishes this task. It correlates the indications of Chapters 2 and 3, and discusses the potential strengths and weaknesses of the combined results.

As in Chapter 2, we commence the review of dependency metrics using tools known as treemaps* to provide a top-level view of all sectors and how they relate to one another from the perspective of first inbound, then outbound information and data dependency.

For comprehension purposes, the dependency scale has been aggregated into high, medium, and low data dependency where high is the top of all dependency scores across all sectors, for a given sector. Medium is the middle and low is the bottom of all dependency scores for a given sector. The ranks are color coded according to the following scale:

| Value | Color | Metric (Score) Range |
|---|---|---|
| High | ☐ White | 5.15–10.00 |
| Medium | ▨ Gray | 3.75–5.14 |
| Low | ■ Black | 1.00–3.74 |

Below is a map for inbound data dependency. Figure 3.4 at the highest level represents the total sum of all median scores for inbound dependency. Within the

---

* Treemaps are tools developed by Ben Shneiderman at the University of Maryland in the 1990s to display complex and multi-layers data sets. http://www.cs.umd.edu/hcil/treemap-history/.

total score are boxes for each sector, which represent the proportional size of each sector's inbound median sum relative to the other sectors. Within each sector box are smaller boxes for each inbound relationship with all other sectors, such that the size of the box is proportional to the size of each sectors' contribution to the inbound median score for the specific sector.

Figure 3.4 provides a comprehensive perspective on inbound dependency among the CI sectors. For instance, the inbound dependency nature of Energy becomes much more evident, although the relative isolation of Food, Water, and Communications and IT also stand out due to the size of their boxes. Meanwhile, it becomes obvious that sectors like Manufacturing and Communications and IT (again) have inbound dependencies composed of either intense or mild relationships. Either they place a high value on the assurance of information and data from

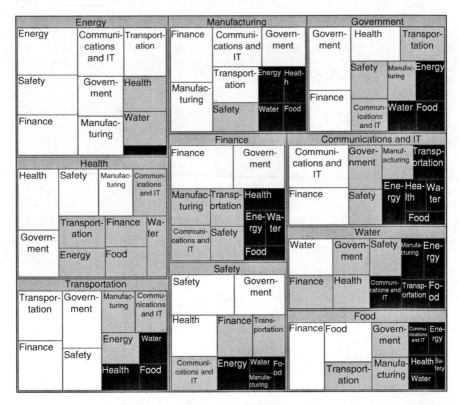

**FIGURE 3.4**  White denotes high inbound dependency; gray denotes medium inbound dependency; and black denotes low inbound dependency. Each sector block is proportional to the size of its inbound dependency score relative to the other sectors. Each square within each sector block indicates the proportional size of inbound dependecy scores from each sectors. Recall that inbound dependency is equivalent to the vulnerability of the CI sector to threats from other sectors.

a given sector or a very low value; there is little middle ground (grey) in the boxes relative to white and black.

Next is a map for outbound dependency. Figure 3.5 represents the total sum of median scores for outbound dependency. Within the total score are boxes for each sector, which represent the proportional size of each sector's outbound median sum. Within each sector's box are smaller boxes for each outbound relationship with all other sectors, such that the size of the box is proportional to the size of each sectors' contribution to the outbound median sum. Finally, to facilitate intersector analysis, the weighting for each sector output for each sector box is coded by high, medium, and low dependency relative to all sectors.

As was the case for the inbound dependency map, the scale for the outbound dependency map has been aggregated into high, medium, and low data dependencies where high is the top of all dependency scores across all sectors, for a given sector;

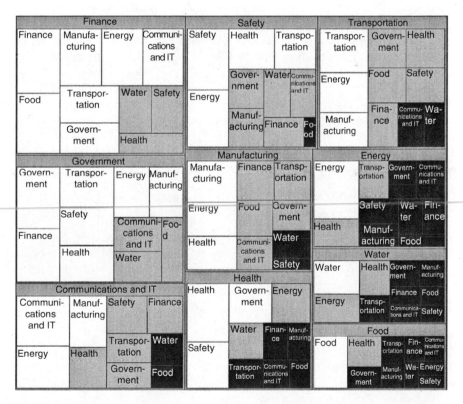

**FIGURE 3.5** White denotes high outbound dependency; gray denotes medium outbound dependency; and black denotes low outbound dependency. Each sector block is proportional to the size of its outbound dependency score relative to the other sectors. Each square within each sector block indicates the proportional size of outbound dependecy scores from each sectors. Recall that outbound dependency is equivalent to the vulnerability of the CI sector to threats from other sectors.

medium is the middle and low is the bottom of all dependency scores for a given sector. The ranks are color coded according to the following scale:

| Value | Color | Metric (Score) Range |
|-------|-------|----------------------|
| High | ☐ White | 5.15–10.00 |
| Medium | ▨ Gray | 3.75–5.14 |
| Low | ■ Black | 1.00–3.74 |

Above is a map for outbound dependency. Figure 3.5 represents the total sum of all median scores for outbound dependency. Within the total score are boxes for each sector, which represent the proportional size of each sector's inbound median sum relative to the other sectors. Within each sector box are smaller boxes for each inbound relationship with all other sectors, such that the size of the box is proportional to the size of each sectors contribution to the inbound median sum for the specific sector.

Figure 3.5 provides a perspective on outbound dependency. For instance, the outbound dependency of Finance in contrast to the inbound of Energy becomes much more evident, although the relative isolation of Food especially stands out. Meanwhile, that sectors like Manufacturing and Communications and IT which displayed inbound dependencies composed of either intense or mild relationships tend to become more balanced when considered from an outbound perspective: there is a more gradual movement from high to low dependency relationships when Manufacturing and Communications and IT are assessed by their peer infrastructures.

## SECTOR-SPECIFIC DEPENDENCY ANALYSIS

The following section examines each CI sector individually, from the perspectives of both inbound and outbound dependence on information and data. Some of the discussion to follow is critical of the indications; further analysis of the accuracy of the metrics is discussed in Chapter 4, where the econometrics from Chapter 2 is correlated with the metrics presented here.

### TORNADO DIAGRAMS AND INBOUND/OUTBOUND DEPENDENCY RATIO

Two tools are applied for the analysis of each CI sector to follow. Tornado diagrams and the more familiar inbound–outbound ratio.

A tornado diagram is used to show the inbound and outbound median results for each sector in a side by side fashion so that readers can see exactly how they compare for each sector-to-sector relationship. Every tornado is divided vertically by an axis which is valued at zero. On the left side and right side of the axis are the inbound and outbound median values, respectively. Strongest inbound dependency relationships (the highest inbound median value) are placed at the top left of the tornado. The left side is then organized in descending order, that is, from the highest inbound value to the lowest inbound value. On the left side of the tornado are the reciprocal outbound values for each of the sectors. Within the context of this chapter, the left side (inbound) represents the relative data dependency vulnerability experienced by a given sector, while the right side (outbound) is the threat posed by a sector to other sectors. All tornados are on a scale from 0 to 10 to the either side of the axis.

The inbound–outbound ratio is the result of dividing the inbound median value by the outbound media value. When less than zero, the inbound–outbound ratio indicates that the sector has a positive data dependency relationships with a reciprocal sector. A value above 1 indicates that the sector relationship is dependent or negative; there is more dependency on information and data received/consumed than on the information and data produced by the sector. The higher this value is above 1, the more unbalanced the data dependency relationship is between sectors.

## ENERGY SECTOR DATA DEPENDENCIES

Energy, as defined under the current CI definitions, is centered on electric power generation and transmission, oil, and gas production and storage.

The Energy sector is a large consumer of data from other CI sectors and expresses the highest overall inbound dependency and vulnerability. Energy's inbound requirements are heightened relative to other sectors by the high delivery-assurance standards around energy supplies mandated by clients and government, plus a large volume of consumer-based transactions and publicly listed status which drives regulatory pressures for data assurance (Table 3.6).

Energy is the largest consumer of its own information and data as a result of the tight supply-chain linkages between different business entities. For instance, in production versus distribution of both electricity and fossil energies.

During interviewing, Energy executives maintain that fundamental operations will continue if information and data flows abruptly cease, but will degrade as the ability to control the infrastructure and business as a whole is impaired. The specific speed of service degradation varies according to energy industry and specific rates of decay are not known. This reinforces the observation under the sector aggregations which stated that data dependency is not specifically a measure of the likelihood of a production failure; rather, loss of communications and data from different sectors increases vulnerabilities to a greater or lesser extent. For instance, loss of data flows from within the Energy sector itself is most likely to create a serious vulnerability, which might be exploited by a variety of different threats such as an inability to coordinate load shedding or pipeline pressures.

## TABLE 3.6
### Energy Inbound–Outbound Ratio

|  | Energy | Commu-nications and IT | Finance | Health | Food | Water | Transpor-tation | Safety | Govern-ment | Manufac-turing |
|---|---|---|---|---|---|---|---|---|---|---|
| Ratio | 1.00 | 2.06 | 3.11 | 1.16 | 0.70 | 1.58 | 1.67 | 2.24 | 1.57 | 1.85 |

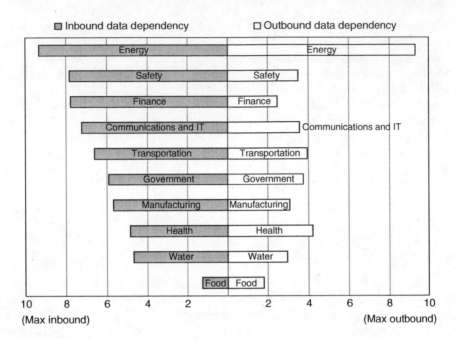

**FIGURE 3.6**    Energy sector data dependency.

Information and data from the Safety sector is the second highest inbound dependency for Energy, reflecting again the observation that loss of data flows creates vulnerabilities to potential threats to exploit with greater probabilities than if information and data were flowing. For Safety, the inability to receive security reports greatly impairs Energy's ability to prepare and respond to incidents which might impact operations.

Table 3.5 shows Energy as having the third lowest outbound dependency, meaning that information and data from the Energy sector is rated as a relatively low priority among the CI sectors, slightly higher that that of Food and Water. A quick review of Figure 3.6 reveals how this is so. Every sector except the Energy sector itself consistently rates the information and data from the Energy sector a lower priority that Energy applies to the reciprocal information.

A low outbound score for Energy is not to imply that CI sector executives felt that energy supplies themselves were a low-priority input to production. Not at all! This illustrates two issues at least: first, energy supplies and their assurance are assumed to a large extent and backup systems (batteries/generators) will fill the temporary gap of occasional outages. This in turn indicates a preparedness and planning profile focused on short-term incidents around energy supplies and little planning or preparedness related to extended outages. The threat in this case is the inability to manage incidents beyond the shortest-term brownouts or blackouts.

The second point illustrated by a low outbound score represents a threat to Energy. Energy's assumptions related to the other sector's responsiveness or collaboration during incident may be inaccurate. For instance, Energy organizations use the core telecommunications infrastructure for managing remote, infield assets. In the event of a pandemic which reduced workforce availability in the Communications and IT sector, Energy might find itself in the middle of a long queue for urgent maintenance although it had expected to be at the front.

## FINANCE SECTOR DATA DEPENDENCIES

Finance, as defined under the current CI definitions, is centered on banking, transaction processing currency storage and disbursement, investment exchange, and securities management (Figure 3.7).

As Figure 3.3 indicates Finance possesses the highest overall outbound dependency of any sector, which means that taken as a whole, the CI sectors rate financial information and data as the most important to operations and the greatest threat if assurance is compromised.

Like all CI sectors except Food (discussed later), the Finance sector is most dependent on information flowing within itself. Data interchange is at the heart of the Finance industry and as an obvious result, the sector's executives rate information from other players in the sector as the most important to the continuity of operations.

Finance executives cite government regulation and reporting as a major operational requirement and vulnerability, as a result, information from the Government sector is the second highest rated information source. Table 3.7 shows that government is also the only CI sector to have an inbound–outbound ratio of greater than 1— indicating that it is the only sector which Finance rates higher than it is itself rated by that sector.

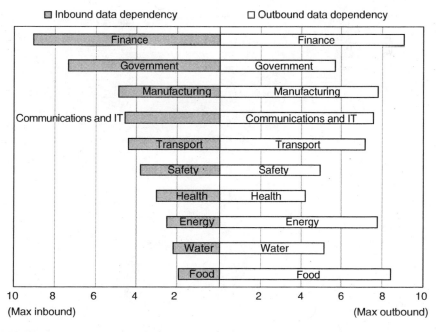

**FIGURE 3.7** Finance sector data dependency.

**TABLE 3.7**

**Finance Inbound–Outbound Ratio**

|  | Energy | Communications and IT | Finance | Health | Food | Water | Transportation | Safety | Government | Manufacturing |
|---|---|---|---|---|---|---|---|---|---|---|
| Ratio | 0.32 | 0.60 | 1.00 | 0.72 | 0.23 | 0.42 | 0.52 | 0.80 | 1.30 | 0.48 |

Aside from the Government sector, all sectors rely heavily upon data flows from Finance—either for conducting day-to-day business or for protecting sensitive competitive or personal information. Food is the most dependent according to the inbound–outbound dependency ratio, indicating the importance of short-term receivables and the nature of trading in perishable goods combined with many smaller producers of primary inputs such as meats, grains, and vegetables. The loss of assurance in the information and data from Finance is the largest threat to the Food CI sector.

## COMMUNICATIONS AND IT SECTOR DATA DEPENDENCIES

Communications and IT, as defined under the current CI definitions, is centered on telecommunications and information technology, broadcasting systems, software, hardware, and networks including the Internet (Figure 3.8).

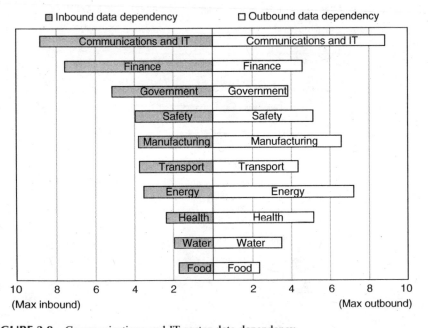

**FIGURE 3.8** Communications and IT sector data dependency.

**TABLE 3.8**

**Communications and IT Inbound–Outbound Ratio**

| | Energy | Commu-nications and IT | Finance | Health | Food | Water | Transpor-tation | Safety | Govern-ment | Manufac-turing |
|---|---|---|---|---|---|---|---|---|---|---|
| Ratio | 0.48 | 1.00 | 1.66 | 0.46 | 0.73 | 0.56 | 0.87 | 0.77 | 1.34 | 0.58 |

Communications and IT is most dependent on information and data flowing within the sector because data interchange is essential to coordinate the delivery of telecommunications services to clients among the various independent service providers, and coordination of intrasector supply chains. Similar to Energy and Finance, intrasector dependencies are both the greatest vulnerabilities and threats.

Finance is a highly important client and supplier to Communications and IT firms. Further, with the exception of government, it is the only sector with a positive dependency relationship. Information and data from Finance is considered to be important due to both the consumer-based transactional properties of the telecommunications industry and the large sums of money that are managed by many service providers due to the scope and scale of operations. (They are large businesses!) Frequently, these firms will be managing cash flows in millions of dollars daily, managing large assets and debts on a daily basis within the treasury departments. Information and data from the Finance sector is critical to clearing and approving transactions and financial management.

The Finance sector places lower assurance requirements upon information and data from Communications and IT as indicated by the inbound–outbound ratio in Table 3.8; in discussions, Finance executives cite the extensive investments they have made in redundant telecommunications services and data centers, which improves their resiliency and reduces dependency on information and data from service providers to maintain operations.

Government possesses a positive inbound dependency relationship with Communications and IT due to the highly regulated nature of much of the sector. The Safety sector frequently requires close cooperation with the Communications and IT industry for the purposes of law enforcement and lawful access (wiretap) purposes.

All sectors require data communications services but do not necessarily maintain any formal, directed Communications with the service providers themselves, relying upon public domain data. In the case of Food and Water, little to no formal communications with communications and IT is maintained, as indicated by sector scores just above 1—which can mean either none or public domain information only.

Communications and IT seems to consume data from other sectors either very intensely, or barely at all. Almost half the total inbound dependency value is from two of ten sectors: Communications (intrasector) and Finance. Notable among the sectors not rated highly by Communications and IT for inbound dependency is the Energy sector—even though Energy and especially electricity is a critical input to the provision of telecommunications services. If the theory of proxy indicators is to be applied, a possible explanation for the lower rating of Energy is that the

Communications and IT sector tends to invest heaviest of all sectors in safeguards around power failures. Backup generators and high-availability are the hallmark of all modern carriers and service providers. To a certain extent, Communications and IT service providers have insulated themselves first and foremost from threats associated with energy disruptions and the inbound dependency (vulnerability) of the Energy sector is rated accordingly.

## HEALTH SECTOR DATA DEPENDENCIES

Health, as defined under the current CI definitions, is centered on hospitals, ambulances, blood banks, laboratories, surveillance, and personal health services (Figure 3.9).

Health is most dependent on data and information flowing within the Health sector itself because of data interchange between services such as laboratories, clinics, hospitals, and private practices.

Under normal operating conditions (versus crisis conditions), formal or directed outbound communications with the Health sector is a secondary concern for most sectors with the exception of Government and Safety. Government is both a regulator and a major funder of the Health sector and therefore, information and data from government is valued by Health highest of all sectors outside Health. To a very similar degree, Safety is a partner-first-responder to Health and regular communications is a matter of day-to-day business (receiving victims of accidents or conducting tests on unknown and possibly dangerous substances).

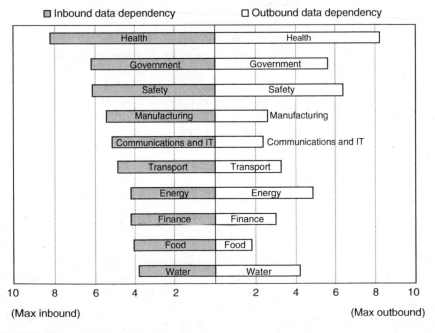

**FIGURE 3.9**   Health sector data dependency.

## TABLE 3.9
## Health Inbound–Outbound Ratio

|  | Energy | Communications and IT | Finance | Health | Food | Water | Transportation | Safety | Government | Manufacturing |
|---|---|---|---|---|---|---|---|---|---|---|
| Ratio | 0.86 | 2.17 | 1.40 | 1.00 | 2.25 | 0.91 | 1.49 | 0.96 | 1.10 | 2.08 |

Government sector, as a regulator and a major funder of the Health sector, values the outbound information and data from the Health sector under all conditions (Table 3.9). Government is intimately accountable for public health issues and requires the constant day-to-day support of the private and public health entities to fulfill this responsibility to the public. To a similar degree, safety, as a partner-first-responder, places a higher outbound value upon the information and data from Health and maintains constant communications as a matter of day-to-day business (managing response traffic accidents to fires). As far the other sectors are concerned, information and data from the Health sector is of significantly less value under normal conditions; for these sectors there is low perceived threat to the business associated with an outage in Health.

On the topic of dependency indications, which do not appear to make sense: Health is dependent on Food services to feed the patients and the staff under its care; yet information and data from the Food sector is considered to be barely of significance for Health, ranked almost the same (but lower) than dependency on information and data from Finance. This may be an indication that Food services tend to be a fragmented business, with many points of contact. A similar inconsistency exists in the case of information and data from the Water sector. During interviewing, Health executive stated that both potable water sources and the ability to dispose of wastewater are fundamental to the functioning of most hospitals and laboratories to maintain the necessary sanitary conditions. Similarly, water testing for biological and chemical contaminates is a significant responsibility of the Water sector, where samples are processed by the Health industry. Presumably, this business relationship is well known inside the Health sector but for some reason this has not been indicated by the inbound Health rating for Water. (Water does acknowledge this relationship in the outbound ranking for Health information and data to the Water sector. See Water Sector Data Dependencies.) This lack of communications between Health and Food may very well be an indication of reality not living up to an operational requirement; the Health sector faces a serious interdependency vulnerability from Food.

### FOOD SECTOR DATA DEPENDENCIES

Food, as defined under the current CI definitions, is centered on agriculture, distribution, and safety (Figure 3.10).

The Food sector is one of only two sectors to not have the overall highest inbound and outbound dependencies associated with intrasector information and data. Food production is a balkanized industry; possibly indicating individual

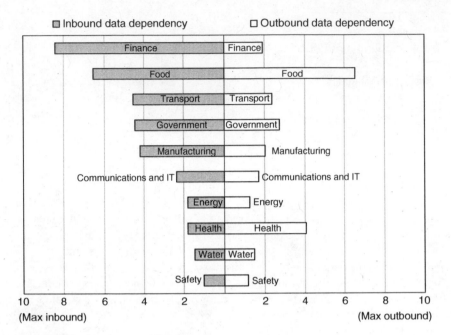

**FIGURE 3.10**   Food sector data dependency.

producers depend more on transactions with the Finance sector than with each other. However, the relationship is one-sided because Finance does not apply any particular importance to data arriving from Food. The inbound–outbound ratio between Food and Finance is the highest of any interdependency indicators among all CI sectors, underscoring the impression that Food is most vulnerable to its interdependency relationship with Finance (Table 3.10).

Aside from intrasector supply-chain relationships, the only significant outbound dependency related to the Food sector is from Health due to the importance of food services to patients and staff. Ironically, Food disclaims any significant degree of information or data coming from Health—even for the purposes of laboratory testing, because such information is generally relayed through governmental sources (regulators). The dependency questionnaire was intended to map information and data flows between sectors. This lack of communications between Food and Health may very well be an indication of reality not living up to an operational requirement, where Food poses a serious interdependency threat to Health.

**TABLE 3.10**

**Food Inbound–Outbound Ratio**

|  | Energy | Communications and IT | Finance | Health | Food | Water | Transportation | Safety | Government | Manufacturing |
|---|---|---|---|---|---|---|---|---|---|---|
| Ratio | 1.43 | 1.37 | 4.38 | 0.44 | 1.00 | 0.99 | 1.90 | 0.86 | 1.62 | 2.08 |

Relative to all other CI sectors (Figure 3.3), Food possesses the lowest outbound dependency indicating that few formal or consistent means of communicating with other sectors are maintained to and from Food. In the event of a crisis, or emergency, Food may be the most difficult to coordinate during a planned response. Similarly, in the event of an incident which required multi-sector response, Food may represent the weakest link in the response chain and may be therefore most likely to catalyze intensifications of impacts.

The outbound dependency of the Food sector is barely over one fourth of either the Government or Finance outbound dependencies. This may reflect an underlying assumption among sector managers that Food is a personal matter for employees and not a business problem. Health has the largest outbound dependency for Food, in partial recognition of their unique requirement to feed patients in hospitals.

## WATER SECTOR DATA DEPENDENCIES

Water, as defined under the current CI definitions, is centered on drinking water and wastewater management treatment (Figure 3.11).

Water management is a sector characterized by independent operators with few physical interconnection points among the many distinct operators. In other words, Water infrastructure operators as a whole tend not to mechanically interconnect with other infrastructures. This is more the case for small infrastructures than for large water infrastructures, like those found in are highly urbanized areas. Relative to other CI sectors, Water has no high inbound dependencies (see Figure 3.2), indicating an

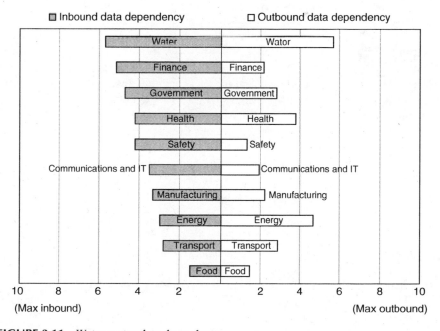

**FIGURE 3.11** Water sector data dependency.

## TABLE 3.11
## Water Inbound–Outbound Ratio

|       | Energy | Commu- nications and IT | Finance | Health | Food | Water | Transpor- tation | Safety | Govern- ment | Manufac- turing |
|-------|--------|-------------------------|---------|--------|------|-------|------------------|--------|--------------|-----------------|
| Ratio | 0.63   | 1.78                    | 2.36    | 1.10   | 1.01 | 1.00  | 0.97             | 3.14   | 1.66         | 1.48            |

isolated production system and probably a production process which is least data-intensive relative to all other sectors. Under this assessment, Water faces the smallest interdependency vulnerabilities.

Information and data from the Health and Safety sectors is important for the purposes of water-quality testing and emergency response, but communications channels are not consistently prioritized, formalized, or standardized. This fact is apparent such that, relative to other sectors, the inbound dependency scores assigned to Health and Safety are relatively low—less than five in both cases (Table 3.11). Conversely, Health and especially Safety do not recognize the dependence of the water infrastructure. This may be especially concerning in the case of Safety, because Water places a strong dependency on the information and data flowing from Safety for the purposes of reacting to impacts and threats on the water sources. For instance, if a truck with chemicals falls off a bridge, Water needs to know to shut down intake valves, and this information comes from Safety.

Energy has the lowest inbound–outbound ratio with Water of all CI sectors. This indicates that the Energy sector places a higher value on the information and data from Water, although Water does not seem to recognize the moderate dependence of the Energy sectors. Among all sectors, Water poses the greatest interdependency threat to Energy.

Water possesses the lowest cumulative outbound dependency (see Figure 3.3) indicating that few formal or consistent means of communicating with this sector is maintained by the other sectors. In the event of a crisis, or emergency, Water may be difficult to coordinate during a planned response. Similarly, in the event of an incident which required multi-sector response, Water may be the catalyst and intensify impacts for lack of an ability to maintain information and data channels to the sectors which require their cooperation and coordination.

## TRANSPORTATION SECTOR DATA DEPENDENCIES

Transportation, as defined under the current CI definitions, is centered on aviation, mass transit, rail, marine, and road (Figure 3.12).

Intrasector information and data dependency within transport is a reflection of the tight supply-chain linkages associated with modern delivery logistics. The movement of goods and services means that airports, rail yards, terminals, and a wide variety of transport infrastructures are in constant contact; for instance, truckers communication with railways, airlines, and shipping to coordinate the final delivery leg of many goods. The intrasector communications is intense and constant.

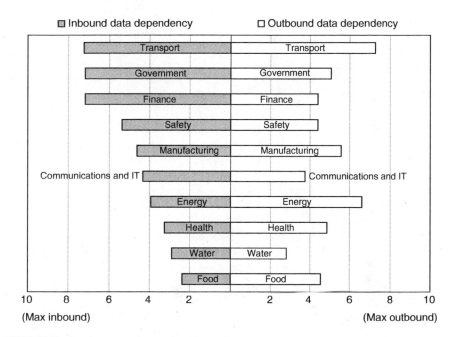

**FIGURE 3.12** Transport sector data dependency.

Unlike most other sectors, Transportation rates information and data from two other key suppliers as very nearly important as its own internal flows: Government and Finance. Government is deemed critical due to the many regulations around the different modes of transportation and especially for border crossings, where government moderates the flows of goods explicitly. Finance is also highly important to many forms of transportation because of the need to execute many transactions for loads that might leave the station/port/terminal/warehouse: loads can even be individual passengers on each plane paying for their own ticket. Loads can be many different goods from many different manufacturers on the same train—all paying their own bills. This granular accounting requirement is coupled with the fact that there are many especially time-sensitive inputs into Transportation, which require many transactions: from independent contract-truckers to discreet purchases of fuel to the publicly traded reporting requirements.

An interesting observation from the data dependency interviews with Transport executives is that they do not place as high a priority on information from the Safety sector as they do for Government and Finance. Although the Transportation sector is a known target for security incidents, the sector does not give security information priority over operational information and communications. This lower level of communications between Transport and Safety may be an indication of reality not living up to an operational requirement resulting in an operational vulnerability because regulatory information and data takes precedence over security information and data.

Energy has the highest outbound information and data dependency with Transport of all the CI sectors, significantly higher the reciprocal dependency from Transport. Although Transportation executive recognizes the overwhelming importance of

## TABLE 3.12
### Transport Inbound–Outbound Ratio

|       | Energy | Communications and IT | Finance | Health | Food | Water | Transportation | Safety | Government | Manufacturing |
|-------|--------|-----------------------|---------|--------|------|-------|----------------|--------|------------|---------------|
| Ratio | 0.60   | 1.16                  | 1.64    | 0.67   | 0.53 | 1.03  | 1.00           | 1.22   | 1.43       | 0.83          |

energy to their business, much of the energy they consume is stockpiled for their purposes (tank yards, generators at ports and terminals) and not necessarily delivered on demand (such as through a gas pipeline). For this reason, short-term interruptions in the Energy sector will not necessarily have any impact on the Transportation sector, goes the reasoning. Conversely, Energy relies to a higher degree upon Transportation and short-term outages have greater, relative impacts due to the delivery of sector inputs, whether they are spare parts for equipment or bulk commodity inputs like liquid hydrogen for turbine-coolant or coal for generator fuel. Therefore, the loss of information and data from Transport poses the largest threat to the Energy sector among all CI sectors, with Health in second place (Table 3.12).

### SAFETY SECTOR DATA DEPENDENCIES

Safety, as defined under the current CI definitions, is centered on law enforcement, fire, search and rescue, and emergency services (Figure 3.13).

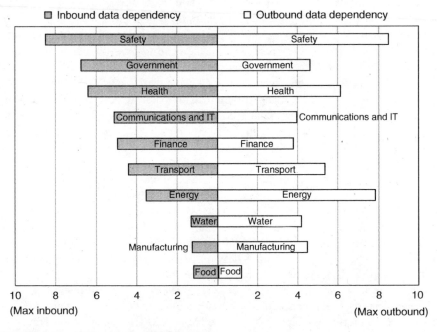

**FIGURE 3.13**  Safety sector data dependency.

**TABLE 3.13**

**Safety Inbound–Outbound Ratio**

|  | Energy | Commu- nications and IT | Finance | Health | Food | Water | Transpor- tation | Safety | Govern- ment | Manufac- turing |
|---|---|---|---|---|---|---|---|---|---|---|
| Ratio | 0.45 | 1.29 | 1.30 | 1.04 | 1.17 | 0.32 | 0.82 | 1.00 | 1.45 | 0.28 |

The Safety sector reports the highest dependence with intrasector information and data exchange—substantially higher than any of the nearest inbound dependency ratings—indicating that other sectors are not comparably essential to normal operations in the opinion of Safety executives.

The Energy sector posseses the largest difference between inbound and outbound dependencies, with Energy citing a very large outbound dependency on Safety—the largest for all of the non-safety sectors (Table 3.13). This indicates clearly that under normal operating conditions, there is a distinct imbalance between Safety and Energy, with the loss of information and data from Safety posing a significant threat to Energy. Conversely, Safety does not consider itself particularly vulnerable or interdependent with Energy sector.

As an inbound–outbound ratio, Water actually has a lower ratio and an even greater proportional imbalance with Safety. Safety is considered an important source of operational data for the Water system and a critical element to preserving public health; yet again the Safety executives interviewed indicated that water has the lowest overall operational inbound dependency for the Safety sector. Additionally, safety routinely requests support from the Water sector for handling day-to-day incidents due to its ability to open and close transportation routes (bridges over dams and waterways), and of course the management of the drinking water supply. Awareness of the requirement for data and information sharing and assurance between Water and Safety is not pervasive for these critical activities. Therefore, the indications are that there is a fundamental interdependency which is not necessarily acknowledged by Safety and is a vulnerability not expressed by Safety executives.

## GOVERNMENT SECTOR DATA DEPENDENCIES

Government, as defined under the current CI definitions, is centered on social services and regulation (Figure 3.14).

The Government sector reports the highest dependence with government-to-government information and data exchange. Government has the highest overall outbound dependency rating among all the sectors, indicating that government is on the critical path for operations in all sectors. This is illustrated through the inbound–outbound ratios for government, which in all cases is less than one. (Anything less than one indicates that the sector assesses information and data from a given sector with a lower level of assurance than the other sector applies to

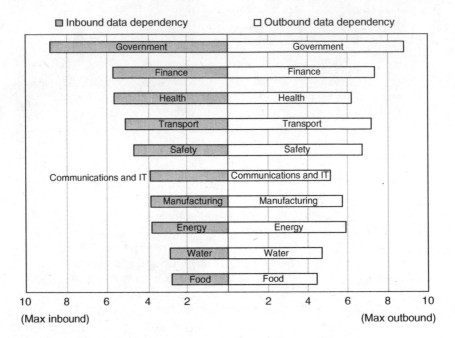

**FIGURE 3.14** Government sector data dependency.

reciprocal information and data. For instance, Energy has a 0.63 ratio with government. A simple translation of this number is that government assesses its assurance requirements around Energy information on a data only about 63 percent as important as Energy assesses incoming information and data from government.) As a result, information and data from government is a net, interdependency threat to all CI sectors (Table 3.14).

This theme of an uneven dependency relationship between government and the other CI sectors is recurrent through this chapter and shows up obviously at every level of analysis. Government has placed itself on the critical path of interdependency through regulation, but appears to underrate this relationship relative to the regulated industries themselves! This type of result indicates that government may not fully understand or be prepared to manage incidents impacting CI sectors due to the fact that they do not appear ready to support

**TABLE 3.14**

**Government Inbound–Outbound Ratio**

|  | Energy | Commu-nications and IT | Finance | Health | Food | Water | Transpor-tation | Safety | Govern-ment | Manufac-turing |
|---|---|---|---|---|---|---|---|---|---|---|
| Ratio | 0.64 | 0.75 | 0.77 | 0.91 | 0.62 | 0.60 | 0.70 | 0.69 | 1.00 | 0.66 |

the information and data-assurance expectations of these sectors under normal operating conditions.

## MANUFACTURING SECTOR DATA DEPENDENCIES

Manufacturing, as defined under the current CI definitions, is centered on the production of chemicals and defense industrial base, which is considered aerospace for practical purposes (Figure 3.15). See Chapter 2 for a brief discussion on defense industrial base in the section "Mapping NAICS to CI Sectors".

Manufacturing is the second sector to have a more intense dependency relationship with an external sector than within the sector itself. In this case, Manufacturing places a higher degree of inbound dependency on the information and data arriving from the Finance sector with intrasector information and data rated approximately 11 percent less important (Finance is rated 7.82 inbound rating, while Manufacturing-to-Manufacturing is rated 7.03 inbound rating, see Table 3.3). Thus Manufacturing indicates more interdependency vulnerability with the financial sector than from within its own sector.

Transaction services and communications with partners and clients are critical supply-chain inputs to Manufacture sector firms. As a result, information and data from software companies (Communications and IT) is rated next most important after the intrasector information and data and third overall for Manufacturing.

From an outbound perspective, the appreciation of the dependence of Manufacturing on Communications and IT and Finance is not fully returned. This appears as

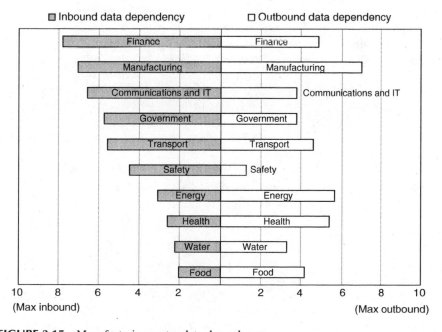

**FIGURE 3.15** Manufacturing sector data dependency.

**TABLE 3.15**

**Manufacturing Inbound–Outbound Ratio**

|  | Energy | Commu-nications and IT | Finance | Health | Food | Water | Transpor-tation | Safety | Govern-ment | Manufac-turing |
|---|---|---|---|---|---|---|---|---|---|---|
| Ratio | 0.54 | 1.73 | 1.60 | 0.48 | 0.48 | 0.68 | 1.21 | 3.51 | 1.51 | 1.00 |

an understandable result for Finance and Communications and IT because the designated industries within the Manufacturing sector are not obvious or primary inputs into either Finance or Communications and IT as a whole (see Tables 2.7 and 2.8).

The inbound–outbound ratio for the Safety sector is 3.51, which indicates a very large imbalance between the assurance placed upon information and data from Safety by Manufacturing, and the reciprocal relationship (Table 3.15). Given that the industries defined for the Manufacturing sector are concerned with either hazardous goods or defense, this is surprising. These are the sectors that might be expected to attract the most significant degree of communications assurance to support national security and emergency response. Consequently, Manufacturing likely faces its most significant interdependency vulnerability from the Safety sector.

## CONCLUSIONS AND INDICATED RISKS

The metrics described and analyzed in this chapter are an expression of how CI sectors rely upon information and data flowing among themselves, and the degree to which the production of goods and services becomes vulnerable when there is an impact in the assurance (confidentiality, integrity, availability) of information and data.

This chapter considers the measurement of information and data dependency among CI sectors as an indicator for overall interdependency of the goods and services. As a stand-alone metric, information and data dependency is not sufficient to make conclusions about CI interdependency; it is merely indicative. In some cases, the results of information and data dependency analysis are even counterintuitive. For this reason, indications from this chapter are correlated with the statistical indications from I–O analysis from Chapter 2. In Chapter 4, a more formal critique and set of observations are made.

### INDICATIONS FROM DATA

The following discussion is a summary of the indications from information and data dependency around CI interdependency, which was covered in depth throughout this chapter.

Canadian CI sector dependency risk is a high-level display of the results of CI interdependencies based upon inbound and outbound information and data dependency for each defined CI sector (Figure 3.16).

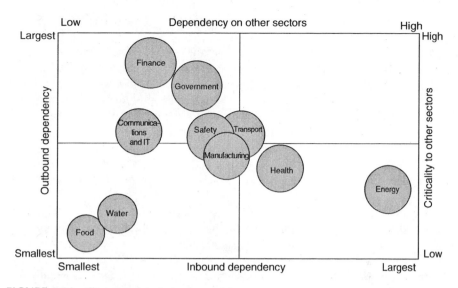

**FIGURE 3.16**   CI sector data dependency risk.

Figure 3.16 shows the position of each CI sector relative to the median inbound dependency score ($x$-axis/horizontal axis/abscissa) and the median outbound dependency score ($y$-axis/vertical axis/ordinate). The inbound score ranges from a minimum of 1 to a maximum of 10 and indicates how important the assurance (confidentiality, integrity, and availability) of information and data from within and among the CI sectors is to a given sector. Inbound dependency is also discussed as a form of interdependency vulnerability of a given sector. The outbound score ranges from a minimum of 1 to a maximum of 10 and indicates how important the assurance of information and data from a given sectors is to the other CI sectors. Outbound dependency is also considered as a form of threat that a sector poses to other sectors. The size of each sector bubble is relative to the combined sum of both inbound and outbound scores.

The top right quadrant represents the highest interdependency risk; sectors in this quadrant would be in a position of being both highly vulnerable to information and data incidents and a significant source of interdependency threats. Sectors in this quadrant possess the greatest risk of suffering impacts and then cascading these impacts into other CI sectors.

The top left quadrant contains sectors that possess the greatest risk of catalyzing cascading events thought information and data interdependencies. Sectors in this quadrant have high outbound and low inbound dependencies. The bottom right quadrant contains sectors possessing the greatest vulnerability to a second-order impact due to an incident in another interdependent CI sector organization. These sectors have higher inbound and lower outbound dependencies. The top right quadrant contains sectors that possess the greatest potential to relay an impact from one CI sector to another (seemingly unrelated) CI sector. These sectors have large inbound and outbound dependencies. The bottom left quadrant indicates low risks (as revealed through data dependency analysis) to CI assurance. Sectors in this quadrant possess both low inbound and low outbound information and data dependencies and are least likely to either propagate or cascade an impact to other CI sectors, or themselves be impacted by an incident in other CI sectors.

Figure 3.16 shows how Energy is clearly the largest consumer of information and data from other CI sectors and rates itself (through the executive interview processes) highly dependent upon other sectors. The indication is that Energy is a very outward-looking CI sector, and likely becomes the most vulnerable to incidents and impacts when information and data assurance is disrupted. Another valid interpretation of the chart in Figure 3.16 and the indications to CI interdependency as a whole is that Energy is the sector to which the most attention needs to be applied because of the risks associated with failures.

The Finance and Government sectors are also among the top CI sectors in terms of the criticality of their information and data to other CI sectors, but for different reasons than Energy. In these instances, both sectors are large producers of information and data (large outbound scores) for the other sectors while being light consumers of information and data (small inbound scores). Taken as a proxy indication of interdependency, Finance and Government are central sectors from which vulnerabilities in other sectors can be catalyzed. Similar to Energy, Finance and Government sectors require particular attention because of their ability to impact other sectors in the event of an incident.

Food and Water sectors, when considered from the perspective of information and data dependency, represent the lowest risks to CI through interdependency relationships. Figure 3.16 shows that both these sectors are rated very low for both inbound and outbound dependencies. On this basis, impacts within either the Food or the Water sectors are less likely to propagate or cascade out of these sectors and into other sectors. Similarly, impacts in other sectors are less likely to propagate or cascade into the Food or Water sectors from other CI sectors experiencing impacts. However, the more realistic interpretation of these findings around Food and Water is that they likely pose significant interdependency threat to most sectors due to the chronic underestimation of their importance in the economic ecosystem. As discussed earlier, critiques of these indications are considered in Chapter 4.

Consider now an alternate view of the same inbound and outbound dependency metrics. If the reader wishes to simply consider the one-to-one intensity of dependency from the relationships in Table 3.2, a picture of the potential for cascading impacts starts to emerge as displayed in Figure 3.17. One-to-one intensity is based upon the sectors with the fewest negative dependency relationships (inbound–outbound ratio >1), tracing downward according to which sectors have the most positive overall I–O dependency. (I–O ratio <1).

A specific sector primacy picture develops from the review of information and data dependency relationships indicated by inbound and outbound metrics. This primacy does not imply a specific order of importance; it displays a view starting with the sector with least number of negative dependency (I–O ratio <1) relationships, namely government. Figure 3.17 shows potential routes of cascading impacts when the sector with the largest outbound rating is placed at the top, and the sectors with the strongest relationship to the top sector are subsequently placed beneath. Below those points are the sectors with the strongest relationships with the "second level" seconds—though this is not an attempt to rank the sectors.

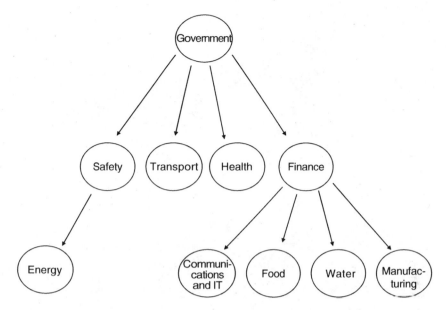

**FIGURE 3.17** CI dependency flow according to inbound–outbound data.

Government has no negative dependency relationships. The sector with the next least number of negative dependency relationships is Finance. However, Safety, Transport, and Health all have their largest dependency relationship with government too. At one degree of separation from government are the remaining CI sectors. Communications and IT, Food, Water, and Manufacturing have their largest dependency with Finance, while Energy has its largest dependency with Safety.

## ACKNOWLEDGMENT

The material presented in this chapter has begun with the work done by the author for the Canadian federal government, Department of Public Safety between October 2006 and July 2007.* The metrics and findings within this chapter reflect updated material and expanded data sets from those delivered to the government. Specifically, the sample set has been expanded to include more U.S. specific responses within the overall sample to dilute for potential Canadian basis in the interdependency indications.

* Public Safety Canada, Cyber-Interdependencies within Canada's key infrastructure sectors, July 2007, delivered by Bell Canada.

# 4 Correlation, Dependency Latency, and Vulnerabilities of Critical Infrastructure

## INTRODUCTION

To create a figure or picture of any sort, at least two dimensions need to be applied: height and width. More advanced artists or perhaps architects might apply a third dimension, depth. Two dimensions allow representations of reality to be placed on paper and expressed to others. A single dimension would literally amount to a dot on a page. Not much information can be communicated by a dot on a page. Consider Chapter 2 as a statistical dimension of critical infrastructure (CI) interdependency and Chapter 3 as an information-flow dimension of interdependency. Neither of these dimensions is perfect in its representation of the reality of CI interdependency, but they both contain a certain amount of accuracy. Where they agree on an indication of interdependency, then the likelihood that the indication is accurate increases. Where these dimensions disagree on an indication of interdependency, then the likelihood that one or both are inaccurate increases.

One approach to understanding the amount of agreement between the metrics from Chapters 2 and 3 is the correlation. Correlation is the extent to which the metrics from two distinct series move up or down in relation to one another. This chapter will discuss the extent to which the CI interdependency metrics from Chapters 2 and 3 correlate, and what these correlations might indicate about CI interdependency as a whole. In this chapter we also engage in adjustments of metrics to improve correlations with the objective of applying subject matter expert option to obtain more accurate results than this current generation of data would allow with pure mathematical formulas.

As discussed in Chapter 1, the use of subject matter expert opinion to tune the final CI interdependency metrics can be viewed as problematic because the results become potentially unrepeatable. All adjustments and manipulations are disclosed and discussed in this chapter, but for some people this approach will be unsatisfactory due to differing perceptions about the value and legitimacy of expert opinion versus repeatable, mathematical algorithms. We consider expert opinion to be an essential element of interdependency assessment, the use of which is well precedented in disciplines such as financial risk management. Please see the author's Web site, http://www.tysonmacaulay.com, for white papers discussing the application of purely mathematical manipulations to the raw CI metrics data.

This chapter also introduces the dimension of time as it relates to interdependencies, vulnerabilities, and cascading events where dependency relationships result in impacts being conducted from CI sector to sector. Up to this point, interdependency has been assessed without the context of time: each dependency relationship was considered to exist at the time of impact. The reality is that different sectors possess different dependency latencies, which must be accounted for when modeling cascading events.

This chapter will be of interest to all readers. In the following pages we engage in the final assessment of the metrics, which we discussed in detail in Chapters 2 and 3. This chapter contains the central fruit of this work and is the culmination of interdependency analysis and the catalog of interdependency vulnerabilities in CI, which have been indicated. If you are an executive within a CI sector, a policy maker, and insurer/risk manager or a contract lawyer this chapter will be valuable concerning purposes of assessing risks because it outlines the sector-level vulnerabilities in an all-hazards context.

Before we head further into this chapter, a quick review of the metrics (dimensions) gathered in Chapters 2 and 3 would be useful.

Applied in Chapter 2, statistical input–output (I–O) data from the U.S. Bureau of Economic Analysis and Statistics, Canada, served as the basis of the first set of CI interdependency metrics. I–O is represented by large tables of "make" and "use" data from industries as classified under the North American Industry Classification System (NAICS). Make data is cited in millions of dollars and records how much value in goods or services a given industry created in the record year, 2005 in the case of the United States and 2003 for Canada. Use data is also cited in millions of dollars and records how much value in goods and services a given industry consumed in the record year. Both make and use are broken down by individual industry sector, allowing us to view in detail how the different CI sectors bought and sold goods and services to each other. This trade among CI is considered a form of interdependency and a proxy-indicator for CI interdependency as a whole.

Chapter 3 discussed the development of the concept of information and data dependency as the second set of CI interdependency metrics. Dependency metrics are the result of executive-level interviews throughout the CI sectors, which gathered qualitative information about how a given sector consumes the information and data flowing from other CI sectors. For instance, what are the assurance requirements (confidentiality, integrity, and available) that Energy sector places on the information and data (voice, e-mail, web, fax, EDI, etc.) from another sector such as Water or Finance. Dependency metrics are categorized as inbound (information and data arriving) and outbound (information and data leaving) on a scale from 1 to 10, where 1 means little or no assurance requirements or nothing is received directly (other than public domain media) and 10 means the assurance of the information and data is critical to continuing operations.

## OBJECTIVE

Familiarizing the reader with correlation analysis will be the first task of this chapter. Not in great detail but just enough so that the data presented is meaningful. Sticking with the notion that anecdotes are more compelling than statistics, we will continue to apply visual anecdotes to all the findings using some of the latest techniques for data and information visualization. As discussed throughout this book, the subject matter of CI interdependency is vastly complex and the numbers and statistics associated with vulnerabilities and threats do not in anyway simplify matters.

The second task of this chapter will be introducing the element of time into the assessment of vulnerabilities and cascading impacts among CI sectors. Layering in a time dimension to the interdependency metrics is a critical element of interdependency assessment, given the metrics available. "Time" is associated with the duration of an incident impacting CI sectors and the relationship between cascading vulnerabilities and time—dependency latency.

Visualization is a key element to successfully communicate the findings of this chapter to decision makers. To that end, we will attempt to produce visual representations of the interdependency relationships and resulting vulnerabilities that this research as ultimately aimed at exposing.

Visualization tools have been developed for CI interdependency based upon work around "adjacency matrixes,"* which are undemanding tools for reviewing otherwise complex many-to-many relationships and have been named more descriptively cascade matrixes for the purposes of this book. The cascade matrixes that are developed for each sector are intended to document not only the first-order dependencies associated with a sector but also the secondary and tertiary interdependencies—cascading impacts and vulnerabilities. Recall that first-order dependencies are the dependencies relationships between a given sector and all the other sectors directly, i.e., direct dependencies with varying, distinct degrees of intensity. Second-order dependencies are a measure of how and which sectors might feel an impact due to the first-order impact, i.e., a degree of separation away from the original source of the incident. Tertiary Dependencies Model which sectors might also receive an impact as a result of a cascade from the first to the second and finally the third sector due to the initial impact, i.e., possibly two degree of separation away from the original source.

Only a small part of the potential cascading impacts are visualized using cascade matrixes. Specifically, only the strongest dependency relationship is indicated for each level of cascading events. For instance, there are nine sectors in total (Safety and Government had to be combined for econometric correlation). If $N = 9$ then there are $N(N-1) = 9 \times 8 = 72$ different first-order impacts available to review.

We will review each of these impacts individually in the following sections. However, once we start to consider second-order impacts we need to revert to only the top/strongest dependency relationships because, if $N = 9$ then there are $N(N-1)^2 = 9(8)^2 = 576$ different intersector second-order impacts available to review.

Similarly, in the consideration of tertiary impacts from secondary impact, we need to revert to only the top/strongest dependency relationships because, if $N = 9$ then there are $N(N-1)^3 = 9(8)^3 = 4608$ different intersector tertiary impacts available to review.

Each CI sector will be individually examined and the process of correlation laid out for the reader. The outcome of correlation analysis will be discussed from the

---

* IEEE-VGTC Symposium on Visualization 2007, *Path Visualization for Adjacency Matrices*, Zeqian Shen and Kwan-Liu Ma, University of California.

perspective of strengths and weakness. Depending on the weakness of the correlation result and the observed metrics, some attempts to correct observed metrics and improve correlations may be attempted using professional opinion and in some cases comment sense as a guideline. Such instances will be clearly identified and will involve the manipulation of dependency metrics, which are qualitative and more prone to error than the quantitative I–O metrics, which are derived directly from official government sources.

## CORRELATION OF INTERDEPENDENCY METRICS

First, a word about correlation and how it will be applied to CI interdependency analysis. A simple definition of correlation is the abandonment of independent movement for synchronized movement. In the case of the CI indicators for interdependency, we are assessing correlation between I–O statistics and data dependency. Ideally, the metrics will tend to indicate the same thing from sector to sector even though they are derived from very distinct and independent sources.

Correlation analysis will be conducted at the sector level for both inbound and outbound metrics. For instance, all inbound I–O metrics for the Transportation sector will be correlated with all dependency metrics from the Transportation sector.

United States and Canadian correlations will be conducted separately because I–O statistics from the two countries is distinct. Both the countries will be correlated against the same dependency data set, because the data set comprises information and metrics gathered from many multinational firms with a presence in both Canada and the United States. However, the data dependency metric set is weighted toward a Canadian sampling especially in the sectors, which are either public or publicly funded such as Safety, Government, Water, and to a certain extent Health.

The reader may have observed that the CI sectors of Government and Safety are managed differently in Chapter 2 (I–O econometrics) and Chapter 3 (data dependency). As discussed earlier in Chapters 1 and 2, Government and Safety are not divisible for econometrics analysis. The tasks which define Government and Safety are considered distinct industries and classifications under NAICS, which is used to organize the I–O statistics in Canada and the United States; however, the I–O is not broken down to those levels of granularity. For this reason, Government and Safety must be combined into a single sector for I–O analysis. To correlate the I–O metrics with the data dependency metrics, the Government and Safety sector from the data dependency metric had to be combined. (You cannot mathematically correlate data series with different number or data points. They have to have the same number of data points.) Government and Safety data dependency metrics were averaged into a single, combined Government/Safety metric to support correlation with I–O metrics.

A summary on how correlations are reported and interpretation of the size of a correlation follows. Correlation scores may range from $-1$ to $1$, where $-1$ is a perfect negative correlation and $1$ is a perfect positive correlation. A perfect negative correlation indicates that the variable moves in opposite direction whenever there is a change, e.g., for every six degrees variable A moves up variable B moves down exactly six degrees. A perfect positive correlation or simply correlation, for the purposes of this book (sorry to the statisticians and purists out there), is the opposite of negative correlation; for every 23 degrees variable A moves up, variable B also moves up exactly 23 degrees.

Quoting from Wikipedia:

Several authors have offered guidelines for the interpretation of a correlation coefficient. Cohen (1988), for example, has suggested the following interpretations for correlations in psychological research, in the table below.

| Correlation | Negative | Positive |
|---|---|---|
| Small | −0.29 to −0.10 | 0.10 to 0.29 |
| Medium | −0.49 to −0.30 | 0.30 to 0.49 |
| Large | −1.00 to −0.50 | 0.50 to 1.00 |

As Cohen himself has observed, however, all such criteria are in some ways arbitrary and should not be observed too strictly. This is because the interpretation of a correlation coefficient depends on the context and purposes. A correlation of 0.9 may be very low if one is verifying a physical law using high-quality instruments, but may be regarded as very high in the social sciences where there may be a greater contribution from complicating factors.*

## TIME AND DEPENDENCY LATENCY

Time is a dimension which is not included in the interdependency proxy-indicators, the metrics—already discussed in this book. For the purposes of both the quantitative econometric I–O statistics and the qualitative data dependency metrics, impacts were deterministic: they were assumed to have occurred. This approach was required for the reason that I–O statistics do not possess a time dimension any more granular that one year. Therefore, applying a time dimension to the data dependency metrics would have been mooted because the two metrics would have been measuring fundamentally different things. However, the data dependency discussions did include discussions around latency of dependency and this information has been applied here.

Latency of dependency is the amount of time between the commencement of an incident and the point at which a impact is felt: the latency between occurrence and impact. This is an important concept in CI interdependency assessment because an incident in a given CI sector will not necessarily invoke first-order, second-order, or tertiary impacts in all other sectors at the same time. Certain sectors have very short dependency latencies, meaning that an incident in that sector will impact dependent sectors very quickly. Other sectors will have long latencies, meaning that an incident in that sector may not have any effect until a certain period of time passes, after which the impact is felt.

Dependency latency is a characteristic of each CI sector. Can the goods or services be stockpiled or cached for use during incidents and outages? Can temporary substitutes be applied on short notice? How long can a substitute be expected to last? At what point in time does operational or strategic risk start to increase after an

---

* http://en.wikipedia.org/wiki/Correlation.

## TABLE 4.1
### Dependency Latency Intervals

| Name | Incident Duration | Description |
|------|-------------------|-------------|
| T1 | Less than one seconds to sixty minutes | Impacts felt in the form of unrecoverable financial losses or significantly elevated operating risks if the incident persists for up to 60 minutes |
| T2 | One to eight hours | Impacts felt in the form of unrecoverable financial losses or significantly elevated operating risks if incident continues for one to eight hours |
| T3 | Greater than eight hours | Impacts felt in the form of unrecoverable financial losses or significantly elevated operating risks if the incident continues for more than eight hours |

outage occurs? That is, increasing financial risks? Increasing production risks? Increasing regulatory risks? Increasing contractual (service-level-maintenance) risks? Increasing reputation (public relations) risks? Increasing market (loss of market share) risks?

Dependency may also be characterized by the dependent CI sector's unique requirement for the supplying sectors' goods or services. For instance, Health would have a shorter dependency latency with the Water sector than Finance, because Health requires clean water and waste disposal to run the hospital in a hygienic fashion.

The time dimension will be applied to the correlated CI interdependency metrics based upon information gathered during the executive interview process described in Chapter 3. Time will be applied as an overlay of the correlated interdependency matrixes at three intervals. Each interval indicates the timeframe within which an impact related to an incident in a CI sector will negatively change the operating environment either through the commencement of accumulating financial losses or the elevation of operating risks. Such a change may consist of production stoppage, product slowdowns, reductions in quality or regulatory breaches. Table 4.1 outlines the dependency latency intervals applied for the purposes of modeling cascading events at different incident durations.

## CANADIAN CORRELATED DEPENDENCY METRICS

Tables 4.2 through 4.4 present the data dependency metrics, which have been modified according to correlation analysis to most strongly indicate interdependencies between CI sectors. The details of the correlation analysis and modifications for each sector are to follow.

Table 4.2 is the complete, correlated CI sector-to-sector interdependency metrics expressed as a purely determinant impact (no dependency latency) for Canada. These are the metrics that would also apply at T3—incidents greater than eight hours when all interdependencies come into play across all CI sectors.

Table 4.3 represents the correlated CI sector-to-sector interdependency metrics as they are assessed from the time of impact to 60 minutes after impact. As opposed to Table 4.2 where only sector-to-sector interdependencies which come into effect

**TABLE 4.2**

**T3 (Greater Than Eight Hours) Correlated Canadian Interdependency Metrics**

| | | Inbound Dependencies | | | | | | | |
|---|---|---|---|---|---|---|---|---|---|
| CI Sector | Energy | Comms & IT | Fin | Health Care | Food | Water | Trans | Gov/ Safety | Manf |
| Energy | 9.33 | 3.50 | 2.50 | 4.19 | 1.80 | 5.00 | 7.00 | 3.62 | 6.75 |
| Comms & IT | 7.23 | 8.83 | 7.50 | 5.14 | 2.33 | 3.48 | 4.33 | 4.47 | 6.56 |
| Fin | 7.77 | 7.59 | 9.06 | 4.19 | 8.45 | 5.15 | 4.00 | 5.31 | 5.50 |
| Health Care | 4.86 | 2.37 | 3.00 | 8.24 | 1.80 | 4.20 | 3.25 | 7.00 | 2.61 |
| Food | 3.50 | 1.71 | 1.93 | 4.05 | 9.00 | 1.48 | 2.39 | 1.96 | 2.02 |
| Water | 4.69 | 1.96 | 2.19 | 4.90 | 1.47 | 5.68 | 2.89 | 2.08 | 2.24 |
| Trans | 5.50 | 3.75 | 4.38 | 4.86 | 4.53 | 2.81 | 7.24 | 4.71 | 5.57 |
| Gov/ Safety | 6.86 | 4.54 | 5.58 | 6.17 | 2.73 | 4.44 | 6.28 | 7.16 | 5.11 |
| Manf | 5.68 | 3.79 | 4.88 | 4.00 | 4.20 | 3.31 | 4.61 | 2.53 | 7.03 |

(Left axis label: Outbound Dependencies)

within the first 60 minutes after the impact are displayed. All other dependencies are set to zero (0.00) because they will result in neither financial losses nor operating risks during an interval of only 60 minutes or less from impact.

Table 4.4 represents the correlated CI sector-to-sector interdependency metrics as they are assessed from the time of impact up to eight hours after impact. All other dependencies are set to zero because they will result in neither financial losses or operating risks during an interval of eight hours or less from impact.

## Sector Dependency Latency and Cascading Threats

To arrive at better metrics, the authors have taken the opportunity to selectively revise certain data dependency scores, where they appear obviously out of sync with executive comments, professional opinion, and common sense. However, data dependency metrics are not revised indiscriminately. Only revisions that have a substantial strengthening effect on both inbound and outbound correlations are considered. Similarly, certain revisions that would have had a strengthening effect are not applied if they conflicted with executive comments, professional opinion, and empirical observations. All changes will be noted in the analysis tables for each sector. Within the analysis tables, all modifications to interdependency metrics will be documented.

**TABLE 4.3**

**T1 (Zero to Sixty Minutes) Dependency Latency Correlated Canadian Interdependency Metrics**

| | CI Sector | Inbound Dependencies | | | | | | | | |
|---|---|---|---|---|---|---|---|---|---|---|
| | | Energy | Comms & IT | Fin | Health Care | Food | Water | Trans | Gov/ Safety | Manf |
| Outbound Dependencies | Energy | 9.33 | 3.50 | 2.50 | 4.19 | 0.00 | 0.00 | 0.00 | 0.00 | 0.00 |
| | Comms & IT | 0.00 | 8.83 | 7.50 | 0.00 | 0.00 | 0.00 | 0.00 | 0.00 | 0.00 |
| | Fin | 0.00 | 0.00 | 9.06 | 0.00 | 0.00 | 0.00 | 0.00 | 0.00 | 0.00 |
| | Health Care | 0.00 | 0.00 | 0.00 | 0.00 | 0.00 | 0.00 | 0.00 | 0.00 | 0.00 |
| | Food | 0.00 | 0.00 | 0.00 | 0.00 | 0.00 | 0.00 | 0.00 | 0.00 | 0.00 |
| | Water | 0.00 | 0.00 | 0.00 | 0.00 | 0.00 | 0.00 | 0.00 | 0.00 | 0.00 |
| | Trans | 0.00 | 0.00 | 0.00 | 0.00 | 0.00 | 0.00 | 0.00 | 0.00 | 0.00 |
| | Gov/ Safety | 0.00 | 0.00 | 0.00 | 0.00 | 0.00 | 0.00 | 0.00 | 0.00 | 0.00 |
| | Manf | 0.00 | 0.00 | 0.00 | 0.00 | 0.00 | 0.00 | 0.00 | 0.00 | 0.00 |

Any modifications will involve changes to the dependency metrics to improve correlations with the econometrics and therefore provide stronger indications of interdependency. In the few cases where modifications are applied to the dependency metrics, the original metric will be displayed in brackets alongside the modified metric which will be used for the purposes of visualization of cascading risks in each section.

*Canadian Energy Sector*

Table 4.5 displays Canadian Energy sector econometrics (I–O) and the data dependency metrics (North American) side by side with the resulting correlations. Modifications to improve correlations are shown with the legacy (original) values in brackets.

There are strong correlations for both inbound and outbound interdependencies between Canadian econometrics and data dependency metrics for the Energy sector.

Four specific changes were applied to the Energy dependency data to correct what appears to be inconsistent in metrics which also improve correlations significantly, indicating that the corrections might result in a closer representation of reality.

## TABLE 4.4
## T2 (1–8 Hours) Dependency Latency Correlated Canadian Interdependency Metrics

| | | | | Inbound Dependencies | | | | | |
|---|---|---|---|---|---|---|---|---|---|
| CI Sector | Energy | Comms & IT | Fin | Health Care | Food | Water | Trans | Gov/ Safety | Manf |
| Energy | 9.33 | 3.50 | 2.50 | 4.19 | 1.80 | 5.00 | 7.00 | 3.62 | 6.75 |
| Comms & IT | 7.23 | 8.83 | 7.50 | 5.14 | 2.33 | 3.48 | 4.33 | 4.47 | 6.56 |
| Fin | 7.77 | 7.59 | 9.06 | 0.00 | 8.45 | 0.00 | 4.00 | 5.31 | 0.00 |
| Health Care | 0.00 | 0.00 | 0.00 | 8.24 | 0.00 | 0.00 | 0.00 | 7.00 | 0.00 |
| Food | 0.00 | 0.00 | 0.00 | 4.05 | 9.00 | 0.00 | 2.39 | 0.00 | 0.00 |
| Water | 4.69 | 1.96 | 0.00 | 4.90 | 1.47 | 5.68 | 0.00 | 0.00 | 0.00 |
| Trans | 0.00 | 0.00 | 4.38 | 4.86 | 4.53 | 0.00 | 7.24 | 4.71 | 5.57 |
| Gov/ Safety | 0.00 | 0.00 | 5.58 | 6.17 | 0.00 | 4.44 | 6.28 | 7.16 | 0.00 |
| Manf | 0.00 | 0.00 | 0.00 | 0.00 | 0.00 | 0.00 | 4.61 | 0.00 | 7.03 |

(Outbound Dependencies — row axis label)

The inbound dependency metrics (columns of the data dependency matrix) associated with Food sector were adjusted upward for the primary reason that it was rated substantially lower than all other sectors by Energy; possibly, inappropriately low given that amount of money that the Food sector spends on Energy. (In Canada, Food is the second largest spender after Government.) By increasing the dependency metrics for Food alone, substantial strength was gained in correlations.

An opportunity to further increase the correlation strength for inbound Energy metrics which was not applied is related to Water. Decreasing the dependency metrics for Water would have had positive effects for correlation, but would not make much sense given the fact that the Water sector and Energy are often business partners for the generation of electricity. Furthermore, the correlation score for Energy is already strong and the dependency metrics should be taken at face value wherever possible.

Outbound dependency metrics (rows of the data dependency matrix) for Energy were also altered in three instances. First, Water in this case the impact was to do with the Water sector's own inbound correlation and not the outbound Energy correlations, which was virtually un-impacted. The Water metric was substantially

## TABLE 4.5
## Canadian Energy Metrics Correlation

| Canadian Energy Sector | | | |
|---|---|---|---|
| | Canadian Inputs (C$ in Millions) | Inbound Dependency | Correlation Coefficient |
| Energy | 22,337 | 9.33 | Canadian inbound |
| Communications and IT | 2,045 | 7.23 | correlation |
| Finance | 5,007 | 7.77 | 0.77 (0.64) |
| Health | 39 | 4.86 | |
| Food | 131 | 3.50 (1.26) | Large |
| Water | 22 | 4.69 | |
| Transportation | 828 | 6.58 | |
| Safety/Government | 616 | 6.86 | |
| Manufacturing | 358 | 5.68 | |
| | Canadian Outputs (C$) | Outbound Dependency | |
| Energy | 22,337 | 9.33 | Canadian outbound |
| Communications and IT | 540 | 3.50 | correlation |
| Finance | 1,672 | 2.50 | 0.75 (0.92) |
| Health | 1,064 | 4.19 | |
| Food | 2,553 | 1.80 | Large |
| Water | 121 | 5.00 (2.96) | |
| Transportation | 5,229 | 7.00 (3.94) | |
| Safety/Government | 2,735 | 3.62 | |
| Manufacturing | 394 | 6.75 (3.07) | |

increased to make Energy the second most important sector from the dependency perspective. The intent was to better reflect the role of Water infrastructure such as dams and waterways, in the generation of power. Similarly, all Water infrastructure relies upon power to run pumps, gates, and purification systems. These systems may frequently have good redundancy built into them—but not necessarily any substantial capability around back-up power. It does not make particular sense that Finance was rated more highly than Energy before adjustment. In the end, this moderate change to Outbound energy metrics resulted in a major improvement in Water correlation. This adjustment and the impact on correlation indicate a substantial, unrecognized threat to Water originating from the Energy. Put differently, Water appears to have an unacknowledged degree of vulnerability to the Energy sector that has been partially but not fully controlled for in this adjustment.

The second CI sector to have its dependency metrics increased for Energy was the Transport sector. In this case, Energy is the second largest trading partner for the Energy sector and a well know and heavy consumer of energy products. Because the outbound metric for Energy is in effect the inbound metric for the Transportation sector, the change impacted both sectors and substantially improved correlations. This adjustment and the impact on correlation indicate a substantial, unrecognized threat to the Transportation sector originating from the Energy sector. Put differently, Transportation appears to have an unacknowledged degree of vulnerability to the Energy sector that has been partially but not fully controlled for in this adjustment.

The third CI sector to have its dependency metric increased for Energy is the Manufacturing sector. Manufacturing is the only one of the two sectors, which has a large balance of trade with another sector as opposed to within its own sector; in this case the designated Manufacturing industries spend more on Energy that they do internally. This indicates a significant degree of supply-chain dependency with the Energy sector and the dependency metric was increased to represent this observation. Because the outbound metric for Energy is in effect the inbound metric for the Manufacturing sector, the change impacted both sectors and substantially improved correlations. This adjustment and the impact on correlation indicate a substantial, unrecognized threat to the Manufacturing sector originating from the Energy sector. Put differently, Manufacturing appears to have an unacknowledged degree of vulnerability to the Energy sector that has been partially but not fully controlled for in this adjustment.

### Cascading Energy Threats in Canada

The cascade matrixes plot the first three levels of impact beyond the Energy sector impact, according to the primary dependency relations for all of the other sectors. For instance, each sector is assumed to receive a first-order impact from an Energy-related incident. Each sector then impacts other sectors, but only the strongest dependency relationship is displayed because it is the most likely to be catalyzed by the first-order impact. This is the second-order impact. Finally, using the same method, the second-order impact is tracked as a tertiary impact from the second-order-impact sector to the sector with which it has the strongest dependency relationship.

The following cascade matrixes illustrate the cascading threats from the Canadian Energy sector at T1 (zero to sixty minutes).

Figure 4.1 indicates that the first zero to sixty minutes of an incident in the Canadian Energy sector is most likely to pose cascading threats as tallied in Table 4.6. Finance, in addition to suffering the original impact, faces the possibility of a second impact cascading back to it through its interdependency relationships with Communications and IT.

Figure 4.2 illustrates the cascading threats from the Canadian Energy sector at T2 (one to eight hours). It indicates that the first one to eight hours of an incident in the Canadian Energy sector is most likely to pose cascading threats as tallied in Table 4.7. During this period, the Health and Food sectors indicate the most impacts when cascading impacts are included, followed closely by Transportation and Manufacturing.

Figure 4.3 illustrates the cascading threats from the Canadian Energy sector at T3 (beyond eight hours), showing all interdependency relationships coming into play. It indicates that an incident in the Canadian Energy sector is most likely to pose cascading threats as tallied in Table 4.8. Energy, in addition to suffering the original impact, faces the possibility of an additional five impacts cascading back to it through its interdependency relationships with other CI sectors. These "rebounding"

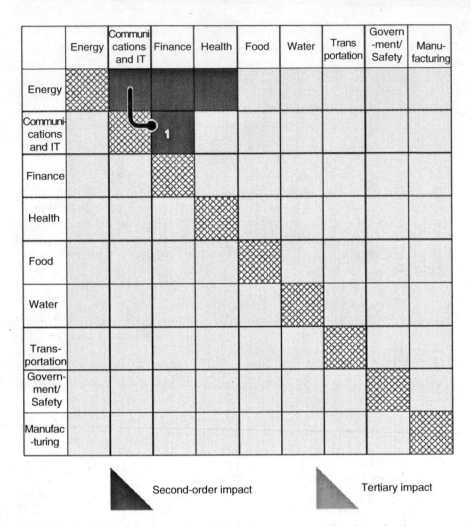

**FIGURE 4.1** T1 (zero to sixty minutes) Canadian energy cascading dependencies.

## TABLE 4.6
### T1 (Zero to Sixty Minutes) Canadian Energy Cascading Threats

|  | Energy | Commu-nications and IT | Finance | Health | Food | Water | Trans-portation | Safety/Govern-ment | Manu-facturing |
|---|---|---|---|---|---|---|---|---|---|
| First-order | 1 | 1 | 1 |  |  |  |  |  |  |
| Second-order |  |  | 1 |  |  |  |  |  |  |
| Tertiary |  |  |  |  |  |  |  |  |  |
| Total | 1 | 1 | 2 |  |  |  |  |  |  |

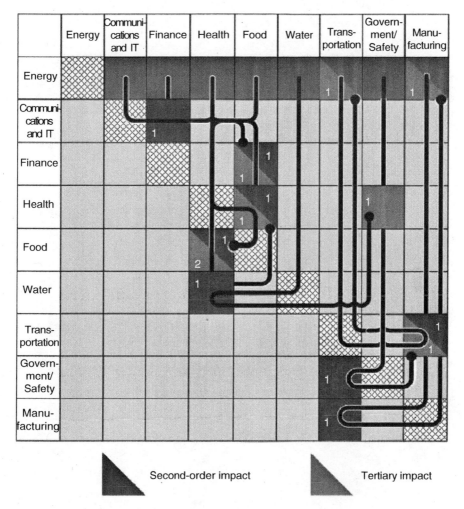

**FIGURE 4.2**   T2 (one to eight hours) Canadian Energy sector cascading impacts.

## TABLE 4.7
## T2 (One to Eight Hours) Canadian Energy Sector Cascading Impacts

| | Energy | Commu-nications and IT | Finance | Health | Food | Water | Trans-portation | Safety/Govern-ment | Manu-facturing |
|---|---|---|---|---|---|---|---|---|---|
| First-order | 1 | 1 | 1 | 1 | 1 | 1 | 1 | 1 | 1 |
| Second-order | | | 1 | 2 | 2 | | 2 | | 1 |
| Tertiary | | | | 2 | 2 | | 1 | 1 | 2 |
| Total | 1 | 1 | 2 | 5 | 5 | 1 | 4 | 2 | 4 |

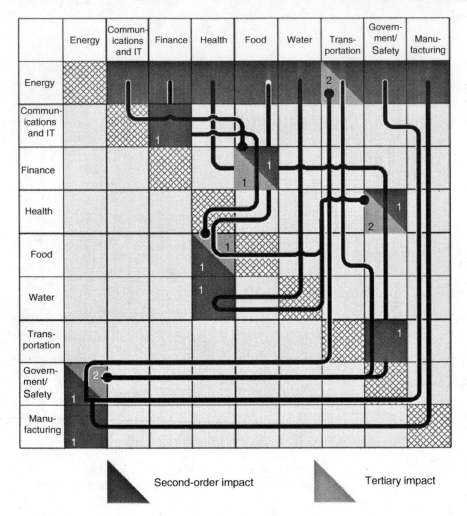

**FIGURE 4.3**  T3 (greater than eight hours) Canadian energy cascading dependencies.

**TABLE 4.8**

**T3 (Full) Canadian Energy Cascading Threats**

|  | Energy | Commu-nications and IT | Finance | Health | Food | Water | Trans-portation | Safety/Govern-ment | Manu-facturing |
|---|---|---|---|---|---|---|---|---|---|
| First-order | 1 | 1 | 1 | 1 | 1 | 1 | 1 | 1 | 1 |
| Second-order | 2 |  | 1 | 2 | 1 |  |  | 2 |  |
| Tertiary | 2 |  |  | 1 | 1 |  | 2 | 2 |  |
| Total | 5 | 1 | 2 | 4 | 3 | 1 | 3 | 5 | 1 |

impacts present a substantial risk of amplifying the original impact and intensifying the original incident. Similarly, Health, Transportation, and Government will encounter a large series of cascading threats as a result of a failure in Energy.

### Canadian Communications and IT Sector

Table 4.9 displays Canadian Communications and IT sector econometrics (I–O) and the data dependency metrics (North American) side by side with the resulting correlations. Modifications to improve correlations are shown with the legacy (original) values in brackets.

There are strong correlations for both inbound and outbound interdependencies between Canadian econometrics and data dependency metrics from the Communications and IT sector.

A single specific change was applied to the Communications and IT outbound dependency metric to correct what appears to be inconsistency in metrics and improve correlations significantly, with the result that corrections might result in a closer representation of reality.

## TABLE 4.9
## Canadian Communications and IT Metrics Correlation

| | Canadian Communications and IT Sector | | |
|---|---|---|---|
| | Canadian Inputs (C$ in Millions) | Inbound Dependency | Correlation Coefficient |
| Energy | 540 | 3.50 | Canadian inbound |
| Communications and IT | 7,062 | 8.83 | correlation |
| Finance | 2,025 | 7.59 | 0.85 (0.85) |
| Health | 61 | 2.37 | |
| Food | 126 | 1.71 | Large |
| Water | 25 | 1.96 | |
| Transportation | 393 | 3.75 | |
| Safety/Government | 398 | 4.54 | |
| Manufacturing | 143 | 3.79 | |
| | Canadian Outputs (C$) | Outbound Dependency | |
| Energy | 2,045 | 7.23 | Canadian outbound |
| Communications and IT | 7,062 | 8.83 | correlation |
| Finance | 7,798 | 7.50 (4.57) | 0.64 (0.36) |
| Health | 1,232 | 5.14 | |
| Food | 1,026 | 2.33 | Large |
| Water | 106 | 3.48 | |
| Transportation | 692 | 4.33 | |
| Safety/Government | 4,629 | 4.47 | |
| Manufacturing | 330 | 6.56 | |

An outbound dependency metric (rows of the data dependency matrix) for Communications and IT was also altered in the instance of the Finance sector. The Finance metric was substantially increased to improve the outbound correlation for Communications and IT, although the inbound correlation of the Finance sector degraded very slightly as a result. The outbound correlation for Communications and IT improved by 28 points with this change, although the inbound correlation for Finance decreased by a single point. This change was deemed appropriate given that spending on Communications and IT by Finance is by far the largest CI expenditure outside the Finance sector itself. When viewed from the perspective of the very large improvement in the outbound correlation in Communications and IT, this modification in a single Finance sector metric seems to indicate that Finance is perhaps underestimating its vulnerability to Communications and IT incidents.

## Cascading Communications and IT Threats in Canada

The cascade matrixes plot the first three levels of impact beyond the Communications and IT sector impact, according to the primary dependency relations for all of the other sectors. For instance, each sector is assumed to receive a first-order impact from a Communications and IT-related incident. Each sector then impacts other sectors, but only the strongest dependency relationship is displayed because it is the most likely to be catalyzed by the first-order impact. This is the second-order impact. Finally, using the same method, the second-order impact is tracked as a tertiary impact from the second-order-impact sector to the sector with which it has the strongest dependency relationship.

At T1 (zero to sixty minutes) there is a single impact outside the Communications and IT industry, within the financial sector. Although there may be some intrasector impacts associated with these incidents, the impacts do not result in unrecoverable financial losses or elevated operating risks in any interdependent CI sectors.

Figure 4.4 indicates that the first zero to sixty minutes of an incident in the Canadian Communications and IT sector is most likely to pose cascading threats as tallied in Table 4.10. Finance, in addition to suffering the original impact, faces the possibility of an additional impact cascading back to it through its interdependency relationships with Communications and IT.

Figure 4.5 illustrates the cascading threats from the Canadian Communications and IT sector at T2 (one to eight hours). It indicates that the first one to eight hours of an incident in the Canadian Energy sector is most likely to pose cascading threats as tallied in Table 4.11. During this period, the Transportation sector indicates the most impacts when cascading effects are included, followed closely by Manufacturing and Health.

Figure 4.6 illustrates the cascading threats from the Canadian communications and IT sector at T3 (beyond eight hours), showing all interdependency relationships coming into play. It indicates that an incident in the Canadian Communications and IT sector is most likely to pose cascading threats as tallied in Table 4.12. Energy, in addition to suffering the original impact, faces the possibility of an additional four impacts cascading back to it through its interdependency relationships with other CI sectors. Transportation, Health, Safety/Government will encounter a large series of cascading second and tertiary threats as a result of a failure in Communications and IT.

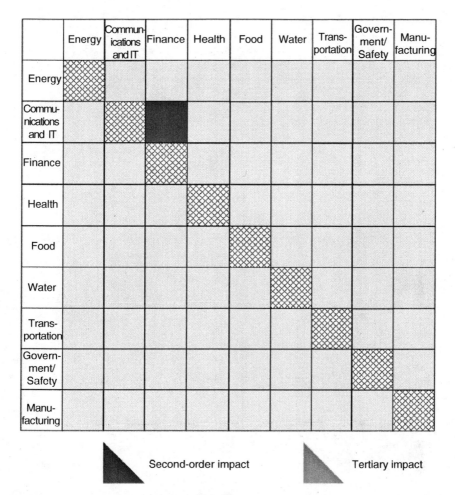

**FIGURE 4.4**    T1 (zero to sixty minutes) Canadian Communications and IT cascading impacts.

**TABLE 4.10**

**T1 (Zero to Sixty Minutes) Canadian Communications and IT Cascading Threats**

|  | Energy | Commu-nications and IT | Finance | Health | Food | Water | Trans-portation | Safety/Govern-ment | Manu-facturing |
|---|---|---|---|---|---|---|---|---|---|
| First-order |  | 1 | 1 |  |  |  |  |  |  |
| Second-order |  |  |  |  |  |  |  |  |  |
| Tertiary |  |  |  |  |  |  |  |  |  |
| Total |  | 1 | 1 |  |  |  |  |  |  |

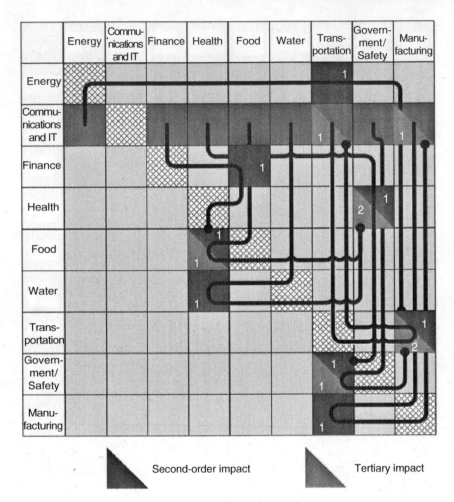

**FIGURE 4.5**   T2 (one to eight hours) Canadian Communications and IT cascading impacts.

**TABLE 4.11**

**T2 (One to Eight Hours) Canadian Communications and IT Cascading Impacts**

| | Energy | Commu-nications and IT | Finance | Health | Food | Water | Trans-portation | Safety/ Govern-ment | Manu-facturing |
|---|---|---|---|---|---|---|---|---|---|
| First-order | 1 | 1 | 1 | 1 | 1 | 1 | 1 | 1 | 1 |
| Second-order | | | | 2 | 1 | | 3 | 1 | 1 |
| Tertiary | | | | 1 | | | 2 | 2 | 3 |
| Total | 1 | 1 | 1 | 4 | 2 | 1 | 6 | 5 | 5 |

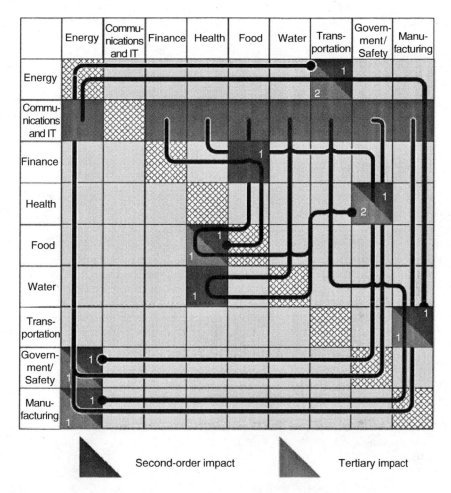

**FIGURE 4.6** T3 (greater than eight hours) Canadian Communications and IT cascading impacts.

**TABLE 4.12**

**Canadian Communications and IT Sector Cascading Impacts**

| | Energy | Commu-nications and IT | Finance | Health | Food | Water | Trans-portation | Safety/ Govern-ment | Manu-facturing |
|---|---|---|---|---|---|---|---|---|---|
| First-order | 1 | 1 | 1 | 1 | 1 | 1 | 1 | 1 | 1 |
| Second-order | 2 | | | 2 | 1 | | 1 | 1 | 1 |
| Tertiary | 2 | | | 1 | | | 2 | 2 | 1 |
| Total | 5 | 1 | 1 | 4 | 2 | 1 | 4 | 4 | 3 |

*Canadian Finance Sector*

Table 4.13 displays Canadian Finance sector econometrics (I–O) and the data dependency metrics (North American) side by side with the resulting correlations. Modifications to improve correlations are shown with the legacy (original) values in brackets.

There are strong correlations for both inbound and outbound interdependencies between Canadian econometrics and data dependency metrics for the Finance sector.

Three specific changes were applied to the Finance dependency data to correct what appears to be inconsistent in metrics which also improve correlations significantly, indicating that the corrections might result in a closer representation of reality.

The inbound dependency metrics (columns of the data dependency matrix) associated with Communications and IT sector were adjusted upward for the primary reason that it was rated very close to the median dependency score, yet it supplies four times the value of services to Finance as the nearest, largest supplier (Energy). Therefore, the rating appears inappropriately low given the amount of money that the Finance sector spends on Communications and IT. However, the change does not

## TABLE 4.13
## Canadian Finance Metrics Correlation

| Canadian Finance Sector | | | |
|---|---|---|---|
| | Canadian Inputs (C$ in Millions) | Inbound Dependency | Correlation Coefficient |
| Energy | 1,672 | 2.50 | Canadian inbound |
| Communications and IT | 7,798 | 7.50 (4.57) | correlation |
| Finance | 22,365 | 9.06 | 0.82 (0.63) |
| Health | 163 | 3.00 | |
| Food | 149 | 1.93 | Large |
| Water | 117 | 2.19 | |
| Transportation | 1,322 | 4.38 | |
| Safety/Government | 950 | 5.58 | |
| Manufacturing | 129 | 4.88 | |
| | Canadian Outputs (C$) | Outbound Dependency | |
| Energy | 5,007 | 7.77 | Canadian outbound |
| Communications and IT | 202 | 7.59 | correlation |
| Finance | 22,365 | 9.06 | 0.63 (0.54) |
| Health | 916 | 4.19 | |
| Food | 1,905 | 8.45 | Large |
| Water | 195 | 5.15 | |
| Transportation | 1,502 | 4.00 (7.19) | |
| Safety/Government | 2,084 | 5.31 | |
| Manufacturing | 419 | 5.5 (7.82) | |

in reality affect the overall inbound correlation for Finance, but it does have a substantial affect on the related outbound correlation score for Communications and IT. When viewed from the perspective of the very large improvement in the outbound correlation in Communications and IT, this modification in a single Finance sector metric seems to indicate that Finance is perhaps seriously underestimating its vulnerability to Communications and IT incidents.

Outbound dependency metrics (rows of the data dependency matrix) for Finance were also altered in two instances: for the Transportation sector and the Manufacturing sector. The Transportation and the Manufacturing metrics were substantially decreased to improve both the outbound correlation for Finance and the inbound correlation of the Transport and Manufacturing sectors. These changes were deemed appropriate given that spending on Transport and Manufacturing is moderate within the Finance sector. Furthermore, the outbound metrics are supplied by the sector executive to which the metric applies; in this case Transportation and Manufacturing executives. Therefore, we are actually modifying the response-metrics of these executives—not Finance executives—and we will discuss these changes in the context of inbound dependency within the Transportation and Manufacturing discussions to follow.

These adjustments and the impact on correlation indicate a potential and substantial, unrecognized threat to at least the Finance sector through the lack of inclusion of certain industries within the CI definitions currently in place. Alternately, Transport and Manufacturing may be overestimating dependency on Finance and under-applying resources to controls and safeguards associated with other CI relationships.

### Cascading Finance Threats in Canada

The cascade matrixes plot the first three levels of impact beyond the Finance sector impact, according to the primary dependency relations for all of the other sectors. For instance, each sector is assumed to receive a first-order impact from a Finance-related incident. Each sector then impacts other sectors, but only the strongest dependency relationship is displayed because it is the most likely to be catalyzed by the first-order impact. This is the second-order impact. Finally, using the same method, the second-order impact is tracked as a tertiary impact from the second-order-impact sector to the sector with which it has the strongest dependency relationship.

As per Table 4.3, the only Canadian sector experiencing an unrecoverable financial loss or significantly elevated operating risks when there is an incident of less than 60 minutes with the Finance sector is the Finance sector itself. No cascading impacts are proposed for incidents within the Finance sector lasting 60 minutes or less.

Figure 4.7 illustrates the cascading threats from the Canadian Finance sector at T2 (one to eight hours duration). It indicates that the first one to eight hours of an incident in the Canadian Finance sector is most likely to pose cascading threats as tallied in Table 4.14. During this period, the Transport sector indicates the most impacts when cascading impacts. The Manufacturing receives impacts only from cascades—it not directly suffers nonrecoverable financial losses or elevated operational risks directly from Finance incidents—but it may as a result of cascading impacts from Government/Safety and Transportation.

Figure 4.8 illustrates the cascading threats from the Canadian Finance sector (beyond eight hours), showing all interdependency relationships coming into play.

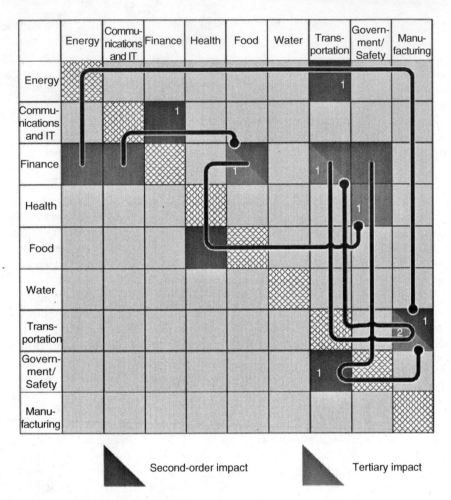

**FIGURE 4.7**   T2 (one to eight hours) Canadian Finance sector cascading impacts.

**TABLE 4.14**

**T2 (One to Eight Hours) Canadian Finance Cascading Impacts**

| | Energy | Communications and IT | Finance | Health | Food | Water | Transportation | Safety/Government | Manufacturing |
|---|---|---|---|---|---|---|---|---|---|
| First-order | 1 | 1 | 1 | | 1 | | 1 | 1 | |
| Second-order | | | 1 | 1 | | 1 | 1 | | 1 |
| Tertiary | | | | 1 | | | 2 | 1 | 1 |
| Total | 1 | 1 | 2 | 1 | 2 | 1 | 4 | 2 | 2 |

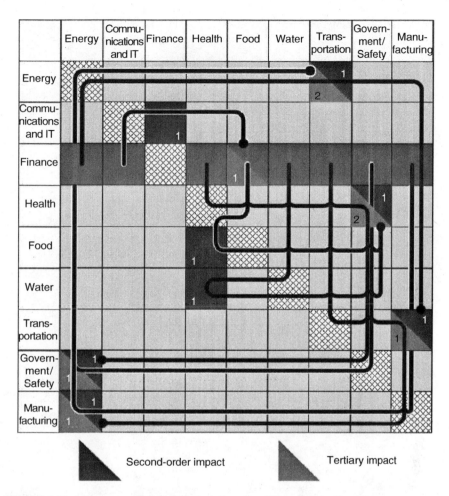

**FIGURE 4.8** T3 (greater than eight hours) Canadian Finance cascading threats.

It indicates that an incident in the Canadian finance sector is most likely to pose cascading threats as tallied in Table 4.15. Finance, in addition to suffering the original impact, faces the possibility of an additional impact cascading back to it

**TABLE 4.15**

**T3 (Greater Than Eight Hours) Canadian Finance Cascading Threats**

| | Energy | Commu- nications and IT | Finance | Health | Food | Water | Trans- portation | Safety/ Govern- ment | Manu- facturing |
|---|---|---|---|---|---|---|---|---|---|
| First-order | 1 | 1 | 1 | 1 | 1 | 1 | 1 | 1 | 1 |
| Second-order | 2 | | 1 | 2 | | | 1 | 1 | 1 |
| Tertiary | 2 | | | | 1 | | 2 | 2 | 1 |
| Total | 5 | 1 | 2 | 3 | 2 | 1 | 4 | 4 | 3 |

through its interdependency relationships with Communications and IT. Transportation and Energy especially will encounter a large series of cascading threats as a result of a failure in Finance.

## Canadian Health Sector

Table 4.16 displays Canadian Health sector econometrics (I–O) and the data dependency metrics (North American) side by side with the resulting correlations. Modifications to improve correlations are shown with the legacy (original) values in brackets.

There are strong correlations for both inbound and outbound interdependencies between Canadian econometrics and data dependency metrics for the Health sector.

Two specific changes are applied to the inbound dependency metrics for the Health sector to improve correlations and also controls for econometric patterns that are not necessarily representative of real consumption. First, changes to Water metrics for the Health sector. Water is known to be an important input to hospital

## TABLE 4.16
## Canadian Health Metrics Correlation

| Canadian Health Sector | | | |
|---|---|---|---|
| | Canadian Inputs (C$ in Millions) | Inbound Dependency | Correlation Coefficient |
| Energy | 1,064 | 4.19 | Canadian inbound |
| Communications and IT | 1,232 | 5.14 | correlation |
| Finance | 916 | 4.19 | 0.74 (0.73) |
| Health | 2,055 | 8.24 | |
| Food | 435 | 4.05 | Large |
| Water | 72 | 4.90 (3.81) | |
| Transportation | 229 | 4.86 | |
| Safety/Government | 339 | 6.17 | |
| Manufacturing | 120 | 4.00 (5.43) | |
| | Canadian Outputs (C$) | Outbound Dependency | |
| Energy | 39 | 4.86 | Canadian outbound |
| Communications and IT | 61 | 2.37 | correlation |
| Finance | 163 | 3.00 | 0.59 (0.48) |
| Health | 2,055 | 8.24 | |
| Food | 16 | 1.80 | Large |
| Water | 1 | 4.20 | |
| Transportation | 27 | 3.25 | |
| Safety/Government | 21,154 | 7.00 (6.01) | |
| Manufacturing | 9 | 2.61 | |

and laboratories because it is central to waste management, cleaning, and mainten-ance of sterile environments. In Chapter 2, we noted that spending on water by the Health sector is not necessarily accurately represented by the econometrics because municipal water bills for hospitals and government-funded laboratories might be paid for by sources within Safety and Government sector, and do not show up as an input to health. In Chapter 3, we highlighted the fact that the low level of commu-nications and data flowing between the Water sector and the Health sector represents a vulnerability to health. Together, the evidence is that a substantial increase of the Water metrics from 3.81 to 4.90 is warranted, moving Water from the last place of importance to the fourth place. The second change applied was to the Manufacturing sector that had its metric reduced from 5.43 (third place) to 4.00 (last place). The justification for this is driven by the fact that, as discussed in Chapters 2 and 3, Manufacturing in the context of health is primarily industrial chemicals and gases, but does not include the significantly larger amounts spend on pharmaceut-icals, which is contained within the Canadian Health sector itself under current definitions. This is a detailed distinction that may have not been evident to executives during questioning and increased importance was applied to Manufacturing under the assumption that this sector currently includes pharmaceutical manufacturing— which it does not.

An outbound dependency metric (rows of the data dependency matrix) for Health was also altered in one instance: for the Government and Safety sector. The Government and Safety metrics were increased to improve the outbound correlation for Health, although the inbound correlation of the Health sector was un-impacted as a result. The outbound correlation for Health improved by 12 points with this change. This change was deemed appropriate given that spending on Health by Government is by far the largest CI expenditure for Health as a whole, and Health is publicly funded in Canada. When viewed from the perspective of the very large improvement in the outbound correlation in Health, this modification in a single Government and Safety sector metric seems to indicate that Government and Safety is perhaps underestimating its vulnerability to Health incidents.

### Cascading Health Threats in Canada

The cascade matrixes plot the first three levels of impact beyond the Health sector impact, according to the primary dependency relations for all of the other sectors. For instance, each sector is assumed to receive a first-order impact from an Health-related incident. Each sector then impacts other sectors, but only the strongest dependency relationship is displayed because it is the most likely to be catalyzed by the first-order impact. This is the second-order impact. Finally, using the same method, the second-order impact is tracked as a tertiary impact from the second-order-impact sector to the sector with which it has the strongest dependency relationship.

At T1 (zero to sixty minutes) there are no impacts to other interdependent CI sectors indicated through the executive interviewing process. Although there may be some intrasector impacts associated with these short duration incidents, the impacts do not result in unrecoverable financial losses or elevated operating risks in any interdependent CI sectors.

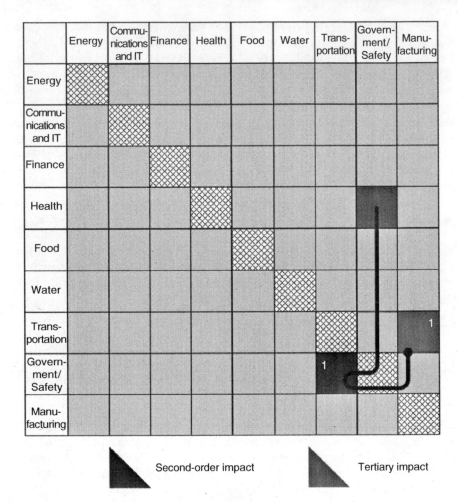

FIGURE 4.9   T2 (one to eight hours) Canadian Health sector cascading impacts.

Figure 4.9 illustrates the cascading threats from the Canadian Health sector at T2 (one to eight hours). It indicates that the first one to eight hours of an incident in the Canadian Health sector is most likely to pose cascading threats as tallied in Table 4.17.

**TABLE 4.17**

**T2 (One to Eight Hours) Canadian Health Cascading Impacts**

| | Energy | Commu- nications and IT | Finance | Health | Food | Water | Trans- portation | Safety/ Govern- ment | Manu- facturing |
|---|---|---|---|---|---|---|---|---|---|
| First-order | | | | 1 | | | | 1 | |
| Second-order | | | | | | | 1 | | |
| Tertiary | | | | | | | | 1 | 1 |
| Total | | | | | | | 1 | 2 | 1 |

During this period, Safety/Government sectors are the only sectors to be an impacted related to a Health incident lasting less than eight hours; however, Manufacturing and Transport are still prone to cascading impacts.

Figure 4.10 illustrates the cascading threats from the Canadian Health sector at T3 (beyond eight hours), showing all interdependency relationships coming into play. It indicates that an incident in the Canadian Health sector is most likely to pose cascading threats as tallied in Table 4.18. Relative to some of the other observed cascades, an impact in the Health sector seems to spread itself over a larger number of CI sectors, rather than being concentrated in a few sectors. Health itself experiences at least three different rebound impacts from other CI sectors. Energy suffers a substantial number of secondary and tertiary

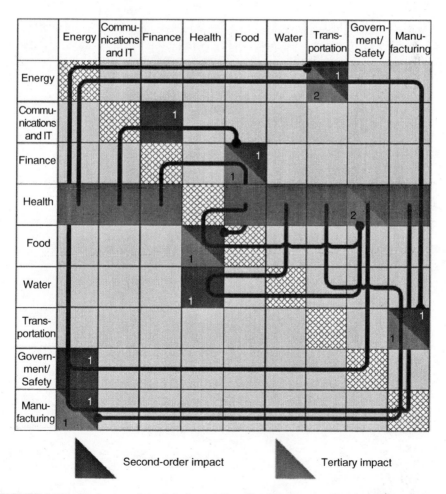

**FIGURE 4.10** T3 (greater than eight hours) Canadian Health cascading impacts.

## TABLE 4.18
### Canadian Health Cascading Threats

| | Energy | Communications and IT | Finance | Health | Food | Water | Transportation | Safety/Government | Manufacturing |
|---|---|---|---|---|---|---|---|---|---|
| First-order | 1 | 1 | 1 | 1 | 1 | 1 | 1 | 1 | 1 |
| Second-order | 2 | | 1 | 2 | 1 | | 1 | | 1 |
| Tertiary | 1 | | | 1 | 1 | | 2 | 2 | 1 |
| Total | 4 | 1 | 2 | 4 | 3 | 1 | 4 | 3 | 3 |

impacts—but Transportation and Health are also impacted similarly due to its dependence on Energy.

### Canadian Food Sector

Table 4.19 displays Canadian Food sector econometrics (I–O) and the data dependency metrics side by side with the resulting correlations. Modifications to improve correlations are shown with the legacy (original) values in brackets.

## TABLE 4.19
### Canadian Food Metrics Correlation

| Canadian Food Sector | | | |
|---|---|---|---|
| | Canadian Inputs (C$ in Millions) | Inbound Dependency | Correlation Coefficient |
| Energy | 2,553 | 1.80 | Canadian inbound |
| Communications and IT | 1,026 | 2.33 | correlation |
| Finance | 1,905 | 8.45 | 0.67 (0.46) |
| Health | 16 | 1.80 | |
| Food | 36,838 | 9.00 (6.53) | Large |
| Water | 52 | 1.47 | |
| Transportation | 1,531 | 4.53 | |
| Safety/Government | 249 | 2.73 | |
| Manufacturing | 130 | 4.20 | |
| | Canadian Outputs (C$) | Outbound Dependency | |
| Energy | 131 | 3.50 (1.26) | Canadian outbound |
| Communications and IT | 126 | 1.71 | correlation |
| Finance | 149 | 1.93 | 0.94 (0.88) |
| Health | 435 | 4.05 | |
| Food | 36,838 | 9.00 (6.53) | Large |
| Water | 1 | 1.48 | |
| Transportation | 105 | 2.39 | |
| Safety/Government | 330 | 1.96 | |
| Manufacturing | 65 | 2.02 | |

There are strong correlations for both inbound and outbound metrics between Canadian econometrics and data dependency metrics for the Food sector.

A single specific change was applied to the intrasector Food inbound/outbound dependency data to correct what appears to be inconsistency in metrics and improve correlations significantly, with the result that the corrections might result in a closer representation of reality. This is the only instance in the series of modifications that an intrasector metric is adjusted. Food consumes more goods and services from itself than all the other sectors combined by a factor of 5, and is the largest CI sector by dollar value. The intrasector metric for Food was raised from 6.54 to 9—the highest rating in the series, and resulted in an upward movement in the correlation of 19 points. The indication in this case is that Food, although maintaining that the industry is relatively balkanized during interviewing, is not really that dissegregated. Therefore, Food may pose both a threat and a vulnerability to itself by under-assessing the importance of its own native supply chain relative to the other CI sectors.

Two outbound dependency metric (rows of the data dependency matrix) for Food was also altered. The Government and Safety metrics were increased to improve the outbound correlation for Food, although the outbound correlation of the Energy sector was also improved as a result. This change was deemed appropriate given that Food was rated conspicuously low by Energy for inbound dependency—even though spending is stronger than other sectors and other workplace safety issues drove higher rating for Health and Water. When viewed from the perspective of the improvement in the outbound correlation in Food, this modification in the Energy sector metric seems to indicate that Energy is perhaps underestimating its vulnerability to Food incidents.

*Cascading Food Threats in Canada*
The cascade matrix plots the first three levels of impact beyond the Food sector impact, according to the primary dependency relations for all of the other sectors. For instance, each sector is assumed to receive a first-order impact from a Food-related incident. Each sector then impacts other sectors, but only the strongest dependency relationship is displayed because it is the most likely to be catalyzed by the first-order impact. This is the second-order impact. Finally, using the same method, the second-order impact is tracked as a tertiary impact from the second-order-impact sector to the sector with which it has the strongest dependency relationship.

At T1 (zero to sixty minutes) there are no impacts to interdependent CI sectors indicated through the executive interviewing process. Although there may be some intrasector impacts associated with these short duration incidents, the impacts do not result in unrecoverable financial losses or elevated operating risks in any interdependent CI sectors.

Figure 4.11 illustrates the cascading threats from the Canadian Food sector at T2 (one to eight hours). It indicates that the first one to eight hours of an incident in the Canadian Food sector is most likely to pose cascading threats as tallied in Table 4.20. During this period, the Health and Transportation sectors are the only sectors to indicate an impact related to a Food incident last up to eight hours; however, Safety/

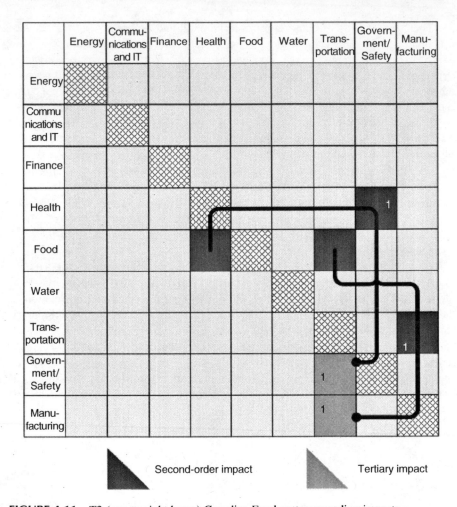

**FIGURE 4.11**   T2 (one to eight hours) Canadian Food sector cascading impacts.

**TABLE 4.20**

**T2 (One to Eight Hours) Canadian Food Cascading Impacts**

|  | Energy | Commu-<br>nications<br>and IT | Finance | Health | Food | Water | Trans-<br>portation | Safety/<br>Govern-<br>ment | Manu-<br>facturing |
|---|---|---|---|---|---|---|---|---|---|
| First-order |  |  |  | 1 | 1 |  | 1 |  |  |
| Second-order |  |  |  |  |  |  |  | 1 | 1 |
| Tertiary |  |  |  |  |  |  | 2 |  |  |
| Total |  |  |  | 1 | 1 |  | 3 | 1 | 1 |

Government and Manufacturing are still prone to cascading impacts. Overall, Transport appears to bare the brunt of a Food impact due to cascading impacts from Safety/Government and Manufacturing.

Figure 4.12 illustrates the cascading threats from the Canadian Food sector at T3 (beyond eight hours), showing all interdependency relationships coming into play. It indicates that an incident in the Canadian Food sector is most likely to pose cascading threats as tallied in Table 4.21. Relative to some of the other observed cascades, an impact in the Food sector seems to result in at least two different rebound impacts from other CI sectors. Energy suffers a substantial number of secondary and tertiary impacts, but Transportation is also impacted heavily due to its dependence on Energy.

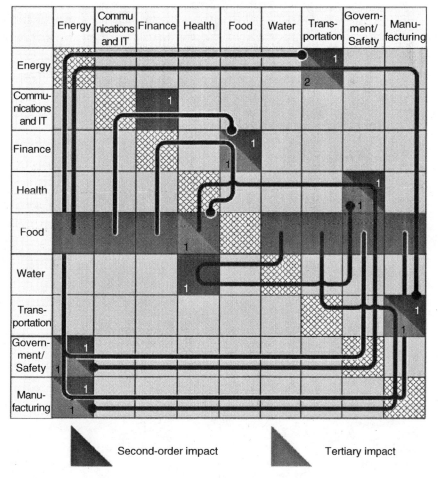

**FIGURE 4.12**    T3 (greater than eight hours) Canadian Food cascading impacts.

**TABLE 4.21**

**Canadian Food Cascading Threats**

| | Energy | Communications and IT | Finance | Health | Food | Water | Transportation | Safety/Government | Manufacturing |
|---|---|---|---|---|---|---|---|---|---|
| First-order | 1 | 1 | 1 | 1 | 1 | 1 | 1 | 1 | 1 |
| Second-order | 2 | | 1 | 1 | 1 | | 1 | 1 | 1 |
| Tertiary | 2 | | | 1 | 1 | | 2 | 1 | 1 |
| Total | 5 | 1 | 2 | 3 | 3 | 1 | 4 | 3 | 3 |

*Canadian Water Sector*

Table 4.22 displays Canadian Water sector econometrics (I–O) and the data dependency metrics (North American) side by side with the resulting correlations. Modifications to improve correlations are shown with the legacy (original) values in brackets.

**TABLE 4.22**

**Canadian Water Metrics Correlation**

| Canadian Water Sector | | | |
|---|---|---|---|
| | Canadian Inputs (C$ in Millions) | Inbound Dependency | Correlation Coefficient |
| Energy | 121 | 5.00 (2.96) | Canadian inbound |
| Communications and IT | 106 | 3.48 | correlation |
| Finance | 195 | 5.15 | 0.41 (0.22) |
| Health | 1 | 4.20 | |
| Food | 1 | 1.48 | Medium |
| Water | 1 | 5.68 | |
| Transportation | 8 | 2.81 | |
| Safety/Government | 21 | 4.44 | |
| Manufacturing | 6 | 3.31 | |
| | Canadian Outputs (C$) | Outbound Dependency | |
| Energy | 22 | 4.69 | Canadian outbound |
| Communications and IT | 25 | 1.96 | correlation |
| Finance | 117 | 2.19 | −0.58 (−0.64) |
| Health | 72 | 4.90 (3.81) | |
| Food | 52 | 1.47 | Small |
| Water | 1 | 5.68 | |
| Transportation | 35 | 2.89 | |
| Safety/Government | 170 | 2.08 | |
| Manufacturing | 13 | 2.24 | |

Water is the most problematic Canadian CI sector to assess using I–O and data dependency correlation, because it is often a service paid for by municipal government. Municipal government then bills users through taxes and property levies. For this reason, the flow of payments (outputs) to Water is obfuscated within Government revenues.

There are moderate correlations for inbound interdependencies between Canadian econometrics and data dependency metrics for the Water sector, and essentially no positive correlations for outbound dependencies.

A single modification was applied to the inbound dependencies to try and strengthen correlation from weak to a moderate level. This was achieved by raising the Energy inbound dependency rating from 2.96 to 5.00, which had the effect of providing Energy with the second highest intersector dependency along with the second highest intersector spending. This modification was considered rational because Water and Energy frequently have collaborative agreements for the production of power. These agreements may require a significant amount of coordination, communication, and integration. For instance, information and data from the Energy sector would be important to the generation or sale of power. Similarly and probably more importantly, the Water infrastructure amounts to a form of heavy industry, consuming significant amount of energy resources in the management of potable and wastewater. This infrastructure cannot be readily supported for extended periods with back-up power such as might be generated on-site. The indication is that Water underestimates the threat associated with a loss of Energy supplies, and believes itself to be substantially isolated from all infrastructures for operational purposes. Given that Energy is the largest expense for Water outside financial services, it is fair to assume that Energy is a central operational input to Water.

At least two potential modifications to inbound Water metrics were not applied, but would have increased correlation substantially. First, Finance dependency metrics could have been raised given that in Canada the Water sector spends a significant amount on these services; however, given that no sectors, including Energy, received high ratings from Water it was determined that a modification was not appropriate because Finance already has the highest overall dependency rating in Canada. Second, the dependency metrics for water could have been substantially lowered to also increase the overall correlation; however, large intrasector dependency is the rule not the acceptation to CI interdependency. To lower the intrasector Water dependency metric would have been very much against executive perceptions and the precedent in other sectors.

One specific change is applied to the outbound dependency metrics for the Water sector to improve correlations and also control for econometric patterns that are not necessarily representative of real consumption: changes to Water metrics for the Health sector. Water is known to be an important input to hospitals and laboratories because it is central to waste management, cleaning, and the maintenance of sterile environments. In Chapter 2, we noted that spending on water by the Health sector is not necessarily accurately represented by the econometrics because municipal water bills for hospital and government-funded laboratories might be paid for both sources within Safety and Government sector, and do not show up as an input to Health. In Chapter 3, we highlighted the fact that the low level of communications and data flowing between the water and the Health sectors represents vulnerability. Together, the evidence is that a substantial increase of the Water metrics from 3.81 to 4.90 is warranted, moving Health from the fourth place of importance to the second place only after intrasector dependency.

## Cascading Water Threats in Canada

The cascade matrixes plot the first three levels of impact beyond the Water sector impact, according to the primary dependency relations for all of the other sectors. For instance, each sector is assumed to receive a first-order impact from a Water-related incident. Each sector then impacts other sectors, but only the strongest dependency relationship is displayed because it is the most likely to be catalyzed by the first-order impact. This is the second-order impact. Finally, using the same method, the second-order impact is tracked as a tertiary impact from the second-order-impact sector to the sector with which it has the strongest dependency relationship.

At T1 (zero to sixty minutes) there are no impacts to interdependent CI sectors, as indicated through the executive interviewing process. Although there may be some intrasector impacts associated with these incidents, the impacts do not result in unrecoverable financial losses or elevated operating risks in any interdependent CI sectors.

Figure 4.13 illustrates the cascading threats from the Canadian Water sector at T2 (one to eight hours). It indicates that the first one to eight hours of an incident, the Canadian Water sector is most likely to pose cascading threats as tallied in Table 4.23. During this period, the Energy, Communications and IT, Health, and Food sectors indicate an impact related to a Water incident last up to eight hours. However, Finance, Transportation, and Safety/Government are still prone to cascading impacts.

Figure 4.14 illustrates the cascading threats from the Canadian Water sector at T3 (beyond eight hours), showing all interdependency relationships coming into play. It indicates that an incident in the Canadian Water sector is most likely to pose cascading threats as tallied in Table 4.24. Relative to some of the other observed cascades, an impact in the Water sector seems to spread itself over a larger number of CI sectors, rather than being concentrated in a few sectors. Energy, as usual, suffers a substantial number of secondary and tertiary impacts—but Food is also impacted similarly due to its dependence on Water.

## Canadian Transportation Sector Correlations

Table 4.25 displays Canadian Transportation sector econometrics (I–O) and the data dependency metrics (North American) side by side with the resulting correlations. Modifications to improve correlations are shown with the legacy (original) values in brackets.

There are strong correlations for both inbound and outbound interdependencies between Canadian econometrics and data dependency metrics for the Transportation sector.

Two inbound dependency modifications were made to the Canadian Transportation sector to try and strengthen correlation from moderate to a strong level. First, the metric associated with Energy sector dependency was raised from 3.94 to 7.0; from the sixth highest to the second highest. This modification was justified because

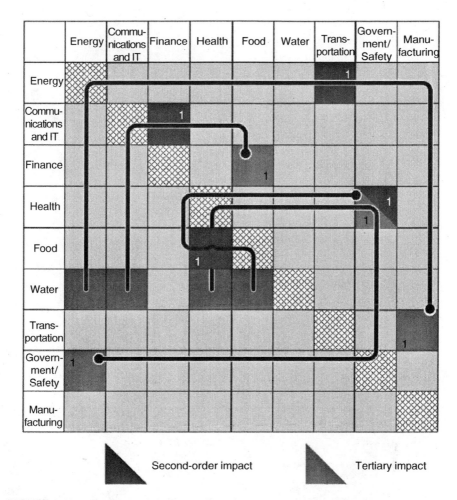

**FIGURE 4.13** T2 (one to eight hours) Canadian Water sector cascading impacts.

**TABLE 4.23**

**T2 (One to Eight Hours) Canadian Water Cascading Impacts**

| | Energy | Commu-nications and IT | Finance | Health | Food | Water | Trans-portation | Safety/ Govern-ment | Manu-facturing |
|---|---|---|---|---|---|---|---|---|---|
| First-order | 1 | 1 | | 1 | 1 | | | | |
| Second-order | | | 1 | 1 | | | 1 | 1 | |
| Tertiary | 1 | | | | | | | 1 | 1 |
| Total | 2 | 1 | 1 | 2 | 1 | 1 | 1 | 2 | 1 |

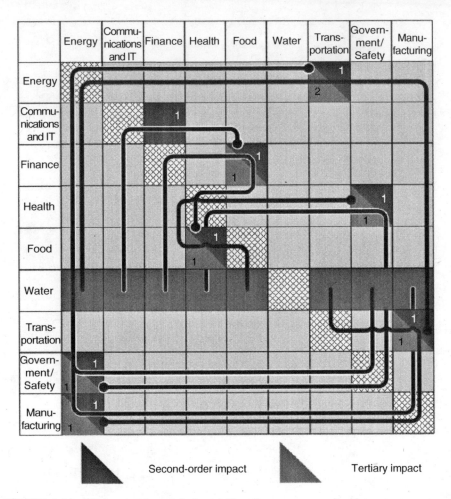

**FIGURE 4.14**   T3 (greater than eight hours) Canadian water cascading impacts.

**TABLE 4.24**

**T3 (Greater Than Eight Hours) Canadian Water Cascading Impacts**

| | Energy | Commu-nications and IT | Finance | Health | Food | Water | Trans-portation | Safety/Govern-ment | Manu-facturing |
|---|---|---|---|---|---|---|---|---|---|
| First-order | 1 | 1 | 1 | 1 | 1 | 1 | 1 | 1 | 1 |
| Second-order | 2 | | 1 | 1 | 1 | | 1 | 1 | 1 |
| Tertiary | 2 | | | 1 | 1 | | 2 | 1 | 1 |
| Total | 5 | 1 | 2 | 3 | 3 | 1 | 4 | 3 | 3 |

**TABLE 4.25**
**Canadian Transportation Metrics Correlation**

| | Canadian Transportation Sector | | |
|---|---|---|---|
| | **Canadian Inputs (C$ in Millions)** | **Inbound Dependency** | **Correlation Coefficient** |
| Energy | 5,229 | 7.00 (3.94) | Canadian inbound |
| Communications and IT | 692 | 4.33 | correlation |
| Finance | 1,502 | 4.00 (7.19) | 0.80 (0.46) |
| Health | 27 | 3.25 | |
| Food | 105 | 2.39 | Large |
| Water | 35 | 2.89 | |
| Transportation | 6,115 | 7.24 | |
| Safety/Government | 452 | 6.28 | |
| Manufacturing | 347 | 4.61 | |
| | **Canadian Outputs (C$)** | **Outbound Dependency** | |
| Energy | 828 | 6.58 | Canadian outbound |
| Communications and IT | 393 | 3.75 | correlation |
| Finance | 1,322 | 4.38 | 0.76 (0.66) |
| Health | 229 | 4.86 | |
| Food | 1,531 | 4.53 | Large |
| Water | 8 | 2.81 | |
| Transportation | 6,115 | 7.24 | |
| Safety/Government | 1,324 | 4.71 | |
| Manufacturing | 302 | 5.57 | |

Energy is the single largest supplier to the Canadian Transportation sector, with spending on the Energy sector almost equal to intrasector Transportation spending.

A second modification was applied to the inbound dependencies by lowering the Finance inbound dependency rating from 7.19 to 4.00, which had the effect of lowering Finance from the second highest dependency rating to the fourth highest rating for Transportation. This modification was considered rational because Transportation is a sector with very large, regulated security obligations concerning the movement of goods and people and Safety and Government is a critical dependency. Placing Finance above this regulatory and security dependency does not appear rational. Similarly, the Transportation industry is built upon logistics management in many regards and the underlying infrastructure to support logistics is the Communications and IT sector, another critical operational input. Finally, maintenance and the amortization of capital equipment are central to the profitability of the various business within the Transport sectors; all of which are capital intensive, communication with manufacturers to support maintenance and uptime of equipment has a direct impact upon the viability of the sector businesses. All this is not to minimize the importance of the Finance sector to Transportation, especially because Finance is the third largest expenditure. The indication is that Transport overestimates the threat associated with a loss of financial services relative to other suppliers of goods and services.

No modifications were applied to the outbound dependency information for the Transportation sector.

## Cascading Transportation Threats in Canada

The cascade matrixes plot the first three levels of impact beyond the Transportation sector impact, according to the primary dependency relations for all of the other sectors. For instance, each sector is assumed to receive a first-order impact from a Transportation-related incident. Each sector then impacts other sectors, but only the strongest dependency relationship is displayed because it is the most likely to be catalyzed by the first-order impact. This is the second-order impact. Finally, using the same method, the second-order impact is tracked as a tertiary impact from the second-order-impact sector to the sector with which it has the strongest dependency relationship.

At T1 (zero to sixty minutes) there are no impacts to other interdependent CI sectors indicated through the executive interviewing process. Although there may be some intrasector impacts associated with these incidents, the impacts do not result in unrecoverable financial losses or elevated operating risks in any interdependent CI sectors.

Figure 4.15 illustrates the cascading threats from the Canadian Transportation sector at T2 (one to eight hours). It indicates that the first one to eight hours of an incident in the Canadian Transportation sector is most likely to pose cascading threats as tallied in Table 4.26. During this period, the Finance, Health, Food, Safety and Government, and Manufacturing sectors all indicate an impact related to a Transportation incident lasting up to eight hours; however, the Transportation sector itself receives among the most overall impact not only due to intrasector effects but cascading impacts from other sectors which can exacerbate the incident.

Figure 4.16 illustrates the cascading threats from the Canadian Transportation sector at T3 (beyond eight hours), showing all interdependency relationships coming into play. It indicates that an incident in the Canadian Transportation sector is most likely to pose cascading threats as tallied in Table 4.27. An impact in the Transportation sector seems concentrate impacts within the Energy, Health and Safety/Government sectors. The Transportation sector itself will be impacted by another three cascading impacts from other CI sectors associated, in addition to intrasector impacts.

## Canadian Safety and Government Sector Correlations

In Chapter 2, Safety and Government were grouped together into a single sector because the different infrastructure roles were not available individually at the econometric I–O level. Police, fire, and other safety services are necessarily grouped with other government services such as regulation and social services. The methodology employed in Chapter 3 for the collection of interdependency metrics (executive interviewing) made it possible to keep metrics for the Safety and Government sectors separate. To correlate these metrics, it becomes necessary to have an equal

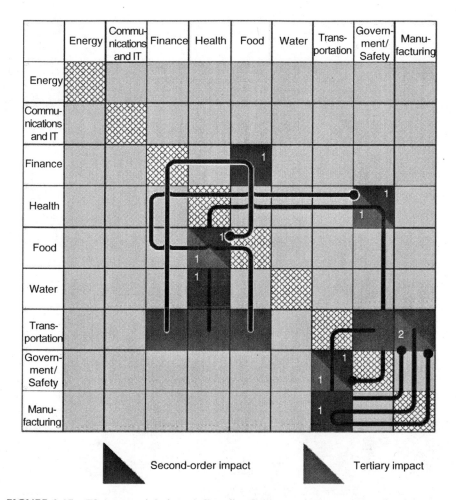

**FIGURE 4.15** T2 (one to eight hours) Canadian Transportation sector cascading impacts.

**TABLE 4.26**

**T2 (One to Eight Hours) Canadian Transportation Cascading Impacts**

| | Energy | Commu- nications and IT | Finance | Health | Food | Water | Trans- portation | Safety/ Govern- ment | Manu- facturing |
|---|---|---|---|---|---|---|---|---|---|
| First-order | | | 1 | 1 | 1 | | | 1 | 1 |
| Second-order | | | | 1 | 1 | | 2 | 1 | |
| Tertiary | | | | 1 | | | 1 | 1 | 2 |
| Total | | | 1 | 3 | 2 | | 3 | 3 | 3 |

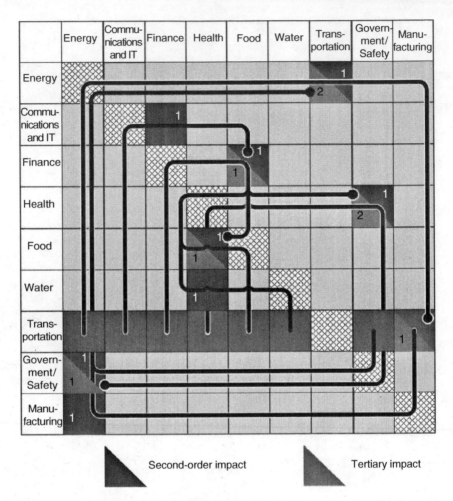

**FIGURE 4.16**   T3 (greater than eight hours) Canadian Transportation cascading impacts.

**TABLE 4.27**

**T3 (Greater Than Eight Hours) Canadian Transportation Cascading Impacts**

| | Energy | Commu-nications and IT | Finance | Health | Food | Water | Trans-portation | Safety/Govern-ment | Manu-facturing |
|---|---|---|---|---|---|---|---|---|---|
| First-order | 1 | 1 | 1 | 1 | 1 | 1 | 1 | 1 | 1 |
| Second-order | 2 | | 1 | 2 | 1 | | 1 | 1 | |
| Tertiary | 1 | | | 1 | 1 | | 2 | 2 | 1 |
| Total | 4 | 1 | 2 | 4 | 3 | 1 | 4 | 4 | 2 |

number of metrics, therefore the Safety and Government metrics for data dependency (Chapter 3 metrics) have to be combined into a single metric. This was accomplished through simple averaging of the two different metrics for each inbound and outbound relationship.

*Canadian Correlations*

Table 4.28 displays Canadian Safety/Government sector econometrics (I–O) and the data dependency metrics (North American) side by side with the resulting correlations. Modifications to improve correlations are shown with the legacy (original) values in brackets.

There are strong correlations for both inbound and outbound interdependencies between Canadian econometrics and data dependency metrics for the Canadian Safety/Government sector.

A single modification was applied to the inbound dependencies to try and strengthen correlation for the Canadian Safety and Government sector. This was achieved by raising the Health inbound dependency rating from 6.01 to 7.00, which did not impact the ordinal placement of Health but improved correlation by 12 points. This modification was considered rational because Health is by far the largest source

## TABLE 4.28
## Canadian Safety/Government Metrics Correlation

| Canadian Safety/Government Sector | | | |
| --- | --- | --- | --- |
| | Canadian Inputs (C$ in Millions) | Inbound Dependency | Correlation Coefficient |
| Energy | 2,735 | 3.62 | Canadian inbound |
| Communications and IT | 4,629 | 4.47 | correlation |
| Finance | 2,084 | 5.31 | 0.67 (0.54) |
| Health | 21,154 | 7.00 (6.01) | |
| Food | 330 | 1.96 | Large |
| Water | 170 | 2.08 | |
| Transportation | 1,324 | 4.71 | |
| Safety/Government | 4,845 | 7.16 | |
| Manufacturing | 312 | 2.53 | |
| | Canadian Outputs (C$) | Outbound Dependency | |
| Energy | 616 | 6.86 | Canadian outbound |
| Communications and IT | 398 | 4.54 | correlation |
| Finance | 950 | 5.58 | 0.52 (0.52) |
| Health | 339 | 6.17 | |
| Food | 249 | 2.73 | Large |
| Water | 21 | 4.44 | |
| Transportation | 452 | 6.28 | |
| Safety/Government | 4,845 | 7.16 | |
| Manufacturing | 68 | 5.11 | |

of spending for Canadian Safety and Government and therefore it is expected that there would be a significant amount of this present in the supply chain for Safety and Government. All this is not to minimize the importance of other sectors to Safety and Government; however the indication is that Safety and Government underestimates the threat associated with a loss of Health services relative to other suppliers of goods and services.

No modifications were applied to the outbound dependency information for the Canadian Safety and Government sector.

### Cascading Safety/Government Threats in Canada

The cascade matrixes plot the first three levels of impact beyond the Safety/Government sector impact, according to the primary dependency relations for all of the other sectors. For instance, each sector is assumed to receive a first-order impact from a Safety/Government-related incident. Each sector then impacts other sectors, but only the strongest dependency relationship is displayed because it is the most likely to be catalyzed by the first-order impact. This is the second-order impact. Finally, using the same method, the second-order impact is tracked as a tertiary impact from the second-order-impact sector to the sector with which it has the strongest dependency relationship.

At T1 (zero to sixty minutes) there are no impacts to other interdependent CI sectors indicated through the executive interviewing process. Although there may be some intrasector impacts associated with these incidents, the impacts do not result in unrecoverable financial losses or elevated operating risks in any interdependent CI sectors.

Figure 4.17 illustrates the cascading threats from the Canadian Safety/Government sector at T2 (one to eight hours). It indicates that the first one to eight hours of an incident impacting the Canadian Safety/Government sector, it is most likely to pose cascading threats as tallied in Table 4.29. During this period, the Transportation and Health sectors indicate the largest number of impacts related to cascades from other CI sectors. The Safety and Government sector itself receives one additional cascading impacts to exacerbate an incident.

Figure 4.18 illustrates the cascading threats from the Canadian Safety/Government sector at T3 (beyond eight hours), showing all interdependency relationships coming into play. It indicates that an incident in the Canadian Safety/Government sector is most likely to pose cascading threats as tallied in Table 4.30. An impact in the Safety and Government sector spreads cascading impacts almost evenly across the entire Canadian CI sector-economy relative to some of the concentrations seen in other cascade matrixes. Although Communications and IT and Water do not appear to suffer any cascading impacts from an incident in Safety and Government, it must be recalled that only the most potent dependency relationships are traced for the purposes of adjacency matrixes. Table 4.30 should be interpreted to mean that Communications and IT and Water are not primary targets for cascades from Safety and Government, but may certainly still be vulnerable to cascades through second- or third-order relationships not illustrated here.

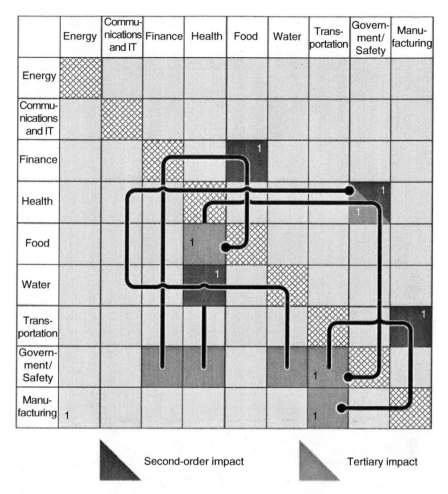

**FIGURE 4.17**  T2 (one to eight hours) Canadian Safety/Government sector cascading impacts.

**TABLE 4.29**

**T2 (One to Eight Hours) Canadian Safety/Government Cascading Impacts**

| | Energy | Commu-nications and IT | Finance | Health | Food | Water | Trans-portation | Safety/ Govern-ment | Manu-facturing |
|---|---|---|---|---|---|---|---|---|---|
| First-order | | | 1 | 1 | | 1 | 1 | 1 | |
| Second-order | | | | 1 | 1 | | | 1 | 1 |
| Tertiary | 1 | | | 1 | | | 2 | | |
| Total | 1 | | 1 | 3 | 1 | 1 | 3 | 2 | 1 |

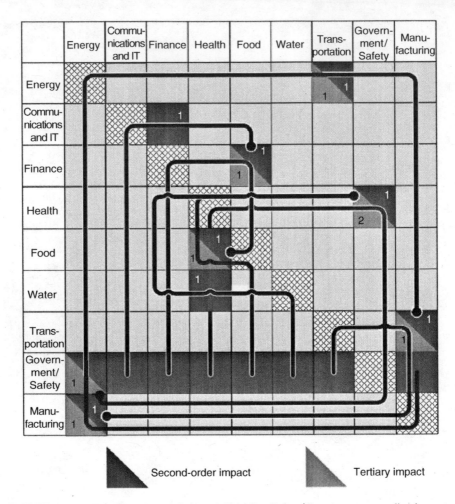

**FIGURE 4.18**  T3 (greater than eight hours) Canadian Safety/Government cascading impacts.

**TABLE 4.30**

**T3 (Greater Than Eight Hours) Canadian Safety/Government Cascading Impacts**

|  | Energy | Commu-nications and IT | Finance | Health | Food | Water | Trans-portation | Safety/Govern-ment | Manu-facturing |
|---|---|---|---|---|---|---|---|---|---|
| First-order | 1 | 1 | 1 | 1 | 1 | 1 | 1 | 1 | 1 |
| Second-order | 1 |  | 1 | 2 | 1 |  | 1 | 1 | 1 |
| Tertiary | 2 |  |  | 1 | 1 |  | 1 | 2 | 1 |
| Total | 4 | 1 | 2 | 4 | 3 | 1 | 3 | 4 | 3 |

*Canadian Manufacturing Sector*

Table 4.31 displays Canadian Manufacturing sector econometrics (I–O) and the data dependency metrics (North American) side by side with the resulting correlations. Modifications to improve correlations are shown with the legacy (original) values in brackets.

There are strong correlations for both inbound and outbound interdependencies between Canadian econometrics and data dependency metrics for the Canadian Manufacturing sector.

A modification was applied to the inbound Energy metric to increase it to the second highest from fifth. This change was rationalized on the basis of the large spending of the Transportation sector on Energy goods and services. This spending is in fact one of only two instances where intrasector spending was exceeded by a single sector of the supply chain. The indication related to this change is that designated Manufacturing industries underestimate the threat associated with a loss of Energy goods and services relative to other CI suppliers of goods and services.

A second modification was applied to the inbound dependencies to try and strengthen correlation for the Canadian Manufacturing sector. This was achieved by lowering the Finance inbound dependency rating from 7.82 to 5.50, which had the impact of moving Finance from the highest ranking inbound dependency to the

**TABLE 4.31**

**Canadian Manufacturing Sector Metrics Correlation**

| | Canadian Manufacturing Sector | | |
|---|---|---|---|
| | **Canadian Inputs (C$ in Millions)** | **Inbound Dependency** | **Correlation Coefficient** |
| Energy | 3,553 | 6.75 (3.07) | Canadian inbound |
| Communications and IT | 394 | 6.56 | correlation |
| Finance | 753 | 5.50 (7.82) | 0.67 (0.21) |
| Health | 93 | 2.61 | Large |
| Food | 96 | 2.02 | |
| Water | 78 | 2.24 | |
| Transportation | 520 | 5.57 | |
| Safety/Government | 180 | 5.11 | |
| Manufacturing | 3,351 | 7.03 | |
| | **Canadian Outputs (C$)** | **Outbound Dependency** | |
| Energy | 528 | 5.68 | Canadian outbound |
| Communications and IT | 192 | 3.79 | correlation |
| Finance | 167 | 4.88 | 0.75 (0.70) |
| Health | 339 | 4.00 (5.43) | Large |
| Food | 309 | 4.20 | |
| Water | 8 | 3.31 | |
| Transportation | 355 | 4.61 | |
| Safety/Government | 445 | 2.53 | |
| Manufacturing | 3,351 | 7.03 | |

fourth ranking. This modification was considered rational and applied for two primary reasons. First, the dependency seemed clearly out of proportion relative to the spending on financial services, and relative to the dependencies applied to other sectors with econometric inputs very similar to Manufacturing. The second reason this change appeared rational was because of the substantial improvement it generated in the outbound correlations for the Finance sector, improving the outbound Finance correlation by 0.11. The indication related to this change is that Manufacturing overestimates the threat associated with a loss of financial services relative to other suppliers of goods and services.

The second change applied was to the outbound Health sector, which had its metric reduced from 5.43 (third place) to 4.00 (fourth place). The justification for this is driven by the fact that, as discussed in Chapter 2 and also in Chapter 3, Manufacturing in the context of Health is primarily industrial chemicals and gases, but does not include the significantly larger amounts spend on pharmaceuticals, which in Canada is considered part of the Health sector itself. This is a detailed distinction which may have not been evident to executives during questioning and increased importance was applied to Manufacturing under the assumption that this sector currently includes pharmaceutical manufacturing—which it does not.

## Cascading Manufacturing Threats in Canada

The cascade matrixes plot the first three levels of impact beyond the Manufacturing sector impact, according to the primary dependency relations for all of the other sectors. For instance, each sector is assumed to receive a first-order impact from a Manufacturing-related incident. Each sector then impacts other sectors, but only the strongest dependency relationship is displayed because it is the most likely to be catalyzed by the first-order impact. This is the second-order impact. Finally, using the same method, the second-order impact is tracked as a tertiary impact from the second-order-impact sector to the sector with which it has the strongest dependency relationship.

At T1 (zero to sixty minutes) there are no impacts to other interdependent CI sectors indicated through the executive interviewing process. Although there may be some intrasector impacts associated with these incidents, the impacts do not result in unrecoverable financial losses or elevated operating risks in any interdependent CI sectors.

Figure 4.19 illustrates the cascading threats from the Canadian Manufacturing sector at T2 (one to eight hours). It indicates that the first one to eight hours of an incident in the Canadian Manufacturing sector is most likely to pose cascading threats as tallied in Table 4.32. During this period, the Manufacturing sector indicates the least number of impacts related to cascades to and from other CI sectors. Only Transportation is impacted by an incident for up to eight hours in the Manufacturing sector. This sensitivity is attributed to the availability of maintenance and technical data needed to support the capital equipment central to the Transportation industry.

Figure 4.20 illustrates the cascading threats from the Canadian Manufacturing sector at T3 (beyond eight hours), showing all interdependency relationships coming into play. It indicates that an incident in the Canadian Manufacturing sector is most likely to pose cascading threats as tallied in Table 4.33. Of the most heavily impacted sectors, Energy, Health, and Transportation appear to receive the largest

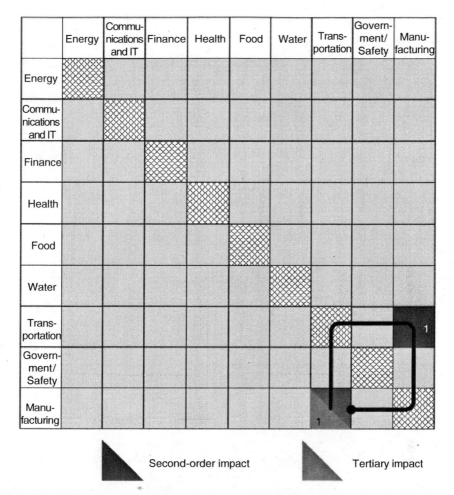

**FIGURE 4.19**  T2 (one to eight hours) Canadian Manufacturing sector cascading impacts.

**TABLE 4.32**

**T2 (One to Eight Hours) Canadian Manufacturing Cascading Impacts**

| | Energy | Communi- cations and IT | Finance | Health | Food | Water | Trans- portation | Safety/ Govern- ment | Manu- facturing |
|---|---|---|---|---|---|---|---|---|---|
| First-order | | | | | | | 1 | | 1 |
| Second-order | | | | | | | | | 1 |
| Tertiary | | | | | | | 1 | | |
| Total | | | | | | | 2 | | 2 |

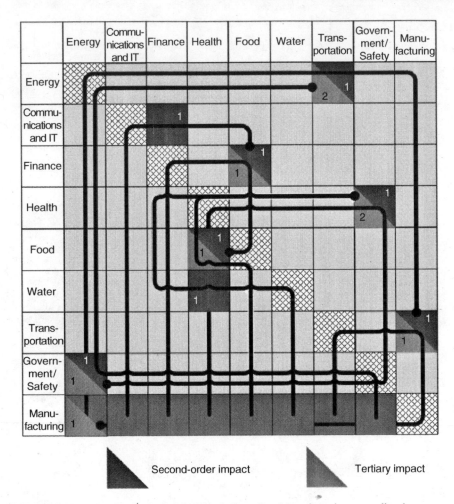

FIGURE 4.20  T3 (greater than eight hours) Canadian Manufacturing cascading impacts.

TABLE 4.33
**T3 (Greater Than Eight Hours) Canadian Manufacturing Cascading Impacts**

|  | Energy | Commu-nications and IT | Finance | Health | Food | Water | Trans-portation | Safety/Govern-ment | Manu-facturing |
|---|---|---|---|---|---|---|---|---|---|
| First-order | 1 | 1 | 1 | 1 | 1 | 1 | 1 | 1 | 1 |
| Second-order | 1 |  | 1 | 2 | 1 |  | 1 | 1 | 1 |
| Tertiary | 2 |  |  | 1 | 1 |  | 1 | 2 | 1 |
| Total | 4 | 1 | 2 | 4 | 3 | 1 | 3 | 4 | 3 |

number of cascading impacts. Similar to the Safety and Government indications, Communications and IT and water do not appear to suffer cascading impacts from an incident in Manufacturing sector. (It must be recalled that only the most potent dependency relationships are traced for the purposes of adjacency matrixes.) Table 4.33 should be interpreted to mean that Communications and IT and Water are not primary targets for cascades from Manufacturing, and may certainly still be vulnerable to cascades through second- or third-order relationships not shown.

## U.S. Correlated Interdependency Metrics

Tables 4.34 through 4.36 present the data dependency metrics that have been modified according to correlation analysis to most strongly indicate interdependencies between U.S. CI sectors. The details of the correlation analysis for each sector are to follow.

Table 4.34 is a complete, correlated CI sector-to-sector interdependency metrics expressed as a purely determinant impact (no dependency latency) for the United States. These are the metrics that would also apply at T3—incidents greater than eight hours when all interdependencies come into play across all CI sectors.

Table 4.35 represents the correlated CI sector-to-sector interdependency metrics as they are assessed from the time of impact to 60 minutes after impact. As opposed

### TABLE 4.34
### T3 (Greater Than Eight Hours), Correlated U.S. Interdependency Metrics

| | CI Sector | Energy | Comms & IT | Fin | Health Care | Food | Water | Trans | Gov/ Safety | Manf |
|---|---|---|---|---|---|---|---|---|---|---|
| | | | | | Inbound Dependencies | | | | | |
| Outbound Dependencies | Energy | 9.83 | 3.50 | 2.50 | 4.19 | 1.80 | 5.50 | 7.00 | 6.00 | 3.07 |
| | Comms & IT | 7.23 | 8.83 | 4.57 | 5.14 | 2.33 | 3.48 | 4.33 | 7.00 | 5.00 |
| | Fin | 7.77 | 7.59 | 9.06 | 7.75 | 8.45 | 5.15 | 7.19 | 5.31 | 6.50 |
| | Health Care | 4.86 | 2.37 | 3.00 | 8.24 | 1.80 | 4.20 | 3.25 | 6.01 | 2.61 |
| | Food | 3.50 | 1.71 | 1.93 | 4.05 | 6.53 | 1.48 | 2.39 | 1.96 | 2.02 |
| | Water | 4.69 | 1.96 | 2.19 | 4.90 | 1.47 | 5.68 | 2.89 | 2.08 | 2.24 |
| | Trans | 6.58 | 3.75 | 4.38 | 4.86 | 4.53 | 2.81 | 7.24 | 4.71 | 5.57 |
| | Gov/ Safety | 6.86 | 4.54 | 5.58 | 6.17 | 2.73 | 4.44 | 6.28 | 7.16 | 5.11 |
| | Manf | 5.68 | 3.79 | 4.88 | 7.50 | 4.20 | 3.31 | 4.61 | 6.25 | 7.75 |

**TABLE 4.35**

**T1 (Zero to Sixty Minutes) Dependency Latency Correlated U.S. Interdependency Metrics**

|  |  | Inbound Dependencies | | | | | | | | |
|---|---|---|---|---|---|---|---|---|---|---|
|  | CI Sector | Energy | Comms & IT | Fin | Health Care | Food | Water | Trans | Gov/ Safety | Manf |
| Outbound Dependencies | Energy | 9.33 | 3.50 | 2.50 | 4.19 | 0.00 | 0.00 | 0.00 | 0.00 | 0.00 |
|  | Comms & IT | 0.00 | 8.83 | 4.57 | 0.00 | 0.00 | 0.00 | 0.00 | 0.00 | 0.00 |
|  | Fin | 0.00 | 0.00 | 9.06 | 0.00 | 0.00 | 0.00 | 0.00 | 0.00 | 0.00 |
|  | Health Care | 0.00 | 0.00 | 0.00 | 0.00 | 0.00 | 0.00 | 0.00 | 0.00 | 0.00 |
|  | Food | 0.00 | 0.00 | 0.00 | 0.00 | 0.00 | 0.00 | 0.00 | 0.00 | 0.00 |
|  | Water | 0.00 | 0.00 | 0.00 | 0.00 | 0.00 | 0.00 | 0.00 | 0.00 | 0.00 |
|  | Trans | 0.00 | 0.00 | 0.00 | 0.00 | 0.00 | 0.00 | 0.00 | 0.00 | 0.00 |
|  | Gov/ Safety | 0.00 | 0.00 | 0.00 | 0.00 | 0.00 | 0.00 | 0.00 | 0.00 | 0.00 |
|  | Manf | 0.00 | 0.00 | 0.00 | 0.00 | 0.00 | 0.00 | 0.00 | 0.00 | 0.00 |

to Table 4.34 where all dependency metrics are displayed, only sector-to-sector interdependencies that come into effect within the first 60 minutes after the impact are displayed. All other dependencies are set to zero (0.00) because they will result in neither financial losses nor operating risks during an interval of only 60 minutes from impact.

Table 4.36 represents the correlated CI sector-to-sector interdependency metrics as they are assessed from the time of impact up to eight hours after impact. All other dependencies are set to zero because they will result in neither financial losses nor operating risks during an interval of only eight hours from impact.

## Sector Dependency Latency and Cascading Threats

All tables within this section represent the correlation of the two indicator metrics from Chapter 2 (I–O econometrics) and Chapter 3 (data dependency metrics) for the CI sector in the United States. Two specific correlations are offered to the reader for each sector. The first correlation is the result of tuning the data dependency metrics according to what appear to be inconsistency in results, possibly due to errors during the interview phases of the data dependency, collection phase, or financial flows not

## TABLE 4.36
## T2 (One to Eight Hours) Dependency Latency Correlated
## U.S. Interdependency Metrics

| | Inbound Dependencies | | | | | | | | |
|---|---|---|---|---|---|---|---|---|---|
| CI Sector | Energy | Comms & IT | Fin | Health Care | Food | Water | Trans | Gov/ Safety | Manf |
| Energy | 9.33 | 3.50 | 2.50 | 4.19 | 1.80 | 5.50 | 7.00 | 6.00 | 3.07 |
| Comms & IT | 7.23 | 8.83 | 4.57 | 5.14 | 2.33 | 3.48 | 4.33 | 7.00 | 5.00 |
| Fin | 7.77 | 7.59 | 9.06 | 0.00 | 8.45 | 0.00 | 7.19 | 5.31 | 0.00 |
| Health Care | 0.00 | 0.00 | 0.00 | 8.24 | 0.00 | 0.00 | 0.00 | 6.01 | 0.00 |
| Food | 0.00 | 0.00 | 0.00 | 4.05 | 6.53 | 0.00 | 2.39 | 0.00 | 0.00 |
| Water | 4.69 | 1.96 | 0.00 | 4.90 | 1.47 | 5.68 | 0.00 | 0.00 | 0.00 |
| Trans | 0.00 | 0.00 | 4.38 | 4.86 | 4.53 | 0.00 | 7.24 | 4.71 | 5.57 |
| Gov/ Safety | 0.00 | 0.00 | 5.58 | 6.17 | 0.00 | 4.44 | 6.28 | 7.16 | 0.00 |
| Manf | 0.00 | 0.00 | 0.00 | 0.00 | 0.00 | 0.00 | 4.61 | 0.00 | 7.75 |

(Outbound Dependencies — row axis label)

accurately depicted by the econometric statistics. (For instance, Government may procure certain inputs sectors such as Health or Water, and therefore see the input values attributed to itself when they are really destined for Health or Water.)

To arrive at better metrics, the authors have taken the opportunity to selectively revise certain data dependency scores, where they appear obviously out of sync with executive comments, professional opinion, and conventional wisdom. However, data dependency metrics are not revised indiscriminately. Only revisions that have a substantial strengthening effect on both inbound and outbound correlations are considered. Similarly, certain revisions that would have had a strengthening effect are not applied if they conflicted with executive comments, professional opinion, and conventional wisdom. All changes will be noted in the analysis tables for each sector. Within the analysis tables all modifications to interdependency metrics will be documented. Any modifications will involve changes to the dependency metrics to improve correlations with the econometrics and therefore provide stronger indications of interdependency. In the few cases where modifications are applied to the dependency metrics, the original metric will be displayed in brackets alongside the modified metric which will be used for the purposes of visualization of cascading risks in each section.

*U.S. Energy Sector*

Table 4.37 displays U.S. Energy sector econometrics (I–O) and the data dependency metrics (North American) side by side with the resulting correlations. Modifications to improve correlations are shown with the legacy (original) values in brackets.

There are strong correlations for both inbound and outbound interdependencies between U.S. econometrics and data dependency metrics.

One specific change was applied to the Energy dependency data to correct inconsistencies in metrics, which also improve correlations significantly, indicating that the corrections might result in a closer representation of reality.

The inbound dependency metric (columns of the data dependency matrix) associated with the Food sector was adjusted upward for the primary reason that it was rated substantially lower than all other sectors by Energy; possibly, inappropriately low given that the amount of money that the Food sector spends on Energy. (In the United States, Food is the fourth largest spender after Government, Transportation, and Manufacturing.) By increasing the dependency metrics for Food alone, substantial strength was gained in overall Energy correlations for the United States.

An opportunity to further increase the correlation strength for inbound Energy metrics which was not applied is related to Water. Decreasing the dependency

**TABLE 4.37**

**U.S. Energy Metrics Correlation**

| | **U.S. Energy Sector** | | |
| --- | --- | --- | --- |
| | **U.S. Inputs (US$ in Millions)** | **Inbound Dependency** | **Correlation Coefficient** |
| Energy | 439,786.90 | 9.33 | |
| Communications and IT | 2,713.79 | 7.23 | |
| Finance | 10,345.35 | 7.77 | U.S. inbound |
| Health | 0.00 | 4.86 | correlation |
| Food | 78.59 | 3.50 (1.26) | 0.67 (0.55) |
| Water | 18.67 | 4.69 | Large |
| Transportation | 39,712.02 | 6.58 | |
| Safety/Government | 0.00 | 6.86 | |
| Manufacturing | 6,150.31 | 5.68 | |
| | **U.S. Outputs (US$)** | **Outbound Dependency** | |
| Energy | 439,787 | 9.33 | |
| Communications and IT | 5,008 | 3.50 | |
| Finance | 12,256 | 2.50 | U.S. outbound |
| Health | 12,627 | 4.19 | correlation |
| Food | 28,694 | 1.80 | 0.78 (0.94) |
| Water | 2,299 | 5.50 (2.96) | Large |
| Transportation | 75,519 | 3.94 | |
| Safety/Government | 85,226 | 6.00 (3.62) | |
| Manufacturing | 39,974 | 3.07 | |

metrics for Water would have had positive effects for correlation, but would not make much sense given the fact that the Water and Energy sectors are often business partners for the generation of electricity. Furthermore, the correlation score for Energy is already strong and the dependency metrics should be taken at face value wherever possible.

Outbound dependency metrics for Energy (rows of the data dependency matrix) were altered in two instances: Water, again, and Government/Safety. In the case of Water, the change in the Energy metric was to do with the Water sector's own inbound correlation and not the outbound Energy correlations, which was virtually un-impacted. The Water metric was substantially increased to make Energy the second most important sector from the dependency perspective. The intent was to better reflect the role of Energy in powering Water services and infrastructure such as pumps and gateways, in the management of water. All Water infrastructure relies upon power to run pumps, gates, and purification systems. These systems may frequently have good redundancy built into them—but not necessarily any sub-stantial capability around back-up power. It does not make particular sense that Finance was rated more highly than Energy before adjustment. In the end, this moderate change to outbound Energy metrics resulted in a major improvement in Water correlation. This adjustment and the impact on correlation indicate a substantial, unrecognized threat to water originating from the Energy. Put differently, Water appears to have an unacknowledged degree of vulnerability to the Energy sector.

Similar to the Water sector adjustments that impacted the outbound dependency metrics for energy, the adjustments for Government and Safety substantially improve the inbound metrics for this sector, although have a very minor impact on the correlations for energy. Energy is the largest source of spending (according to I–O analysis) for Government and Safety, yet the inbound data dependency metrics from Chapter 3 were established as the second lowest—below all but the Food sector. This adjustment and the impact on correlation indicate a substantial, unrec-ognized threat to Government and Safety originating from the Energy. Put differ-ently, Government and Safety appears to have an unacknowledged degree of vulnerability to the Energy sector.

## Cascading Energy Threats in United States

The cascade matrix plots the first three levels of impact beyond the U.S. Energy sector impact, according to the primary (largest) dependency relationships for all of the other sectors. For instance, each sector is assumed to receive a first-order impact from an Energy-related incident. Each sector then impacts other sectors, but only the strongest dependency relationship is displayed because it is the most likely to be catalyzed by the first-order impact. This is the second-order impact. Finally, using the same method, the second-order impact is tracked as a tertiary impact, from the second-order-impact sector to the sector with which it has the strongest dependency relationship.

Figure 4.21 illustrates the cascading threats from the U.S. Energy sector. It indicates that the first zero to sixty minutes of an incident in the U.S. Energy sector is most likely to pose cascading threats as tallied in Table 4.38. Finance, in addition to

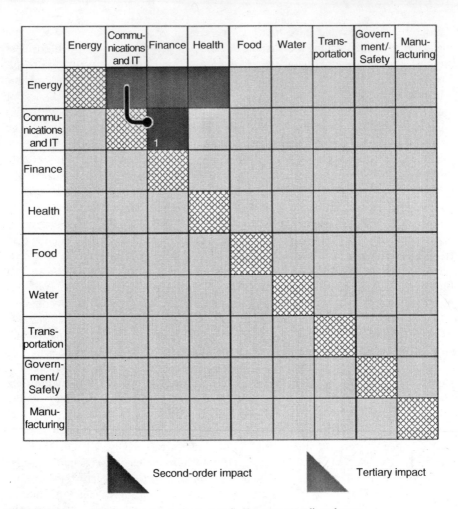

FIGURE 4.21    T1 (zero to sixty minutes) U.S. Energy cascading threats.

TABLE 4.38

**T1 (Zero to Sixty Minutes) U.S. Energy Cascading Threats**

|  | Energy | Finance | Commu-nications and IT | Health | Food | Water | Trans-portation | Safety/ Govern-ment | Manu-facturing |
|---|---|---|---|---|---|---|---|---|---|
| First-order | 1 | 1 | 1 | | | | | | |
| Second-order | | | 1 | | | | | | |
| Tertiary | | | | | | | | | |
| Total | 1 | 1 | 2 | | | | | | |

suffering the original impact, faces the possibility of an additional impact cascading back to it through its interdependency relationships with Communications and IT.

Figure 4.22 illustrates the cascading threats from the U.S. Energy sector at T2 (one to eight hours). It indicates that the first one to eight hours of an incident in the U.S. Energy sector is most likely to pose cascading threats as tallied in Table 4.39. During this period, the Food, Health, and Transportation sectors indicate the most impacts when cascading impacts are considered, followed closely by Manufacturing.

Figure 4.23 illustrates the cascading threats from the U.S. Energy sector at T3 (beyond eight hours), showing all interdependency relationships coming into play. It indicates that an incident in the U.S. Energy sector is most likely to pose cascading threats as tallied in Table 4.40. Safety and Government faces the possibility of an additional four impacts cascading back to it through its interdependency relationships

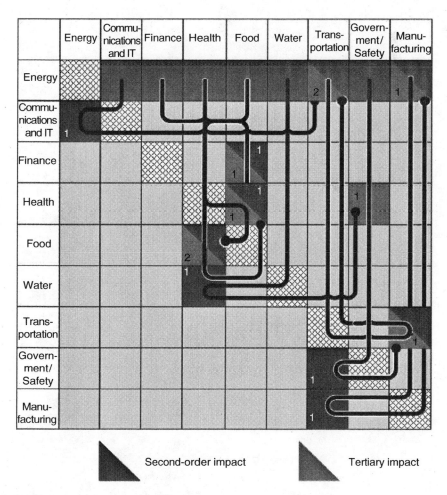

**FIGURE 4.22**  T2 (one to eight hours) U.S. Energy cascading threats.

**TABLE 4.39**

**T3 (One to Eight Hours) U.S. Energy Cascading Threats**

| | Energy | Commu-nications and IT | Finance | Health | Food | Water | Trans-portation | Safety/ Govern-ment | Manu-facturing |
|---|---|---|---|---|---|---|---|---|---|
| First-order | 1 | 1 | 1 | 1 | 1 | 1 | 1 | 1 | 1 |
| Second-order | 1 | | | 2 | 2 | | 2 | | 1 |
| Tertiary | | | | 2 | 2 | | 2 | | 2 |
| Total | 2 | 1 | 1 | 5 | 5 | 1 | 5 | 1 | 4 |

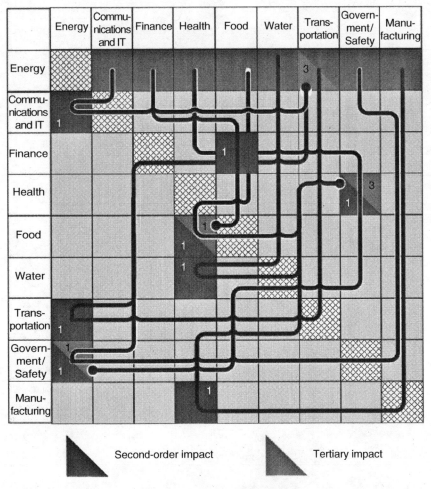

**FIGURE 4.23**   T3 (greater than eight hours) U.S. Energy sector cascading impacts.

## TABLE 4.40
### T3 (Greater Than Eight Hours) U.S. Energy Cascading Threats

| | Energy | Commu-nications and IT | Finance | Health | Food | Water | Trans-portation | Safety/ Govern-ment | Manu-facturing |
|---|---|---|---|---|---|---|---|---|---|
| First-order | 1 | 1 | 1 | 1 | 1 | 1 | 1 | 1 | 1 |
| Second-order | 3 | | | 3 | 1 | | | 1 | |
| Tertiary | 1 | | | 1 | | | 3 | 3 | |
| Total | 5 | 1 | 1 | 5 | 2 | 1 | 4 | 5 | 1 |

with other CI sectors. Rebounding impacts to Energy also present a substantial risk of amplifying the original impact and intensifying the original incident.

### U.S. Communications and IT Correlations
Table 4.41 displays U.S. Communications and IT sector econometrics (I–O) and the data dependency metrics (North American) side by side with the resulting correlations.

## TABLE 4.41
### U.S. Communications and IT Metrics Correlation

| U.S. Communications and IT Sector | | | |
|---|---|---|---|
| | U.S. Inputs (US$ in Millions) | Inbound Dependency | Correlation Coefficient |
| Energy | 5,008 | 3.50 | U.S. inbound |
| Communications and IT | 160,548 | 8.83 | correlation |
| Finance | 31,851 | 7.59 | 0.81 (0.81) |
| Health | 2 | 2.37 | |
| Food | 1 | 1.71 | Large |
| Water | 83 | 1.96 | |
| Transportation | 7,457 | 3.75 | |
| Safety/Government | 0 | 4.54 | |
| Manufacturing | 1,429 | 3.79 | |
| | **U.S. Outputs (US$)** | **Outbound Dependency** | |
| Energy | 2,713 | 7.23 | U.S. outbound |
| Communications and IT | 160,548 | 8.83 | correlation |
| Finance | 33,590 | 4.57 | 0.74 (0.59) |
| Health | 23,467 | 5.14 | |
| Food | 5,579 | 2.33 | Large |
| Water | 4 | 3.48 | |
| Transportation | 13,335 | 4.33 | |
| Safety/Government | 68,459 | 7.00 (4.47) | |
| Manufacturing | 3,386 | 5.00 (6.56) | |

Modifications to improve correlations are shown with the legacy (original) values
in brackets.

There are strong correlations for both inbound and outbound interdependencies
between U.S. econometrics and data dependency metrics.

Two changes were applied to the U.S. Communications and IT outbound
dependency data to correct what appears to be inconsistent in metrics. These changes
improved correlations significantly, resulting in a closer representation of reality.

An outbound dependency metric (rows of the data dependency matrix) for
U.S. Communications and IT was altered upward for the Government and Safety
sector. The U.S. Government and Safety metrics were substantially increased to
improve the outbound correlation for Communications and IT, although the inbound
correlation of the sectors was un-impacted by this change. These changes were
deemed appropriate given that spending on Communications and IT by Government
and Safety is by far the largest CI expenditure outside the Communications and
IT sector itself. When viewed from the perspective of the very large improvement
in the outbound correlation in Communications and IT, this modification seems
to indicate that U.S. Government and Safety is perhaps underestimating its vulnerability to Communications and IT incidents.

Outbound dependency metrics for U.S. Government and Safety were adjusted
downward for the Manufacturing sector. This reflects a modification of Manufacturing's inbound metrics and the responses derived from Manufacturing executives.
For this reason, the modification will be analyzed in detail in the Manufacturing
sector to follow. However, briefly put, this adjustment and the impact on correlation
indicate a substantial, overestimated threat to U.S. Manufacturing originating from
the U.S. Communications and IT sector. The result of this overestimation may be a
misallocation of resources to perceived risks associated with the Communications
and IT sector, although leaving other more substantial risks related to other sectors
unaddressed.

### Cascading Communications and IT Threats in United States

The cascade matrixes plot the first three levels of impact beyond the U.S. Communications and IT sector impact, according to the primary (largest) dependency
relationships for all of the other sectors. For instance, each sector is assumed to
receive a first-order impact from a Communications and IT-related incident. Each
sector then impacts other sectors, but only the strongest dependency relationship is
displayed because it is the most likely to be catalyzed by the first-order impact. This
is the second-order impact. Finally, using the same method, the second-order impact
is tracked as a tertiary impact from the second-order-impact sector to the sector with
which it has the strongest dependency relationship.

The following cascade matrix illustrates the cascading threats from the
U.S. Communications and IT sector at T1 (zero to sixty minutes).

The first zero to sixty minutes of an incident in the U.S. Communications
and IT sector is most likely to pose cascading threats as tallied in Table 4.42.
Finance, in addition to suffering the original impact, faces the possibility of an
additional impact cascading back to it through its interdependency relationships
with Communications and IT.

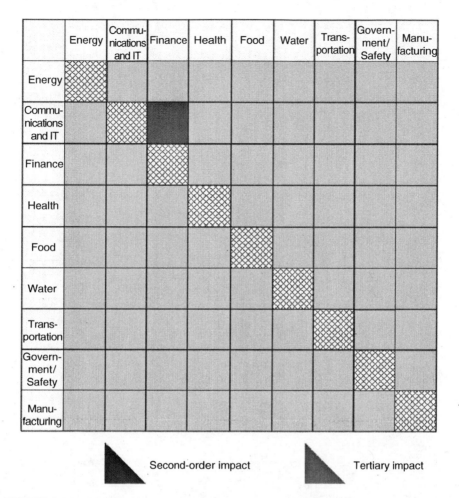

**FIGURE 4.24** T1 (zero to sixty minutes) U.S. Communications and IT cascading impacts.

**TABLE 4.42**

**T1 (Zero to Sixty Minutes) U.S. Communications and IT Cascading Threats**

| | Energy | Commu-nications and IT | Finance | Health | Food | Water | Trans-portation | Safety/ Govern-ment | Manu-facturing |
|---|---|---|---|---|---|---|---|---|---|
| First-order | | 1 | 1 | | | | | | |
| Second-order | | | | | | | | | |
| Tertiary | | | | | | | | | |
| Total | | 1 | 1 | | | | | | |

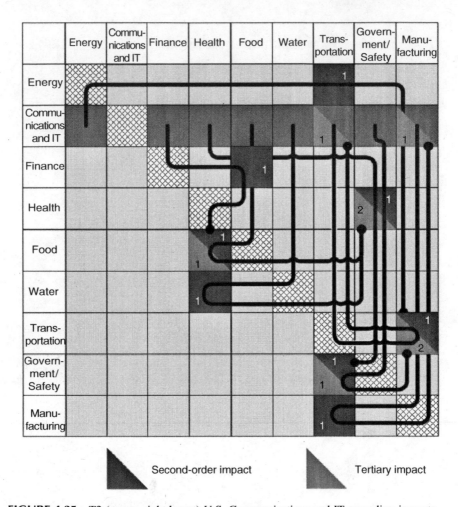

**FIGURE 4.25**  T2 (one to eight hours) U.S. Communications and IT cascading impacts.

Figure 4.25 illustrates the cascading threats from the U.S. Communications and IT sector at T2 (one to eight hours). It indicates that the first one to eight hours of an incident in the U.S. Communications and IT sector is most likely to pose cascading threats as tallied in Table 4.43. During this period, the Transportation sector indicates the most impacts related to an incident in Communications and IT when cascading impacts are included, followed by Manufacturing.

Figure 4.26 illustrates the cascading threats from the U.S. Communications and IT sector at T3 (beyond eight hours), showing all interdependency relationships coming into play. It indicates that an incident in the U.S. Communications and IT sector is most likely to pose cascading threats as tallied in Table 4.44. Communications and IT does not appear to face the possibility of additional impacts cascading back to it through its interdependency relationships with other CI sectors. Health and Safety/Government will encounter a large series of cascading threats as a result of a failure in U.S. Communications and IT.

**TABLE 4.43**

**T2 (One to Eight Hours) U.S. Communications and IT Sector Cascading Impacts**

| | Energy | Communications and IT | Finance | Health | Food | Water | Transportation | Safety/ Government | Manufacturing |
|---|---|---|---|---|---|---|---|---|---|
| First-order | 1 | 1 | 1 | 1 | 1 | 1 | 1 | 1 | 1 |
| Second-order | | | | 2 | 1 | | 3 | 1 | 1 |
| Tertiary | | | | 1 | | | 2 | 2 | 3 |
| Total | 1 | 1 | 1 | 4 | 2 | 1 | 6 | 4 | 5 |

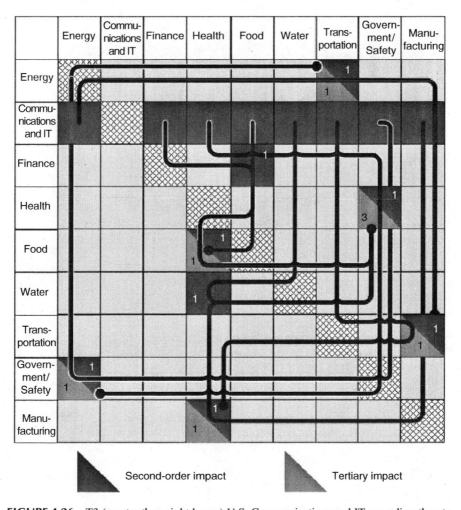

**FIGURE 4.26**  T3 (greater than eight hours) U.S. Communications and IT cascading threats.

## TABLE 4.44

### T3 (Greater Than Eight Hours) U.S. Communications and IT Cascading Threats

| | Energy | Commu-nications and IT | Finance | Health | Food | Water | Trans-portation | Safety/Govern-ment | Manu-facturing |
|---|---|---|---|---|---|---|---|---|---|
| First-order | 1 | 1 | 1 | 1 | 1 | 1 | 1 | 1 | 1 |
| Second-order | 1 | | | 3 | 1 | | 1 | 1 | 1 |
| Tertiary | 1 | | | 2 | | | 1 | 3 | 1 |
| Total | 3 | 1 | 1 | 6 | 2 | 1 | 3 | 5 | 3 |

### U.S. Finance Sector

Table 4.45 displays U.S. Finance sector econometrics (I–O) and the data dependency metrics (North American) side by side with the resulting correlations. Modifications to improve correlations are shown with the legacy (original) values in brackets.

There are strong correlations for both inbound and outbound interdependencies between U.S. econometrics and data dependency metrics.

## TABLE 4.45

### U.S. Finance Metrics Correlation

| U.S. Finance Sector | | | |
|---|---|---|---|
| | U.S. Inputs (US$ in Millions) | Inbound Dependency | Correlation Coefficient |
| Energy | 12,256 | 2.50 | U.S. inbound |
| Communications and IT | 33,590 | 4.57 | correlation |
| Finance | 463,502 | 9.06 | 0.82 (0.82) |
| Health | 0 | 3.00 | Large |
| Food | 0 | 1.93 | |
| Water | 179 | 2.19 | |
| Transportation | 14,673 | 4.38 | |
| Safety/Government | 0 | 5.58 | |
| Manufacturing | 13 | 4.88 | |
| | U.S. Outputs (US$) | Outbound Dependency | |
| Energy | 10,345 | 7.77 | U.S. outbound |
| Communications and IT | 31,851 | 7.60 | correlation |
| Finance | 463,502 | 9.10 | 0.57 (0.49) |
| Health | 40,520 | 7.75 (4.19) | Large |
| Food | 50,535 | 8.45 | |
| Water | 53 | 5.15 | |
| Transportation | 21,579 | 7.19 | |
| Safety/Government | 36,703 | 5.31 | |
| Manufacturing | 31,481 | 6.50 (7.82) | |

Two specific changes were applied to the Energy–Finance dependency data in order to correct what appears to be inconsistencies in metrics based upon subject matter expert opinion. These changes improved outbound correlations significantly, indicating that the corrections and resulting composite metrics may be a closer representation of reality.

In the case of the U.S. Finance sector, only outbound metrics were modified because the inbound metrics were already very strong at 0.82. Attempting to improve the inbound Finance beyond this point would have implied that there was a nearly perfect representation of reality with the U.S. Finance dependency set. Such an impression would be misleading based upon the discussions throughout this book, especially related to the flawed nature of the CI definitions to begin with and the fact that much intersector spending (especially in the United States) is partially obscured through financial holding companies and the nonpublication of many details of government spending for security reasons.

Outbound dependency metrics for Health were adjusted significantly upward. This in essence reflects a modification of Health's inbound metrics and the responses derived from Health executives. For this reason, the modification will be analyzed in detail in the Health sector to follow. However, briefly put, this adjustment and the impact on correlation indicate a substantial, unrecognized threat to Health originating from U.S. Finance. Put differently, Health appears to have an unacknowledged degree of vulnerability to the U.S. Finance sector.

Meanwhile, outbound dependency metrics for U.S. Manufacturing were adjusted significantly downward. Again, this reflects a modification of Manufacturing's inbound metrics and the responses derived from Manufacturing executives. For this reason, the modification will be analyzed in detail in the Manufacturing sector to follow. However, briefly put, this adjustment and the impact on correlation indicate a substantial, overestimated threat to U.S. Manufacturing originating from the U.S. Finance sector. The result of this overestimated threat may be a misallocation of resources to risks associated with the Finance sector, although leaving other more substantial risks related to other sectors unaddressed.

## Cascading Finance Threats in United States

The cascade matrixes plot the first three levels of impact beyond the U.S. Finance sector impact, according to the primary (largest) dependency relationships for all of the other sectors. For instance, each sector is assumed to receive a first-order impact from a Finance-related incident. Each sector then impacts other sectors, but only the strongest dependency relationship is displayed because it is the most likely to be catalyzed by the first-order impact. This is the second-order impact. Finally, using the same method, the second-order impact is tracked as a tertiary impact from the second-order-impact sector to the sector with which it has the strongest dependency relationship.

As per Table 4.35, The only U.S. sector experiencing an impact resulting in unrecoverable financial losses or significantly elevated operating risks when there is an incident within the Finance sector is the Finance sector itself. No cascading impacts to other CI sectors are proposed for incidents within the Finance sector lasting 60 minutes or less.

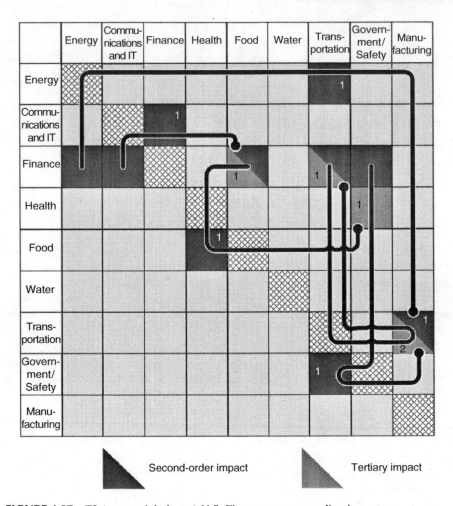

**FIGURE 4.27**   T2 (one to eight hours) U.S. Finance sector cascading impacts.

Figure 4.27 illustrates the cascading threats from the U.S. Finance sector at T2 (one to eight hours). It indicates that the first one to eight hours of an incident in the U.S. Finance sector is most likely to pose cascading threats as tallied in Table 4.46. During this period, the Transport sector indicates the most cascading impacts, and the Manufacturing receives impacts only from cascades—it does not directly suffer nonrecoverable financial losses or elevated operational risks directly from Finance incidents—but it may as a result of cascading impacts from Government/Safety, Transportation, and Energy.

Figure 4.28 illustrates the cascading threats from the U.S. Finance sector (beyond eight hours), showing all interdependency relationships coming into play. It indicates that an incident in the U.S. Finance sector is most likely to pose cascading threats as tallied in Table 4.47. Finance does not appear to face the possibility of additional impacts cascading back to it through its interdependency

**TABLE 4.46**

**T2 (One to Eight Hours) U.S. Finance Cascading Impacts**

| | Energy | Commu-nications and IT | Finance | Health | Food | Water | Trans-portation | Safety/ Govern-ment | Manu-facturing |
|---|---|---|---|---|---|---|---|---|---|
| First-order | 1 | 1 | 1 | | 1 | | 1 | 1 | |
| Second-order | | | 1 | 1 | | | 2 | | 1 |
| Tertiary | | | | | 1 | | 1 | 1 | 2 |
| Total | 1 | 1 | 2 | 1 | 2 | | 4 | 2 | 3 |

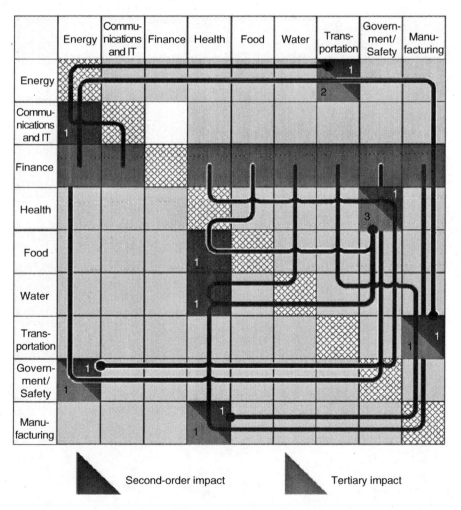

**FIGURE 4.28**   T3 (greater than eight hours) U.S. Finance sector cascading impacts.

## TABLE 4.47
### T3 (Greater Than Eight Hours) U.S. Finance Cascading Threats

| | Energy | Communications and IT | Finance | Health | Food | Water | Transportation | Safety/Government | Manufacturing |
|---|---|---|---|---|---|---|---|---|---|
| First-order | 1 | 1 | 1 | 1 | 1 | 1 | 1 | 1 | 1 |
| Second-order | 2 | | | 3 | | | 1 | 1 | 1 |
| Tertiary | 1 | | | 1 | | | 2 | 3 | 1 |
| Total | 4 | 1 | 1 | 5 | 1 | 1 | 4 | 5 | 3 |

relationships with other CI sectors. Health, Energy, and Transportation will encounter a large series of cascading threats as a result of a failure in Finance.

### U.S. Health Sector

Table 4.48 displays U.S. Health sector econometrics (I–O) and the data dependency metrics (North American) side by side with the resulting correlations. Modifications to improve correlations are shown with the legacy (original) values in brackets.

## TABLE 4.48
### U.S. Health Metrics Correlation

| U.S. Health Sector | | | |
|---|---|---|---|
| | U.S. Inputs (US$ in Millions) | Inbound Dependency | Correlation Coefficient |
| Energy | 12,635 | 4.19 | U.S. inbound |
| Communications and IT | 23,467 | 5.14 | correlation |
| Finance | 40,520 | 7.75 (4.19) | 0.53 (−0.09) |
| Health | 10,185 | 8.24 | |
| Food | 6,197 | 4.05 | Large |
| Water | 176 | 4.90 (3.81) | |
| Transportation | 10,937 | 4.86 | |
| Safety/Government | 0 | 6.17 | |
| Manufacturing | 38,030 | 7.50 (5.43) | |
| | U.S. Outputs (US$) | Outbound Dependency | |
| Energy | 0 | 4.86 | U.S. outbound |
| Communications and IT | 2 | 2.37 | correlation |
| Finance | 0 | 3.00 | 0.80 (0.80) |
| Health | 10,185 | 8.24 | |
| Food | 0 | 1.80 | Large |
| Water | 0 | 4.20 | |
| Transportation | 123 | 3.25 | |
| Safety/Government | 13,401 | 6.01 | |
| Manufacturing | 0 | 2.61 | |

In the case of the U.S. Health sector there are both moderate and strong correlations for both inbound and outbound interdependencies, respectively, for U.S. econometrics and data dependency metrics.

Four changes were considered, but only three applied, to the U.S. Health inbound dependency data to correct what appears to be inconsistency in metrics and improve correlations significantly, with the result that the corrections might result in a closer representation of reality. The symbol "*" indicates that no change was applied, even though it would have resulted in significantly improved correlations.

The nature of U.S. economic measurement of Health sector outputs (who is buying the services) has made correlation with data dependency metrics problematic, and apparently results in significantly lower inbound correlations. In fact the inbound correlation was negative before modifications. The difficultly in comparing U.S. econometrics to data dependency is that the Bureau of Economic Analysis (BEA) records most of the U.S. Health sector spending under "personal consumption expenditures," which accounts for most Health sector outputs at approximately US$1.5 trillion. Spending by industries on health benefits or employee subsidies is hardly present within the U.S. I–O metrics next to $1.5 trillion. However, what little spending that is recorded by CI sectors in the United States does show moderate correlations with a modification to the Finance sector metric.

A further problem associated with the Health sector correlations is that Safety and Government spending in this area (such as for employee benefits/military) is not made available through the BEA I–O econometrics. The $0 reported by the BEA significantly impacts correlations given that Safety and Government executive reports Health data dependency in Chapter 2 as the second most important input, only after intrasector communications.

The inbound dependency metric (columns of the data dependency matrix) associated with U.S. Finance sector was adjusted upward for the primary reason that is by far the largest input to Health. Therefore, the rating appears inappropriately low given that amount of money that the Finance sector spends on Health. Similarly, the U.S. health care system being a largely private system is mediated and permeated with financial transactions between providers, Health Maintenance Organizations (not considered CI), and employers. This change to inbound financial metric results in a massive 47 point swing in the Health correlation. When viewed from the perspective of the very large improvement in the inbound correlation in U.S. Health sector, this modification in a single Finance sector metric seems to indicate that Finance interdependency is perhaps seriously underestimated as a potential threat to the Health sector.

The inbound dependency metric for the Water sector was adjusted upward from 3.81 to 4.90. Water is known to be an important input to hospital and laboratories because it is central to waste management, cleaning, and maintenance of sterile environments. In Chapter 2, we noted that spending on Water by the Health sector is not necessarily accurately represented by the econometrics because municipal water bills for hospital and government-funded laboratories might be paid for by sources within Safety and Government sector or holding companies within the U.S. Finance sector, and are not showed as an input to Health. In Chapter 3, we highlighted the fact that the low level of communications and data flowing between the Water sector and the Health sector represents vulnerability. Together, the evidence is that a substantial increase of the Water metrics from 3.81 to 4.90 is warranted, moving Water from last place of importance to fifth place.

The third change applied was to. the Manufacturing sector that had its metric increased from 5.43 (third place) to 7.5 (still third place). The justification for this is the fact that, as discussed in Chapters 2 and 3, Manufacturing in the context of Health is primarily industrial chemicals and gases, and in the case of the U.S. I–O data includes pharmaceuticals. This is a detailed distinction that may have not been evident to executives during questioning and increased importance was applied to U.S. Manufacturing under the assumption that this sector currently includes pharmaceutical manufacturing.

The modification to the inbound dependency metrics for the U.S. Safety and Government sectors are considered but not implemented, although lowering this metric would have raised the overall correlation substantially. The specific reasons that this modification was not considered appropriate were (a) there is no value for Government and Safety inputs, any change cannot really be judged for the purposes of correlation because the correlation is with nonzero number in the series and (b) Government and Safety are a critical regulatory and welfare payer in the United States and must be reasonably assumed to be an important element of the Health supply chain.

## Cascading Health Threats in United States

The cascade matrixes plot the first three levels of impact beyond the U.S. Health sector impact, according to the primary (largest) dependency relationships for all of the other sectors. For instance, each sector is assumed to receive a first-order impact from a Health-related incident. Each sector then impacts other sectors, but only the strongest dependency relationship is displayed because it is the most likely to be catalyzed by the first-order impact. This is the second-order impact. Finally, using the same method, the second-order impact is tracked as a tertiary impact, from the second-order-impact sector to the sector with which it has the strongest dependency relationship.

At T1 (zero to sixty minutes) there are no impacts to other interdependent CI sectors indicated through the executive interviewing process. Although there may be some intrasector impacts associated with these incidents, the impacts do not result in unrecoverable financial losses or elevated operating risks in any interdependent CI sectors.

Figure 4.29 illustrates the cascading threats from the U.S. Health sector at T2 (one to eight hours). It indicates that the first one to eight hours of an incident in the U.S. Health sector is most likely to pose cascading threats as tallied in Table 4.49. During this period, the Food and Safety/Government sectors are the only sectors to indicate an impact related to a Health incident lasting less than eight hours. However, Manufacturing and Transport are still prone to cascading impacts.

Figure 4.30 illustrates the cascading threats from the U.S. Health sector at T3 (beyond eight hours), showing all interdependency relationships coming into play. It indicates that an incident in the U.S. Health sector is most likely to pose cascading threats as tallied in Table 4.50. Health faces the possibility of additional impacts cascading back to it through its interdependency relationships with other CI sectors.

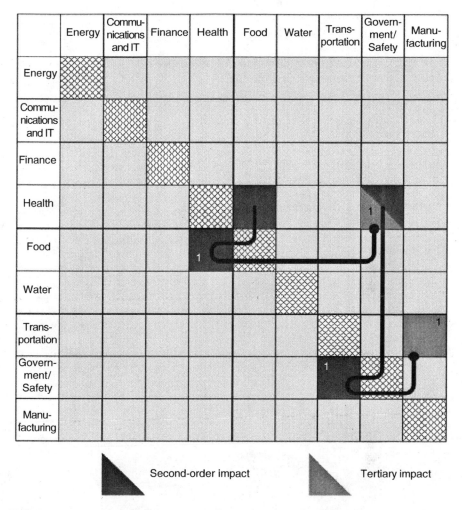

**FIGURE 4.29**   T2 (one to eight hours) U.S. Health sector cascading impacts.

---

**TABLE 4.49**

**T2 (One to Eight Hours) U.S. Health Cascading Impacts**

| | Energy | Commu- nications and IT | Finance | Health | Food | Water | Trans- portation | Safety/ Govern- ment | Manu- facturing |
|---|---|---|---|---|---|---|---|---|---|
| First-order | | | | 1 | 1 | | | 1 | |
| Second-order | | | | 1 | | | 1 | | |
| Tertiary | | | | | | | | 1 | 1 |
| Total | | | | 2 | 1 | | 1 | 2 | 1 |

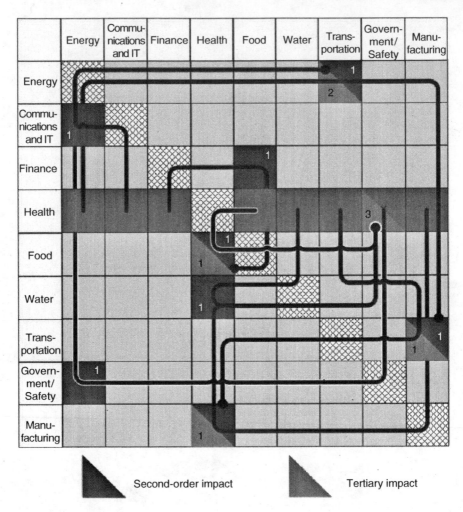

FIGURE 4.30    T3 (greater than eight hours) U.S. Health cascading impacts.

## TABLE 4.50
## T3 (Greater Than Eight Hours) U.S. Health Cascading Impacts

| | Energy | Commu-<br>nications<br>and IT | Finance | Health | Food | Water | Trans-<br>portation | Safety/<br>Govern-<br>ment | Manu-<br>facturing |
|---|---|---|---|---|---|---|---|---|---|
| First-order | 1 | 1 | 1 | 1 | 1 | 1 | 1 | 1 | 1 |
| Second-order | 2 | | | 3 | 1 | | 1 | | 1 |
| Tertiary | | | | 2 | | | 2 | 3 | 1 |
| Total | 3 | 1 | | 6 | 2 | 1 | 4 | 4 | 3 |

Government and Safety, Health, and Transportation will encounter a large series of cascading threats as a result of a failure in U.S. Health sector, although Health will be subject to a series of up to six rebounding cascading failures.

## U.S. Food Sector

Table 4.51 displays U.S. Food sector econometrics (I–O) and the data dependency metrics (North American) side by side with the resulting correlations. Modifications to improve correlations are shown with the legacy (original) values in brackets.

In the case of the U.S. Food sector there are large correlations for both inbound and outbound interdependencies, respectively, for U.S. econometrics and data dependency metrics.

A single change was applied, to the U.S. Food sector outbound dependency for the Energy sector. This modification was applied for the purposes of improving the Energy inbound dependency correlation, but has the reciprocal impact of actually lowering the Food sector's outbound correlation. The improvement in the inbound energy correlation of 11 points (from 0.55 to 0.66) was considered worth the slight

**TABLE 4.51**

**U.S. Food Metrics Correlation**

| | U.S. Food Sector | | |
|---|---|---|---|
| | U.S. Inputs (US$ in Millions) | Inbound Dependency | Correlation Coefficient |
| Energy | 28,758 | 1.80 | U.S. inbound |
| Communications and IT | 5,578 | 2.33 | correlation |
| Finance | 50,535 | 8.45 | 0.58 (0.57) |
| Health | 0.00 | 1.80 | Large |
| Food | 262,737 | 6.53 | |
| Water | 242 | 1.47 | |
| Transportation | 23,844 | 4.53 | |
| Safety/Government | 0.00 | 2.73 | |
| Manufacturing | 23,270 | 4.20 | |
| | U.S. Outputs (US$) | Outbound Dependency | |
| Energy | 78 | 3.50 (1.26) | U.S. outbound |
| Communications and IT | 1.20 | 1.71 | correlation |
| Finance | 0.30 | 1.93 | 0.85 (0.88) |
| Health | 6,196 | 4.05 | Large |
| Food | 262,737 | 6.53 | |
| Water | 0.01 | 1.48 | |
| Transportation | 251 | 2.39 | |
| Safety/Government | 16,468 | 1.96 | |
| Manufacturing | 2,871 | 2.02 | |

reduction to the Food sector correlation, because the outbound correlation for the U.S. Food sector remained very strong at 0.85. The indication from this adjustment is that the Energy sector may be underestimating the potential of an impact in the Food sector to pose a threat to the Energy sector, resulting in unaddressed vulnerabilities.

### Cascading Food Threats in United States

The cascade matrixes plot the first three levels of impact beyond the U.S. Food sector impact, according to the primary (largest) dependency relationships for all of the other sectors. For instance, each sector is assumed to receive a first-order impact from a Food-related incident. Each sector then impacts other sectors, but only the strongest dependency relationship is displayed because it is the most likely to be catalyzed by the first-order impact. This is the second-order impact. Finally, using the same method, the second-order impact is tracked as a tertiary impact, from the second-order-impact sector to the sector with which it has the strongest dependency relationship.

At T1 (zero to sixty minutes) there are no impacts to other interdependent CI sectors indicated through the executive interviewing process. Although there may be some intrasector impacts associated with these incidents, the impacts do not result in unrecoverable financial losses or elevated operating risks in any interdependent CI sectors.

Figure 4.31 illustrates the cascading threats from the U.S. Food sector at T2 (one to eight hours). It indicates that the first one to eight hours of an incident in the U.S. Food sector is most likely to pose cascading threats as tallied in Table 4.52. During this period, the Health and Transportation sectors are the only sectors to indicate an impact related to a Food incident less than eight hours. However, Manufacturing and Safety and Government are still prone to cascading impacts.

Figure 4.32 illustrates the cascading threats from the U.S. Food sector at T3 (beyond eight hours), showing all interdependency relationships coming into play. It indicates that an incident in the U.S. Food sector is most likely to pose cascading threats as tallied in Table 4.53. Health faces the greatest possibility of impacts cascading to it through its interdependency relationships with other CI sectors. Government and Safety and Energy will encounter a large series of cascading threats as a result of a failure in U.S. Food sector.

### U.S. Water Sector Correlations

Table 4.54 displays U.S. Water sector econometrics (I–O) and the data dependency metrics (North American) side by side with the resulting correlations. Modifications to improve correlations are shown with the legacy (original) values in brackets.

Water is the most problematic U.S. CI sector to assess using I–O and data dependency correlation, because it is often a service paid for by municipal government. Municipal government then bills users through taxes and property levies. For this reason, the flow of payments (outputs) to Water is obfuscated within Government revenues.

There are moderate correlations for inbound interdependencies between U.S. econometrics and data dependency metrics for the U.S. Water sector, and essentially no positive correlations for outbound dependencies.

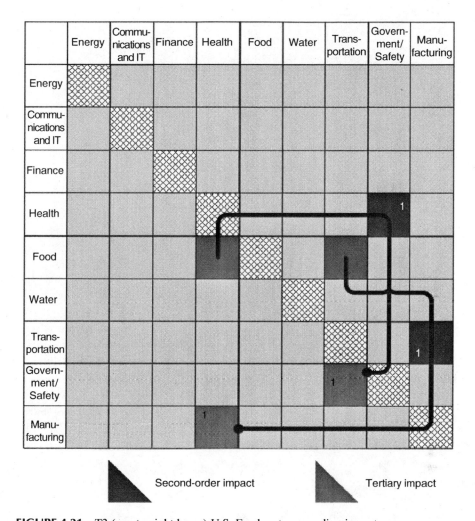

**FIGURE 4.31**   T2 (one to eight hours) U.S. Food sector cascading impacts.

## TABLE 4.52
## T2 (One to Eight Hours) U.S. Food Cascading Impacts

|  | Energy | Communications and IT | Finance | Health | Food | Water | Transportation | Safety/Government | Manufacturing |
|---|---|---|---|---|---|---|---|---|---|
| First-order |  |  |  | 1 | 1 |  | 1 |  |  |
| Second-order |  |  |  |  |  |  |  | 1 | 1 |
| Tertiary |  |  |  | 1 |  |  | 1 |  |  |
| Total |  |  |  | 2 | 1 |  | 2 | 1 | 1 |

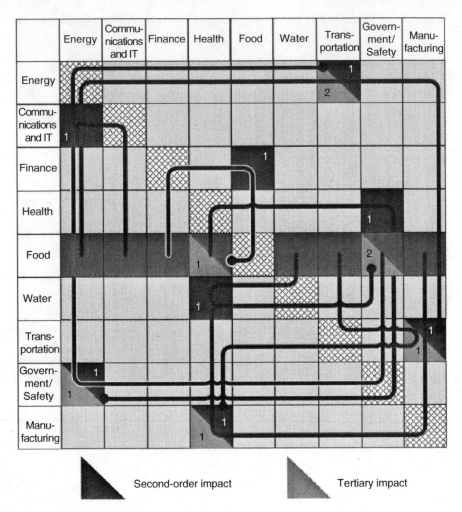

**FIGURE 4.32**   T3 (greater than eight hours) U.S. Food cascading impacts.

**TABLE 4.53**

**T3 (Greater Than Eight Hours) U.S. Food Cascading Impacts**

|  | Energy | Commu-nications and IT | Finance | Health | Food | Water | Trans-portation | Safety/Govern-ment | Manu-facturing |
|---|---|---|---|---|---|---|---|---|---|
| First-order | 1 | 1 | 1 | 1 | 1 | 1 | 1 | 1 | 1 |
| Second-order | 2 |  |  | 2 | 1 |  | 1 | 1 | 1 |
| Tertiary | 1 |  |  | 2 |  |  | 2 | 2 | 1 |
| Total | 4 | 1 | 1 | 5 | 2 | 1 | 4 | 4 | 3 |

**TABLE 4.54**

**U.S. Water Metrics Correlation**

| U.S. Water Sector | | | |
|---|---|---|---|
| | U.S. Inputs (US$ in Millions) | Inbound Dependency | Correlation Coefficient |
| Energy | 2,776 | 5.50 (2.96) | U.S. inbound |
| Communications and IT | 4 | 3.48 | correlation |
| Finance | 53 | 5.15 | 0.32 (−0.22) |
| Health | 0 | 4.20 | Medium |
| Food | 0 | 1.48 | |
| Water | 0 | 5.68 | |
| Transportation | 34 | 2.81 | |
| Safety/Government | 0 | 4.44 | |
| Manufacturing | 3 | 3.31 | |
| | U.S. Outputs (US$) | Outbound Dependency | |
| Energy | 21 | 4.69 | U.S. outbound |
| Communications and IT | 83 | 1.96 | correlation |
| Finance | 179 | 2.19 | −0.30 (−0.30) |
| Health | 176 | 4.90 (3.81) | Small |
| Food | 243 | 1.47 | |
| Water | 0 | 5.68 | |
| Transportation | 14 | 2.89 | |
| Safety/Government | 2,400 | 2.08 | |
| Manufacturing | 38 | 2.24 | |

A single modification was applied to the inbound dependencies to try and strengthen correlation from a negative to a moderate level. This was achieved by raising the Energy inbound dependency rating from 2.96 to 5.50, which had the effect of providing Energy with the highest dependency outside the Water sector itself. This modification was also considered rational because Energy is the largest input to U.S. water by approximately 75 times. Similarly, Water and Energy frequently have collaborative agreements for the production of power, and these agreements may require a significant amount of coordination, communication, and integration. For instance, information and data from the Energy sector would be important to the generation or sale of power. Similarly and probably more importantly, the Water infrastructure amounts to a form of heavy industry, consuming significant amount of energy resources in the management of potable and wastewater. This infrastructure is typically not supportable for extended periods with back-up power such as might be generated on-site. The indication is that Water underestimates the threat associated with a loss of Energy supplies, and believes itself to be substantially isolated from all infrastructures for operational purposes. Given that Energy is the largest expense for Water outside financial services, it is fair to assume that Energy is a central operational input to Water.

A single outbound dependency metric was changed for the U.S. Water sector in the case of the Health metric, which was raised from 3.81 to 4.9. This change was considered rational because of the increased strength that was realized in the Health inbound correlation, and especially due to the acknowledged importance of the Water infrastructure in the maintenance of the sterile conditions in hospital and laboratories. This change primarily reflects more a possible underestimation of the importance of the Water sector by Health, as opposed to any vulnerability within Water itself.

At least three potential modifications to Water metrics were not applied, but would have increased correlation substantially. First, the outbound Energy metric could be substantially lowered to increase outbound correlations. This modification was not applied due to the power-generation relationship between Energy and Water discussed above, and the fact that the inbound correlation for Energy would also have decreased. Second, Finance dependency metrics could have been raised given that in United States the Water sector spends a significant amount on these services. However, given that no sectors, including Energy, received high ratings from water it was determined that a modification was not appropriate because Finance already has the highest overall dependency rating in the United States. Finally, the dependency metrics for Water could have been substantially lowered to also increase the overall correlation; however, large intrasector dependency is the rule not the exception to CI interdependency. To lower the intrasector Water dependency metric would have been very much against executive perceptions and the precedent in other sectors.

## Cascading Water Threats in United States

The cascade matrixes plot the first three levels of impact beyond the U.S. Water sector impact, according to the primary (largest) dependency relationships for all of the other sectors. For instance, each sector is assumed to receive a first-order impact from a Water-related incident. Each sector then impacts other sectors, but only the strongest dependency relationship is displayed because it is the most likely to be catalyzed by the first-order impact. This is the second-order impact. Finally, using the same method, the second-order impact is tracked as a tertiary impact from the second-order-impact sector to the sector with which it has the strongest dependency relationship.

At T1 (zero to sixty minutes) there are no impacts to other interdependent CI sectors indicated through the executive interviewing process. Although there may be some intrasector impacts associated with these incidents, the impacts do not result in unrecoverable financial losses or elevated operating risks in any interdependent CI sectors.

Figure 4.33 illustrates the cascading threats from the U.S. Water sector at T2 (one to eight hours). It also indicates that the first one to eight hours of an incident in the U.S. Water sector is most likely to pose cascading threats as tallied in Table 4.55. During this period, the Energy, Communications and IT, Health, and Food sectors indicate an impact related to a Water incident that lasts up to eight hours. However, Transportation and Safety/Government are the most prone to cascading impacts.

Figure 4.34 illustrates the cascading threats from the U.S. Water sector at T3 (beyond eight hours), showing all interdependency relationships coming into play. It indicates that an incident in the U.S. Water sector is most likely to pose cascading threats as tallied in Table 4.56. Government and Safety and Energy will encounter a large series of cascading threats as a result of a failure in U.S. Water sector.

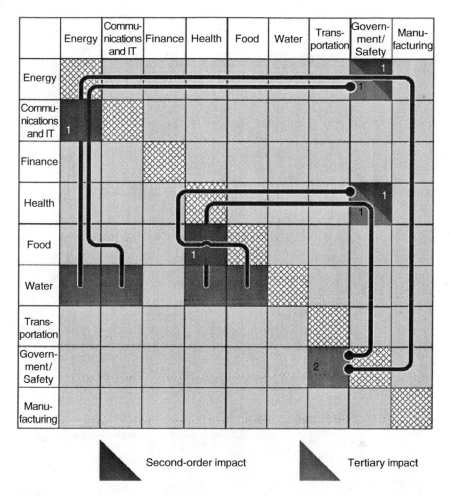

**FIGURE 4.33**  T2 (one to eight hours) U.S. Water sector cascading impacts.

**TABLE 4.55**

**T2 (One to Eight Hours) U.S. Water Cascading Impacts**

| | Energy | Commu-nications and IT | Finance | Health | Food | Water | Trans-portation | Safety/Govern-ment | Manu-facturing |
|---|---|---|---|---|---|---|---|---|---|
| First-order | 1 | 1 | | 1 | 1 | | | | |
| Second-order | | | | 1 | | | | 2 | |
| Tertiary | 1 | | | | | | 2 | 2 | |
| Total | 2 | 1 | | 2 | 1 | | 2 | 4 | |

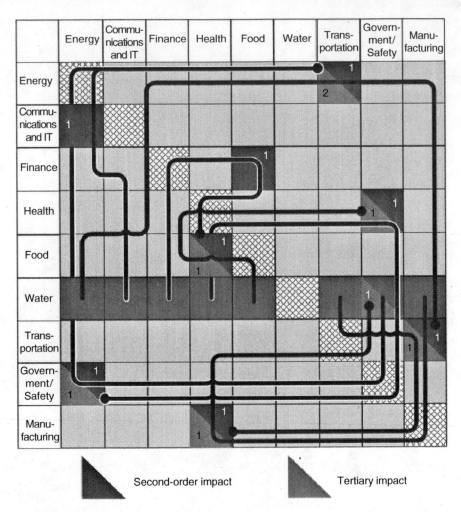

**FIGURE 4.34**  T3 (greater than eight hours) U.S. Water cascading impacts.

**TABLE 4.56**

**T3 (Greater Than Eight Hours) U.S. Water Cascading Threats**

| | Energy | Commu- nications and IT | Finance | Health | Food | Water | Trans- portation | Safety/ Govern- ment | Manu- facturing |
|---|---|---|---|---|---|---|---|---|---|
| First-order | 1 | 1 | 1 | 1 | 1 | 1 | 1 | 1 | 1 |
| Second-order | 2 | | | 2 | 1 | | 1 | 1 | 1 |
| Tertiary | 1 | | | 2 | | | 2 | 2 | 1 |
| Total | 4 | 1 | 1 | 5 | 2 | 1 | 4 | 4 | 3 |

*U.S. Transportation Sector*

Table 4.60 displays U.S. Transportation sector econometrics (I–O) and the data dependency metrics (North American) side by side with the resulting correlations. Modifications to improve correlations are shown with the legacy (original) values in brackets.

There are strong correlations for inbound interdependencies between U.S. econometrics and data dependency metrics for the U.S. Transportation sector, and strong correlations for outbound dependencies.

A single inbound dependency metric was modified to substantially improve correlations for the U.S. Transportation sector. The metric associated with Energy sector dependency was raised from 3.94 to 7.0; from fifth highest to third highest. This modification was justified because Energy is the single largest supplier to the U.S. Transportation sector, with spending on the Energy sector exceeding even intra-sector Energy spending. See Chapter 3, U.S. Transportation sector for a detailed discussion of these dependency metrics.

*U.S. Transportation Sector*

Table 4.57 displays U.S. Transportation Sector econometrics (I–O) and the data dependency metrics (North American) side by side with the resulting correlations.

**TABLE 4.57**

**U.S. Transportation Metrics Correlation**

| U.S. Transportation Sector | | | |
|---|---|---|---|
| | **U.S. Inputs (US$ in Millions)** | **Inbound Dependency** | **Correlation coefficient** |
| Energy | 75,519 | 7.00 (3.94) | U.S. inbound |
| Communications and IT | 13,335 | 4.33 | correlation |
| Finance | 21,579 | 7.19 | 0.71 (0.38) |
| Health | 128 | 3.25 | Strong |
| Food | 661 | 2.39 | |
| Water | 17 | 2.89 | |
| Transportation | 72,843 | 7.24 | |
| Safety/Government | 0 | 6.28 | |
| Manufacturing | 8,365 | 4.61 | |
| | **U.S. Outputs (US$)** | **Outbound Dependency** | |
| Energy | 39,712 | 6.58 | U.S. outbound |
| Communications and IT | 7,457 | 3.75 | correlation |
| Finance | 14,673 | 4.38 | 0.87 (0.61) |
| Health | 14,004 | 4.86 | Strong |
| Food | 25,227 | 4.53 | |
| Water | 643 | 2.81 | |
| Transportation | 72,843 | 7.24 | |
| Safety/Government | 32,286 | 4.71 | |
| Manufacturing | 16,473 | 5.57 | |

Modifications to improve correlations are shown, with the legacy (original) values is brackets.

## Cascading Transportation Threats in United States

The cascade matrixes plot the first three levels of impact beyond the U.S. Transportation sector impact, according to the primary (largest) dependency relationships for all of the other sectors. For instance, each sector is assumed to receive a first-order impact from a Transportation-related incident. Each sector then impacts other sectors, but only the strongest dependency relationship is displayed because it is the most likely to be catalyzed by the first-order impact. This is the second-order impact. Finally, using the same method, the second-order impact is tracked as a tertiary impact from the second-order-impact sector to the sector with which it has the strongest dependency relationship.

At T1 (zero to sixty minutes) there are no impacts to other interdependent CI sectors indicated through the executive interviewing process. Although there may be some intrasector impacts associated with these incidents, the impacts do not result in unrecoverable financial losses or elevated operating risks in any interdependent CI sectors.

Figure 4.35 illustrates the cascading threats from the U.S. Transportation sector at T2 (one to eight hours). It indicates that the first one to eight hours of an incident in the U.S. Transportation sector is most likely to pose cascading threats as tallied in Table 4.58. During this period, the Finance, Health, Food, Water, Safety and Government, and Manufacturing sectors all indicate an impact related to a Transportation incident lasting up to eight hours. However, the Transportation sector itself along with Health receives the most overall impact not only due to intrasector effects but also due to cascading impacts from other sectors, which can exacerbate the incident.

Figure 4.36 illustrates the cascading threats from the U.S. Transportation sector at T3 (beyond eight hours), showing all interdependency relationships coming into play. It indicates that an incident in the U.S. Transportation sector is most likely to pose cascading threats as tallied in Table 4.59. Health, Energy, and Safety/Government will encounter a large series of cascading threats as a result of a failure in U.S. Transportation sector. The Transportation sector itself will be impacted by another three cascading impacts from other CI sectors associated, in addition to intrasector impacts.

## U.S. Safety and Government Sector Correlations

In Chapter 2, Safety and Government were grouped together into a single sector because the different infrastructure roles were not available individually at the econometric I–O level. Police, fire, and other safety services are grouped with other government services such as regulation and social services. The methodology employed in Chapter 3 for the collection of interdependency metrics (executive interviewing) made it possible to keep metrics for the Safety and Government sectors separate. To correlate these metrics, it becomes necessary to have an equal number of metrics, therefore the Safety and Government metrics for data dependency (Chapter 3 metrics) have to be combined into a single metrics. This was accomplished through simple averaging of the two different metrics for each inbound and outbound relationship.

Table 4.60 displays U.S. Safety/Government sector econometrics (I–O) and the data dependency metrics (North American) side by side with the resulting

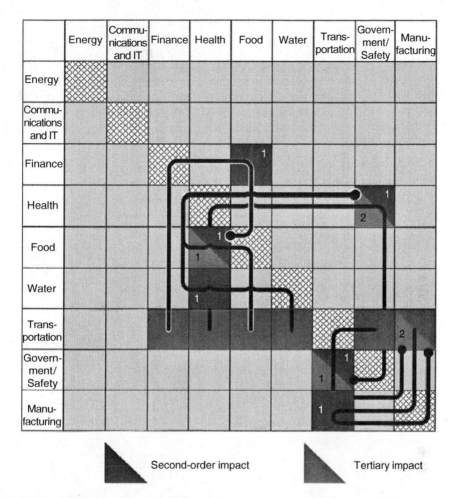

**FIGURE 4.35** T2 (one to eight hours) U.S. Transportation sector cascading impacts.

**TABLE 4.58**

**T2 (One to Eight Hours) U.S. Transportation Cascading Impacts**

| | Energy | Commu-nications and IT | Finance | Health | Food | Water | Trans-portation | Safety/ Govern-ment | Manu-facturing |
|---|---|---|---|---|---|---|---|---|---|
| First-order | | | 1 | 1 | 1 | 1 | 1 | 1 | 1 |
| Second-order | | | | 2 | 1 | | 2 | 1 | |
| Tertiary | | | | 1 | | | 1 | 2 | 2 |
| Total | | | 1 | 4 | 2 | 1 | 4 | 4 | 3 |

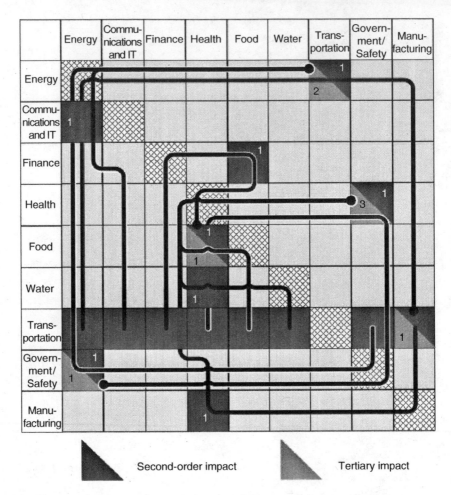

**FIGURE 4.36**   T3 (greater than eight hours) U.S. Transportation cascading impacts.

**TABLE 4.59**

**T3 (Greater Than Eight Hours) U.S. Transportation Cascading Threats**

|  | Energy | Communications and IT | Finance | Health | Food | Water | Transportation | Safety/Government | Manufacturing |
|---|---|---|---|---|---|---|---|---|---|
| First-order | 1 | 1 | 1 | 1 | 1 | 1 | 1 | 1 | 1 |
| Second-order | 2 |  |  | 3 | 1 |  | 1 | 1 |  |
| Tertiary | 1 |  |  | 1 |  |  | 2 | 3 | 1 |
| Total | 4 | 1 | 1 | 5 | 2 | 1 | 4 | 5 | 2 |

**TABLE 4.60**

**U.S. Safety/Government Metrics Correlation**

| U.S. Safety/Government Sector | | | |
|---|---|---|---|
| | **U.S. Inputs (US$ in Millions)** | **Inbound Dependency** | **Correlation Coefficient** |
| Energy | 85,435.79 | 6.00 (3.62) | U.S. inbound |
| Communications and IT | 68,459.10 | 7.00 (4.47) | correlation |
| Finance | 36,703.20 | 5.31 | 0.44 (−0.22) |
| Health | 13,401.00 | 6.01 | Medium |
| Food | 16,468.76 | 1.96 | |
| Water | 2,399.51 | 2.08 | |
| Transportation | 30,226.90 | 4.71 | |
| Safety/Government | 0.00 | 7.16 | |
| Manufacturing | 62,718.90 | 6.25 (2.56) | |
| | **U.S. Outputs (US$)** | **Outbound Dependency** | |
| Energy | 0.00 | 6.86 | U.S. outbound |
| Communications and IT | 0.00 | 4.54 | correlation |
| Finance | 0.00 | 5.58 | NA |
| Health | 0.00 | 6.17 | |
| Food | 0.00 | 2.73 | |
| Water | 0.00 | 4.44 | |
| Transportation | 0.00 | 6.28 | |
| Safety/Government | 0.00 | 7.16 | |
| Manufacturing | 0.00 | 5.11 | |

correlations. Modifications to improve correlations are shown with the legacy (original) values in brackets.

There are moderate correlations for inbound interdependencies between U.S. econometrics and data dependency metrics for the U.S. Safety/Government sector, although correlations are not available for outbound dependencies due to the BEA practice of not reporting details about Safety and Government selling patterns.

Three specific modifications were applied to the Safety and Government dependency metrics, where the metrics were raised (increased in strength). The Energy sector was raised from 3.62 to 6.00, which reflects moving from the seventh place of importance for Safety and Government to fourth place. This increase is partially justified by the fact that the Energy sector is the largest single input (supplier) to the Safety and Government sector among all the CI sectors. A further increase in Energy was not undertaken because the reciprocal impacts on the correlations for outbound Energy dependency would have been disproportionately negative. Similar to Energy, the Finance dependency metric was raised from 4.47 to 7.00, reflecting a movement from sixth to second place of importance to the Safety and Government sector. This increase is partially justified by the fact that the Finance sector is the second largest input (supplier) to the Safety and Government sector among the CI sectors. A further increase in Finance was not undertaken because the reciprocal impacts on the correlations for outbound Finance dependency would have been disproportionately negative. Finally, the Manufacturing inbound dependency metrics were raised from 2.56 (sixth place) to 6.25 (seventh place) to reflect the large amount of Government and Safety spending the other transportation/aerospace component of manufacturing, which is the defense industrial base component. Possibly more importantly, and as previously noted, there was a bias toward Canadian interviewees for the data dependency portion of Safety and Government sectors. Given the smaller spending level of Canada upon defense relative to the United States, an increase in the U.S. inbound dependency metric for manufacturing was further justified to account for differing national security strategies.

At least two modifications to Safety and Government were resisted, even though they would have substantially improved the inbound correlation of Safety and Government itself, and the outbound correlations for the Water sector specifically. First, Safety and Government: no modification was applied to the intrasector dependency metric which is the highest at 7.16. Because there are no statistics available from the BEA about value flows within Safety and Government, the value is set to $0, which equates to the lowest econometric input in contrast to the highest data dependency (7.16). As this information is not available, indications from other sectors need to be considered. The following two considerations lead to the conclusion that the intrasector dependency rating should remain unchanged: (1) all other sectors rate intrasector dependency as the highest and (2) Canadian intrasector econometrics indicate substantial value transfers between government entities, support the idea that they also exist among U.S. government entities.

*Cascading Safety/Government Threats in United States*

The cascade matrixes plot the first three levels of impact beyond the U.S. Safety/Government sector impact, according to the primary (largest) dependency relationships for all of the other sectors. For instance, each sector is assumed to receive a first-order impact from a Safety/Government-related incident. Each sector then impacts other sectors, but only the strongest dependency relationship is displayed because it is the most likely to be catalyzed by the first-order impact. This is the second-order impact. Finally, using the same method, the second-order impact is tracked as a tertiary impact from the second-order-impact sector to the sector with which it has the strongest dependency relationship.

At T1 (zero to sixty minutes) there are no impacts to other interdependent CI sectors indicated through the executive interviewing process. Although there may be some intrasector impacts associated with these incidents, the impacts do not result in unrecoverable financial losses or elevated operating risks in any interdependent CI sectors.

Figure 4.37 illustrates the cascading threats from the U.S. Safety/Government sector at T2 (one to eight hours). It indicates that the first one to eight hours of an incident in the U.S. Safety/Government sector is most likely to pose cascading threats as tallied in Table 4.61. During this period, the Transportation sector indicates the latest number of impacts related to cascades from other CI sectors, although the Safety and Government sector itself receives two additional cascading impacts to exacerbate the incident.

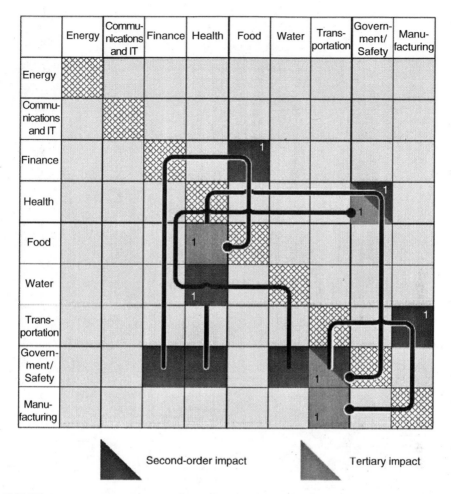

**FIGURE 4.37**  T2 (one to eight hours) U.S. Safety/Government sector cascading impacts.

**TABLE 4.61**

**T2 (One to Eight Hours) U.S. Safety/Government Cascading Impacts**

|  | Energy | Commu-nications and IT | Finance | Health | Food | Water | Trans-portation | Safety/ Govern-ment | Manu-facturing |
|---|---|---|---|---|---|---|---|---|---|
| First-order |  |  | 1 | 1 |  | 1 | 1 | 1 |  |
| Second-order |  |  |  | 1 | 1 |  |  |  | 1 |
| Tertiary |  |  |  | 1 |  |  | 3 | 1 |  |
| Total |  |  | 1 | 3 | 1 | 1 | 4 | 2 | 1 |

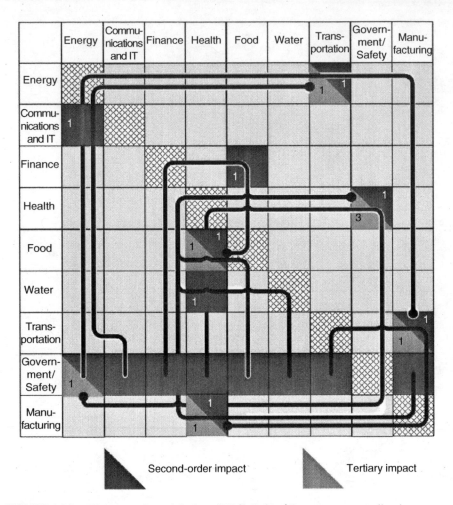

**FIGURE 4.38**   T3 (greater than eight hours) U.S. Safety/Government cascading impacts.

Figure 4.38 illustrates the cascading threats from the U.S. Safety/Government sector at T3 (beyond eight hours), showing all interdependency relationships coming into play. It indicates that an incident in the U.S. Safety/Government sector is most likely to pose cascading threats as tallied in Table 4.62. An impact in the Safety and Government sector results in cascading impact effect in Health, Energy, and Transportation mostly, but also circle back and re-impact safety and Government itself. Although Communications and IT, Finance, and Water do not appear to suffer cascading impacts from an incident in Safety and Government, it must be recalled that only the most potent (one-to-one) dependency relationships are traced for the purposes of adjacency matrixes. Table 4.62 should be interpreted to mean that Communications and IT and Water are indicated as primary targets for cascades, and may certainly still be vulnerable to cascades through second- or third-order relationships not shown.

**TABLE 4.62**

**T3 (Greater Than Eight Hours) U.S. Safety/Government Cascading Threats**

|  | Energy | Commu-nications and IT | Finance | Health | Food | Water | Trans-portation | Safety/Govern-ment | Manu-facturing |
|---|---|---|---|---|---|---|---|---|---|
| First-order | 1 | 1 | 1 | 1 | 1 | 1 | 1 | 1 | 1 |
| Second-order | 1 |  |  | 3 | 1 |  | 1 | 1 | 1 |
| Tertiary | 1 |  |  | 2 |  |  | 1 | 3 | 1 |
| Total | 3 | 1 | 1 | 6 | 2 | 1 | 3 | 5 | 3 |

## U.S. Manufacturing Sector Correlations

Table 4.63 displays U.S. Manufacturing sector econometrics (I–O) and the data dependency metrics (North American) side by side with the resulting correlations. Modifications to improve correlations are shown with the legacy (original) values in brackets.

There are strong correlations for inbound and outbound interdependencies between U.S. econometrics and data dependency metrics for the U.S. Manufacturing sector.

**TABLE 4.63**

**U.S. Manufacturing Metrics Correlation**

| U.S. Manufacturing Sector | | | |
|---|---|---|---|
|  | U.S. Inputs (US$ in Millions) | Inbound Dependency | Correlation Coefficient |
| Energy | 41,708 | 3.07 | U.S. inbound |
| Communications and IT | 3,386 | 5.00 (6.56) | correlation |
| Finance | 31,481 | 6.50 (7.82) | 0.66 (0.46) |
| Health | 0 | 2.61 | Large |
| Food | 2,871 | 2.02 | |
| Water | 38 | 2.24 | |
| Transportation | 14,177 | 5.57 | |
| Safety/Government | 0 | 5.11 | |
| Manufacturing | 149,104 | 7.75 (7.03) | |
|  | **U.S. Outputs (US$)** | **Outbound Dependency** | |
| Energy | 6,183 | 5.68 | U.S. outbound |
| Communications and IT | 1,429 | 3.79 | correlation |
| Finance | 13 | 4.88 | 0.76 (0.49) |
| Health | 38,030 | 7.50 (5.43) | Large |
| Food | 23,271 | 4.20 | |
| Water | 3 | 3.31 | |
| Transportation | 6,974 | 4.61 | |
| Safety/Government | 62,719 | 6.25 (2.56) | |
| Manufacturing | 149,104 | 7.03 | |

Three specific modifications were applied to the Manufacturing inbound dependency metrics, where the metrics were both lowered (decreased in strength) and raised. The Communications and IT sector inbound dependency was lowered from 6.56 to 5.75, which reflects a "hold" in its relative ranking among the CI sectors. This decrease is justified by the fact that Communications and IT is a relatively small input to Manufacturing and actually five times smaller than the nearest comparable dependency score from the Transportation sector. A further increase was not undertaken because of the reciprocal impacts on the correlations for outbound Communications and IT dependency would have been disproportionately negative. Similar to the inbound score for Communications and IT, the Finance dependency metric lowered from 7.82 to 6.5 reflected a movement from first to second place of importance to the U.S. Manufacturing sector. This decrease is justified by the fact that Finance possessed the highest overall inbound dependency rating, higher even than intrasector dependency but with approximately one fifth the trade flow as that within the Manufacturing sector itself. A further increase was not undertaken because of the reciprocal impacts on the correlations for outbound Finance dependency would have been disproportionately negative. Finally, the inbound dependency metric for intrasector dependency was raised from second to first place. This decision was justified by the large volume of intrasector trade and the fact that defense industrial base companies are known to be highly integrated and delivery of goods and services to their common customer—Government and Safety.

Two specific modifications were applied to the Manufacturing outbound dependency metrics, where the metrics were both increased in strength.

The first outbound change applied was to the Health sector, which had its metric increased from 5.43 to 7.5. The justification for this is driven by the fact that, as discussed in Chapters 2 and 3, Manufacturing in the context of Health is primarily industrial chemicals and gases, but in the case of the U.S. I–O data includes the significant amounts spent on pharmaceuticals. This is a detailed distinction that may have not been evident to executives during questioning on data dependency and increased importance was applied to Manufacturing under the assumption that this sector currently does not include pharmaceutical manufacturing.

The second outbound change applied was to the Safety and Government sector, which is the largest client for Manufacturing goods and services by almost twice the nearest sector. Under the contemporary CI definitions, defense industries are specifically included in the CI definition for Manufacturing and therefore represent a matter of national security to the Safety and Government sector, not simply regulation and social-service delivery. For this reason, the input metrics for the Manufacturing were raised substantially from the metrics provided by executives from this sector. Similarly, the sample from which Safety and Government executives were drawn was more biased toward Canadians than the other sectors. This Canadian bias in the data dependency samples from Chapter 3 could easily have skewed the representation of national defense concerns and the Manufacturing sector dependency downward.

## Cascading Manufacturing Threats in United States
The cascade matrixes plot the first three levels of impact beyond the U.S. Manufacturing sector impact, according to the primary (largest) dependency relationships for

all of the other sectors. For instance, each sector is assumed to receive a first-order impact from a Manufacturing-related incident. Each sector then impacts other sectors, but only the strongest dependency relationship is displayed because it is the most likely to be catalyzed by the first-order impact. This is the second-order impact. Finally, using the same method, the second-order impact is tracked as a tertiary impact from the second-order-impact sector to the sector with which it has the strongest dependency relationship.

At T1 (zero to sixty minutes) there are no impacts to other interdependent CI sectors indicated through the executive interviewing process. Although there may be some intrasector impacts associated with these incidents, the impacts do not result in unrecoverable financial losses or elevated operating risks in any interdependent CI sectors.

Figure 4.39 illustrates the cascading threats from the U.S. Manufacturing sector at T2 (one to eight hours). It indicates that the first one to eight hours of an incident in

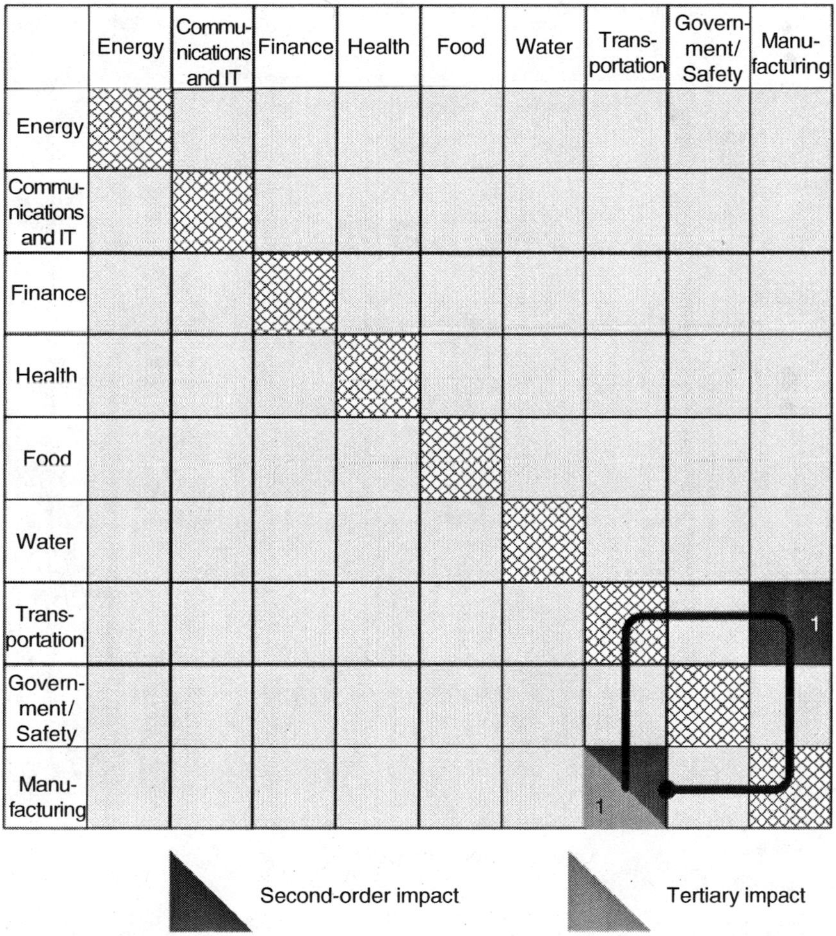

FIGURE 4.39    T2 (one to eight hours) U.S. Manufacturing sector cascading impacts.

**TABLE 4.64**

**T2 (One to Eight Hours) U.S. Manufacturing Sector Cascading Impacts**

| | Energy | Communications and IT | Finance | Health | Food | Water | Transportation | Safety/ Government | Manufacturing |
|---|---|---|---|---|---|---|---|---|---|
| First-order | | | | | | | 1 | | 1 |
| Second-order | | | | | | | | | 1 |
| Tertiary | | | | | | | 1 | | |
| Total | | | | | | | 2 | | 2 |

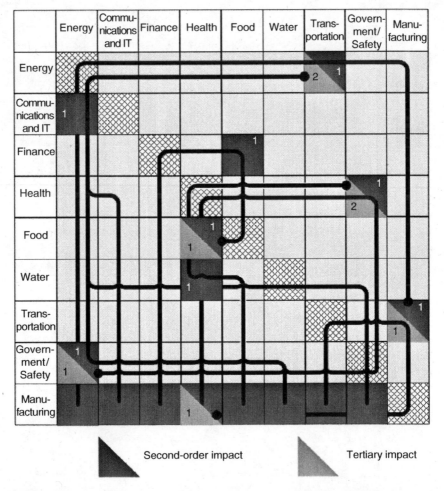

**FIGURE 4.40**  T3 (greater than eight hours) U.S. Manufacturing cascading impacts.

**TABLE 4.65**

**T3 (Greater Than Eight Hours) U.S. Manufacturing Sector Cascading Impacts**

| | Energy | Commu-<br>nications<br>and IT | Finance | Health | Food | Water | Trans-<br>portation | Safety/<br>Govern-<br>ment | Manu-<br>facturing |
|---|---|---|---|---|---|---|---|---|---|
| First-order | 1 | 1 | 1 | 1 | 1 | 1 | 1 | 1 | 1 |
| Second-order | 2 | | | 2 | 1 | | 1 | 1 | 1 |
| Tertiary | 1 | | | 2 | | | 2 | 2 | 1 |
| Total | 4 | 1 | 1 | 5 | 2 | 1 | 4 | 4 | 3 |

the U.S. Manufacturing sector is most likely to pose cascading threats as tallied in Table 4.64. During this period, the Manufacturing sector indicates the least number of impacts related to cascades to and from other CI sectors. Only Transportation is impacted by an incident of less than eight hours in the Manufacturing sector. This sensitivity is attributed to the availability of maintenance and technical data needed to support the capital equipment central to the Transportation industry.

Figure 4.40 illustrates the cascading threats from the U.S. Manufacturing sector at T3 (beyond eight hours), showing all interdependency relationships coming into play. It indicates that an incident in the U.S. Manufacturing sector is most likely to pose cascading threats as tallied in Table 4.65. An impact in the Manufacturing sector spreads cascading impacts most heavily between Energy and Transportation. Similar to the Safety and Government indications, Communications and IT, Finance, and Water do not appear to suffer cascading impacts from an incident in Manufacturing sector. (It must be recalled that only the most potent dependency relationships are traced for the purposes of adjacency matrixes.) Table 4.65 should be interpreted to mean that Communications and IT, Finance, and Water are indicators of primary targets for cascades, and may certainly still be vulnerable to cascades through second- or third-order relationships not shown.

## CONCLUSIONS AND INDICATED RISKS

A lot of very granular data has been presented in this chapter, and yet we have only scratched the surface of the possible depth of interdependency analysis. At the start of this chapter we did a little math and defined how many potential secondary and tertiary cascading impacts are possible in this $9 \times 9$ matrix of CI sectors: 576 and 4608, respectively.

In this chapter, we managed to cover all first-order impacts by simulating an impact in each sector and mapping how it spills out across the other CI sectors, but from that point we pull back and assess only the strongest dependency relationships for both second and tertiary impacts. In other words, we only assessed the strongest secondary cascade relationship out of potentially nine relationships, and then only the strongest tertiary relationship associated with the strongest secondary relationship out of a possible eighty tertiary relationships. This means of a total possible set of 4608 different cascading impacts possible across the 9 CI sector (when you assess down to the tertiary impact level), we reviewed 216 impacts and 64 different cascading patterns—slightly less than 5 percent.

This issue of assessing large variations of cascading impacts dramatically increases the overall difficulty of assessing CI interdependency. Cascading impacts mean that the effects of an incident spread far and wide through the CI ecosystem; if and where cascading impacts might meet or accumulate is difficult to assess. Much like waves traveling through water, where cascading impacts meet they might combine to form a larger impact than the original. Similarly, when a given CI sector suffers an impact it will be relying upon CI sectors within its supply chain to support it during recovery. The manner in which dependency relationships flow (the metrics associated with these relationships) not only indicate how impacts might flow down into the supply chain, but also how support and assurance might flow up the supply chain to the sector suffering the impact.

In 2007, Defense Research and Development Canada augmented and enhanced the PageRank* algorithm that underlies the eponymous Google search engine to create AssetRank.[†] PageRank functions by assigning weights to web pages based not only on the contents of the page but also the number and weight of pages, which point to a given page. In turn, each pointing page is assigned a weight according to the number of pages and weights of these pages, which point to them. Pages pass weight down to the pages they point to. In this manner, Google determines how much weight every page has according to the value of upstream pages and the number of downstream pages. AssetRank extends the functionality of PageRank by allowing starting weight (the intrinsic value) for pages/assets to be set differently, although PageRank assumes all pages/assets are initially equal.

AssetRank has been applied to the correlated dependency metrics from both Canada (Figure 4.41) and the United States (Figure 4.42) in the charts below to assess the outcome of thousands of potential cascading impacts and assign weights to all CI sectors according to their overall importance to the CI sector ecosystem. Although the correlated dependency metrics inherently possess weights relative to each other, these are before the effects of cascades have been modeled or considered. The benefit of the following piece of analysis is to reveal the extent a CI sector may be over or underestimated in its criticality among the CI sectors once cascading impacts accumulate, for instance, during a major incident impacting CIs for days or more.

Figures 4.41 and 4.42 reveals that for the most part, correlated weights tend to be similar to AssetRank weights, which take into consideration the cumulated effects of cascading impacts and relationships. This is a good news for high-level CI interdependence assessment because it indicates that at the highest levels of assessment, there are probably no hidden landmines among the dependency relationships. However, a few notable variations between the AssetRank and the correlated weights do appear, specifically in Finance, Communications and IT, and Manufacturing.

---

* Page, L., Brin, S., Motwani, R., and Winograd, T., 1999, *The PageRank Citation Ranking: Bringing Order to the Web.*

† Sawilla and Burrell, *General Interpretation of AssetRank*, Defence research and development Canada 2007.

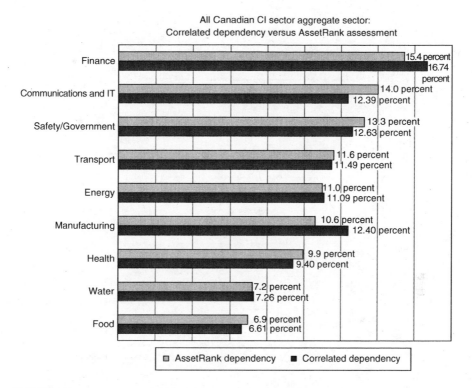

**FIGURE 4.41**   Canadian correlate versus AssetRank weights.

In these cases, AssetRank is indicating the following information about the importance of these sectors among all CI sectors: Finance as a whole is less important to all
CI sector as an aggregate measure once the potential of cascading impacts is
considered. Communications and IT is more important to all CI sector as an
aggregate measure once the potential of cascading impacts is considered. And
finally, Manufacturing as a whole is less important to all CI sector as an aggregate
measure once the potential of cascading impacts is considered. The core message in
these findings is that the criticality of CI sectors can shift in perhaps non-intuitive
ways as incident are prolonged.

Another feature of AssetRank is the ability to establish unique intrinsic values
(starting weights) for different assets. In the case of applying AssetRank to CI
interdependency assessment, this generates the ability to model and impact in a
given sector and assess the cascading impacts from the perspective of which sectors
will be most important to support recover in the impacted sector. Chapter 6 is a case-
study chapter demonstrating this application of AssetRank.

Application of AssetRank to U.S. data dependency figures reveals a distinctly
different picture from Canada. Although in Figure 4.41 that Canadian correlated
weights tend to be similar to AssetRank weights, some U.S. ranking and weighting
change substantially. For instance, the AssetRank weight for Finance increases as
does the Communications and IT rank, although the Energy and Health rankings

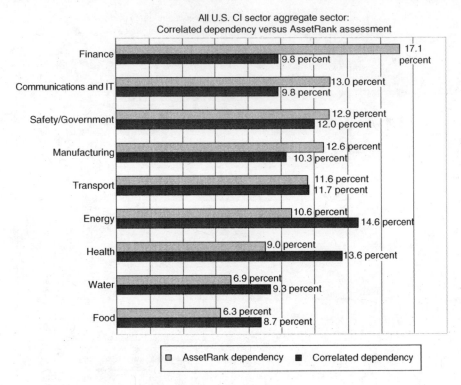

**FIGURE 4.42**   U.S. correlated versus AssetRank weights.

decrease. The indication from this finding is that taking into account the complexity
of the economic ecosystem and the overall dependencies of all sectors, Finance and
Communications and IT are under-assessed by the correlated dependency metrics.
This possibly means that the sheer size of the Energy and Health sectors in the U.S.
has distorted prima facie dependencies. Energy is big, but Finance is still hugely
important when all the interrelationships among the sectors are taken into account.
Another notable element of the AssetRank indications is that the differences between
the Canadian and U.S. dependencies start to disappear under this form of assessment.
In Chapter 2, an econometric review had shown Communications and IT in Canada
and Energy in the United States to be the strongest CI sectors with the most over
dependent relationships. Similarly, in Chapter 3 a data dependency review had
shown the Government was the sector with the least dependent relationships due
to its regulatory powers. It is striking to note that under AssetRank assessment,
neither Communications and IT, Energy, nor Government are ranked at the top.
In both Canada and the U.S. Finance is ranked at the top. To some people this is a
non-intuitive outcome, but it reflects empirical observations, quantitative analysis,
and ultimately the distinction between being operational and being profitable for
many CI sectors: there is a substantially reduced incentive to keep the lights on,
send e-mail and make calls, or remain compliant with regulations, if you cannot
be profitable!

Another feature of AssetRank is the ability to establish unique intrinsic values (starting weights) for different assets. In the case of applying AssetRank to CI interdependency assessment, this generates the ability to model and impact in a given sector and assess the cascading impacts from the perspective of which sectors will be most important to support recover in the impacted sector.

## CASCADING IMPACT CONCENTRATIONS

One of the most interesting aggregations that is available from the large amount of information presented in this chapter is a consideration of which sectors are subject to the most, and the least, cascading impacts. And at what points in time are they subject to differing levels of cascading impacts?

This information is useful to operational risk assessors and business continuity managers who need to consider not only internally generated impacts to their organization, but externally catalyzed impacts. Although a sector might be able to cope with one or even two concurrent impacts, how ready are they to deal with a cascading series of up to four or five impacts or more from different sources? In the past this sort of event was considered either too complex to model or too unlikely to consider; the aggregations that follow show that it is not only possible, but probable, that an impact in a single CI sector will generate multiple cascading impacts from multiple sources.

Some CI sectors are more susceptible to cascading impacts than others. The following six aggregations show how Canadian and U.S. CI sectors are vulnerable to cascading impacts from incidents in other sectors during the timeframes T1 (zero to sixty minutes), T2 (one to eight hours), and T3 (greater that eight hours). These aggregations show all cascading impacts to the extend they have been assessed here and are indicative of the totals that might exist if a full assessment was undertaken. (Recall that less than 5 percent cascading impacts patterns have been assessed.)

Figure 4.43 indicates that only four CI sectors are likely to be operationally impacted by any CI incidents lasting less than one hour. Of these sectors, Finance will be impacted by an outage of less than one hour in three of the nine sectors, and will even have a potential for a secondary cascading impact within this timeframe. For instance, Finance may potentially suffer intrasector impacts (among financial sector entities), and impacts from outages in other CI sectors such as Energy or Communications and IT. (Refer to the Finance sector discussion earlier in this chapter.) In the cases of Health and Energy which show one, single impact for outages of less than one hour—this single impact is the intrasector impact.

Figure 4.44 indicates that a large regional or national incident with an impact on all nine CI sectors lasting up to eight hours is likely to trigger risk conductance and cascades among all the sectors. Of these sectors, Transportation will be potentially impacted directly by six of the nine sectors, meaning that it is most likely that Transport will be impacted through CI interdependency for incidents last up to eight hours. And even if Transportation is not directly impacted, it has the largest number of potential secondary and tertiary vulnerabilities. The indication is that even if not directly in the line of fire, an impact will be partially or fully conducted down to

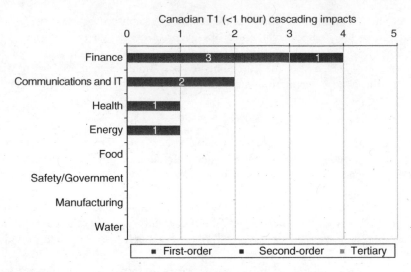

**FIGURE 4.43**   Canadian T1 (less than one hour) cascading impacts.

Transportation. Meanwhile, at the other end of this scale is Communications and IT, which indicates that only an impacts on four out of nine CI sectors (which includes itself) will have an operational impact if the duration is less than eight hours. Communications and IT does not indicate susceptibility to any cascading impacts from other sectors during an incident lasting less than eight hours.

Figure 4.45 indicates that a large regional or national incident with an impact on all nine CI sectors, lasting more than eight hours is likely to trigger risk conductance and cascades among all the sectors. The indication is that all sectors are susceptible

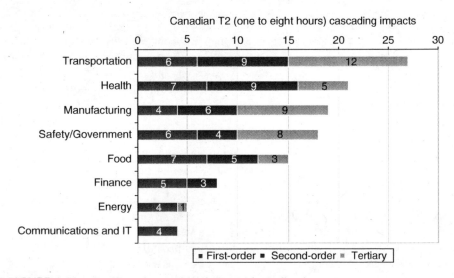

**FIGURE 4.44**   Canadian T2 (one to eight hours) cascading impacts.

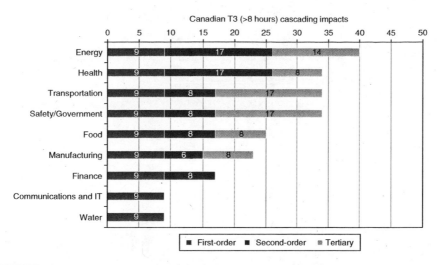

**FIGURE 4.45**  Canadian T3 (greater than eight hours) cascading impacts.

to impacts from all other sectors—hence the common score of 9 for first-order impacts. Put another way, an impact to any one sector of more than eight hours—due to a determinant threat—will impact all eight other sectors directly. Of the sectors, Energy is the most susceptible to cascading impacts, such that it will be impacted directly by the sector that has had a threat materialize into an incident, plus impacts conducted from other sectors. In total, among all second-order impacts assessed (72 in total), Energy had the strongest potential for impact in 26 of 72 cases. Similarly, among all tertiary impacts assessed (72 in total), Energy had the strongest potential for impact in 14 of 72 cases. Meanwhile, at the other end of this scale is Water and Communications and IT, which indicate susceptibility to only direct hits from the other CI sectors, but not necessarily any cascading impacts even for unspecified durations.

This information in Figure 4.45 does not imply that the Energy sector will be impacted 50 times from its CI sector relationships with every given incident. It would literally take a major catastrophe such as a hurricane or act of war to impact all CI sector simultaneously. But if and when they are impacted all at the same time—the amplification of these concurrent impacts would be felt most in the Energy sector. This in turn will make the Energy sector the most difficult to restore justifying the resilience and precautions innate to Energy providers. The importance of this observation is that stakeholder needs to understand that some of the sectors will be required to cope with much more than a single impact at a time.

Identical to the Canadian indications, Figure 4.46 indicates that only four U.S. CI sectors are likely to be operationally impacted by any CI incidents lasting less than one hour. Of these sectors, Finance will be impacted by an outage of less than 60 minutes in three of nine sectors, and will even have a potential for a secondary cascading impact within this timeframe. For instance, Finance will suffer intrasector impacts (among financial sector entities), and impacts from outages in other CI sectors such as Energy or Communications and IT. (Refer to the Finance sector discussion in this

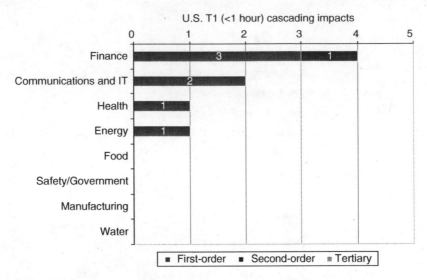

**FIGURE 4.46**   U.S. T1 (less than one hour) cascading impacts.

chapter.) In the cases of Health and Energy, which show one, single impact for outages of less than one hour—this single impact is the intrasector impact.

Figure 4.47 indicates that a large regional or national incident lasting up to eight hours is likely to trigger both impacts: risk conductance and cascades among all the sectors. Of these sectors, Transportation will be potentially impacted directly by six of nine sectors, meaning that it is most likely that Transport will be impacted through CI interdependency for incidents last up to eight hours. And even if Transportation is not directly impacted, it has the largest number of potential secondary and tertiary

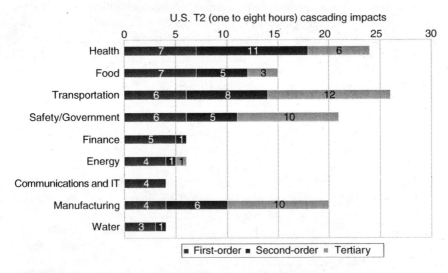

**FIGURE 4.47**   U.S. T2 (one to eight hours) cascading impacts.

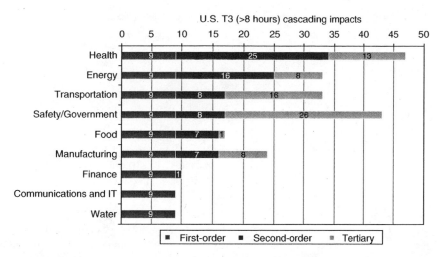

**FIGURE 4.48** U.S. T3 (greater than eight hours) cascading impacts.

vulnerabilities. The indication is that even if not directly in the line of fire, an impact will be partially or fully conducted down to Transportation. Meanwhile, at the other end of this scale is Water, which indicates that only a direct hit on three of the nine CI sectors (including itself) will have an operational impact if the duration is less than eight hours. Water also indicates that it has a single vulnerability to a cascading secondary impact in the less than eight-hour window.

Figure 4.48 indicates that a large regional or national incident lasting more than eight hours is likely to impact all sectors and trigger risk conductance and cascades among most of the sectors. The first indication is that all sectors are susceptible to impacts from all other sectors—hence the common score of 9 for first-order impacts. Put another way, an impact to any one sector—due to a determinant threat—will have an impact on all eight other sectors directly if its duration is beyond eight hours. Of the sectors, Energy is the most susceptible to cascading impacts, such that it will be impacted directly by the sector that has had a threat materialize into an incident, plus impacts conducted from other sectors. In total, among all second-order impacts assessed (72 in total), Energy had the strongest potential for impact in 26 of 72 cases. Similarly, among all tertiary impacts assessed (72 in total), Energy had the strongest potential for impact in 14 of 72 cases. Meanwhile, at the other end of this scale is Water and Communications and IT, which indicate susceptibility to only direct hits from the other CI sectors, but not necessarily any cascading impacts even for unspecified durations.

Similar to the Canadian indications, the information in Figure 4.48 does not imply that the Energy sector will be impacted 50 times from its CI sector relationships with every given incident. It would literally take a major catastrophe such as a hurricane or act of war to impact all CI sector simultaneously. But if and when they are impacted all at the same time—the amplification of these concurrent impacts would be felt most in the Energy sector. This in turn will make the Energy sector the most difficult to restore and aggregate overall CI restoration further. The importance of this observation is that stakeholder needs to understand that some of the sectors will be required to cope with much more than a single impact at a time.

## CORRELATED DEPENDENCY MAPS

### Canada

We will conclude this chapter on correlated dependency metrics using a visualization tool that was also employed in Chapters 2 (econometric analysis) and 3 (data dependency analysis). As in Chapters 2 and 3, we will review the correlated dependency metrics using tools known as treemaps* to provide a top-level view of all sectors and how they relate to one another from the perspective of inbound, and then outbound information and data dependency.

For comprehension purposes the dependency scale has been aggregated into high, medium, and low data dependency where "high" is the top third of all dependency scores across all sectors, for a given sector, "medium" is the middle third, and "low" is the bottom third of dependency scores for a given sector. The ranks are color coded according to the following scale:

| Value | Color | Metric (Score) Range |
|---|---|---|
| High | ☐White | 5.31–10.00 |
| Medium | ▨Grey | 3.62–5.30 |
| Low | ■Black | 1.00–3.62 |

Below is a map for Canadian correlated inbound data dependency. Figure 4.49 at the highest level represents the total sum of all median scores for inbound dependency. Within the total score are boxes for each sector, which represent the proportional size of each sector's inbound median sum relative to the other sectors. Within each sector box are smaller boxes for each inbound relationship with all other sectors, such that the size of the box is proportional to the size of each sectors' contribution to the inbound median sum for the specific sector. Figure 4.49 provides a comprehensive perspective on Canadian correlated inbound dependency among the CI sectors.

Next is a map for Canadian correlated outbound dependency. Figure 4.50 represents the total sum of median scores for Canadian correlated outbound dependency. Within the total score are boxes for each sector, which represent the proportional size of each sector's outbound median sum. Within each sector box are smaller boxes for each outbound relationship with all other sectors, such that the size of the box is proportional to the size of each sectors' contribution to the outbound median sum. Finally, to facilitate intersector analysis, the weighting for each sector output for each sector box is coded by high, medium, and low dependency relative to all sectors.

---

* Treemaps are tools developed by Ben Shneiderman at the University of Maryland in the 1990s to display complex and multilayer data sets. http://www.cs.umd.edu/hcil/treemap-history/.

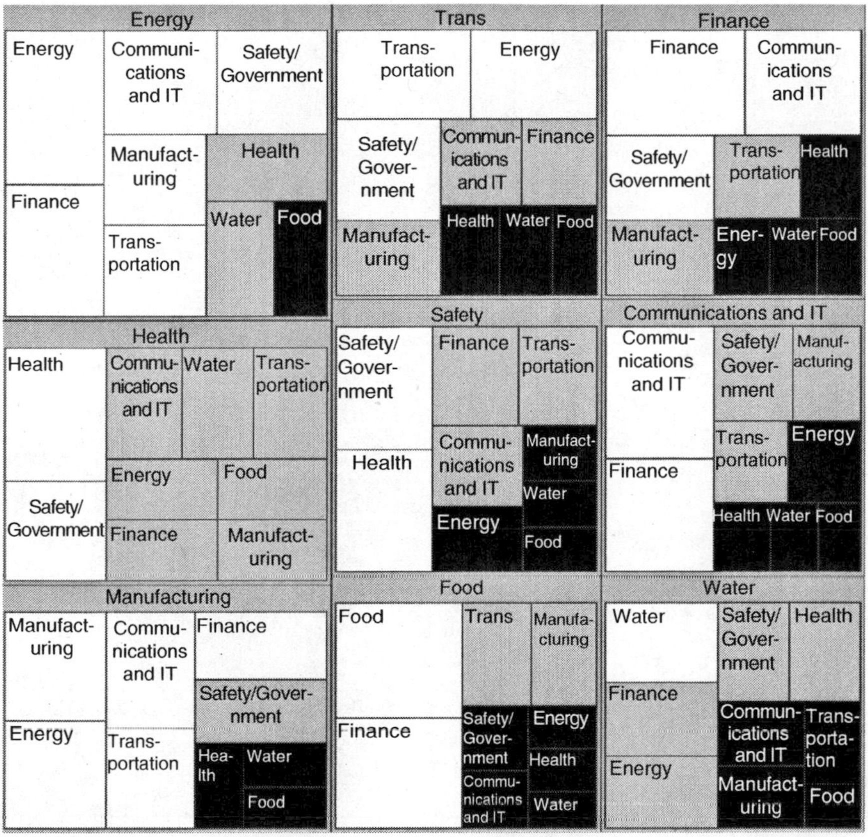

| Energy | | | Trans | | | Finance | | |
|---|---|---|---|---|---|---|---|---|
| Energy | Communi-cations and IT | Safety/ Government | Trans-portation | Energy | | Finance | Commun-ications and IT | |
| | Manufact-uring | Health | Safety/ Gover-nment | Commun-ications and IT | Finance | Safety/ Government | Trans-portation | Health |
| Finance | | Water / Food | | Health / Water / Food | | Manufact-uring | Ener-gy / Water / Food | |
| | Trans-portation | | Manufact-uring | | | | | |

| Health | | | | Safety | | | Communications and IT | | |
|---|---|---|---|---|---|---|---|---|---|
| Health | Commu-nications and IT | Water | Trans-portation | Safety/ Gover-nment | Finance | Trans-portation | Commu-nications and IT | Safety/ Gover-nment | Manuf-acturing |
| | Energy | Food | | Health | Commu-nications and IT | Manufact-uring / Water | Finance | Trans-portation | Energy |
| Safety/ Government | Finance | Manufact-uring | | | Energy | Food | | Health / Water / Food | |

| Manufacturing | | | Food | | | | Water | | |
|---|---|---|---|---|---|---|---|---|---|
| Manufact-uring | Commu-nications and IT | Finance | Food | Trans | Manufa-cturing | | Water | Safety/ Gover-nment | Health |
| | | Safety/Gover-nment | | Safety/ Gover-nment | Energy | | Finance | Commun-ications and IT | Trans-porta-tion |
| Energy | Trans-portation | Hea-lth / Water | Finance | | Health | | Energy | Manufact-uring | Food |
| | | Food | | Commu-nications and IT | Water | | | | |

**FIGURE 4.49** Canadian correlated inbound data dependency map. White □ = high inbound dependency. Gray ▪ = medium inbound dependency. Black ■ = low inbound dependency. Each sector block is proportional to the size of its inbound dependency score relative to the other sectors. Each square within each sector block indicates the proportional size of inbound dependency scores from each sectors. Recall that inbound dependency is equivalent to the vulnerability of the CI sector to threats from other sectors.

As was the case for the correlated inbound dependency map, the scale for the correlated outbound dependency map has been aggregated into high, medium, and low data dependency where high is the top third of dependency scores for a given sector, medium is the middle third, and low is the bottom third of dependency scores for a given sector. The ranks are color coded according to the following scale:

| Value | Color | Metric (Score) Range |
|---|---|---|
| High | □ White | 5.31–10.00 |
| Medium | ▪ Grey | 3.62–5.30 |
| Low | ■ Black | 1.00–3.61 |

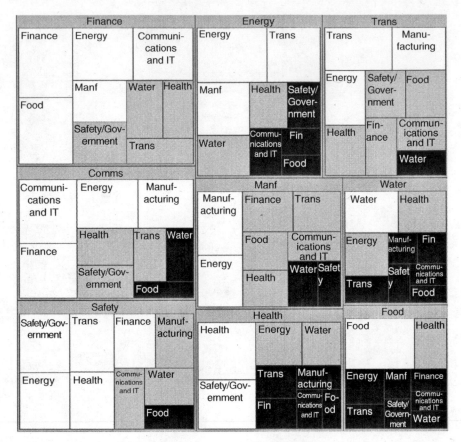

**FIGURE 4.50** Canadian correlated outbound dependency map. White □ = high outbound dependency. Gray ▦ = medium outbound dependency. Black ■ = low outbound dependency. Each sector block is proportional to the size of its outbound dependency score relative to the other sectors. Each square within each sector block indicates the proportional size of outbound dependency scores from each sectors. Recall that outbound dependency is equivalent to the threat posed by a CI sector to other sectors.

And to conclude this chapter, Figure 4.50 represents the total sum of all median scores for outbound dependency. Within the total score are boxes for each sector, which represent the proportional size of each sector's outbound median sum relative to the other sectors. Within each sector box are smaller boxes for each outbound relationship with all other sectors, such that the size of the box is proportional to the size of each sectors contribution to the outbound median sum for the specific sector.

## United States

We will conclude this chapter on correlated dependency metrics using a visualization tool, which was also employed in Chapters 2 (econometric analysis) and 3 (data dependency analysis). As in Chapters 2 and 3, we will review the correlated dependency metrics using treemap tools to provide a top-level view of all sectors and how they relate to one another from the perspective of first inbound, then outbound information and data dependency.

For comprehension purposes the dependency scale has been aggregated into high, medium, and low data dependency where high is the top third of all dependency scores across all sectors, for a given sector, medium is the middle third, and low is the bottom third of dependency scores for a given sector. The ranks are color coded according to the following scale:

| Value | Color | Metric (Score) Range |
|--------|----------|----------------------|
| High | ☐White | 5.68–10.00 |
| Medium | ▨Grey | 3.75–5.67 |
| Low | ■Black | 1.00–3.74 |

Below is a map for U.S. correlated inbound data dependency. Figure 4.51 at the highest level represents the total sum of all median scores for inbound dependency. Within the total score are boxes for each sector, which represent the proportional size of each sector's inbound median sum relative to the other sectors. Within each sector box are smaller boxes for each inbound relationship with all other sectors, such that the size of the box is proportional to the size of each sectors' contribution to the inbound median sum for the specific sector. Figure 4.51 provides a comprehensive perspective on U.S. correlated inbound dependency among the CI sectors.

Following is a map for U.S. correlated outbound dependency. Figure 4.52 represents the total sum of median scores for U.S. correlated outbound dependency. Within the total score are boxes for each sector, which represent the proportional size of each sector's outbound median sum. Within each sector box are smaller boxes for each outbound relationship with all other sectors, such that the size of the box is proportional to the size of each sectors' contribution to the outbound median sum. Finally, to facilitate intersector analysis, the weighting for each sector output for each sector box is coded by high, medium, and low dependency relative to all sectors.

As was the case for the correlated inbound dependency map, the scale for the correlated outbound dependency map has been aggregated into high, medium, and low data dependency where high is the top third of dependency scores for a

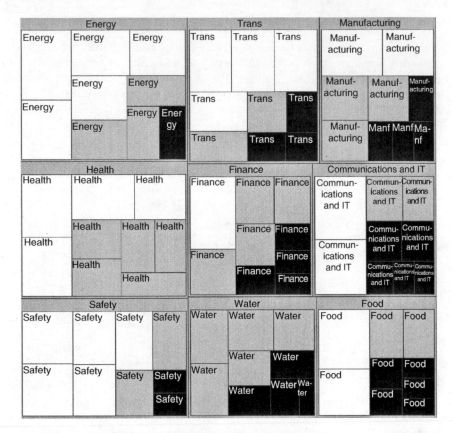

**FIGURE 4.51** U.S. correlated inbound data dependency map. White □ = high inbound dependency. Gray ■ = medium inbound dependency. Black ■ = low inbound dependency. Each sector block is proportional to the size of its inbound dependency score relative to the other sectors. Each square within each sector block indicates the proportional size of inbound dependency scores from each sectors. Recall that inbound dependency is equivalent to the vulnerability of the CI sector to threats from other sectors.

given sector, medium is the middle third, and low is the bottom third of dependency scores for a given sector. The ranks are color coded according to the following scale:

| Value | Color | Metric (Score) Range |
|---|---|---|
| High | □ White | 5.68–10.00 |
| Medium | ■ Grey | 3.75–5.67 |
| Low | ■ Black | 1.00–3.74 |

To conclude this chapter, Figure 4.52 represents the total sum of all median scores for outbound dependency. Within the total score are boxes for each sector, which

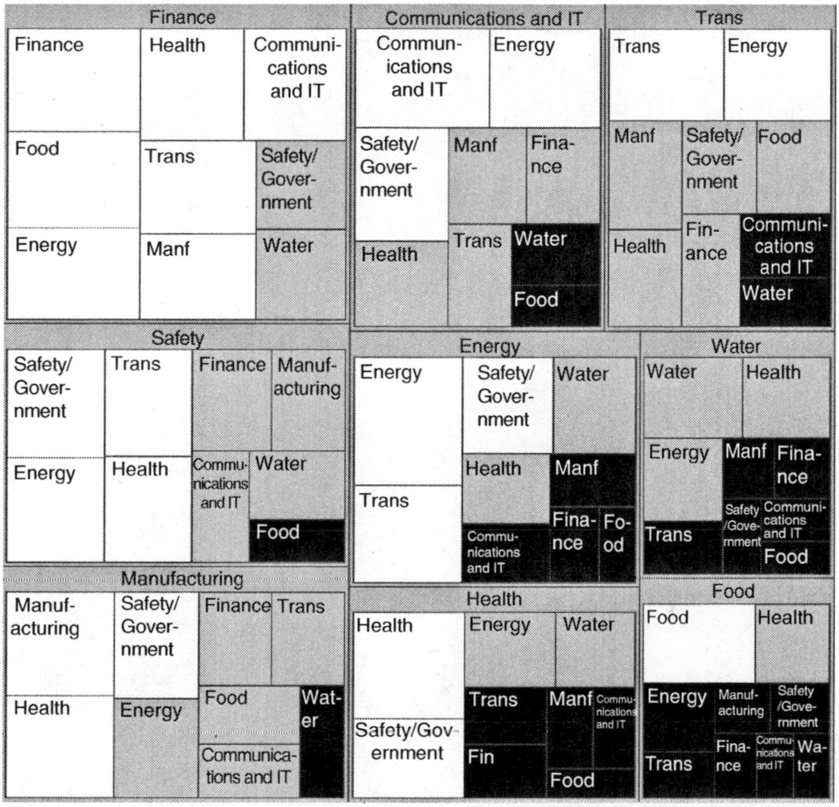

**FIGURE 4.52** U.S. correlated outbound dependency map. White □ = high outbound dependency. Gray ▨ = medium outbound dependency. Black ■ — low outbound dependency. Each sector block is proportional to the size of its outbound dependency score relative to the other sectors. Each square within each sector block indicates the proportional size of outbound dependency scores from each sectors. Recall that outbound dependency is equivalent to the threat posed by a CI sector to other sectors.

represent the proportional size of each sector's outbound median sum relative to the other sectors. Within each sector box are smaller boxes for each outbound relationship with all other sectors, such that the size of the box is proportional to the size of each sectors contribution to the outbound median sum for the specific sector.

# 5 Critical Infrastructure Threat–Risk

## Contributed by David McMahon

## INTRODUCTION

This chapter describes the relevance of threat-to and threat-from analysis to effective risk management. The resultant threat-vector and dependency-flow theories will be illuminated with examples, and include a discussion on possible threat metrics associated with critical infrastructure (CI) interdependency. These examples are intended to illustrate how to apply the material from the earlier chapters into risk assessment activities around CI sectors.

The common threads that bind all CI include money and information flows, both of which are incubated in cyberspace. Financial and energy control grids run directly over cyberspace. It necessarily follows that threats to the fabric of cyberspace conduct risks across all sectors.* These exposures precipitate both logical and physical impacts. Shared risks in cyberspace are conducted at the speed of light. Thus, the health of cyberspace is a good early indicator for the condition of all CI. This preamble explains why there is clear emphasis on cyber throughout this chapter.

How does one go about managing something a chaotic as threat–risk? Although it may not be possible to measure threat–risk absolutely, complete understanding of the threat–risk is not necessary to begin to take correct action in mitigating overall risk.

Most nominal threat–risk assessments produced today contain limited threat, vulnerability, or incident metrics. They typically represent compliance audits against common, general practices. It is also beyond the capabilities for most organizations to gather definitive threat metrics and perform the necessarily complex threat–risk-likelihood calculation.

What is the effective difference between deploying security safeguards to meet the requirements of an audit to a given standard, and a threat–risk assessment? For one thing, security standards are environmentally agnostic and expect uniform deployment of security. Organizational security often experiences regression to the mean that is based upon their neighborhood and fixed security budgets (keep up with the Jones'—no more no less). Similarly, security standards tend to espouse homogenous strategies. This is somewhat analogous to placing your limited supply

---

* Macaulay, T., 2007. Risk conductors, *Information Systems Security Journal*, January.

sandbags right around your foxhole at an equal height, even though the enemy is most predominant to your front, and most likely to advance from that direction.

This is the whole point of an effective threat–risk assessment. We now understand that given a fixed or limited security budget, an accurate threat–risk assessment is essential to deploying security in the most efficacious manner—placing most of the sandbags between you and the enemy rather than between you and your own forces. The direction of a deliberate attack against an infrastructure will have a vector in physical or logical space. The two end points of this threat-vector are determined by threats-to and threats-from analysis. Thus, a predictive threat–risk assessment can buy your organization time and precision within a dynamic threat environment.

The magnitude and direction (vector) of a threat event is influenced by the presence of risk conductors. The most insidious of which are generated along lines of interdependencies.

The metrics that most often define interdependencies are money, data flows, and geospatial proximity. Conversely, if two organizations trade no goods, nor services, have no communications and are not colocated, then there is likely no direct interdependency. However, there may well exist indirect dependencies through an intermediary or supply chain. This is where most organizations get burnt and have little security.

## LAY PERCEPTIONS OF RISK

There is tendency to talk in terms of risk scenarios that loosely combine threat, vulnerability, assets, impacts, and likelihood into some form of narrative. The discussion often takes on a distinctive asset-availability focus because this is what is tangible for most people. Threat attacks against confidentiality and integrity are the least understood, are nearly undetectable and by far the most likely events to damage an organization. One cannot talk about vulnerabilities without alluding to threat. Similarly, vulnerability-from and threat-to discussions share common ground.

The prevalent asset-vulnerability-centric strategy is focused on protection and recovery based upon a potential loss of availability while neglecting to detect, interdict, predict, and disrupt the threat preemptively or deal primarily with confidentiality and integrity. Remember the axiom which points out that "an ounce of prevention in worth a pound of cure." Let us revisit the definition of risk in more depth and breadth in the context of CIs.

### SCALE AND BREADTH

We can think big and bad with the doctrinal tenets of information warfare (IW). IW operations and network-centric warfare are concepts evolved from electronic warfare first pioneered with radio signals in WWI, becoming an intense practice in the 1980s. Nation states have since defined formidable capabilities to conduct warfare in cyberspace (over telecommunications networks). Many countries are fully operational and now constitute a measurable and persistent threat to a nation's CI. The risk is exacerbated by the convergence of the globalization of supply chains, the introduction of disruptive technologies, and the criminalization of cyberspace.

We begin by stating that network-centric operations (NCO) or computer network operations (CNO) are not new theories of warfare. They represent a confluence of signals intelligence (SIGINT) and the emergence of the Internet. Doctrine and battle tactics dating thousands of years has just been dusted off and applied to the information age. Warfare in the physical and logical spaces is fused, both theoretically and in practice. One only has to look to the Yugoslavian conflict, both Gulf Wars, and Estonia for poignant examples of physical and logical (data flows) infrastructure targeting.

CNO includes computer network attack (CNA), computer network exploitation (CNE), and computer network defense (CND). CNA represents actions taken through the use of computers to disrupt, deny, degrade, or destroy information resident in computers and networks, or the machines themselves. CND uses information communications technology (ICT) to protect, monitor, analyze, detect, and respond to malicious activity targeted against information systems and computer networks. CNE enables operations and intelligence collection capabilities which are conducted through the use of computer networks. CNE is the most rampant and least detectable activity launched against our infrastructures.

The following is adapted from Dr. Robert Garigue, on information peacekeeping*:

> Information Operations (IO), formally known as Information Warfare (IW) strikes with a composite of Physical, Syntactical, and Semantic weapons of force. The use of a physical weapon will result in the permanent destruction of physical components and denial of service. A Syntactical weapon will focus on attacking the operating logic of a system and introduce delays, permit unauthorized control or create unpredictable behaviours. A Semantic weapon will focus its effects on destroying the trust and truth maintenance components of the system.
>
> It often takes a total loss of availability before most infrastructure owners take notice. Degradation of services is attributed to gremlins in the system, and the erosion of integrity credited to ghosts in the machine. The compromise of confidentiality is out-of-sight and out-of-mind. Information Warfare Operations can be characterized in this way, but is a small subset of a much broader debate within of what is the computational life cycle of knowledge. And organizations run on knowledge. Do you know where your information is at all times? How it is communicated? Created, used and destroyed? And who has had access to it from cradle to grave? The composition of the primary material itself is changing–data and information–is being changed from "dumb" and passive and has started to becoming "smarter" and more active. It all has to do with the rise of the new protocols. New semantically capable computational technologies will permit a completely new range of processing more akin to reasoning than calculating. The use of Ontologies, Declarative Logic, and Unsupervised Concepts Learning will change both the nature and exploitation of content. This also means that the data and

* Information peacekeeping—Dr. Robert Garigue, Information Warfare. Developing a Conceptual Framework 1995, Managing Ontological Ambiguity: Extending the Knowledge Management Framework 2003, http://http-server.carleton.ca/~rgarigue/.

information is actionable computationally and within a few internet based technology cycles blur the distinction between what is an application and what is content. The intellectual property of your organization becomes alive and vulnerable on new plains of existence.

Computational epistemology is vitally important in the context of universal systems theory and quantifying risk in critical infrastructures. If you don't appreciate the language of knowledge, it is very hard to accurately measure the risk to intellectual properties and real wealth. All wealth is, at most, one step from the Internet.

There is no such thing as a closed system. Trending forces of convergence, globalization, systemization, and virtualization, to name a few, have created an information environment where your organization and the World most dangerous terrorist group are connected at the speed of light.

Because information operations (IO) in an integrative framework it extends beyond just one organization. IO is not just the concern of one group. To be effective it has to be democratized into all fields of human activities. IO needs to integrate medical, social, economic, geographic, political, cultural and religious data, information and events. Notwithstanding, the telecom and financial sectors are the current custodians of IO. In the end, IO will restructure organizations along a new set of shared accountabilities based upon market forces and a measurable value at risk. The complexity of the problem begets the complexity of the organization that will try to manage it.

Information Warfare Operations and Information Peacekeeping are powerful concepts that will help recast and reframe strategic analysis. The Information Operation, analytical framework, as not just integrates of the roles of Information Warfare Operations and Information Peacekeeping into a total continuum of conflict management and conflict resolution but offers the road map to higher levels of technical and organizational performance. This is the concern of all infrastructure owners and governments, because the "Matrix" connects all things.

The 1999 Report of the Special Senate Committee on security and intelligence stated that

> Threat actors are bent on causing harm have an array of techniques to destroy, steal or interfere with electronically stored or transmitted information. This malicious activity is referred to as Information Operations (IO). Foreign intelligence services are using the Internet to conduct espionage operations. The rationale proffered for intelligence service activity in this area, is that it is a simple, low-cost, non-threatening and relatively risk-free way for to collect classified, proprietary or sensitive information. The growth of and our increased reliance on critical infrastructures, combined with their complexity, have made them potential targets for physical or cyber-attacks.

The United States has begun to address vulnerabilities of CIs beginning with Presidential Directive 39 in 1995. Later, on May 22, 1998 the president issued Presidential Directive 63 which organized the U.S. economy and government into sectors, with an assigned agency. The purpose was to build a system to identify, detect, protect, and prevent natural and man-made (deliberate) threats.

Marshall McLuhan wrote that "World War III would be a guerrilla information war with no division between the civilian and military populations." Prophetically, today the telecoms and financial sectors are fighting on the front line in cyberspace. IW operations against CIs are conducted on a global scale.

## DEEP DIVE INTO UNIVERSAL RISK

A universal integrated risk theory addresses the full-spectrum of threats in a predictive and scientific manner and tackles the human perceptions of risk. The method creates the framework and model for probable and possible outcomes to be presented, qualified with metrics, and communicated effectively to decision makers. The primary purpose of any threat–risk assessment is to allocate security resources most effectively and proactively. This is a far better way of implementing security than reacting to a crisis in an ad hoc manner driven by the emotion of the incident.

## EXISTING METHODOLOGIES

Current risk assessment methodologies are basically security compliance audits based upon common and best practices. They are simplistic and are not currently designed for complex, converged systems. More sophisticated methodologies are required for real-world security ecosystems such as CIs—not something you can easily capture in a checklist. The fidelity of risk modeling has always been challenging. It necessarily involves a cross-disciplinary approach that addresses the equities between defensive and offensive domains, considers the physical, logic, and semantic layers of the security model, and introduces the most important human factor. A study into the effects of CI risks requires experimental methods, behavioral observations, fused with both qualitative and qualitative (relativistic) analysis.

## REAL THREAT METRICS

Understanding infrastructure/infostructure technology, strategy and the threat is paramount to designing realistic and effective risk model and mitigation strategies. An organization cannot make a determination of risk without direct or indirect access to current and accurate threat intelligence. Conversely, organizations must be collecting intelligence on those entities which pose the greatest threat—not just well-known traditional ones.

## PREVENTION VERSUS RESPONSE

Risk mitigation includes both reducing the effects of events as well as preventing events from occurring in the first place. Most communities appear to be content with letting a threat event occur, and paying for the cleanup afterward. Just look at the money invested into fixing people who make themselves sick (obesity, smoking) compared to a preemptive investment in fitness. Prevention and response merge when considering how early warning and preparedness can serve to prevent as well as to mitigate the effects of natural or man-made disasters.

Nowadays, organizations need to be security agile and risk tolerant. Too often, we see evidence of walled gardens of static security and risk adverse corporate behavior are seen.

The goal of organizational security should be predictive threat assessment and effective near-real-time integrated risk management deploying an adaptive and active-defense-in-depth strategy, against a singular converged threat (all hazards approach), and around the enterprises' most valued assets. Generalists will always win over a specialist in no-rules no-bound warfare owing to the generalists' ability to change the mode and line of attack away from the specialist's strengths and turn toward weaknesses. This age-old strategy is thought of in terms of provisioning a homogeneous or holistic security posture. We need the stimulus of a threat to evolve and build immunities but cannot be a slave reacting to the threat.

Congruently, it also follows that one cannot win a threat-engagement purely through defensive means. History has taught this again and again. The organization must be prepared to undertake proactive operations; ideally at distance in time and space: we can refer to this as active-defense. This concept is poignant within a universe where threats are converging, because traditionally fortified/protected enclaves will find themselves under siege on many fronts and in many dimensions. Sieges against an organization's valuable assets will not endure for years, as they did in the crusades, but could be over in a matter of seconds. No longer will a particular threat-to an asset come from a traditional threat-from source agent or vector, who manifests the attack in an entirely standard bounded and defendable manner. There is no perimeter, no clear approach along which an attack will come. It will come from any direction and dimension at the speed of light. The only defense against surprise is not to be surprised.

## ATTRIBUTES OF GOOD UNIVERSAL RISK MANAGEMENT

Having a sophisticated integrated Risk Management Framework and crisis readiness expertise available to both evaluate the universal risks associated with an infrastructure investment does several things:

- Provides a good story for those entrusted with security and emergency preparedness
- Demonstrates assurance and compliance
- Creates greater confidence that key risks are being proactively managed to reduce insurance costs
- Enables more effective governance, command, and control

Key attributes of risk expertise that characterize good capabilities in the field include a good understanding of the universal risk management process and infrastructure security across a wide range of industrial interfaces; an insightful appreciation of how assurance and risk transfer solutions have a role in risk management; a strong quantitative, statistical, investigative, and economic analytical background is required to understand how risks adversely affect hard and soft asset values, supply chains and customers, and an inventory of intangible assets like reputation and goodwill; and most usefully, valid and timely threat-to information.

## Universal Risk Methodology for CIP

A universal risk methodology* for CIs must be based upon

- Solid and incontrovertible theoretical foundation, notably the synthesis of critical infrastructure protection (CIP) and sophisticated risk analytics with the universal
- Pragmatics of real infrastructures that are influenced by advanced research in contagion-borne interdependencies, technological and threat convergence, globalization, risk conductance, IO, and critical node analysis
- Qualitative statistical findings from thorough consultation with CI owners, which is validated and contrasted with comprehensive quantitative (empirical) metrics from statistically relevant synaptic and semantic coverage of the national information infrastructure
- Applied mature analytical processes, like hypodeductive reasoning, formal and inductive (fuzzy) logic, critical, and alternative analytics, within an Integrated Risk Management Framework
- Systems theory that most correctly addresses the chaotic behavior of complex dynamic and open systems

The outcome should be an adaptive model of high-fidelity and capable of predictive accuracy. These thoughts represent an essential departure from relying on doctrine and security policy as the common means of managing risk. "You can't manage what you cannot measure."

## Pragmatic Threat–Risk Analysis Methodology

Threat–risk analysis is a process of inquiry that often requires hypodeductive reasoning. Deduction takes the form of predictions, or hypotheses, that we seek to either prove or disprove categorically. Hypotheses are tentative answers to a question or are possible causes of an outcome. However, a generalization based upon inductive reasoning or intuition is not a hypothesis. In this day and Internet age, a risk analyst must cross-train as a computational epistemologist and an experimentalist.

When induction is reasoning from a set of specific observations to reach a general conclusion, deductive reasoning flows in the opposite direction. More

---

* The universal systems theory is a multiperspective domain, synthesizing principles and concepts from computational epistemology, ontology, engineering, cybernetics, morphological analysis, statistical thermodynamics (entropy), self-organization, catastrophe, chaos, uncertainty, and complexity theory. The universal systems theory is a means of modeling infrastructure risk with a high degree of precision and deterministic uncertainty, when tuned by pragmatics and empirical data from the matrix.

The behavioral model of infrastructures comprise of people, processes, and technology that is continually under the influence of dynamic actors, and is prone to errors or accidents. Real systems are open, chaotic, multi-order, recursively interdependent, widely dynamic, and nonlinear. This is where an infinitesimal threat catalyst can create widespread catastrophic impact, as substantiated by the butterfly effect. Understanding risk in, and between, CIs requires that an analyst has a means of modeling systems-of-systems at both macro and down to microscales.

specific outcomes are extrapolated from general premises, and these outcomes are expected if all the premises are true, and the logic is valid.

Hypotheses may reflect past experience with similar questions. They are educated propositions about cause. Multiple hypotheses should be proposed wherever possible. These are alternative explanations. Hypotheses can be eliminated, but not confirmed with absolute certainty. Hypothesis must be testable. Herein, the analyst must move beyond a paper exercise and garner real-world metrics. It is not possible to repeat an experiment that will show that something will never happen. Risk analysis constantly runs into this conundrum.

Analysis of competing hypotheses requires an analyst to explicitly identify all reasonable alternatives and test them against each other rather than dealing with them one at a time. Start by listing significant threat evidence and arguments for and against each hypothesis. Then, tune or reduce the matrix of evidence and arguments by reducing those that have no diagnostic value. The irrelevancy of the risk scenarios needs to be thought out. The analyst needs to draw tentative conclusions relative to likelihood as an intermediary step. Judgment should be deferred until the complete risk assessment can be reviewed critically and alternative or contrary analysis has been completed.

One objective should be to try to disprove hypotheses. Of the remaining solutions, one should analyze how sensitive each remaining conclusions are to critical items of evidence and state the consequences of a wrong analysis. Separate proven and disproved hypothesis from unproven; then identify inconsistencies or knowledge gaps.

It is common that conclusions of an assessment are based upon lack of evidence. The first stage is to identify what you know, and what you know you do not know, and measure what you do not know you do not know through null steerage techniques.* It is possible to draw inferences from gaps in information because there is a distinct lack of plausible arguments against the hypothesis. In real terms, there is a big difference to stating that you have nothing that would indicate a terrorist attack because (1) you have infiltrated the group and know everything that has been said; or (2) you have no coverage whatsoever. The former has rigor whereas the latter is a conclusion based upon ignorance. The most often neglected factor in risk analysis is an educated and valid measurement of uncertainty.

After identifying gaps, the analyst can use null steering to infer compelling evidence or construct reasonable arguments, which fit into the analysis. For example, if an extremist group has the means, opportunity, and motivation to carry out an infrastructure attack in Toronto and yet none has occurred, this should cause the analyst to revisit the fidelity of the threat model.

Once the analyst has quantified what they know and what they know they do not know, and run through several risk scenarios, the missing variables are the unknowns. Even this can be quantified and reported as uncertainty or confidence level associated with the analysis. It is important that, when the assessment reports its risk findings, there is some contingency; the conclusions are wrong, what would be the magnitude of the error, and in what direction would the outcome take?

---

* Null steerage refers to a passive inference toward the conspicuous absence of information, reasoning or sensory data. One example is the acoustic hole that someone creates when walking into a room, or passive radar that detects the hole an aircraft leaves in the RF spectrum.

## RELATIVISTIC THREAT ANALYSIS

Weighted analysis means that all statements about threat–risk need to be assigned meaningful relative metrics, which should further be anchored to absolute measurements. Applying high, medium, and low, red orange, and yellow risk levels is of limited utility to most analysts. It is like asking how high is up. Notwithstanding, it may not always be possible to determine risk in absolute terms, but some relativistic analysis is required to enumerate magnitudes of risk scenarios relative to each other. Later, the analyst can determine absolute risk of one of these scenarios and will be in a better position to state all risks in absolute terms because they are linked.

Relative residual risk assessment can be performed by selective security safeguards to the analysis, and calculating or observing changes to the overall risk. The direction and magnitude of the shift in risk can indicate which security measures are most cost effective even if you do not know the risk in absolute terms.

## REAL-TIME RISK

Real-time, empirical observations of threat activity should be given precedence over intuitive risk calculations. There is no rule that deliberate threat agents have to act rationally, or even in their best interests. The same guidance is applicable to those targets selected by a threat agent. The model may suggest that people may act a certain way in response to an event, but a strong leader may influence behavior along another path. It is important to build the model with the capability to recognize and adapt to real-world warnings and indicators, which may signal a departure away from the primary, rational analysis.

## CRITICAL ANALYSIS

Threat and risk analysis requires a structured objective approach starting with correct presuppositions, true premises, performing valid logical reasoning to develop a high-fidelity threat–risk model. Adequate room must be made in the assessment to facilitate out-of-the-box thinking and creativity. Foremost, 9/11 was a failure to think creatively. Particularly, threat events involving deliberate threat agents often occur chaotically and without historical precedence. What actually happens may not be the most probable, but should always be contained in the analysis. Therefore, a full threat and risk assessment must contain critical analysis and alternate views that consider the less probable but important.

Utility theory is a normative theory of human behavior not intended to describe how people actually behave, but how they should behave if they were rational.*

---

* Utility theory—http://en.wikipedia.org/w/index.php?title = Utility&oldid = 171835763. Utility theory— Daniel Bernoulli (1738) gave the earliest known written statement of this hypothesis as a way to resolve the St. Petersburg Paradox. In the expected utility theorem, v. Neumann and Morgenstern proved that any normal preference relation over a finite set of states can be written as an expected utility. (Therefore, it is also called von-Neumann–Morgenstern utility.)

Unfortunately, deliberate threat agents are often neither always rational nor predictable in tactical time frames. Their plans do not necessarily go the way they predicted. For every deliberate threat event, there are frequently multiple agendas or reasons. Threat agent behavior is fraught with irony, change, chaos, fluidity, paradox, and errors. Threat agents are far more predictable on strategic scales versus discreet, specific, tactical measures.

The prospect theory observes that most people place more intrinsic value on loss than the value on gain.* This influences people's behavior in a way which is not always apparent in a quantitative predictive-analysis (e.g., the impact of losing $5 feels worse than finding $5). This is an important factor in calculating risk conductance and work factors for deliberate threat agents.

Natural forces divert energy toward the path of least resistance at a rate and amount proportionally to the resistance presented by the other routes. Similarly, of the attack scenarios known to a deliberate (thinking) threat agent, the path of least resistance will be chosen orders of magnitude more often. Resistance to a threat agent, in this context, represents the ease of the attack, risk to the attacker, and return on investment. As an illustration, if one attack scenario is perceived as offering half the resistance compared with other options, then it is at least ten times more likely to be chosen. It is similarly important to note that, when threatened, people will often choose to avoid the threatening situation by taking the perceived safest course of action the vast majority of time. For example, if a bucket has two holes, where one hole was twice as big as the other, then there it would be reasonable to assume twice the flow. Yet, for humans, if it were twice the risk to go outside than to stay inside during a terrorist incident, then nearly everyone would stay put, given the variable of informed choice. Curiously, with physical threats, people react more acutely where the consequences are more gruesome, immediate, or uncertain even when the similar outcomes are no less likely. In other words, people fear and take measures to avoid uncertain and scary threat scenarios in favor of high-risk familiar alternatives. For instance, it is common to see trampling fatalities with fire outbreak.

As a threat agent could launch an attack for all the wrong reasons or crowds can act irrationally influenced by "group think," in response to an incident, the analyst needs to consider threat events and responses out of the boundaries of the plausible, particularly high impact—low probability scenarios and plan accordingly. A study ought to identify the triggers which signal a departure from rational behavior for both threat agents and their targets. The pitfall in this alternative analysis is that it should not substitute for a thoughtful analysis of higher risk scenarios. Clever, convoluted, and implausible threat scenarios do not translate to more serious risk. Likewise, scenarios with more serious impact do not necessarily mean that they are not more likely nor do they actually present more risk.

---

* Prospect Theory—http://en.wikipedia.org/w/index.php?title = Prospect_theory&oldid = 172503617. Prospect theory was developed by Daniel Kahneman and Amos Tversky in 1979 as a psychologically realistic alternative to expected utility theory.

In parcel with critical analysis comes the notion of parallel trends analysis and the virtue of contrary thinking.* These concepts challenge the presuppositions and initial premises used in the mainstream analysis or offer alternative branches, and ultimately different conclusions from those presented in the primary assessment. The value of contrary thinking, parallel trends analysis, and alternative analysis is to demonstrate diligence in considering all possibilities. It guards against a distortion of judgment by the biases of the analyst. It prepares ready-made risk contingencies should the situation change or the premises change. It may help to identify blind-stops within the analysis.

Presuppositions and initial premises used throughout a threat or risk assessment can suffer from perils of inaccurate or stale intelligence. Besides obvious review, revision, and culling of material, an analyst needs to establish warning and indicators, which should trigger a reevaluation. It should be described in the initial assessment which indicators would substantially change analysis. These could include real incidents that defy reason, or irrational attacks. Warnings and indicators not only need involve scenarios which follow the predicted path but also indications of the unpredicted path. In quantitative analysis, what would mark a flaw in the fidelity of the risk behavioral model?

## Contextual Concepts of Risk Management

The following discussion is adapted from the authors work on an Integrated Risk Management Framework.[†]

Over the years, I contributed philanthropically to thought on more evolved risk management approaches. Consequently, much of my earlier writings have appeared in public sector doctrine on integrated risk management. I consider it fair use to talk to CI risks in the context of those earlier writings.

There are important contextual aspects to consider in modeling behavioral responses to actual and perceived threats and to decision making bound to effective risk management.

Notwithstanding, there is inherent risk in all decisions. It must be recognized that there is a relationship between the cost of any particular action and the cost of not acting, i.e., the actions to avoid minimize risks cannot be taken at whatever the cost. In practical terms, the implications of a given risk must be measured against the cost of addressing that risk, or directing resources to other priorities. Furthermore,

---

* Parallel trends analysis is the author's theory and is based upon alternative and critical analysis. See similar ideas from The CIAs Sherman Kent Center for Intelligence Analysis, ref: Logic of Alternative Analysis, Making Sense of Transnational Threats, The Sherman Kent Center for Intelligence Analysis, Occasional Papers: Vol. 3, No. 1, October 2004, Warren Fishbein and Gregory Treverton, Sherman Kent Center.

† Integrated Risk Management Framework, http://www.tbs-sct.gc.ca/pubs_pol/dcgpubs/RiskManagement/rmf-cgr_e.asp, Treasury Board of Canada, March 2000; Risk Management for Canada and Canadians: Report of the ADM Working Group on Risk Management, PCO, March 2000; Building Risk Management Capacity in the Public Service. Stephen Hill, Post-doctoral fellow NSERC/SSHRC Chair Program in Risk Communication and Public Policy Haskayne School of Business University of Calgary and Geoff Dinsdale, Research and Policy Analyst and Coordinator of CCMD's Action-Research Roundtables Canadian Centre for Management Development.

avoiding or ignoring risk is to mismanage and ultimately accept the risk. A risk ignored is a risk accepted.

Infrastructure owners are accountable to societal values and the public's, shareholder's, or partner's willingness to take the risk are relevant and legitimate considerations for decision making, whether or not they are consistent with rational assessment of the risk. The common perception of risk must be taken into account, as does the human behavioral response to a threat stimulus.

As stated, there is a correlation between the tolerance for risk and the perception of control over the activity generating a given incident. In this book, measurements of qualitative perceptions of cyber threats and actual quantitative metrics show a gap between real and imagined vulnerabilities related to CI interdependency. Analysts must make a clear distinction between actions driven by knowledge, uninformed opinion, and irrational beliefs.

## PRECAUTIONARY APPROACH

The precautionary approach to risk management was defined in the 1992 Rio Declaration on Environment and Development:

> In order to protect the environment, the precautionary approach shall be widely applied by states according to their capabilities. Where there are threats of serious or irreversible damage, lack of full scientific certainty shall not be used as a reason for postponing cost-effective measures to prevent environmental degradation.

Risk typically has a negative connotation, but there are also positive opportunities arising from risk taking. Innovation and risk coexist frequently. Today's compliance and legal systems will hold executives responsible for ensuring prudent risk management; this not only includes showing wise risk mitigation but also demonstrating appropriate risk taking in pursuing opportunities, and ensuring safety in a proactive manner. In risk analysis, exposures owing to inaction are tabled as losses or negative impacts.

A precautionary approach is an increasingly important element of risk management particularly as it applies to the uncertainties of a risk assessment. This approach forces a conscious risk management decision to act or to not act. The precautionary approach should be applied where there are potential impacts on irreversible damage. A lack of full rational certainty is not acceptable, as a reason for postponing cost-effective measures to mitigate an event. It is no longer acceptable for a lack of knowledge about possible risks of a given situation to be used as an excuse to avoid some positive action. Integrated risk management including a precautionary approach to addressing risk has been slow to be operationalized within in CI sectors owing to the level familiarity with these concepts.

There is need for a deeper understanding of risk management and a more systematic and consolidated approach to managing risk. Infrastructure risk management and national security are involved in the process of transitioning private sector to the public sector. It is no surprise that the majority of targets of deliberate asymmetric threats (terrorism, espionage, and organized crime) have been commercial entities and citizens. Similarly, the private sector is much more decisively engaged in predicting detecting, disrupting, interdicting, and countering deliberate threats unilaterally.

An integrated risk management framework provides an organization with a means to develop an overall approach to manage strategic risks by creating conditions to evaluate substantially different risks on the same page. Risk is bound to the uncertainty that surrounds future events and outcomes. It is the expression of the likelihood and impact of an event with the potential to influence operational objectives. An expression of the likelihood and impact of an event implies that, as a minimum, some form of quantitative or qualitative analysis is required for making decisions concerning major risks.

Formal and de facto standards establish limits and boundaries concerning what are acceptable risk practices and outcomes. It is no longer sufficient to manage risk at the individual activity level or in functional silos. Organizations stand to benefit from a more comprehensive approach to dealing with all their risks.

Integrated risk management is a continuous, proactive, and systematic process to understand, manage, and communicate risk from an organizationwide perspective. It is about making strategic decisions that contribute to the achievement of an organization's overall corporate objectives.

## THREAT EVENTS

The threat event is an undesirable occurrence, which can exploit a given vulnerability. It can be described in the absence of an instigator or likelihood. All threats fall within three broad categories—deliberate, accidental, and natural hazards. Of the three categories, deliberate threats are generally the more difficult to counter because an intelligent adversary, whether working from the inside or outside, will attempt to circumvent existing safeguards, often surreptitiously.

Deliberate threat events are intentionally motivated actions that originate from internal or external agents. They are by definition man-made, and include all manner of harmful actions purposefully directed at a target in a focused or indiscriminate manner. They also target more vulnerable.

## THREAT PERSPECTIVE

Threats are often viewed from two perspectives: threats-to and threats-from. Both approaches are required to provide early warning of threat activities in context with exposures to an organization's valued assets.

### Threats-From

Threat events and agents can be examined without immediately linking them to an incident or victim. It is a common practice for security and criminal intelligence services to gather information on potential groups who have demonstrated potential to precipitate a threat event. The analysis is useful from both a security preparedness point of view and it provides investigative steerage to head off an incident. This analysis involves examining the motives, means, and methods of a threat agent surrounding a potential threat event.

A threats-from analysis is performed from within the threat milieu and is seen as a proactive step to mitigating the risk by addressing the threat directly. The disadvantages of a threats-from approach are preoccupation with traditional threats-agents-events at the expense of emerging threats and more importantly specifically targeted assets.

## Threats-To

Threats-to approach begins by identifying potential targets of the threat, the intrinsic vulnerabilities of the asset, and its exposures. It is complementary to a threats-from viewpoint and has the advantage of being more selective in an examination of threats based upon a given target system. The disadvantage of a threats-to approach is that it is reactionary and provides little early warning of threat activities, intentions, trends, or targets. There is often a gap in the intelligence coverage linking threats-to and threats-from data.

## THREAT-VECTOR

A vector is a measurement of direction and magnitude. Direction in Cartesian space requires both a start and end point.

## IMPORTANCE OF THREAT AGENTS IN FORMING A PREDICTIVE ANALYSIS

A risk-to or vulnerability weighted perspective to threat analysis suggests static protective safeguards to mitigate perceived exposures. The next stage of an analytical process is to apply any threat-from or means-motives, intention, and specific capability modifiers to the risk values. Threats-from has a more significant bearing on the predictive risk analysis in contrast to the historical or empirical testing, and is a good indicator of what detection and response mechanisms should be added. Risk assessments that do not examine threat agents and their victims cannot be predictive. They present a snapshot in time, neither relying on historical data nor intelligence to determine what the risk will be even over a short period. Safeguard selection can only be based upon best practices and addressing vulnerabilities discovered through evaluation. Without accurate threat agent information, an assessment will be unable to determine magnitude of exposures particularly in a dynamic threat environment. It is also impractical to uniformly implement security safeguards and exercise all scenarios across large and complex systems to the highest levels. To do so would raise the business risk (costs) associated with the program to unacceptable levels. Responsible risk management should proceed with an efficacious selection and implementation of security plans guided by a predictive assessment based upon an analysis of the threat agents.

## THREAT AGENTS

Threat agents are the catalysts, which trigger a threat event, and consequentially an asset compromise. They are the actual perpetrator or causal factor in threat scenarios. Awareness about the nature and seriousness of the threat agents posing symmetric and asymmetric attacks against infrastructure is a significant challenge.

## THREAT ACTION

As stated previously, the threat event defines the class of occurrence where the threat agent gives the event focused and enacts the process. Each threat event may lead to a variety of outcomes, either spontaneously or when acted upon by a threat agent, or as a catalyst. Actions may occur in isolation, sequentially, or in combination. Certain actions must occur in a progressive order to be effective. A variety of means can be used in assessing the threat including

- Historical incident attributed to states, groups, or individuals
- Investigations
- Surveillance
- Trends analysis or forecasting

A threat event generally has a primary and secondary effect. For example, an explosion and fire may provoke panic which may ultimately cause most of the damage. The political and economic fallout of the physical 9/11 attacks is a good example of how the secondary effects (air transport industry, Iraq War) to a threat event can be as significant as the primary effect.

Many threat actions are a prerequisite for follow-on actions or events. Before a weapon can be built, the threat agent must gain access to knowledge, facilities, and access. The case is, the greater level of access a threat agent has, the more options present themselves, to the point where attack is more a matter of motivation and objective, than it is means.

Many threat events, natural and man-made, have cascading effects—the topic of the book! A recent example is the ice storm in Canada. The phenomena of cascading effects can be deliberately initiated or taken advantage by a threat Agent. A diversionary tactic may attack in a manner, which preoccupies security forces. In the same vein, a fortuitous event (for the threat agent) like a power outage or pandemic may be taken advantage of. Examining the work factor associated with each threat scenario is an important tool in assigning relative and absolute risk. Understanding the threat agent in question is paramount. Most deliberate threat agents follow the path of least resistance that yields the most profitable returns at the least risk to them. Other threat agents myopically focus on the magnitude impact regardless of risk to themselves.

## IMPACT LIMITATIONS

The precise outcome or consequence of a threat event cannot be calculated with absolute certainty at the macrolevel. Most of the impact uncertainty is associated with how the people will react to a major incident should it occur, the real and long-term losses and perceived value. How much is a human life worth? The cost of stockpiling too much vaccine will impact what other health services and ultimately cost lives.

## THREAT LIMITATIONS

The threat to infrastructures has migrated from military invasions to organized criminal organizations operating abroad with the duplicity of foreign states, to foreign-originated terrorist groups driven by ideology and anti-Western sentiments. Considering that the preparation and planning for attacks is likely to first occur on foreign soil, there is a strong requirement for all-source foreign intelligence collection in ascertaining the nature of any threat, predicting, interdicting, and disrupting.

## MANAGING UNCERTAINTY

Uncertainty can only be limited by committing sufficient resources to quantify the impacts, vulnerabilities, and threats. Risk owing to uncertainty can be mitigated by either increasing protection, transferring the risk, or investing in crisis management and recovery. The cost to limit uncertainty must be balanced with resources allocated to mitigating risk.

At a certain point, it may not be cost effective to seek to achieve absolute certainty. Rather, it would make more sense to allocate resources to protection. When protection mechanisms become too expensive, resources should be redirected to detection and response mechanisms. Active and proactive measures directed against potential threats need to be undertaken when all those mechanisms become inefficient.

Risk is the product of the likelihood and the consequence of an undesirable occurrence. This occurrence is described in terms of a coincidence of both threat and vulnerability, which is called exposure. There must be measurable impact from the occurrence for an exposure to be considered in calculating risk. Impact is directly associated with the value and sensitivity of the system components (including information components) under examination. A system consists of people, processes, services, technology, information, and the operating environment.

People are notoriously poor at recognizing their real risks. They often rely on anecdotal evidence to form an opinion and unduly weighting consequence although ignoring likelihood.

A threat and risk assessment consists of a rigorous examination of human and inanimate assets, intrinsic vulnerabilities (as properties of the asset), threats, and threat agents, which may adversely affect what one is trying to protect, the likelihood and impact of exploitation, and consequential exposure. On the basis of this analysis, a reasoned and informed assessment is made of the risks to the system and the degree to which they ought to be managed.

## INFRASTRUCTURE RISK MITIGATION ERRORS

The common mistakes made by the authority of infrastructure security are listed:

The efforts to eliminate threat–risks are cost preclusive and increase business risk (costs, time, or efficiency) such that overall risk is higher. Too much security can bankrupt a program or cause security mechanisms or procedures to be ignored for the sake of business operations.

Protective measures should not be implemented in such a way that they draw attention to vulnerable points or mark valuable assets. Openly, discussing threat scenarios in the past has directly influenced terrorists to attack precisely in that manner, as was the case with several anthrax incidents.

Every security mechanism creates an alternate or unexpected vector for a threat, just as a protective barrier bars and redirects the movements of those being protected to the next vulnerable point. Risk and responses to events must be reviewed before and after safeguard implementation. Strong and clear protective mechanisms will accelerate the threat-action or decision cycle.

The application of security creates high-pressure gaps between the safeguards that either drive a threat through the seams or overloads other security mechanisms. Care must be taken to understand the effect the addition of security has on the system and engineer appropriately. An enterprise should understand that by closing security gaps, they may well be speeding up the threat decision cycle by reducing perceived options. The organization must therefore plan to react faster to an attack on remaining weak points.

Hard protective measures provide a means for a threat to push against with a direct attack. Mechanisms that absorb or redirect attacks are preferable. Applying security when not needed does more harm than good. Human behavior has never been accurately modeled to the extent that the model itself can predict and react to a deliberate threat event. Some room must be made to redeploy security to an evolving and dynamic threat. Stacking security mechanisms is not layered defense, particularly if it is the same security mechanism positioned on the same threat vector. Chained security measures often provide less security than simpler solutions because the design adds more points to failure and more complexity to the response system. It is no more difficult to circumvent for an attacker.

Mounting a defense without adequate knowledge of offense, leads to inappropriate design and assignment of security. Conversely, carrying out offense operations without knowledge of defense marginalizes success and leaves the organization open to counterattack. An organization's offensive actions can reveal the defensive capabilities. Attacks are often chosen, which are less risky for the attacker, nominally because they perceive them as less defensible. In this manner, an adversary may counterattack along the same line believing that is where the organization is weakest. Generally, the organization should not launch or contemplate attacks that the organization itself cannot defend against. Both defensive and offensive infrastructure work must occur in lockstep. Any study, in the risk factors surrounding the behavioral response to the infrastructure threat and its mitigation, must contemplate both offensive and defensive capabilities and tactics to predict affects and response to any degree of accuracy.

- Failure to provide defense in depth and breadth.
- Failure to set interlocking defenses covered with detection and response mechanisms will permit deliberate threats to slip through the cracks undetected.
- Failure to provide homogeneous security creates weak points and reveals the organizations defensive strategy.

## THREAT IN 2008

Data dependency, econometrics, and geospatial relationships establish interdependencies and risk conductance amongst CIs. Cyberspace is the nervous system, which binds all these sectors. Consider cyber threat-surveillance analogous to health monitoring of the electrical signals in a human body with electrocardiogram (EKG/ECG). What happens in the physical world typically manifests in cyberspace. Conversely, cyber threats can profoundly affect logical and physical spaces. This is why all public and private sector decision makers need to take heed to the cyber threat regardless of how physically grounded their work life and responsibilities appear. Wealth is more often tied up in information where money is ethereal representations of ones and zeros on a computer.

Virtually anonymously, they prowl interconnected networks probing, scanning, and watching. They can attack and withdraw back into the ether at the speed of light. They are the hackers and crackers, telecommunications phreakers, precocious script kiddies to cyber-terrorists, spies, and sophisticated organized criminal syndicates engaged in industrial espionage. Then just when you think you know their identity and tradecraft, your organization is blindsided by the actions of an insider with access to your most sensitive computer files, and a penchant for trouble.

What we believe about security threats is constructed from several perspectives. The most often view is one which is fabricated from our own experience in managing detectable security events within our own organizations. Confidence in this world view is reinforced with open-sourced security hype that is derived for the most part, observation and assessment of threat-from, data and econometrics, while glossing over the more pertinent but difficult to obtain threat-to information. People tend to manage perceived risk. Consequently, the reality of the threat and risk are not mandatory to the evolution of the security landscape.

## COUNTERPOINT ON CYBER THREAT–RISK

Public and private sector organizations are exceedingly reliant on U.S. commercial sources for cyber-vulnerability, threat intelligence, and mitigation code. The statistics most often quoted from branded security vendors show a linear increase in vulnerabilities and exploits. Similar trends in incidents are reported by CERT (Computer Emergency Response Team), based upon the few events that are reported. Although, these metrics are useful in capturing most targeted systems, vulnerabilities and cyber security trends in general, they provide deemphasized view to the wilds of cyberspace.

"You can't manage what you can't measure."

The reality shows a nonlinear increase in zero-day exploits, attacks and a convergence of threat agents, their means, and methods.

Whatever view one takes, the biggest vulnerability remains unpatched/updated system, the delay in receiving patches, dial-up customers, unfiltered access to Internet (unclean pipes), and instant messaging communities.

A strategic understanding the cyber threat must consider both disruptive technology and convergence.

"You can't protect what you can't predict."

## THREAT–RISK CONVERGENCE

Threat–risk convergence applies an inclusive model when classifying threats rather than one that labels threat agents with single purpose yet multifarious motives, means, and methods, i.e., a hacker hacks, and a spy subverts in a way that defines them in a threat class. There has long since existed a one-to-one mapping between mode of attack and mode of defense. So, we have tended to set defenses along expected lines of attack. Moreover, as identified classes of threat agents owned a certain type of attack mode, we could identify the attacker based upon the attack. Organizations have come to expect and plan a defense against a simplistic threat vector, which is dangerous.

The traditionalist view holds threats are most often defined by their actions. They are what they do. It is a view that is bounded by what we perceive and expect from a threat. This leads to less than helpful definitions: "Hackers hack and all who hack are hackers" or "terrorists are those who belong to terrorist organizations. The definition of a terrorist organization is a group made up of terrorists." One would have to discard these political definitions of threat actors as unworkable in the craft of fighting the real threat.

The RAND Corporation's predictions concerning the mapping of evolving social threat networks to emerging interconnected computer networks was prophetic because it showed how the threat is both empowered and bounded by what we now see as convergence. If we can predict, then we can protect.

> The protagonists in Cyberspace are likely to amount to a set of diverse, dispersed "nodes" who share a set of ideas and interests and who often are arrayed to act in a fully connected "all-channel" manner. The potential effectiveness of the networked design compared to traditional hierarchical designs attracted the attention of management theorists as early as the 1960s. Today, in the business world, virtual or networked organizations are heralded as effective alternatives to traditional bureaucracies because of their inherent flexibility, adaptiveness, and ability to capitalize on the talents of all of their members. Networked organizations share three basic sets of features.
>
> First, communication and coordination are not formally specified by horizontal and vertical reporting relationships, but rather emerge and change according to the task at hand. Similarly, relationships are often informal and marked by varying degrees of intensity, depending on the needs of the organization.
>
> Second, internal networks are usually complemented by linkages to individuals outside the organization, often spanning national boundaries. Like internal connections, external relationships are formed and wind down according to the lifecycle of particular joint projects.
>
> Third, both internal and external ties are enabled not by bureaucratic fiat, but rather by shared norms and values, as well as by reciprocal trust. Internally, the bulk of the work is conducted by self-managing teams, while external linkages compose a constellation involving a complex network of contributing firms or groups.*

Analysis ought to consider one singular class of deliberate threat for the purposes of establishing an effective integrated risk management framework. Public and private sectors need to become threat agnostic and risk aware.

In 2008, not only do threat agents covet multiple agendas and act similarly in cyberspace but also the tools themselves have converged. The necromancy of

---

* Arquilla, J. and Ronfeldt, D., Eds., 1999. *Networks and Netwars: The Future of Terror, Crime, and Militancy*, RAND Corporation, Santa Monica, CA.

cyberspace has adopted tools for discovery, manufacturing access, and controlling machines. To understand weaponry, one certainly needs to understand the technology and risks underpinning information networks.

## CONCLUSIONS

1. Risk avoidance rather than risk management is commonplace. A risk ignored is a risk accepted.
2. Security responses will be circumvented if overused or too well exercised; a deliberate threat will build up immunity or learn to predict and avoid. Conversely, lackluster security responses will often invite a direct attack.
3. Safeguards will eventually be circumvented or overrun if an organization implements protection without detection.
4. A deliberate threat agent will successfully breach defenses if there is detection but no response.
5. An organization will not have an effect on the strength of deliberate agent if a defensive strategy is based on reaction without prevention.
6. An enterprise will be in the dark to identifying real risks if the scope of their security is limited to prevention without prediction. A threat agent will be better able to act within their victim's decision cycle (the ability to respond) if there is no predictive threat analysis and warning.
7. Prediction without proaction or interdiction does little to effect or reduce the threat before they have attacks.
8. Often organizations place security against scenarios of high-impact/low-likelihood rather than those of high risk.

# 6 Critical Infrastructure Interdependency Case Studies

## INTRODUCTION

In this chapter, we apply the proposed interdependency metrics and theories established in Chapters 2 through 4 to two distinct case studies. These case studies involve distinct types of incidents impacting initially one critical infrastructure (CI) sector, and propagating out over time and distance to impact other CI sectors to varying degrees.

These case studies will be composites of real, past events rather than purely hypothetical in nature. These case studies will not be related to a specific geographic location, since the metrics presented in this book are compiled at a national-level. Geography always plays a major role in the interdependencies of CI sectors, under normal operation conditions or crisis conditions. To make these case studies as meaningful as possible to the widest possible audience, no specific geographic anomalies have been incorporated such as extreme temperatures, remoteness or the role of bridges, mountains, or waterways.

Although it would be ideal to document a case study of a real event and map the observations back to the indications contained within the book, this would require that publication wait an indefinite period for new events to occur because past events have simply not been documented in the context of CI interdependencies. Virtually all after-action reports related to incidents impacting CI tend to focus on intrasector continuity challenges and vaguely mention CI interdependency as a challenge to be addressed. CI interdependencies are widely acknowledged as being a dark spot in the world of emergency preparedness and management. The typical documentation set and after-action reports related to CI incidents tend to focus overwhelmingly on the intrasector experience; other CI sectors become footnotes. Even to the extent that major interdependency issues are acknowledged and cited as concerns, few metrics or information about the extend of the intersector impacts are provided. In fact, the most common observation about CI interdependencies from after-action reports is that little to nothing is known about CI interdependency!

The case studies presented in this chapter show how the dependency metrics have been analyzed and presented in such detail in this book are applicable to the management and planning associated with crisis conditions. Normal operating conditions are the way in which CI sectors will probably spend 99.5 percent of their time functioning. Normal operating conditions are the point of departure when a crisis strikes; these are the conditions of preparedness and the interrelationships that characterize preparedness. Interdependency metrics based upon normal operating conditions are the baseline from which distinct crisis metrics emerge, and can provide a basic order and latency of impact under an all-hazards approach to CI risk management. Ideally, we possess two distinct metrics for each and every CI interrelationship: normal operating conditions and crisis conditions. Unfortunately, each crisis is as different as the unlimited number of threat agents and events: crisis metrics under one threat/scenario will be completely different from another threat/scenario. For this reason, collecting and presenting crisis interdependency metrics is a vast undertaking and probably of limited value. Interdependency metrics under normal operating conditions provide the basis for appropriate, all-hazards risk management related to CI interdependency. Case studies provided in this chapter utilize normal operating conditions to extrapolate to the likely, levels of dependency and risk during crisis conditions.

## OBJECTIVES

The case studies are intended to provide examples of how to apply the material from the earlier chapters of this book to risk assessment and operational risk management. The case studies are designed to identify gaps within plans, procedures, and systems, and provide the basis for operational risk control and evaluation. The case studies, in addition to discussing incidents within specific CI sectors, will reveal the initial cascading events using a simple methodology that can be applied by stakeholders in any CI sectors. Stakeholders will posses a process to run vulnerability, threat, and risk scenarios against their own assets and organizations to identify the greatest opportunities for improvement. One of the most typically ignored threats among CI sector organizations are interdependency threats. This is not because managers are negligent or unprofessional; the interdependency threat and risk information upon which to base plans has, for the most part, been unavailable. Entities wishing to assess the resiliency of CI sector entities (organizations and companies) for the purposes of partnership or investment will possess a methodology to asses the most insidious threats—interdependency threats.

The case studies and information in this book might also be applied to disaster management exercises, simulations, and evaluations. The interdependency relationships between CI sectors are bounded both by time and the nature of the good or service produced. Information about the potential of cascading events is essential for the development and evaluation of disaster recovery and emergency management exercises. Disaster exercises, especially the most accessible form of tabletop exercise are structured around elapsed time and the changing circumstances as time passes. The inclusion in Chapter 4 of a time dimension associated with interdependency is especially adoptable to creation and execution of strong disaster exercises and the comprehensive demonstration of strengths and weakness associated with emergency and disaster management.

The case-study analysis methodologies employed in the following discussion may also be applied usefully for rapid situational assessment after incidents have occurred. It is certainly not practical or realistic to expect emergency managers to stop and create documentation during the initial phases of disaster response; however, familiarity with these case studies and the techniques employed will provide a broader range of information and inputs upon which to make critical decisions. For instance, although it is certainly true that the impact of the Water sector might be of low priority to a financial service firm in the midst of a major computer failure, at least they will have a higher degree of confidence that traps doors are not around every corner and can focus on the obvious priorities with confidence.

Finally, the case studies attempt to emphasize policy issues as well as operational threats and risks relevant to CI sector incident response. Policy issues will vary greatly from jurisdiction to jurisdiction, so no observations will be made about flaws in specific policy or legislation; however, generally, there are definitely trends and commonalities in many North American jurisdictions related to CI and emergency management. If possible, the case studies will highlight where a policy vacuum might exist, which results in ambiguity and risk in the event of an incident.

## STRUCTURE OF CASE STUDIES

The case studies presented in this chapter follows a consistent format to assist comprehension and comparability. Each starts with a hypothetical scenario which has been developed using a composite of previous, real-life events or simulations (such as large exercises). The descriptions are provided in simple, natural language and are concise because the scenarios are not the focus of the case studies; CI interdependencies resulting from the scenarios are the focus.

Following the scenario descriptions, there is a high-level literature review of known CI interdependencies under the given scenario conditions. The purpose of engaging in the literature review is to show the extent to which conventional wisdom either supports or refutes the CI interdependency indications in this book. The literature review also serves to highlight the current gap between conventional wisdom around CI interdependency and the assessments of this book.

The case studies will involve reviews of all inbound and outbound dependencies impacts at the three time intervals of T1 (0–60 minutes), T2 (one to eight hours) and T3 (greater than eight hours). Inbound dependency discusses how the sector, which is the focal point of the incident-and-response effort, will be impacted from its supply chain, while outbound dependency covers impacts flowing from the impacted sector into its client base or into the supply chain of other CI sectors.

## CASE STUDY 1: PANDEMIC AND INFLUENZA

### SCENARIO

A novel avian flu strain that was being tracked in Asia has obtained a foothold in North America. Initial quarantine measures were applied too late or ineffectively. Fatalities are occurring and the spread is currently unchecked or at least cannot be said to be under control.

## LITERATURE REVIEW

According to RAND Corporation, the Health sector can anticipate an absentee rate of 30–60 percent during a pandemic* plus an impact on health service delivery due to loading associated with treating the sick, symptomatic, and worried well.

The U.S. Department of Health and Human Services (DHHS) Pandemic Flu Plan states that a vaccine will have to be rapidly manufactured as samples of the pandemic are isolated.[†] Antivirals can be stockpiled but vaccine for novel strains of flu cannot be stockpiled.

Information and observations from past, large pandemics will be of limited value in assessing CI interdependency impacts, because data from past pandemics in the United States (1918 and 1958) is not fully applicable due to changes in technology and business models.[‡]

The DHHS has identified 11 key areas of pandemic response[§] within the Health sector. These response areas are

1. *Surveillance* for influenza viruses and disease to monitor the health impact of influenza throughout the pandemic phases.
2. *Laboratory diagnostics* to detect, characterize, and monitor novel subtypes of influenza, including avian influenza A (H5N1) and other viruses with pandemic potential.
3. *Health care planning* for pandemic influenza surveillance, decision-making structures for responding to a pandemic, hospital communications, education and training, patient triage, clinical evaluation and admission, facility access, occupational health, distribution of vaccines and antiviral drugs, surge capacity, and mortuary issues. Planning for the provision of care in nonhospital settings—including residential care facilities, physicians' offices, private home health care services, emergency medical services, federally qualified health centers, rural health clinics, and alternative care sites is also addressed.
4. *Infection control* for limiting the spread of pandemic influenza including the selection and use of personal protective equipment; hand hygiene and safe work practices; cleaning and disinfection of environmental surfaces; handling of laboratory specimens; and postmortem care. The guidance also covers infection control practices related to the management of infectious patients, the protection of persons at high-risk for severe influenza or its complications, and issues concerning occupational health.
5. *Clinical guidelines* for the initial screening, assessment, and management of patients with suspected novel influenza during the interpandemic and pandemic alert periods and for patients with suspected pandemic influenza during the pandemic period.

---

* RAND Centre for Domestic and International Health Security, Tabletop Exercises for the Pandemic Influenza Preparedness in local Public Health Agencies, 2006.
† RAND Centre for Domestic and International Health Security, Tabletop Exercises for the Pandemic Influenza Preparedness in local Public Health Agencies, 2006.
‡ U.S. Department of Health and Human Services, HHS Pandemic Flu Plan, November 2005, Appendix D.
§ U.S. Department of Health and Human Services, HHS Pandemic Flu Plan, November 2005.

6. *Vaccine distribution and use* including priority groups, monitoring of adverse events, tracking of vaccine supply and administration, vaccine coverage and effectiveness studies, communications, legal preparedness, training, data collection on use, effectiveness, safety, and the development of drug resistance.

7. *Antiviral drug distribution and use* for treatment and prophylaxis throughout the pandemic phases, including issues such as procurement, distribution to predefined priority groups, legal preparedness, training, and data collection.

8. *Community disease control and prevention* containment strategies to prevent or decrease transmission during different pandemic phases.

9. *Managing travel-related risks of disease* with containment strategies that can be used during different phases of an influenza pandemic, including strategies that range from distribution of travel health alert notices, to isolation and quarantine of new arrivals, to restriction or cancellation of nonessential travel.

10. *Public health communications* outlines key influenza pandemic risk communications concepts including
    (a) When health risks are uncertain, as likely will be the case during an influenza pandemic, people need information about what is known and unknown, as well as interim guidance to formulate decisions to help protect their health and the health of others.
    (b) Influenza pandemic will generate immediate, intense, and sustained demand for information from the public, health care providers, policy makers, and news media.
    (c) Timely and transparent dissemination of clear, accurate, science-based, culturally competent information about pandemic influenza and the progress of the response can build public trust and confidence.
    (d) Coordination of message development and release of information among federal, state, and local health officials is critical to help avoid confusion that can undermine public trust, raise fear and anxiety, and impede response measures.
    (e) Information to public audiences should be technically correct and sufficiently complete to encourage support of policies and official actions.

11. *Workforce support* psychosocial considerations and information services that will help workers manage emotional stress during the response to an influenza pandemic and resolve related personal, professional, and family issues.

Although the DHHS plan has identified these as being key areas of pandemic response, there is no mention of how other CI sectors might play a supporting role in these activities. From the list above, it can be inferred that Transportation services and Communications services will be crucial to the response: Transportation for moving samples and medicines around and Communications and IT to support first responders. The requirements for isolation and quarantine also implicate government and safety as critical components of the response to manage borders and physically enforce quarantine orders.

The DHHS Flu Plan recognizes certain forms of CI interdependency through proposed guidelines around the allocation of vaccines from stockpiles for industrial sectors considered core to pandemic response.

Groups included in CI are needed to respond to a pandemic and to minimize morbidity and mortality, and include the following sectors:

- Persons directly involved with influenza vaccine and antiviral medication manufacturing and distribution and essential support services and suppliers (e.g., growers of pathogen-free eggs for growth of vaccine virus) production activities
- Key government leaders and health decision-makers who will be needed to quickly move policy forward on pandemic prevention and control efforts
- Public safety workers (firefighters, police, and correctional facility staff, including dispatchers) are critical to maintaining social functioning and order and will contribute to a pandemic response, for example by ensuring order at vaccination clinics and responding to medical emergencies
- Utility service workers (water, power, and sewage management) are prioritized as the services they provide are also essential to the health care system as well as to preventing additional illnesses from lack of these services unrelated to a pandemic
- Transportation workers who maintain critical supplies of food, water, fuel, and medical equipment and who provide public transportation, which is essential for provision of medical care and transportation of health care workers to work and transportation of ill persons for care
- Telecommunication and information technology services critical for maintenance and repairs of these systems are also essential as these systems are now critical for accessing and delivering medical care and in support of all other CI
- Mortuary services will be substantially impacted due to the increased numbers of deaths from a pandemic and the fact that impact will be high in the elderly, a growing segment of the population*

From this guidance, we see that the U.S. Health sector is considered by DHHS dependent upon the following CI sectors to a significant degree during a pandemic situation:

- Safety and Government
- Energy
- Water
- Transportation
- Communications and IT

---

* U.S. Department of Health and Human Services, HHS Pandemic Flu Plan, November 2005, Appendix D.

A further significant observation from the DHHS Flu Plan was that pandemic will likely impact CI sector because of the requirement "to divert flow of CI supplies and materials that normally transit through quarantined areas," implying that the Transportation sector especially could face further disruptions not only related to staffing but also the availability of physical infrastructure.*

The Public Health Agency of Canada (PHAC) has acknowledged the role of CI in pandemic response, but like the DHHS it is limited to discussions of how to allocate vaccines to CI workers in the event of a pandemic. Rationale and guidance is provided in the Canadian Pandemic Plan, 2006,[†] where infrastructure workers were placed in group 2 of four groups for vaccinations after frontline health workers and government. Groups 1 and 2 are quoted below, while groups 3 and 4 describe lifestyles and health status rather than professions.

In keeping with the goal of pandemic response, the prioritization process must consider the impact that the vaccine will have on (1) reducing morbidity and mortality by maintaining the health services response and the protection of high-risk groups and (2) minimizing societal disruption by maintaining the essential services necessary for public health, safety, and security.

Group 1. Health Care Workers, Public Health Responders and Key Health Decision Makers

Rationale: The health care and public Health sectors will be the first line of defense in a pandemic. Maintaining the health service response and the vaccine program is central to the implementation of the response plan in order to reduce morbidity and mortality. Members of this group may be considered in the following work settings for vaccine program planning:

- Acute care hospitals
- Long-term care facilities and nursing homes
- Private physician offices
- Home care and other community care facilities
- Public health offices
- Ambulance and paramedic services
- Pharmacies
- Laboratories
- Government offices

Group 2: Pandemic Societal Responders and Key Societal Decision Makers

Rationale: The ability to mount an effective pandemic response may be highly dependent on persons, within the groups listed below, being in place to maintain key community services. Those individuals who are essential to the response or to maintaining key community services may vary among jurisdictions. Local plans will likely reflect these differences; however, they are likely to include

---

* U.S. Department of Health and Human Services, HHS Pandemic Flu Plan, November 2005, Appendix S-8 22.
† Health Canada, Canadian Pandemic Plan 2006, http://www.phac-aspc.gc.ca/cpip-pclcpi/pdf-e/ CPIP-2006_e.pdf.

- Police
- Firefighters
- Armed forces
- Key emergency response decision makers (e.g., elected officials, essential government workers, disaster services personnel)
- Utility workers (e.g., water, gas, electricity, nuclear power, essential communications systems)
- Funeral service and mortuary personnel
- People who work with institutionalized populations (e.g., corrections)
- Persons who are employed in public transportation and the transportation of essential goods (e.g., food)
- Key government employees/elected officials (e.g., ministers, mayors)*

From this guidance we see that the Canadian Health sector is considered by HPAC dependent upon following CI sectors to a significant degree during a pandemic situation:

- Safety and Government
- Energy
- Transportation

Recommendations made by the SARS Commission of 2005 to strengthen government powers to facilitate management and response to pandemics provides further indications about perceived CI interdependencies. These are powers that are recommended by the SARS Commission for health protection, but do not exist under current statutes and regulations.

STRENGTHENING DAY-TO-DAY PUBLIC HEALTH POWERS[†]

Public health officials require better access to health risk information and greater daily authority, together with more resources and expertise to investigate, intervene, and enforce. The commission has identified seven fields of public health activity that require additional daily authority under the Health Protection and Promotion Act:

- In relation to infectious diseases in hospitals.
- To acquire information necessary for them to protect the public from a health risk.
- To investigate health risks to the public.
- For the chief medical officer of health to establish an adjudication system whereby decisions of local medical officers of health regarding classification of disease may be reviewed.
- For the chief medical officer of health to issue directives to hospitals and other health care institutions.
- To detain, as a last resort, noncompliant individuals infected with a virulent disease who pose a risk to public health.

---

* Health Canada, Canadian Pandemic Plan 2006, Appendix D.
[†] SARS Commission second interim report: SARS and Public legislation, p. 14. http://www.health.gov.on.ca/english/public/pub/ministry_reports/campbell05/campbell05.html.

- To enter, as a last resort, a private dwelling to apprehend a noncompliant person infected with a virulent disease poses a risk to public health.
- Commission sees a greater role for public health in infection control, whether it be in a hospital, long-term care facility, or a private clinic. A medical officer of health must have authority under the Health Protection and Promotion Act to monitor, investigate, and intervene in cases where infectious diseases or inadequate infection control poses a risk to public health.

In this instance, the implication from the commission is that functions provided by Government and Safety sectors represent critical interdependencies due to regulatory decision making and the need to enforce physical remediation measures with the police/safety sector.

The SARS Commission report also indicated an interesting and less obvious CI interdependency between Health, Government, and Finance due to the need to access to and distribution emergency funds to induce public cooperation with quarantine requirements.

Despite criticism that it took too long to bring forward an appropriate compensation package, some observers suggest that the compensation system, once in place, was largely responsible for the success of the voluntary quarantine programme. Dr. James Young has said that compensation for those quarantined was a vital element of Ontario's response to SARS:

During SARS, we were using quarantine for the first time in 50 years. One of the important things in using quarantine was getting people to abide by it. One of the important ways of getting people to abide by it was by offering financial compensation so they would in fact abide by it and stay in quarantine if and when they were ordered by the medical officer of health. We got approval from the Ontario government to institute a quarantine program and to pay people for that. That resulted in us being able to manage the quarantine in an effective manner.

The message is that it is important to plan in advance for the compensation of those whose cooperation in the emergency effort is so vital. It is impossible to predict in advance exactly what form and level of compensation is necessary and affordable for every conceivable emergency. But it is possible to require by legislation that every government emergency plan include a basic blueprint for the most predictable types of compensation packages. And it is possible to legislate that compensation, in a form and amount to be decided by the government.*

On the basis of this analysis of open source documentation related to pandemic response and Health sector CI interdependencies in both Canada and the United States, in no specific order, conventional wisdom deems the following sectors important to a pandemic response:

- Safety and Government
- Energy
- Water

---

* SARS Commission second interim report: SARS and Public legislation, p. 256. http://www.health.gov.on.ca/english/public/pub/ministry_reports/campbell05/campbell05.html.

- Transportation
- Communications and IT
- Finance

No information was available about the level or intensity of interdependency or the timeframes in which the interdependency occurs. Similarly, these interdependencies were in all cases expressed as inbound dependencies: how and why Health needs these sectors.

## FINDINGS: CI INTERDEPENDENCY VULNERABILITY AND RISK ANALYSIS UNDER PANDEMIC CONDITIONS

The following section applies the CI interdependency metrics to the management of Health sector vulnerabilities due to CI interdependency, and vulnerabilities of other CI sectors due to dependencies with the Health sector.

### SUMMARY ANALYSIS

The columns in Table 6.2 represent the inbound dependency metric for a given sector, where inbound refers to the level of assurance required by a sector in the goods or services supplied by another sector. The rows represent the outbound dependency metric for a given sector, where outbound refers to the level of assurance other sectors places upon the goods or services supplied by a given sector.

Metrics are on a scale from 1 to 10 as derived through correlation of quantitative econometric analysis and qualitative executive interviewing, and represent inbound or outbound dependency under normal operating conditions.

The colors in the cells represent the assessed risk around these dependency relationships when a change occurs from normal operating conditions to crisis conditions (Table 6.1).

Table 6.2 is a derivative of the CI dependency matrix developed in Chapter 4, and contains only the Health-related dependency metrics from that chapter and the assessed risk from this case study. Each of the cells associated with Health interdependency are discussed and reasoning provided to support the risk judgments applied.

## TABLE 6.1
## Assessed Risk Definitions

| | |
|---|---|
| Green | Low or unchanged operational risks during pandemic, or mitigating controls and safeguards are largely in place. |
| Yellow | Acknowledged operational risks and impacts during pandemic—mitigating controls or safeguards are planned or under consideration. |
| Red | Large operational risks result due to incomplete understanding of dependency and substantially incomplete mitigation controls and safeguards. |

**TABLE 6.2**
**Correlated Canadian CI Interdependency Metrics for the Health Sector**

| Outbound Dependencies | Inbound Dependencies | | | | | | | | |
|---|---|---|---|---|---|---|---|---|---|
| CI Sector | Energy | Comms and IT | Fin | Health Care | Food | Water | Trans | Gov/ Safety | Manf |
| Energy | | | | 4.19[b] | | | | | |
| Comms and IT | | | | 5.14[c] | | | | | |
| Fin | | | | 4.19[c] | | | | | |
| Health Care | 4.86[a] | 2.37[a] | 3.00[a] | 8.24[b] | 1.80[c] | 4.20[c] | 3.25[c] | 7.00[c] | 2.61[a] |
| Food | | | | 4.05[c] | | | | | |
| Water | | | | 4.90[b] | | | | | |
| Trans | | | | 4.86[b] | | | | | |
| Gov/ Safety | | | | 6.17[b] | | | | | |
| Manf | | | | 4.00[a] | | | | | |

[a] Denotes green.
[b] Denotes yellow.
[c] Denotes red.

## Detailed Risk Analysis of Sector Interdependency under Pandemic Conditions

Interdependencies are considered from the perspective of how Health is dependent upon other CI sectors under pandemic response (inbound dependency) and how might other CI sectors be impacted by pandemic response due to their dependence on the Health sector (outbound dependency).

Sectors are discussed in order of the impact latency. (The amount of time that passes before the impact from the loss of a sector starts to be felt.) *Note*: impact latency does not equate to severity of impact. Dependence on a sector input might not be felt immediacy upon loss, but when felt, the impact may be more debilitating than those of sectors with short impact latencies.

## Health Dependency on Energy

|  | Threat | | Outbound Vulnerability | |
| --- | --- | --- | --- | --- |
|  | Sector | Description | Correlated Dependency Metric | Dependency Latency (Time to Impact) |
| Risk rating | Energy Yellow | Pandemic | 4.19 | <60 minutes |
|  | Acknowledged operational risks and impacts during pandemic—mitigating controls or safeguards are planned or under consideration | | | |

*Comments*

The Energy sector consists of extractors, refiners of liquid fuels, gas, and generators of electricity. This includes major oil, gas, and electricity firms but not independent wholesalers or distributors of energy products.

As observed in the referenced case study material, the Health sector has spent considerable effort to understand intersector dependencies with Energy. Impacts related to power loss are acknowledged but not completely addressed.

Under normal operating conditions, Energy is a critical and an obvious input to the Health sector, the lack of which is immediately evident. Although many hospitals will have backup generators that can operate for hours at a time, many other Health infrastructure elements such as laboratories or dispensing sites may not have backup power available, forcing them to cease operations immediately when power fails.

A failure in Energy (specifically electricity) will require a switch to backup power, typically diesel generators. Once relying upon backup systems, hospitals already in an overload pandemic situation may be forced to stop admitting new patients and move patients elsewhere because backup power is not reliable enough to maintain normal operations. Similarly, prolonged outages of more than a few hours will result in evacuation procedures due to the forced assumption that backup generator fuel could run out. This assumption is based upon the impacts similar to those within the Transportation sector (see below), where drivers and delivery staff may refuse to enter quarantine zones or may be blocked from entering by safety authorities. These circumstances will delay or deny timely treatment to new patients and increase the potential for contagion and higher mortality.

Finally, a pandemic declaration from the Health sector will have a direct, first-order impact upon the Energy sector itself. This impact is manifested through projected absenteeism rates of 20–40 percent.* Operational efficiency will be impacted and significantly complicate effective response in the event of an Energy

---

* PandemicFlu.gov, U.S. federal government, planning assumptions http://www.pandemicflu.gov/plan/pandplan.html.

incident. Thus, a second incident impacting Energy and concurrent to a pandemic would significantly intensify pandemic risks.

## Health Dependency on Other Health Sector Entities

| | Threat | | Outbound Vulnerability | |
|---|---|---|---|---|
| | **Sector** | **Description** | **Correlated Dependency Metric** | **Dependency Latency (Time to Impact)** |
| | Health | Pandemic | 8.24 | One to eight hours |
| Risk rating | Yellow | | | |
| | Acknowledged operational risks and impacts during pandemic—mitigating controls or safeguards are planned or under consideration | | | |

*Comments*

The Health sector consists of hospitals, laboratories, blood and pharmaceutical supply facilities, and ambulatory services.

This scenario is about a direct impact to the Health sector and the inbound and outbound cascading effects on the other CI sectors. Impacts to the Health sector are recorded throughout this analysis.

Under normal operating conditions, the Health sector members are interdependent with other members of the Health sector for services such as testing, drug dispensing, resource and knowledge sharing, and patient care.

Under pandemic response conditions, these conditions continue but with heightened restrictions and controls around the movement of staff between sector members to limit the possibility of contagion.

Although the emergence and recognition of a pandemic condition is of the utmost seriousness, spread of this news and resulting impacts to operational risk and operating conditions is not instantaneous, requiring at least between one and eight hours for analysis and communications strategy activation.

## Health Dependency on Safety and Government

| | Threat | | Outbound Vulnerability | |
|---|---|---|---|---|
| | **Sector** | **Description** | **Correlated Dependency Metric** | **Dependency Latency (Time to Impact)** |
| | Safety and Government | Pandemic | 6.17 | One to eight hours |
| Risk rating | Yellow | | | |
| | Acknowledged operational risks and impacts during pandemic—mitigating controls or safeguards are planned or under consideration | | | |

*Comments*

The Safety sector includes police, fire, and other emergency response services for specific hazards like biological, nuclear, or chemical incidents. Government consists of regulators of critical government services and dispensers of social security programs.

Safety is an important input to Health during a pandemic situation due to the need to support and enforce quarantine operations (under proposed legislation) and to potentially transport victims to treatment locations. An unspecified impact to the Safety sector would be rapidly conducted into a Health infrastructure already trying to cope with a pandemic situation, and exacerbate response efforts but hobbling quarantine efforts and allowing infection to continue with minimal damping. A reduction in the capabilities of the Safety sector during a pandemic response would result in higher mortality and contagion as infected individuals were not transferred to treatment centers efficiently and safely. Finally, the Safety sector may be called upon to secure treatment facilities and medicine stockpiles from panicked persons or mobs.

Government is an important input to Health during pandemic situations because government maintains the legislative fiat to invoke emergency powers and also emergency funding to support voluntary quarantine by individuals with possible infection. Ultimately, government is the major funder and manager of the Health sector in Canada and partially in the United States. Although it is unlikely that short-term legislation would occur during a pandemic response, liaison with government is critical during pandemic response to coordinate public messaging and to ensure that liability under existing legislation is not assumed on the part of the responders unilaterally.

Finally, a pandemic declaration from the Health sector will have a direct, first-order impact upon the Safety and Government sectors themselves. This impact is manifested through projected absenteeism rates of 20–40 percent. Operational efficiency will be impacted and significantly complicate effective response in the event of an incident. Thus, an incident impacting safety or government and concurrent to a pandemic would significantly intensify pandemic risks.

## Health Dependency on Communications and IT

|  | Threat | | Outbound Vulnerability | |
| --- | --- | --- | --- | --- |
|  | Sector | Description | Correlated Dependency Metric | Dependency Latency (Time to Impact) |
|  | Communications and IT | Pandemic | 6.17 | One to eight hours |
| Risk rating | Red | | | |
|  | Large operational risks result due to incomplete    understanding od dependency or substantially incomplete mitigation controls and safegaurds | | | |

*Comments*

Communications and IT includes the data links and telephone lines that connect Health infrastructure assets across physical space. Local area networks and communications within Health assets such as hospitals are not part of the Communications and IT sector. Communications and IT also includes suppliers of computer software, hardware but not data hosting and processing services.

Under normal operating conditions, Communications and IT is essential for coordination among Health infrastructure assets such as hospitals, laboratories, treatment, and dispensing sites. Communications and IT is also essential to coordinate between Health and acknowledged core CI partners such as Safety and Government.

Under normal conditions, a failure of Communications and IT services to the Health sector would be immediately noticed, as with Energy, but treatment of patients and dispensing of care could continue for a short duration without significant impact (one to eight hours). Beyond an eight-hour outage, service-delivery efforts would start to be significantly impaired due to the logistics and coordination among Health sector players which are not colocated, such as between hospitals, hospitals to laboratories, physicians to laboratories and hospitals.

A failure of Communications and IT services under a pandemic scenario would be immediately noticed, but treatment of victims and dispensing of care could continue for a short duration without significant impact (one to eight hours). Beyond an eight-hour outage, response efforts would start to collapse for lack of information flowing to responders and coordination among responders. Under pandemic scenarios, Communications and IT is essential for delivering messages to the public to manage public reaction and control the spread of disease. Public temper and order would start to decay and physical danger in the form of riots by scared, desperate people becomes a distinct possibility—further impairing Health service delivery and adding a new response burden to the Safety sector. A reduction in the capabilities and assurance of the Communications and IT sector during a pandemic response would result in higher mortality and contagion as treatment coordination and management rapidly degrades in efficiency.

Sustained failures in Communications and IT during a pandemic response will also result in cascading impacts and failures in other CI sectors more than any other sector (see Chapter 4).

Data hosting and processing services perform a major Communications and IT function for the Health sector, which outsources many central information-management tasks like patient records and pharmaceuticals management. Data hosting and processing services are not included within CI definitions for Communications and IT. This represents a significant operational risk during pandemics because these agents may not receive the necessary vaccinations on a priority basis.

Finally, a pandemic declaration from the Health sector will have a direct, first-order impact upon the Communications and IT sector itself. This impact is manifested through projected absenteeism rates of 20–40 percent. Operational efficiency will be impacted and significantly complicate effective response in the event of an incident. Thus, an incident impacting Communications and IT and concurrent to a pandemic would significantly intensify pandemic risks.

## Health Dependency on Water

|  | Threat | | Outbound Vulnerability | |
|---|---|---|---|---|
|  | Sector | Description | Correlated Dependency Metric | Dependency Latency (Time to Impact) |
|  | Water | Pandemic | 4.90 | One to eight hours |
| Risk rating | Yellow | | | |
|  | Acknowledged operational risks and impacts during pandemic—mitigating controls or safeguards are planned or under consideration | | | |

*Comments*

Water includes the potable water supply and wastewater management. Water is essential for maintenance of sterile conditions in hospitals and treatment centers because of its application in both cleaning and waste disposal. A failure of Water infrastructure under normal operating conditions would be immediately noticed by Health sector workers and normal operations could continue for only a short period before evacuation procedures would have to commence. A typical time before evacuation might commence after a failure in Water infrastructure is two to four hours. Evacuation would involve the complete diversion of all care-seekers/patients to alternate hospitals and treatment centers, and the transfer of patients through ambulances to other facilities according to their needs.

A reduction in the capabilities and assurance of the Water sector during a pandemic response would result in higher mortality and contagion as infected individuals must be moved and quarantine areas must be reestablished with the inevitable outcome that more people are exposed during this transition.

Sustained failures in Water during a pandemic response will also result in cascading impacts directly impacting the Health sector. For example, the ability to supply Food services to support in-patients and staff will be rapidly disrupted and compound the difficulties of managing the pandemic and Water outage.

Finally, a pandemic declaration from the Health sector will have a direct, first-order impact upon the Water sector itself. This impact is manifested through projected absenteeism rates of 20–40 percent. Operational efficiency will be impacted and significantly complicate effective response in the event of an incident. Thus, an incident impacting Water and concurrent to a pandemic would significantly intensify pandemic risks.

## Health Dependency on Transportation

| | Threat | | Outbound Vulnerability | |
|---|---|---|---|---|
| | Sector | Description | Correlated Dependency Metric | Dependency Latency (Time to Impact) |
| Risk rating | Transportation Yellow | Pandemic | 4.86 | One to eight hours |
| | Acknowledged operational risks and impacts during pandemic—mitigating controls or safeguards are planned or under consideration | | | |

*Comments*

Transportation sector includes goods and modes of transportation such as rail, air, marine, and truck. In Canada, the Transportation sector does not include couriers and messengers by definition.

Transportation services are essential to the delivery of Health services under normal conditions for inputs such as delivery of highly perishable medicines and donor material and medical equipment. In addition, the Transportation sector assures the delivery of certain other CI sector goods such as Food (for patients and staff), Energy (fuel for heating, cooling, and backup generators), and Manufacturing (gases for patient care and anesthesia, and medical equipment).

A failure of Transportation infrastructure under normal operating conditions would be quickly noticed by Health sector workers and normal operations could continue for up to eight hours before significant widespread operational risks developed.

A reduction in the capabilities and assurance of the Transportation sector during a pandemic response would result in higher mortality and contagion as vaccines are not delivered and dispensed according to instructions from the Health sector responders. Infected individuals would not be treated expeditiously and more people would become exposed for lack of treatment of the infected. Simultaneously, Transportation services and workers themselves would suffer exposure and infection as they are required to travel into infected areas to deliver goods and services, and an accelerating cycle of cause-and-effect between Health and Transportation can develop.

Finally, a pandemic declaration from the Health sector has a direct, first-order impact upon the Transportation sector itself. This impact is manifested through projected absenteeism rates of 20–40 percent and a drastic increase in remote work. Operational efficiency is impacted and significantly complicate effective response in the event of an incident. Thus, an incident impacting Transportation and concurrent to a pandemic would significantly intensify energy-dependency risks.

Couriers and messengers perform a major Transportation function for the Health sector but are not included within CI definitions for Transportation. This represents a significant operational risk during pandemics as these agents may not receive the necessary vaccinations of a priority basis as suggested for the Transportation sector.

## Health Dependency on Food

| | | Threat | Outbound Vulnerability | |
|---|---|---|---|---|
| | Sector | Description | Correlated Dependency Metric | Dependency Latency (Time to Impact) |
| | Food | Pandemic | 4.05 | One to eight hours |
| Risk rating | Red | | | |
| | Large operational risks result due to incomplete understanding of dependency and lack or incomplete mitigation controls and safeguards | | | |

*Comments*

Food sector includes both farming and food manufacturing/processing, but not Food services that includes food contractors, mobile food services, catering and restaurants, or bottling.

A failure of Food infrastructure under normal operating conditions would be immediately noticed by Health sector workers and normal operations could continue for not more than a few hours before patients and staff started to miss meals. Once meals are missed, productivity will sharply decrease and employee attrition increase.

A reduction in the assurance of the Food sector during a pandemic response would result in sharply increased staff attrition and impair response capability. Reduced service levels would lead to higher mortality and contagion as treatments and vaccines are dispensed and administered less and less rapidly. Infected individuals would not be treated expeditiously and more people become exposed for lack of treatment of the sick. Simultaneously, Food workers themselves would suffer exposure and infection because they are required to travel into infected areas to deliver goods and services.

Finally, a pandemic declaration from the Health sector will have a direct, first-order impact upon the Food sector itself. This impact is manifested through projected absenteeism rates of 20–40 percent. Operational efficiency is impacted and significantly complicate effective response in the event of an incident. Thus, an incident impacting Food and concurrent to a pandemic would significantly intensify pandemic risks.

Food services (food contracting, food catering, mobile food services) perform a major function for the Health sector but are not included within CI definitions for Food. Food services are essential to the delivery of health services under normal conditions for inputs such as processed and prepared foods for patients and staff. Food is both highly perishable and consumable and cannot be stockpiled to any extensive degree for hospital purposes. This represents a significant operational risk during pandemics because these agents are clearly involved in the support of Food services to the Health sector, but may not receive necessary vaccinations on a priority basis.

## Health Dependency on Finance

| | Threat | | Inbound Vulnerability | |
| --- | --- | --- | --- | --- |
| | Sector | Description | Correlated Dependency Metric | Dependency Latency (Time to Impact) |
| | Finance | Pandemic | 4.19 | Greater than eight hours |
| Risk rating | Yellow | | | |
| | Acknowledged operational risks and impacts during pandemic—mitigating controls or safeguards are planned or under consideration | | | |

*Comments*

Finance sector includes banking services, investment and brokering services, credit card, and other transaction services.

Financial services are important to the viable delivery of Health services under normal conditions for inputs such as payment of staff, contractors, and suppliers.

A failure of financial infrastructure under normal operating conditions would be noticed by Health sector workers possibly within a working day and by contractors and suppliers within several working days. Normal Health sector operations could continue for more than eight hours before staff, contractors, and supplies suffered material impacts.

A reduction in the assurance of the Finance sector during a pandemic response is important due to the role of voluntary quarantine and the transfer of emergency government funds to those personally disadvantaged by quarantine. It has been previously cited in the research of this case study that without compensated quarantine, infection rates and mortality will increase.

Finally, a pandemic declaration from the Health sector will have a direct, first-order impact upon the Finance sector itself. This impact is manifested through projected absenteeism rates of 20–40 percent. Operational efficiency is impacted and significantly complicate effective response in the event of an incident. Thus, an incident impacting Finance and concurrent to a pandemic would significantly intensify pandemic risks.

## Health Dependency on Manufacturing

| | Threat | | Inbound Vulnerability | |
| --- | --- | --- | --- | --- |
| | Sector | Description | Correlated Dependency Metric | Dependency Latency (Time to Impact) |
| | Manufacturing | Pandemic | 4.00 | Greater than eight hours |
| Risk rating | Green | | | |
| | Low or unchanged operational risks during pandemic, or mitigating controls and safeguards are largely in place | | | |

*Comments*

Manufacturing sector includes chemical manufacturing and aerospace/defense industries.

Manufacturing services are important to the delivery of Health services under normal conditions for inputs such as industrial gases for anesthesia, respiratory care, and medical equipment operations.

A failure of Manufacturing infrastructure under normal operating conditions would be quickly noticed by Health sector workers, but normal operations could continue in most cases for more than eight hours due to local stockpiles of Manufacturing sector inputs. A reduction in the assurance of the Manufacturing sector during a pandemic response would likely present lesser challenges to the Health sector.

Finally, a pandemic declaration from the Health sector will have a direct, first-order impact upon the Manufacturing sector itself. This impact manifested through projected absenteeism rates of 20–40 percent and a drastic increase in remote work. Operational efficiency will be impacted and significantly complicate effective response in the event of an incident. Thus, an incident impacting Manufacturing and concurrent to a pandemic would significantly intensify pandemic risks.

## OUTBOUND CASCADING IMPACTS UNDER PANDEMIC CONDITIONS

The following tables review each of the CI sectors and the impact on these sectors of a Health sector largely occupied with pandemic response.

### ENERGY DEPENDENCY ON HEALTH

|             | Threat | | Outbound Vulnerability | |
|-------------|--------|-------------|---------------------------------|---------------------------------|
|             | Sector | Description | Correlated Dependency Metric | Dependency Latency (Time to Impact) |
|             | Energy | Pandemic    | 4.86                            | Greater than eight hours        |
| Risk rating | Green  |             |                                 |                                 |
|             | Low or unchanged operational risks during pandemic | | | |

### Comments

The Energy sector consists of extractors, refiners of liquid fuel, gas, and generators of electricity. This includes major oil, gas, and electricity firms but not independent wholesalers or distributors of energy products.

The Health sector is an important client to the Energy sector and is recognized as being a formal priority customer. A Health sector in distress will heighten awareness and place certain energy resources into an alert mode.

A pandemic condition will likely invoke response plans within the Energy sector that vary widely from company to company and will not be considered within this discussion.

The Health sector does not provide direct inputs into the provision of Energy goods and services, but the availability of Health services is an important component of workplace health and safety. A disruption in the Health sector such as overloading during a pandemic condition will possibly reduce production efficiency, but production will continue at near-normal levels nonetheless.

## SAFETY AND GOVERNMENT DEPENDENCY ON HEALTH

| | Threat | | Outbound Vulnerability | |
| --- | --- | --- | --- | --- |
| | Sector | Description | Correlated Dependency Metric | Dependency Latency (Time to Impact) |
| | Safety/Government | Pandemic | 7.00 | One to eight hours |
| Risk rating | Red | | | |
| | Large operational risks result due to incomplete understanding of dependency and lack or incomplete mitigation controls and safeguards | | | |

## Comments

The Safety sector includes police, fire, and other emergency response services such as biological, nuclear, or chemical incidents. Government consists of regulators of critical government and dispensers of services such as social security programs.

Under normal operating conditions, Health is a critical delivery partner for the Safety sector with constant interaction between the two sectors. Under normal operating conditions, Health is an important input to government because it is a highly regulated service and publicly funded service in Canada and partially funded in the United States.

Under pandemic conditions, the Safety sector is faced with overload conditions much like the Health sector due to the requirement to support quarantine order, keep order during times of potential hysteria, protect medical shipments, and medical staff from panicked or deranged persons or even mobs.

During a pandemic situation, government is held as accountable for the effectiveness of the response as the Health sector itself. During a response, government will be a critical component in public communications and the maintenance of public morale and order. All messaging and communications will have to be closely coordinated with Health sector officials.

Pandemic response consumes large portions of government energy and attention during a pandemic response to the point that most nonprogrammatic (routine and established processes) will be suspended. Legislation, policies, and new programs will be delayed.

Government will be expected to understand and anticipate cascading CI threats and risks and be prepared to mitigate these risks. The current state of understanding of cascading threats and risks among CIs is incomplete.

## COMMUNICATIONS AND IT DEPENDENCY ON HEALTH

| | Threat | | Outbound Vulnerability | |
|---|---|---|---|---|
| | Sector | Description | Correlated Dependency Metric | Dependency Latency (Time to Impact) |
| | Communications and IT | Pandemic | 2.37 | Greater than eight hours |
| Risk rating | Green | | | |
| | Low or unchanged operational risks during pandemic | | | |

## Comments

Communications and IT includes the data links and telephone lines that connect Health infrastructure assets across physical space. Local area networks and equipment within Health assets such as hospitals are not part of the Communications and IT sector. Communications and IT also includes suppliers of computer software, hardware but not data hosting and processing services.

The Health sector is an important client to the Communications and IT sector and is recognized as being a formal priority customer. A Health sector in distress will heighten awareness and place certain Communications and IT resources into an alert mode.

A pandemic condition will likely invoke response plans within the Communications and IT sector that will vary widely from company to company and will not be considered within this discussion.

The Health sector does not provide direct inputs into the provision of Communications and IT goods and services, but the availability of health services is an important component of workplace health and safety. A disruption in the Health sector such as overloading during a pandemic condition will possibly reduce production efficiency, but production will continue at near-normal levels nonetheless.

## WATER DEPENDENCY ON HEALTH

| | Threat | | Outbound Vulnerability | |
|---|---|---|---|---|
| | Sector | Description | Correlated Dependency Metric | Dependency Latency (Time to Impact) |
| | Water | Pandemic | 5.68 | Greater than eight hours |
| Risk rating | Red | | | |
| | Large operational risks result due to incomplete understanding of dependency and lack or incomplete mitigation controls and safeguards | | | |

## Comments

Water sector includes the potable water supply and wastewater management.

The Health sector is an important supplier to the Water sector through the provision of water testing services by laboratories. Water testing is a continual and ongoing process. Samples sent for testing must be processed expeditiously and delays of a working day will have a significant impact on operational risk. While large municipal water systems will have in-house testing laboratories and capability, smaller water utilities will not have in-house capability and will rely upon Health sector services entirely. Notwithstanding, large municipal water services will rely upon the Health sector to verify and validate results and provide critical advice in the event of suspected water quality problem.

A pandemic condition will delay the availability of water quality test results to the Water sector and could result in a contaminate, going undetected long enough to require a boil water advisory or order, or worse an outbreak of diseases such as cholera or hepatitis. Such an impact would further burden a Health sector already overloaded with pandemic response.

## TRANSPORTATION DEPENDENCY ON HEALTH

| | Threat | | Outbound Vulnerability | |
| --- | --- | --- | --- | --- |
| | Sector | Description | Correlated Dependency Metric | Dependency Latency (Time to Impact) |
| | Transportation | Pandemic | 3.25 | Greater than eight hours |
| Risk rating | Red | | | |
| | Large operational risks result due to incomplete understanding of dependency and lack or incomplete mitigation controls and safeguards | | | |

## Comments

Transportation includes goods and modes of transport such as rail, air, marine, and truck. In Canada, the Transportation sector does not include couriers and messengers by definition. A Health sector in distress will heighten awareness and place certain Transportation resources into an alert mode to expedite the delivery of medical goods such as vaccines.

A pandemic condition will invoke response plans within the Transportation sector that includes stepped-up communications between Health/Safety–Government and Transportation related to areas of contagion and precautions to take related to movement and mass transit. The Transportation sector may be required to detour the movement of goods and services around infected or quarantine areas. Similarly, Transportation may need support and protection from the Safety sector to fulfill the logistics requirements of the Health sector.

The Health sector does not provide direct inputs into the provision of Transportation services, but the availability of Health services is an important component of workplace health and safety. A disruption in the Health sector such as overloading during a pandemic condition will possibly reduce production efficiency, but excluding the direct impact of the pandemic declaration on Transportation, production will continue at near-normal levels nonetheless.

Under pandemic conditions, the Transportation sector is faced with overload conditions due to increased demand for logistics services from all elements of the economy; quarantine and sick people will require most goods and services to be

delivered directly to their homes or offices as travel is restricted, both voluntarily and
due to infection.

Finally, it must be noted that messengers and couriers are not considered part of
the Transportation sector, but much of the burden of logistics for the delivery for
vaccine and goods to quarantine people and areas fall into this sector. At this time,
the Transportation sector cannot count on the Health sector to support it adequately
with vaccine and priority service during a pandemic condition relative to the role
Transportation will be expected to play.

## FOOD DEPENDENCY ON HEALTH

|  | Threat | | Outbound Vulnerability | |
| --- | --- | --- | --- | --- |
|  | Sector | Description | Correlated Dependency Metric | Dependency Latency (Time to Impact) |
|  | Food | Pandemic | 1.8 | Greater than eight hours |
| Risk rating | Red | | | |
|  | Large operational risks result due to incomplete understanding of dependency or incomplete mitigation controls and safeguards | | | |

## Comments

Food sector includes both farming and food manufacturing/processing, but not Food
services that includes food contractors, mobile food services, catering and restaurants, or bottling of any variety.

The Health sector is an important client to the Food sector. A Health sector
in distress will heighten awareness and place certain Food resources into an
alert mode to respond to increased demands for food supplies from hospitals and
possibly quarantine facilities. The Food sector as defined does not deliver its goods
directly to hospitals; this would be accomplished either by the Transport sector, or by
commercial caterers, which are not considered part of the Food sector.

A pandemic condition may invoke response plans within the Food sector that will
vary widely among sector players. A pandemic condition will increase operational
risks for the Food sector primarily through the requirement to deal with Transportation
sector workers who will be in direct contact with Health sector workers and first
responders due to the logistics of delivering food and vaccines.

The Health sector is a supplier to the Food sector through the provision of food
testing by laboratories. Food testing is a continual and ongoing process. Samples
sent for testing must be processed expeditiously and delays of more than a working
day will have a significant impact on operational risk. While large food producers
will have in-house testing laboratories and capabilities, smaller processors and
producers will not have in-house capabilities and will rely upon Health sector
services entirely. Notwithstanding, large food processors will rely upon the Health
sector to occasionally verify and validate results and provide critical advice in the
event of suspected food quality problem.

A pandemic condition will delay the availability of food quality test results to the Food sector and could result in a food contaminate going undetected long enough to require an additional public health warning, advisory or order, or worse an outbreak of diseases such as cholera or hepatitis. Such an impact would further burden a Health sector already overloaded with pandemic response.

## FINANCE DEPENDENCY ON HEALTH

| | Threat | | Outbound Vulnerability | |
|---|---|---|---|---|
| | Sector | Description | Correlated Dependency Metric | Dependency Latency (Time to Impact) |
| | Finance | Pandemic | 4.86 | Greater than eight hours |
| Risk rating | Green | | | |
| | Low or unchanged operational risks during pandemic | | | |

## Comments

Finance sector includes banking services, investment and brokering services, credit card, and other transaction services.

The Health sector is an important client to the Finance sector. A Health sector in distress will heighten awareness and place certain financial sector resources into an alert mode.

A pandemic condition will likely invoke response plans within the Finance sector that will vary widely from company to company and involve restrictions of staff movements and telework.

The Health sector does not provide direct inputs into the provision of financial goods and services, but the availability of health services is an important component of workplace health and safety. A disruption in the Health sector such as overloading during a pandemic condition will possibly reduce production efficiency, but production will continue at near-normal levels nonetheless.

## MANUFACTURING DEPENDENCY ON HEALTH

| | Threat | | Outbound Vulnerability | |
|---|---|---|---|---|
| | Sector | Description | Correlated Dependency Metric | Dependency Latency (Time to Impact) |
| | Manufacturing | Pandemic | 2.61 | Greater than eight hours |
| Risk rating | Green | | | |
| | Acknowledged operational risks and impacts during pandemic—mitigating controls or safeguards are planned or under consideration | | | |

## Comments

Manufacturing sector includes chemical Manufacturing and aerospace/defense industries. When the current definition of the Manufacturing sector is applied, the Health sector is a moderate client to the Manufacturing sector. A Health sector in distress will heighten awareness and place certain Manufacturing sector resources into an alert mode.

## ASSETRANK ASSESSMENT ALGORITHM

Large variations of cascading impacts dramatically increase the overall difficulty of assessing CI interdependency. Cascading impacts mean that the effects of an incident spread far and wide through the CI ecosystem. If and where cascading impacts might meet or accumulate is difficult to assess. Much like waves travelling through water, the point where cascading impacts meet might combine to form a larger impact than the original. Similarly, when a given CI sector suffers an impact it will be relying upon CI sectors within its supply chain to support it during recovery. The manner in which dependency relationships flow (the metrics associated with these relationships) not only indicate how impacts might flow down into the supply chain, but also how support and assurance might flow up the supply chain to the sector managing the impact.

The effects of cascading impacts can be studied using the AssetRank algorithm, which is an objective and quantitative method to assign values to the CI sectors based upon the interdependencies of the system. AssetRank is related to Google's PageRank* algorithm, which computes a value for every web page on the Internet based solely upon how that page is linked to and from other pages. Important pages linking to a web page will increase the value of that web page. AssetRank[†] generalizes this idea to assign values to any type of asset in a system. It supports variables that allow unique specifications of asset importance and dependency importance to be applied. It also has parameters that capture the likelihood that each asset must satisfy its dependencies in the model (versus meeting the dependency by using assets or methods not captured in the model). It includes the ability to specify whether an asset requires just one of its dependencies versus requiring all of its dependencies. These features allow the algorithm to be applied in many different contexts including evaluating dependency upon CI sectors. AssetRank is a generalization of PageRank and so PageRank may be considered a special case of the AssetRank algorithm.

By applying AssetRank to the correlated dependency data, we obtain an objective and quantitative analysis of the projected reliance the CI sectors place upon each other. AssetRank requires that the data be represented in a mathematical graph

---

* Lawrence, P., Sergey, B., Rajeev, M., and Terry, W., 1999. The PageRank citation ranking: Bringing order to the Web.
† Sawilla, R. and Ou, X., 2007, Googling Attack Graphs (DRDC Ottawa TM 2007–205), Defence R&D Canada, Ottawa.

consisting of vertices and arcs. The vertices represent the goods and services of the CI sectors. The arcs represent the requirement that a CI sector has on another sector's goods and services.

The algorithm uses a parameter called a damping factor. The damping factor specifies the probability that a consumer of goods and services from a CI sector will continue consuming the goods and services of CI sectors in the graph (versus consuming the goods and services of industries not represented in the graph). A damping factor of 0.75 is assigned. This number helps to compensate for the noninclusiveness of the CI sector definitions and it also accounts for the fact that dependencies may be met by non-CI sectors.

Graph vertices are weighted to reflect their initial importance. The vertex weight of the goods and services of a CI sector specifies the probability that a new consumer that starts consuming the goods and services of CI sectors in the graph will do so at that CI sector. Since we are specifically interested in the dependencies of the Health sector, we place all the weight vertices on the health vertices in the graph. Placing all weight vertices on Health will simulate the importance of the other sectors to Health.

Arcs are weighted to reflect the relative dependence that a CI sector places on the various CI sectors it depends upon. The arc weights from the correlated dependency data are set to obtain the relative dependencies that one sector places upon another.

AssetRank has been applied to the correlated dependency metrics from Canada in the figures below to assess the outcome of thousands of potential cascading impact-patterns and assign weights to all CI sectors according to their overall importance to the CI sector ecosystem. Whereas the correlated dependency metrics possess weights, these are before the effects of cascades have been modeled or considered. The benefit of this piece of analysis is to reveal to what extent a CI sector may be over or under estimated in its criticality among the CI sectors, once cascading impacts are considered.

Figure 6.1 is an AssetRank assessment of the CI sector dependencies of the Health sector. The AssetRank values illustrate the trickle-through of consumption effects, beginning in the Health sector. Imagine that we could attach a token to a random consumption of Health goods and services. Whenever the provision of those goods and services depend upon other sectors, the token replicates itself and attaches itself to the other sectors' goods and services that enable Health's service delivery. Likewise, once the token has replicated itself in another industry, the provision of that industry's goods and services in turn requires still other industries' goods and services (those industries could possibly depend on Health). The token continues replicating itself as the industries meet their requirements for other industries goods and services. The AssetRank value is the percentage of Health tokens in the CI sectors. Hence, the values represent the steady state of Health dependencies taking into account an infinite-order flow-through of the dependencies. These values are compared with the prima facie correlated dependency metrics which give the first-order dependencies that the Health sector has on the other sectors.

Another perspective from which to review the differences between AssetRank and correlated scores is to consider these scores in terms of their relationship to the time, and the duration of the impacting event. AssetRanks scores are related to prolonged impacts in which a large number of cascades may occur, beyond several

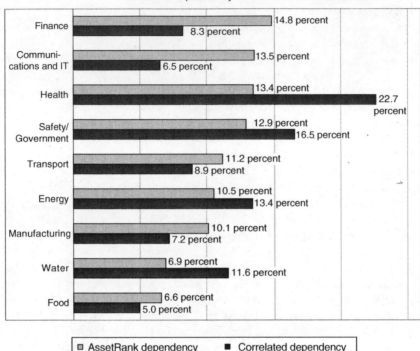

**FIGURE 6.1**　AssetRank assessment of Canadian Health sector dependencies.

days. Therefore, AssetRank might be considered a large or long-term event view of CI interdependency. Correlated scores are related to the initial, short-term effects of an impact, the first few hours to days. As the event unfolds and continues, dependency metrics would rapidly shift from correlated scores to AssetRank scores.

Figure 6.1 illustrates how AssetRank interpretations of cascading effects and CI dependencies differ from the prima facie correlated dependency metrics. AssetRank reveals the dependence that Health has on the other sectors by taking into account not only its direct dependencies on the CI sectors but more importantly, its total dependency on the CI sectors as the effects of cascading dependencies settle into the system. The total dependency includes the indirect dependencies that Health has on the CI sectors.

It is interesting to consider not only the final AssetRank values but also the difference between the AssetRank and correlated dependency scores for a given sector. For example, Finance, Communications and IT, Health, Food, and Water have large differences between the correlated dependency scores and AssetRank values while the remaining sectors have moderate differences. Under an AssetRank analysis, the assurance of the Finance sector and the criticality of these sectors with large differences to Health, shifts substantially.

Under an AssetRank analysis, the assurance of the Finance sector and the Communications and IT sector during pandemic response or any Health crisis are more critical than they first appear, due to their overall criticality to other sectors in the Health supply-chain. Although Finance and Communications and IT might not be intuitively core to pandemic response, especially in the short term, AssetRank is revealing that they are possibly undervalued by the correlated dependency metrics based on normal operating conditions. Similarly, from an AssetRank perspective, the dependency upon the other players in the Health, Safety and Government, and Water is reduced when cascading dependencies are considered and it is realized that a dependence on those sectors places indirect dependence the other sectors.

AssetRank indicates another important point related to pandemic response and Health sector dependency: the spikes associated with the criticality of one sector over another level out and flatten as indirect dependencies are considered. All sectors become comparably important to the Health sector, versus the first-order dependencies (the correlated dependency metrics) where some sectors are rated over four times as important as other sectors.

The above observations are not to say the correlated metrics were wrong—they represent an immediate-term view of the effects of CI interdependency under normal operating conditions. The AssetRank results are indicative of interdependency relationships as impacts and crisis persist and the Health sector relies on the assurance of other CI sectors to manage a crisis within its own sector.

## CASE STUDY 2: CYBER-ATTACK ON WATER INFRASTRUCTURE

### SCENARIO

Desktop computer systems within a large urban water management utility are compromised by a prevalent "botnet" attack and come under the control of unknown entities. The attack constantly morphs its signature and uses a peer-to-peer command and control network that is detected by neither the well-managed and maintained firewalls nor intrusion detection systems in place. From a water utility desktop, the threat entities compromise the utility's Data Historian that manages information from the supervisory control and data acquisition (SCADA) infrastructure. Using the Data Historian as a staging point not the SCADA network, the threat entities reconfigures, slows, and shuts down wastewater pumps, gates, and valves around the city, with the effect that raw sewage is dumped into the local waterways and blackwater sewermains fill and back up all over the city.

### LITERATURE REVIEW

The Water sector-specific plan from the U.S. National Infrastructure Protection Plan is one of the few sources of information about perceived interdependencies between Water and other infrastructures.

> Reliance on another asset or sector for the functioning of certain assets is called a dependency; if two assets depend on one another, they are called interdependent. EPA has undertaken numerous analyses to better understand and evaluate the dependencies and interdependencies between the Water Sector and other infrastructure sectors. Interdependencies within the Water Sector and among the other CI/KR sectors must

be considered when discussing consequences. These interdependencies may have local, regional, or national implications. They are considered to be essential elements of a comprehensive examination of physical and cyber vulnerabilities.*

The Water sector-specific plan also states

Consequences of concern can also include the public health and economic impacts resulting from loss of a wastewater asset's services. Not only can release of untreated sewage into rivers, lakes, and reservoirs cause environmental damage, it can also affect drinking water treatment plants downstream that draw their raw water from these sources.

Therefore, the report identifies Safety/Government, Health, and intrasector Water dependencies as potentially of the highest urgency. Similarly, Communications and IT is highlighted due to

...the Water Sector's increasing reliance on cyber systems (e.g., process control systems), coupled with the downsizing of the sector workforce, has resulted in critical dependency on certain highly skilled human resources.[†]

Energy is also identified up front as an important input to the Water sector:

Interdependencies historically have been considered to be either physical or geographic. For example, the water and power sectors are integrally and often physically linked: the Water Sector needs power to operate its pumps and treatment operations, while the power sector often depends on the Water Sector for cooling water.[‡]

The Water sector-specific plan goes on to identify and discuss specific dependencies among all other CIs and water.

In early 2006, the Blue Cascades III report was issued.[§] Blue Cascades III was a large disaster exercise involving players from across the Pacific North-west region of the United States and western Canada. The report from the exercise contained some interested, ad hoc observations about interdependencies with Water infrastructure which bears mentioning.

Relighting pilot lights after a widespread and prolonged natural gas, propane (LPG), and power disruption was a major problem from a safety standpoint and particularly because of the large numbers of trained technicians and the time required. Likewise water utilities could cause significant damage to buildings should they restore water service prior to checking the integrity of the plumbing systems installed in those buildings.[$]

In this case, there is a significant interdependency issue associated with communications. Property owners need to shut off their water mains until they can be inspected to avoid damage. This communications interdependency might be both technical and

---

* Water Sector Specific Plan—National Infrastructure Protection Plan, Homeland Security, p. 48.
† Water Sector Specific Plan—National Infrastructure Protection Plan, Homeland Security, p. 50.
‡ Water Sector Specific Plan—National Infrastructure Protection Plan, Homeland Security, p. 50.
§ Blue Cascades III http://www.regionalresilience.org/MainMenu/BlueCascades/BlueCascadesIII/tabid/146/Default.aspx.
$ Blue Cascades III, p. 8.

social, where Communications and IT provide the enabling technologies to get the messages out, but government and safety issues the messages for Water.

Blue cascades also revealed certain Safety and Government expectations and dependencies on Water; where the maintenance of public order is based upon assumptions about the planning undertaken by the Water infrastructure managers.

> Encourage critical infrastructure owners and essential service providers to, where possible, establish alternative sources for essential products and services—e.g., for water systems, alternative sources of drinking water and alternative methods of water distribution. State environmental regulators appear unprepared to allow water utilities to access emergency water sources without a timely permitting process.*
>
> Regional organizations are undertaking mitigation measures to deal with large-scale disasters. For example, the Seattle Fire Department and the City of Seattle have been developing alternative water supply, including temporary above ground water mains, improved ability to pump from fireboats on fresh water lakes and reservoirs or Puget Sound. They have procedures for adjusting water use depending on priority water needs.[†]
> Water and wastewater utilities impacted by Katrina lost their as-built drawings and system plans/maps. All utilities should investigate digitizing and backing up important system information outside the geographic area to a site or sites that would not be impacted by earthquake or other disasters striking their facilities.[‡]

A final significant interdependency observation is that the government is expected to play a large supporting role in public communications about the impacts and appropriate countermeasures associated with impacts to the Water infrastructure.

> The public needs education on what a major earthquake or other cascading disaster would cause in terms of disruptions to basic services and awareness of health and safety concerns (e.g., not turning on the electricity before gas fumes are dissipated to avoid igniting fires, and not immediately flushing toilets when water is restored to prevent sewage backup). As one participant said, "the community at large is still unaware of what to expect and what it will take to survive and recover." A water systems representative added, many believe government is prepared to prevent, mitigate, or protect them in events such as this. This misunderstanding will complicate preparing them to care for themselves.[§]

## FINDINGS: CI INTERDEPENDENCY VULNERABILITY AND RISK ANALYSIS UNDER WASTEWATER MANAGEMENT CRISIS CONDITIONS

The columns in Table 6.4 represent the inbound dependency metric for a given sector, where inbound refers to the level of assurance required by a sector in the goods or services supplied by another sector. The rows represent the outbound dependency metric for a given sector, where outbound refers to the level of assurance other sectors places upon the goods or services supplied by a given sector.

---

* Blue Cascades III, p. 31.
[†] Blue Cascades III, p. 31.
[‡] Blue Cascades III, p. 43.
[§] Blue Cascades III, p. 44.

Metrics are on a scale from 1 to 10 as derived through correlation of quantitative econometric analysis and qualitative executive interviewing, and represent inbound or outbound dependency under normal operating conditions.

The colors in the cells represent the assessed risk around these dependency relationships when a change occurs from normal operating conditions to crisis conditions (Table 6.3).

Table 6.4 is a derivative of the CI dependency matrix developed in Chapter 4, and contains only the health-related dependency metrics from that chapter and the assessed risk from this case study. Each of the cells associated with health interdependency are discussed and reasoning provided to support the risk judgments applied.

## DETAILED RISK ANALYSIS OF SECTOR INTERDEPENDENCY UNDER PANDEMIC CONDITIONS

Interdependencies are considered from the perspective of how Water is dependent upon other CI sectors under pandemic response (inbound dependency) and how might other CI sectors be impacted by pandemic response due to their dependence on the Water sector (outbound dependency).

Sectors are discussed in order of the impact latency. (The amount of time that passes before the impact from the loss of a sector starts to be felt.) *Note:* impact latency does not equate to severity of impact. Dependence on a sector input might not be felt immediacy upon loss, but when felt, the impact may be more debilitating than those of sectors with short impact latencies.

## Water Dependency on Water

|  | Threat | | Outbound Vulnerability | |
| --- | --- | --- | --- | --- |
|  | Sector | Description | Correlated Dependency Metric | Dependency Latency (Time to Impact) |
|  | Water | Cyber-attack | 5.68 | One to eight hours |
| Risk rating | Moderate | | | |
|  | Acknowledged operational risks and impacts during pandemic—mitigating controls or safeguards are planned or under consideration | | | |

## TABLE 6.3
## Assessed Risk Definitions

| Green | Low or unchanged operational risks during pandemic, or mitigating controls and safeguards are largely in place |
| --- | --- |
| Yellow | Acknowledged operational risks and impacts during pandemic—mitigating controls or safeguards are planned or under consideration |
| Red | Large operational risks result due to incomplete understanding of dependency and substantially incomplete mitigation controls and safeguards |

**TABLE 6.4**
**Correlated Canadian CI Interdependency Metrics for the Water Sector**

| | | Inbound Dependencies | | | | | | | | |
|---|---|---|---|---|---|---|---|---|---|---|
| | CI Sector | Energy | Comms and IT | Fin | Health Care | Food | Water | Trans | Gov/ Safety | Manf |
| Outbound Dependencies | Energy | | | | | | 5.00[b] | | | |
| | Comms & IT | | | | | | 3.48[c] | | | |
| | Fin | | | | | | 5.15[a] | | | |
| | Health Care | | | | | | 4.20[a] | | | |
| | Food | | | | | | 1.48[a] | | | |
| | Water | 4.69[b] | 1.96[a] | 2.19[a] | 4.90[c] | 1.47[c] | 5.68[b] | 2.89[b] | 2.08[c] | 2.24[b] |
| | Trans | | | | | | 2.81[c] | | | |
| | Gov/ Safety | | | | | | 4.44[b] | | | |
| | Manf | | | | | | 3.31[b] | | | |

[a] Denotes green.
[b] Denotes yellow.
[c] Denotes red.

*Comments*

Water sector includes the potable water supply and wastewater management. Under normal operating conditions, water infrastructure in urban areas may have direct physical interfaces (connecting pipes) and act as backup facilities for another to a certain extent. Impacts in the chemistry and quality of a local water sources may impact all adjacent water infrastructures; therefore, infrastructure managers need to remain in contact with one another and exchange water quality information on a regular basis.

In the event of detected contamination of a local water source, water infrastructure players would need to notify adjacent infrastructures as soon as possible to prevent contaminated water from entering the infrastructure.

A sewage spill into local water sources due to a cyber-attack on the waste management SCADA systems would require rapid communication to adjacent and especially downstream Water infrastructures from drawing contaminated on incompletely treated water into their systems. The impact of a sewage spill into a water source will not have an instantaneous impact on adjacent and downstream infrastructure, but contaminates could reach intakes within a matter of hours and in extreme cases minutes.

Requirements for sharing information between Water infrastructure entities under both normal and abnormal operating are well understood; however, the existence of processes, procedures, and trained person to deal with abnormal operating conditions and crisis events is not comprehensive.

The dependency risk to Water from Water is rated as moderate. Even though the impacted SCADA systems related to wastewater management, the threat to drinking water systems downstream possesses a very high impact. Although documentation and qualified staff are largely in place to address interdependency risks among water infrastructures, a failure in these procedures—which are not automated—would have significant impacts.

## Water Dependency on Energy

|  | Threat | | Outbound Vulnerability | |
| --- | --- | --- | --- | --- |
|  | Sector | Description | Correlated Dependency Metric | Dependency Latency (Time to Impact) |
|  | Energy | Cyber-attack | 5.00 | One to eight hours |
| Risk rating | Moderate | | | |
|  | Acknowledged operational risks and impacts during incident—mitigating controls or safeguards are planned or under consideration | | | |

*Comments*

The Energy sector consists of extractors, refiners of liquid fuels, gas, and generators of electricity. This includes major oil, gas, and electricity firms but not independent wholesalers or distributors of energy products.

Under normal conditions, Water is dependent upon Energy for electricity to run pumps, treatment equipment, and operational systems such as SCADA systems. Energy is a make input to the Water infrastructure, which consumes large amounts of electricity for both water quality management and waste management.

In the event of a power failure, a large Water infrastructure will be equipped with backup power generators which can last for several hours. Additionally, wastewater systems will fail safc and are designed with reservoirs which can sustain several hours to even days of flow without pumps and processing systems operating; therefore, the loss of power will become a significant operational risk between one and eight hours of outage.

Under a cyber-attack condition against Water SCADA infrastructure, Energy would have no particular role to play during either detection, response, or recovery other than to remain available.

The dependency risk to Water from Energy is that procedures, documentation, and qualified staff are not in place to operate equipment using manual methods and bypass modes in the absence of power. Power failure during a cyber-attack would complicate response and recovery but given the compromise of the SCADA system, manual operations might well be the end result regardless.

## Water Dependency on Safety and Government

| | Threat | | Outbound Vulnerability | |
| --- | --- | --- | --- | --- |
| | Sector | Description | Correlated Dependency Metric | Dependency Latency (Time to Impact) |
| | Safety and Government | Cyber-attack | 4.44 | One to eight hours |
| Risk rating | Moderate | | | |
| | Acknowledged operational risks and impacts during incident—mitigating controls or safeguards are planned or under consideration | | | |

*Comments*

The Safety sector includes police, fire, and other emergency response services such as those for specific hazards like biological, nuclear, or chemical incidents. Government consists of regulators of critical government services and dispensers of social security programs.

Under normal conditions, government is important to the Water sector as the primary owner and spending authority. Therefore, business interdependence with municipal government especially is a part of daily operations.

In the event of a cyber-attack on the SCADA system of water treatment infrastructure, government is key source of leadership, funding, and especially communications to the public and other stakeholders. Although the water infrastructure managers might be expected to rapidly notify other water system managers, they need to coordinate general messaging and information with government. Similarly, emergency replacement equipment of temporary solutions such as portable industrial pumps may require out-of-budget costs, which have to be allocated from government quickly.

The dependency risk with the Government sector is that crisis public communications tools and procedures have not been fully developed and communications are not expeditious. Delayed government reaction could result in delayed decision making related to difficult issues such as whether to dump untreated sewage into waterways, into which waterways or ordering evacuations as a result of the need to dump. Similarly, the impact of delayed or incomplete coordination with government results in further cascading CI impacts in sectors other than Water (see outbound impacts to Health and Food).

Dependency risk is rated as moderate because processes and procedures for coordination with government during incidents generally exist, but the indications from this research are that government considers Water as a lower profile infrastructure and awareness of Water's requirements under crisis response may not be proportional to the need or consequences.

## Water Dependency on Communications and IT

| | Threat | | Outbound Vulnerability | |
|---|---|---|---|---|
| Sector | Description | Correlated Dependency Metric | Dependency Latency (Time to Impact) |
| Communication and IT | Cyber-attack | 3.48 | One to eight hours |
| Risk rating | High | | | |
| | Large operational risks result due to incomplete understanding of dependency or substantially incomplete mitigation controls and safeguards | | | |

*Comments*
Communications and IT includes the data links and telephone lines that connect Health infrastructure assets across physical space. Local area networks and communications within Health assets such as hospitals are not part of the Communications and IT sector. Communications and IT also includes suppliers of computer software, hardware but not data hosting and processing services.

Under normal conditions, Communications and IT service plays a central role supporting coordination of operations with other Water infrastructures and government. Communications and IT also provides the foundation capabilities to support SCADA systems and remote management and monitoring of pumps, values, gates, meters and reservoirs, and water sources. A loss of Communications and IT for beyond one hour would start to introduce significant operational risks and manual monitoring and control of some systems and process would have to commence according to defined procedures.

Under a cyber-attack condition, Communications and IT services will be an external staging point for the attack on the internal Water infrastructure systems. Such an attack would probably not involve brute-force and large amounts of traffic, it would be stealthy and leave the network connections intact. Communications and IT service providers may be in a position to detect and probably stem remote attacks against Water perpetrated through their network, but only if such services have been procured in advance by Water. Communications and IT may also support later efforts in forensics and prosecution.

Failure of Communications and IT services under a cyber-attack condition may perversely have both a potentially positive and negative effect. The potentially positive impact would disrupt the threat entitles and cut off their means of access; however, most of the impact of a Communications and IT failure is negative. Water loses a critical tool used for coordination with response partners such as government, emergency response/HazMat teams and other Water infrastructures. Depending on the nature of the Communications and IT failure, cellular services might also be lost in a region, further amplifying the impacts of a cyber-attack as this alternate means of communication is lost. Alternately, if a large number of the Water infrastructure's information-assets were IP-based (VOIP, IP-SCADA, IP-LAN, IP-cameras, and IP-door strikes) then the cyber-attack might also target internal telecommunications devices in parallel with SCADA systems, and bring down virtually all internal communications systems.

The dependency risk for Water on Communications and IT is substantial given that the services provided by communications are central to both business-as-usual operations and emergency response coordination. SCADA systems are obviously IT based and can be manipulated for serious impacts if compromised. The convergence of most communications assets such as voice, data, SCADA, facilities management, and physical access controls to an all-IP network increases the efficient of operations and business, but also the richness of the target. Under a cyber-attack, a lack of adequate risk management controls on Communications and IT can be critical vulnerability.

Dependency risk is rated as high because processes and procedures for recovery of Communications and IT may exist but indications are that Communications and IT are largely assumed by Water, and that response plans associated with concurrent outages of other services (due to converged attacks) are not in place. Furthermore, indications from this research are that Communications and IT considers Water as a lower profile infrastructure and awareness of Water's requirements under crisis response may not be proportional to the need or consequences.

## Water Dependency on Health Sector Entities

|  | Threat | | Outbound Vulnerability | |
|---|---|---|---|---|
|  | Sector | Description | Correlated Dependency Metric | Dependency Latency (Time to Impact) |
|  | Health | Cyber-attack | 4.20 | Greater than eight hours |
| Risk rating | Low | | | |
|  | Low or unchanged operational risks during incident, or mitigating controls and safeguards are largely in place | | | |

*Comments*

The Health sector consists of hospitals, laboratories, blood and pharmaceutical supply facilities, and ambulatory services. Under normal conditions, the Health sector is an important supplier to the Water sector through the provision of water testing services by laboratories. Water testing is a continual and ongoing process. Samples sent for testing must be processed expeditiously and delays of a working day will have a significant impact on operational risk. While large municipal water systems will have in-house testing laboratories and capability, smaller water utilities will not have in-house capability and will rely upon Health sector services entirely. Notwithstanding, large municipal water services will rely upon the Health sector to verify and validate results and provide critical advice in the event of suspected water quality problem.

A cyber-attack condition in the Water sector resulting in the possible discharge of raw sewage into waterways or sewer backup will require consultation with Health officials to support public communications and impacts assessments.

The direct dependency risk to water from Health will be low during a cyber-attack on wastewater systems because public communications and impact assessments will be lead by government which must itself work closely with Health. This assessment should not be confused with the outbound impact on the Health sector of a cyber-attack on waste management systems (see Health Dependency on Water).

## Water Dependency on Transportation

| | Threat | | Outbound Vulnerability | |
| --- | --- | --- | --- | --- |
| | Sector | Description | Correlated Dependency Metric | Dependency Latency (Time to Impact) |
| | Transportation | Cyber-attack | 2.81 | Greater than eight hours |
| Risk rating | High | | | |
| | Large operational risks result due to incomplete understanding of dependency or substantially incomplete mitigation controls and safeguards | | | |

*Comments*

Transportation sector includes goods and modes of transport such as rail, air, marine, and truck. In Canada, the Transportation sector does not include couriers and messengers by definition.

Under normal operating conditions, the Water sector is dependent upon the Transportation for the delivery of treatment chemicals for water quality management, and the delivery of equipment and spares on both a routine and expedited basis. As most chemicals are maintained with several days of stockpile, and most maintenance is scheduled, an outage of less than eight hours in Transportation services will not normally raise operational risks to the Water sector.

Under cyber-attack conditions, urgent requirements to replace damaged equipment or provision treatment chemicals at alternate, emergency treatment locations may be required. As a result, Water may require priority service from Transportation.

Dependency risk is rated as high because processes and procedures for priority service from Transportation may exist but indications are that Transportation is largely assumed by Water, and that response plans associated with concurrent outages of other services (such as truck or rail) are not in place. Furthermore, indications from this research are that Transportation considers Water as a lower profile infrastructure and awareness of Water's requirements under crisis response may not be proportional to the need or consequences.

## Water Dependency on Manufacturing

| | Threat | | Inbound Vulnerability | |
| --- | --- | --- | --- | --- |
| | Sector | Description | Correlated Dependency Metric | Dependency Latency (Time to Impact) |
| Risk rating | Manufacturing Moderate | Cyber-attack | 3.31 | Greater than eight hours |
| | Acknowledged operational risks and impacts during incident—mitigating controls or safeguards are planned or under consideration | | | |

*Comments*
Manufacturing sector includes chemical manufacturing and aerospace/defense industries, but not pharmaceutical manufacturing or the manufacturing of medical equipment.

Under normal operating conditions, the Water sector is dependent upon the manufacturing for treatment chemicals for water quality management. As most chemicals are maintained with several days of stockpile, an outage/loss of availability of less than eight hours in the Manufacturing sector will not normally raise operational risks to the Water sector.

Under cyber-attack conditions, urgent requirements to replace lost, compromised, or stranded stockpiles at alternate, emergency treatment locations may be required. As a result, Water may require priority supplies from manufacturing.

Dependency risk is rated as moderate because processes and procedures for priority service from manufacturing may exist and multiple sources/suppliers for chemical goods are likely available, or stockpiles from other Water infrastructures might be shared. Indications from this research are that manufacturing considers Water as a lower profile infrastructure and awareness of Water's requirements under crisis response may not be proportional to the need or consequences.

## Water Dependency on Food

| | Threat | | Outbound Vulnerability | |
| --- | --- | --- | --- | --- |
| | Sector | Description | Correlated Dependency Metric | Dependency Latency (Time to Impact) |
| Risk rating | Food Low | Cyber-attack | 1.48 | Greater than eight hours |
| | Low or unchanged operational risks during incident, or mitigating controls and safeguards are largely in place | | | |

*Comments*
Food sector includes both farming and food manufacturing/processing, but not food services that includes food contractors, mobile food services, catering and restaurants, or bottling of any variety.

Under normal operating conditions, the Food infrastructure provides some service to waste management systems through the disposal of biosolids used as fertilizer on farms; however, food is largely a workplace health and safety issue for Water sector employees. An impact in the Food sector would not impact operational risk in Water infrastructure for at least eight hours.

Under a cyber-attack condition, water processing may cease and biosolids accumulate, though for reasons unrelated to the Food infrastructure. Otherwise, the Food infrastructure will not have a significant role in crisis response. This statement should not be confused with outbound dependency of the Food sector on Water (see Food Dependency on Water).

Dependency risk is rated as low because Food does not directly support Water's response efforts under a cyber-attack and resulting impacts of sewage backup and dumping.

## Water Dependency on Finance

| | Threat | | Inbound Vulnerability | |
| --- | --- | --- | --- | --- |
| | Sector | Description | Correlated Dependency Metric | Dependency Latency (Time to Impact) |
| | Finance | Cyber-attack | 5.15 | Greater than eight hours |
| Risk rating | Low | | | |
| | Low or unchanged operational risks during incident, or mitigating controls and safeguards are largely in place | | | |

*Comments*

Finance sector includes banking services, investment and brokering services, credit card, and other transaction services.

Under normal operating conditions, the Finance infrastructure provides transaction services to the Water infrastructure for the purposes of payroll and supply payments. For certain Water infrastructure engaged in cogeneration agreements (hydropower from waterways) with power utilities, the Finance sector would also clear and settle transactions associated with selling energy back to the grid. An impact in the Finance sector would not impact operational risk in Water infrastructure for at least eight hours.

Under a cyber-attack condition, the Finance infrastructure will not have a significant role in crisis response. Although the requirement to rapidly procure supplies may be critical to response, there is no requirement for prioritizing transaction processing.

Dependency risk is rated as low because Finance will not directly support Water's response efforts under a cyber-attack and resulting impacts of sewage backup and dumping.

# OUTBOUND CASCADING IMPACTS UNDER CYBER-ATTACK CONDITIONS

The following tables review each of the CI sectors and the impact on these sectors of a Water sector impacted by a cyber-attack on wastewater management SCADA systems.

## HEALTH DEPENDENCY ON WATER

| | Threat | | Outbound Vulnerability | |
|---|---|---|---|---|
| | Sector | Description | Correlated Dependency Metric | Dependency Latency (Time to Impact) |
| | Health | Cyber-attack | 4.90 | One to eight hours |
| Risk rating | High | | | |
| | Large operational risks result due to incomplete understanding of dependency or substantially incomplete mitigation controls and safeguards | | | |

## Comments

The Health sector consists of hospitals, laboratories, blood and pharmaceutical supply facilities, and ambulatory services.

Under normal operating conditions, the Health sector relies heavily upon the Water sector to maintain clean and sterile conditions and is fundamental to workplace health and safety. Additionally, pharmaceutical manufacturing (part of the Health sector) requires water for production processes.

Under a cyber-attack condition in which the wastewater management system has ceased to function, hospitals are forced to stop admitting new patients once they become aware of the failure. Health will not be immediately aware of failure in water infrastructure because drain will not cease functioning instantly; they will likely become aware through coordinated communications channels. Upon notification of a wastewater failure, patients will be redirected to other facilities where wastewater services are functional. In the event that sewer backups or stop water usage orders become probable, health infrastructure will have to start evacuating patients, increasing risks associated with disease spread and general mortality. Even though plans and procedures to support evacuation exist, the risks remain high and evacuation is a last resort.

Under a cyber-attack condition in which sewage must be dumped into water ways, downstream health infrastructures will be placed into alert mode related to waterborne disease which might result. Similarly, boil water advisories or orders may come into effect resulting in overloading as sick people and worried well seek attention. Again, downstream health infrastructure will not be immediately aware of failure in water infrastructure because water from taps will not suddenly turn brown; they will likely become aware through coordinated communications channels.

Dependency risk of the Health sector under a cyber-attack on Water sector SCADA is rated as high, due to the substantial risks posed to life in the event of water infrastructure failure.

## ENERGY DEPENDENCY ON WATER

| | Threat | | Outbound Vulnerability | |
| --- | --- | --- | --- | --- |
| | Sector | Description | Correlated Dependency Metric | Dependency Latency (Time to Impact) |
| | Energy | Cyber-attack | 4.69 | One to eight hours |
| Risk rating | Moderate | | | |
| | Acknowledged operational risks and impacts during incident—mitigating controls or safeguards are planned or under consideration | | | |

## Comments

The Energy sector consists of extractors, refiners of liquid fuels, gas, and generators of electricity. This includes major oil, gas, and electricity firms but not independent wholesalers or distributors of energy products.

Under normal operating conditions, Water is important to different Energy industries for applications as diverse as cooling, steam generation, mining operations and ore processing, refining operations, pollution control, methane and hydrogen generation, and fundamental workplace health and safety. Energy would maintain certain short-term stockpiles of water; however, prolonged outages are not provisioned.

Under cyber-attack conditions, a disruption in the functionality of the Water infrastructure would have an important impact on the Energy sector. Operational risks would develop shortly after the disruption was detected. Risk will take various forms depending on the energy industry in question, but all risks tend to come with extreme consequences in the Energy industry such as loss of life, major damage to expensive capital assets, or idling of expensive production processes.

Dependency risk of the Energy sector under a cyber-attack on Water sector SCADA is rated as moderate, due to the substantial risks posed to life in the event of prolonged Water infrastructure failure. Indications from this research are that Energy considers water as a lower profile infrastructure and awareness of Water's criticality to production processes may not be proportional to the real need or consequences.

## SAFETY AND GOVERNMENT DEPENDENCY ON WATER

| | Threat | | Outbound Vulnerability | |
| --- | --- | --- | --- | --- |
| | Sector | Description | Correlated Dependency Metric | Dependency Latency (Time to Impact) |
| | Safety/ Government | Cyber-attack | 2.08 | One to eight hours |
| Risk rating | High | | | |
| | Large operational risks result due to incomplete understanding of dependency or substantially incomplete mitigation controls and safeguards | | | |

## Comments

The Safety sector includes police, fire, and other emergency response services such as those for specific hazards like biological, nuclear, or chemical incidents. Government consists of regulators of critical government services and dispensers of social security programs.

Under normal operating conditions, government is dependent generally upon Water to maintain a critical service, and specifically to apply water safety standards and regulations to preserve public and environmental health and order. Safety is particularly dependent upon water for the provision of firefighting capabilities (i.e., Water in hydrants).

Under cyber-attack conditions in which wastewater processes are disrupted, government would be heavily dependent upon Water to frequently report status during incidents, share information so that wider response efforts can be coordinated effectively and risks mitigated as far as possible, and repair the damage as quickly as possible to minimize damage to public and environmental health and order. Safety may be impacted by a cyber-attack through the requirement to secure and isolate waterways which have been contaminated by sewage overflows, and to support evacuation orders from critical sites such as hospitals. In these instances, safety will also depend upon Water to frequently report status during incidents, share information so that wider response efforts can be coordinated effectively and risks mitigated as far as possible, and repair the damage fast enough to minimize damage to public and environmental health and order. Finally, government and safety employ large numbers of workers concentrated in centralized locations; these locations would not remain viable for long during a failure of wastewater management services and would have to be evacuated.

Dependency risk of the Safety and Government sector under a cyber-attack on Water sector SCADA is rated as high, due to the substantial risks posed to public and environmental health and order. Indications from this research are that Safety and Government considers Water as a lower profile infrastructure and awareness of Water's criticality to production processes may not be proportional to the real need or consequences.

## COMMUNICATIONS AND IT DEPENDENCY ON WATER

| | Threat | | Outbound Vulnerability | |
|---|---|---|---|---|
| | Sector | Description | Correlated Dependency Metric | Dependency Latency (Time to Impact) |
| | Communications and IT | Cyber-attack | 1.96 | One to eight hours |
| Risk rating | Low | | | |
| | Low or unchanged operational risks during incident, or mitigating controls and safeguards are largely in place | | | |

## Comments

Communications and IT includes the data links and telephone lines that connect Health infrastructure assets across physical space. Local area networks and communications within Health assets such as hospitals are not part of the Communications and IT sector. Communications and IT also includes suppliers of computer software, hardware but not data hosting and processing services.

Under normal operating conditions, Water is important to different Communications and IT industries for applications such as cooling in buildings and central-office locations. While most cooling systems are closed and are not immediately impacted by Water outages, prolonged outages are not provisioned for.

Under cyber-attack conditions, a disruption in the functionality of the Water infrastructure would have a moderate impact on the Energy sector. Operational risks in the form of workplace health and safety risks would develop shortly after a disruption in Water was detected. Communications and IT employ large numbers of workers concentrated in centralized locations; these locations would not remain viable for long during a failure of wastewater management services and would have to be evacuated.

Dependency risk of the Communications and IT sector under a cyber-attack on Water sector SCADA is rated as low, due to the moderate risks posed to Communications and IT in the event of prolonged water infrastructure failure and the existence of short-term alternatives such as shifting work electronically to alternate locations or telework.

## FOOD DEPENDENCY ON WATER

|  | Threat | | Outbound Vulnerability | |
| --- | --- | --- | --- | --- |
|  | Sector | Description | Correlated Dependency Metric | Dependency Latency (Time to Impact) |
| Risk rating | Food | Cyber-attack | 1.47 | One to eight hours |
|  | High | | | |
|  | Large operational risks result due to incomplete understanding of dependency or substantially incomplete mitigation controls and safeguards | | | |

## Comments

Food sector includes both farming and food manufacturing/processing, but not Food services that includes food contractors, mobile food services, catering and restaurants, or bottling of any variety.

Under normal operating conditions, Water is important to different Food industries for applications such as food processing, maintenance of clean facilities, and watering of livestock and irrigation. Food is dependent upon wastewater specifically for the maintenance of clean processing conditions, which represents a highly regulated operational imperative.

Under cyber-attack conditions, a disruption in the functionality of the Water infrastructure would have a significant impact on the Food sector. Operational risks in the form of food quality would develop shortly after a disruption in Water was detected. The Food sector also contains long supply chains, with a variety of different producers and processors providing inputs into even simple products like soup. For instance a can of chicken noodle soup will receive inputs farmers, abattoirs and vegetable processors, flavor and preservative manufacturing, and finally the cannery. Contamination is possible at any point in this production chain and is carefully managed by food professionals. A failure in the water infrastructure may inject risks not just at a single point but possible multiple points and therefore, substantially increase the overall likelihood of a failure. Similarly, individual food processors face potentially devastating strategic risks associated with a compromise in food quality due to loss of reputation and an immediate subsequent collapse in client base.

Dependency risk of the Water sector under a cyber-attack on Water sector SCADA is rated as high, due to the significant risks posed to Water in the event of Water infrastructure failure lasting more than one hour.

## FINANCE DEPENDENCY ON WATER

| | Threat | | Outbound Vulnerability | |
| --- | --- | --- | --- | --- |
| | Sector | Description | Correlated Dependency Metric | Dependency Latency (Time to Impact) |
| | Finance | Cyber-attack | 2.19 | One to eight hours |
| Risk rating | Low | | | |
| | Low or unchanged operational risks during incident, or mitigating controls and safeguards are largely in place | | | |

## Comments

Finance sector includes banking services, investment and brokering services, credit card, and other transaction services. Under normal operating conditions, Water is important to different financial services industries for applications such as cooling in buildings and maintenance of workplace health and safety. Although most cooling systems are closed and are not immediately impacted by Water outages, prolonged outages are not provisioned by landlords.

Under cyber-attack conditions, a disruption in the functionality of the Water infrastructure would have a moderate impact on the Finance sector. Operational risks in the form of workplace health and safety risks would develop within eight hours after a disruption in Water was detected: Finance employ large numbers of workers concentrated in centralized locations; these locations would not remain viable for long during a failure of wastewater management services and would have to be evacuated.

Dependency risk of the Finance sector under a cyber-attack on Water sector SCADA is rated as low, due to the moderate risks posed to Finance in the event of prolonged Water infrastructure failure and the existence of short-term alternatives such as shifting work electronically to alternate locations or telework.

## TRANSPORTATION DEPENDENCY ON WATER

|  | Threat | | Outbound Vulnerability | |
| --- | --- | --- | --- | --- |
|  | Sector | Description | Correlated Dependency Metric | Dependency Latency (Time to Impact) |
|  | Transportation | Cyber-attack | 2.89 | Greater than eight hours |
| Risk rating | Moderate | | | |
|  | Acknowledged operational risks and impacts during incident—mitigating controls or safeguards are planned or under consideration | | | |

## Comments

Transportation sector includes goods and modes of transport such as rail, air, marine, and truck. In Canada, the Transportation sector does not include couriers and messengers by definition.

Under normal operating conditions, water is important to different Transportation industries for applications such as equipment maintenance, and in the case of shipping, management of bridge controls over certain waterways. In the case of air and rail transportation, onboard water and waste systems from airliners must be refreshed frequently.

Under cyber-attack conditions, a disruption in the functionality of the water infrastructure would have a moderate to significant impact on the Transportation sector. A failure of waste management systems at airports would prevent aircraft from being maintained correctly and could result in operational risks associated with stranded aircraft and passengers, as flights are cancelled because onboard septic tanks cannot be emptied. Similarly, airports will have to be evacuated for workplace health and safety reasons if sewers and waste management systems fail for more than a few hours.

Dependency risk of the Transportation sector as a whole under a cyber-attack on Water sector SCADA is rated as moderate, due to the risks posed to Transportation in the event of prolonged water infrastructure failure.

## MANUFACTURING DEPENDENCY ON WATER

|  | Threat | | Outbound Vulnerability | |
| --- | --- | --- | --- | --- |
|  | Sector | Description | Correlated Dependency Metric | Dependency Latency (Time to Impact) |
|  | Manufacturing | Cyber-attack | 2.24 | Greater than eight hours |
| Risk rating | Moderate | | | |
|  | Acknowledged operational risks and impacts during incident—mitigating controls or safeguards are planned or under consideration | | | |

## Comments

Manufacturing sector includes chemical manufacturing and aerospace/defense industries, but not pharmaceutical manufacturing or the manufacturing of medical equipment.

Under normal operating conditions, the Water sector is dependent upon the Manufacturing for treatment chemicals for water quality management. As most chemicals are maintained with several days of stockpile, an outage/loss of availability of less than eight hours in the Manufacturing sector will not normally raise operational risks to the Water sector.

Under normal operating conditions, Water is important to different Manufacturing industries for applications such as cooling, equipment maintenance, and in the case of chemicals, as a direct input into products.

Under cyber-attack conditions, a disruption in the functionality of the Water infrastructure would have a moderate to significant impact on the Manufacturing sector. A failure of waste management systems at manufacturing plants would prevent production by-products from being disposed of on schedule, forcing them to be held in tanks. A prolonged outage of greater than eight hours may require that certain manufacturing processes and production would have to be shut down.

Dependency risk of the Manufacturing sector as a whole under a cyber-attack on Water sector SCADA is rated as moderate, due to the risks posed to Manufacturing in the event of prolonged water infrastructure failure.

## AssetRank Assessment Algorithm

Large variations of cascading impacts dramatically increase the overall difficulty of assessing CI interdependency. Cascading impacts mean that the effects of an incident spread far and wide through the CI ecosystem. If and where cascading impacts might meet or accumulate is difficult to assess. Much like waves travelling through water, the point where cascading impacts meet might combine to form a larger impact than the original. Similarly, when a given CI sector suffers an impact it will be relying upon CI sectors within its supply chain to support it during recovery. The manner in which dependency relationships flow (the metrics associated with these relationships) not only indicate how impacts might flow down into the supply chain but also how support and assurance might flow up the supply chain to the sector managing the impact.

The effects of cascading impacts can be studied using the AssetRank algorithm, which is an objective and quantitative method to assign values to the CI sectors based upon the interdependencies of the system. AssetRank is related to Google's PageRank* algorithm, which computes a value for every Web page on the Internet based solely upon how that page is linked to and from other pages. Important pages linked to a Web page increase the value of that Web page. AssetRank[†] generalizes

---

* Lawrence, P., Sergey, B., Rajeev, M., and Terry, W., 1999. The PageRank citation ranking: Bringing order to the web.
† Sawilla, R. and Ou, X., 2007. Googling Attack Graphs (DRDC Ottawa TM 2007–205), Defence R&D Canada, Ottawa.

this idea to assign values to any type of asset in a system. It supports variables which allow unique specifications of asset importance and dependency importance to be applied. It also has parameters that capture the likelihood that each asset must satisfy its dependencies in the model (versus meeting the dependency by using assets or methods not captured in the model). It includes the ability to specify whether an asset requires just one of its dependencies versus requiring all of its dependencies. These features allow the algorithm to be applied in many different contexts including evaluating dependency upon CI sectors. AssetRank is a generalization of PageRank and so PageRank may be considered a special case of the AssetRank algorithm.

By applying AssetRank to the correlated dependency data, we obtain an objective and quantitative analysis of the projected reliance the CI sectors will place upon each other. AssetRank first requires that the data be represented in a mathematical graph consisting of vertices and arcs. The vertices represent the goods and services of the CI sectors. The arcs represent the requirement that a CI sector has on another sector's goods and services.

The algorithm uses a parameter called a damping factor. The damping factor specifies the probability that a consumer of goods and services from a CI sector will continue consuming the goods and services of CI sectors in the graph (versus consuming the goods and services of industries not represented in the graph). We have assigned a damping factor of 0.75. This number helps to compensate for the non-inclusiveness of the CI sector definitions and it also accounts for the fact that dependencies may be met by non-CI sectors.

Graph vertices are weighted to reflect their initial importance. The vertex weight of the goods and services of a CI sector specifies the probability that a new consumer that starts consuming the goods and services of CI sectors in the graph will do so at that CI sector. Because we are specifically interested in the dependencies of the Health sector, we place all the weight vertices on the health vertices in the graph. Placing all weight vertices on Health will simulate the importance of the other sectors to Health.

Arcs are weighted to reflect the relative dependence that a CI sector places on the various CI sectors it depends upon. We set the arc weights from the correlated dependency data to obtain the relative dependencies that one sector places upon another.

AssetRank has been applied to the correlated dependency metrics from Canada in the figure below to assess the outcome of thousands of potential cascading impact-patterns and assign weights to all CI sectors according to their overall importance to the CI sector ecosystem. Whereas the correlated dependency metrics possess weights before the effects of cascades have been modeled or considered. The benefit of this piece of analysis is to reveal to what extent a CI sector may be over or under estimated in its criticality among the CI sectors, once cascading impacts are considered.

Figure 6.2 is an AssetRank assessment of the CI sector dependencies of the Water sector. The AssetRank values illustrate the trickle-through of consumption effects, beginning in the Water sector. Imagine that we could attach a token to a random consumption of Water goods and services. Whenever the provision of those goods and services depend upon other sectors, the token replicates itself and attaches itself to the other sectors' goods and services that enable water service delivery. Likewise, once

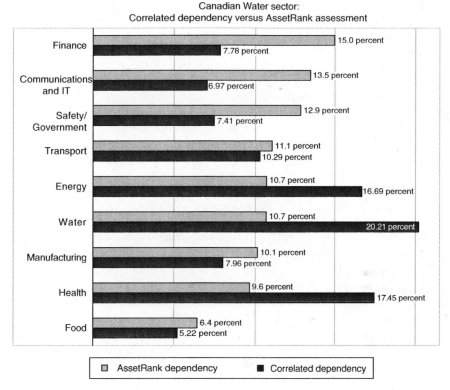

Canadian Water sector:
Correlated dependency versus AssetRank assessment

Finance — 15.0 percent / 7.78 percent

Communications and IT — 13.5 percent / 6.97 percent

Safety/Government — 12.9 percent / 7.41 percent

Transport — 11.1 percent / 10.29 percent

Energy — 10.7 percent / 16.69 percent

Water — 10.7 percent / 20.21 percent

Manufacturing — 10.1 percent / 7.96 percent

Health — 9.6 percent / 17.45 percent

Food — 6.4 percent / 5.22 percent

☐ AssetRank dependency          ■ Correlated dependency

**FIGURE 6.2**  AssetRank assessment of Canadian Water sector dependencies.

the token has replicated itself in another industry, the provision of that industry's goods and services in turn requires still other industries' goods and services (those industries could possibly depend on Water). The token continues replicating itself as the industries meet their requirements for other industries goods and services. The AssetRank value is the percentage of Water tokens in the CI sectors. Hence, the values represent the steady state of Water dependencies taking into account an infinite-order flow-through of the dependencies. These values are compared with the prima facie correlated dependency metrics which give the first-order dependencies that the Water sector has on the other sectors.

Another perspective from which to review the differences between AssetRank and correlated scores is to consider these scores in terms of their relationship to the time, and the duration of the impacting event. AssetRanks scores are related to prolonged impacts in which a large number of cascades may occur, beyond several days. Therefore, AssetRank might be considered a large or long-term event view of CI interdependency. Correlated scores are related to the initial, short-term effects of an impact, the first few hours to days. As the event unfolds and continues, dependency metrics would rapidly shift from correlated scores to AssetRank scores.

Figure 6.2 illustrates how AssetRank interpretations of cascading effects and CI dependencies differ from the prima facie correlated dependency metrics. AssetRank reveals the dependence that Water has on the other sectors by taking into account not only its direct dependencies on the CI sectors but more importantly, its total dependency on the CI sectors as the effects of cascading dependencies settle into the system. The total dependency includes the indirect dependencies that Water has on the CI sectors.

It is interesting to consider not only the final AssetRank values but also the difference between the AssetRank and correlated dependency scores for a given sector. For instance, four out of nine CI sectors have large differences of 3% or more between the correlated dependency scores and AssetRank values while the remaining sectors have moderate differences. This indicates that as the duration of an impact in the Water sector extends, the criticality of these sectors with large differences to Water shifts substantially.

Under an AssetRank analysis, the assurances of the Communications and IT and Transportation sectors during any Water crisis are more critical than they first appear, due to their overall criticality to other sectors in the Water supply chain. While Communications and IT and Transportation might not be intuitively core to a Water crisis response, especially in the short term, AssetRank is revealing that they are possibly undervalued by the correlated dependency metrics based upon normal operating conditions. Similarly, from an AssetRank perspective, the dependency upon the other players in the Water sector, Energy and the Water sector itself, are reduced when cascading dependencies are considered and it is realized that a dependence on those sectors places indirect dependence on the other sectors. Again, the indication is that as an impact in the Water sector persists and extends in duration, dependencies shift as the impact cascades through the supply chain along multiple paths.

AssetRank indicates another important point related to crisis response and Water sector dependency: the spikes associated with the criticality of one sector over another level out and flatten as indirect dependencies are considered. All sectors become comparably important to the Water sector, versus the first-order dependencies (the correlated dependency metrics) where some sectors are rated over four times as important as other sectors.

The above observations are not to say the correlated metrics are wrong; they represent an immediate-term view of the effects of CI interdependency under normal operating conditions. The AssetRank results are indicative of interdependency relationships as impacts and crisis persist and the Water sector relies on the assurance of other CI sectors to manage a crisis within its own sector.

## FURTHER CASE STUDIES

More case studies applying the methodologies and metrics from this book are available from the authors' Web site: http://www.tysonmacaulay.com.

# Index